THE AMERICAN ECONOMY

ISSN 1554-4400

THE AMERICAN ECONOMY

Kim Masters Evans

INFORMATION PLUS® REFERENCE SERIES
Formerly Published by Information Plus, Wylie, Texas

GALE
CENGAGE Learning

Detroit • New York • San Francisco • New Haven, Conn • Waterville, Maine • London

GALE
CENGAGE Learning

The American Economy

Kim Masters Evans

Kepos Media, Inc.: Paula Kepos and Janice Jorgensen, Series Editors

Project Editors: Kathleen J. Edgar, Elizabeth Manar, Kimberley McGrath

Rights Acquisition and Management: Robyn V. Young

Composition: Evi Abou-El-Seoud, Mary Beth Trimper

Manufacturing: Rita Wimberley

© 2013 Gale, Cengage Learning

ALL RIGHTS RESERVED. No part of this work covered by the copyright herein may be reproduced, transmitted, stored, or used in any form or by any means graphic, electronic, or mechanical, including but not limited to photocopying, recording, scanning, digitizing, taping, Web distribution, information networks, or information storage and retrieval systems, except as permitted under Section 107 or 108 of the 1976 United States Copyright Act, without the prior written permission of the publisher.

This publication is a creative work fully protected by all applicable copyright laws, as well as by misappropriation, trade secret, unfair competition, and other applicable laws. The authors and editors of this work have added value to the underlying factual material herein through one or more of the following: unique and original selection, coordination, expression, arrangement, and classification of the information.

For product information and technology assistance, contact us at
Gale Customer Support, 1-800-877-4253.
For permission to use material from this text or product,
submit all requests online at **www.cengage.com/permissions.**
Further permissions questions can be e-mailed to
permissionrequest@cengage.com

Cover photograph: © Steffen Foerster/Shutterstock.com.

While every effort has been made to ensure the reliability of the information presented in this publication, Gale, a part of Cengage Learning, does not guarantee the accuracy of the data contained herein. Gale accepts no payment for listing; and inclusion in the publication of any organization, agency, institution, publication, service, or individual does not imply endorsement of the editors or publisher. Errors brought to the attention of the publisher and verified to the satisfaction of the publisher will be corrected in future editions.

Gale
27500 Drake Rd.
Farmington Hills, MI 48331-3535

ISBN-13: 978-0-7876-5103-9 (set) ISBN-10: 0-7876-5103-6 (set)
ISBN-13: 978-1-4144-8131-9 ISBN-10: 1-4144-8131-4

ISSN 1554-4400

This title is also available as an e-book.
ISBN-13: 978-1-5730-2285-9 (set)
ISBN-10: 1-5730-2285-3 (set)
Contact your Gale sales representative for ordering information.

Printed in the United States of America
2 3 4 5 6 19 18 17 16 15

TABLE OF CONTENTS

Major trade agreements, the International Monetary Fund and the World Bank, economic sanctions, and the increasing trend toward global free trade, or globalization, are also highlighted in this chapter.

PREFACE

The American Economy is part of the Information Plus Reference Series. The purpose of each volume of the series is to present the latest facts on a topic of pressing concern in modern American life. These topics include the most controversial and studied social issues of the 21st century: abortion, capital punishment, care for the elderly, crime, the environment, gambling, gun control, health care, immigration, minorities, national security, social welfare, women, youth, and many more. Even though this series is written especially for high school and undergraduate students, it is an excellent resource for anyone in need of factual information on current affairs.

By presenting the facts, it is the intention of Gale, Cengage Learning to provide its readers with everything they need to reach an informed opinion on current issues. To that end, there is a particular emphasis in this series on the presentation of scientific studies, surveys, and statistics. These data are generally presented in the form of tables, charts, and other graphics placed within the text of each book. Every graphic is directly referred to and carefully explained in the text. The source of each graphic is presented within the graphic itself. The data used in these graphics are drawn from the most reputable and reliable sources, such as from the various branches of the U.S. government and from private organizations and associations. Every effort has been made to secure the most recent information available. Readers should bear in mind that many major studies take years to conduct and that additional years often pass before the data from these studies are made available to the public. Therefore, in many cases the most recent information available in 2013 is dated from 2010 or 2011. Older statistics are sometimes presented as well, if they are landmark studies or of particular interest and no more-recent information exists.

Although statistics are a major focus of the Information Plus Reference Series, they are by no means its only content. Each book also presents the widely held positions and important ideas that shape how the book's subject is discussed in the United States. These positions are explained in detail and, where possible, in the words of their proponents. Some of the other material to be found in these books includes historical background, descriptions of major events related to the subject, relevant laws and court cases, and examples of how these issues play out in American life. Some books also feature primary documents or have pro and con debate sections that provide the words and opinions of prominent Americans on both sides of a controversial topic. All material is presented in an evenhanded and unbiased manner; readers will never be encouraged to accept one view of an issue over another.

HOW TO USE THIS BOOK

The U.S. economy in the 21st century is enormous and extremely complicated. Workers, employers large and small, consumers, the equities markets, the U.S. government, and the world economy are constantly interacting with each other to affect the U.S. economy and, through it, each other. The U.S. economy produces and consumes raw materials, services, manufactured goods, and intellectual property in vast amounts. This book describes the size and scope of the U.S. economy, explains how it functions, and examines some of the challenges it faces, such as inflation, government regulation, outsourcing, and corporate scandals.

The American Economy consists of 10 chapters and three appendixes. Each chapter is devoted to a particular aspect of the U.S economy. For a summary of the information that is covered in each chapter, please see the synopses that are provided in the Table of Contents. Chapters generally begin with an overview of the basic facts and background information on the chapter's topic, then proceed to look at subtopics of particular interest. For example, Chapter 5: The American Worker examines current and historical data related to employment and unemployment. It characterizes U.S. industry overall in terms of industry supersectors, such as manufacturing, and presents employment data and unemployment rates for each supersector. The chapter also describes the development and role of labor unions and provides data regarding the compensation of workers, including wages, salaries, and supplements, such as employer-provided medical insurance. Nontraditional work arrangements including working at home and self-employment are briefly explained. Issues related to foreign workers, both legal and illegal, are explored as are the consequences of U.S. jobs going to foreign countries. The chapter ends with a discussion of government laws and agencies that ensure that workplaces are operated safely and that workers are treated fairly. Readers can find their way through a chapter by looking for the section and subsection headings, which are clearly set off from the text. They can also refer to the book's extensive Index, if they already know what they are looking for.

Statistical Information

The tables and figures featured throughout *The American Economy* will be of particular use to readers in learning about this topic. These tables and figures represent an extensive collection of the most recent and valuable statistics on the U.S. economy—for example, graphics cover the spending habits of the typical consumer, employment in the manufacturing and service industries, the gross domestic product, the trade deficit, and consumer debt levels. Gale, Cengage Learning believes that making this information available to readers is the most important way to fulfill the goal of this book: to help readers understand the issues and controversies surrounding the U.S. economy and reach their own conclusions.

Each table or figure has a unique identifier appearing above it, for ease of identification and reference. Titles for the tables and figures explain their purpose. At the end of each table or figure, the original source of the data is provided.

To help readers understand these often complicated statistics, all tables and figures are explained in the text. References in the text direct readers to the relevant statistics. Furthermore, the contents of all tables and figures are fully indexed. Please see the opening section of the Index at the back of this volume for a description of how to find tables and figures within it.

Appendixes

Besides the main body text and images, *The American Economy* has three appendixes. The first is the Important Names and Addresses directory. Here, readers will find contact information for a number of government and private organizations that can provide further information on aspects of the U.S. economy. The second appendix is the Resources section, which can also assist readers in conducting their own research. In this section, the author and editors of *The American Economy* describe some of the sources that were most useful during the compilation of this book. The final appendix is the Index. It has been greatly expanded from previous editions and should make it even easier to find specific topics in this book.

ADVISORY BOARD CONTRIBUTIONS

The staff of Information Plus would like to extend its heartfelt appreciation to the Information Plus Advisory Board. This dedicated group of media professionals provides feedback on the series on an ongoing basis. Their comments allow the editorial staff who work on the project to continually make the series better and more user-friendly. The staff's top priority is to produce the highest-quality and most useful books possible, and the Information Plus Advisory Board's contributions to this process are invaluable.

The members of the Information Plus Advisory Board are:

- Kathleen R. Bonn, Librarian, Newbury Park High School, Newbury Park, California

- Madelyn Garner, Librarian, San Jacinto College, North Campus, Houston, Texas

- Anne Oxenrider, Media Specialist, Dundee High School, Dundee, Michigan

- Charles R. Rodgers, Director of Libraries, Pasco-Hernando Community College, Dade City, Florida

- James N. Zitzelsberger, Library Media Department Chairman, Oshkosh West High School, Oshkosh, Wisconsin

COMMENTS AND SUGGESTIONS

The editors of the *Information Plus Reference Series* welcome your feedback on *The American Economy*. Please direct all correspondence to:

Editors
Information Plus Reference Series
27500 Drake Rd.
Farmington Hills, MI 48331-3535

CHAPTER 1
THE U.S. ECONOMY: HISTORICAL OVERVIEW

It is not what we have that will make us a great nation;
it is the way in which we use it.

—Theodore Roosevelt, 1886

The workings of the U.S. economy are complex and often mysterious, even to economists. At its simplest, the economy runs on three major sectors: consumers, businesses, and government. (See Figure 1.1.) Consumers earn money and exchange much of it for goods and services from businesses. These businesses use the money to produce more goods and services and to pay wages to their employees. Both consumers and businesses fund the government sector, which spends and transfers money back into the system. The banking system plays a crucial role in the economy by providing the means for all sectors to save and borrow money. Finally, there are the stock markets, which allow consumers to invest their money in the nation's businesses—an enterprise that further fuels economic growth for all sectors. Thus, the U.S. economy is a circular system based on interdependent relationships in which massive amounts of money change hands. The historical developments that produced this system are important to understand because they provide key information about what has made the U.S. economy such a powerful force in the world.

DEFINING THE U.S. ECONOMY

The term *market economy* describes an economy in which the forces of supply and demand dictate the way in which goods and resources are allocated and what prices will be set. The opposite of a market economy is a *planned economy*, in which the government determines what will be produced and what prices will be charged. In a market economy, producers anticipate what products the market will be interested in and at what price, and they make decisions about what products they will bring to market and how these products will be produced and priced. Market economies foster competition among

businesses, which typically leads to lower prices and is generally considered to be beneficial for both workers and consumers. By contrast, a planned economy is directed by a central government that has a far greater degree of influence over prices and production, as well as a tighter regulation of industries and manufacturing procedures. The United States has a mixed economy, which combines aspects of a market economy with some central planning and control of a planned economy to create a system that has both a high degree of market freedom and regulatory agencies and social programs that promote the public welfare.

This mixed economy did not develop overnight. It has evolved over more than two centuries and has been shaped by American experiences at various times with hardship, war, peace, and prosperity.

COLONIZATION THROUGH THE 1800s

When European colonists first began settling in the New World during the late 16th century, they found a vast expanse of land that was inhabited by Native Americans. At first, the colonists were preoccupied with merely surviving. Eventually, they engaged in commerce with Europe by exploiting the natural resources of their new homeland. The main agricultural products of the colonies were tobacco, wheat, rye, barley, rice, and indigo plant. Other important exports were animal furs, products from fish and whales, and timber. Shipbuilding became a major industry in New England.

Frustrated with the political and economic interference of England, the colonists eventually banded together to forge a new nation: the United States of America. The push for independence from Great Britain, which culminated in the Revolutionary War (1775–1783), was driven by economic and political motivations, including the desire for greater self-governance and tax relief. The newly formed United States adopted economic principles

FIGURE 1.1

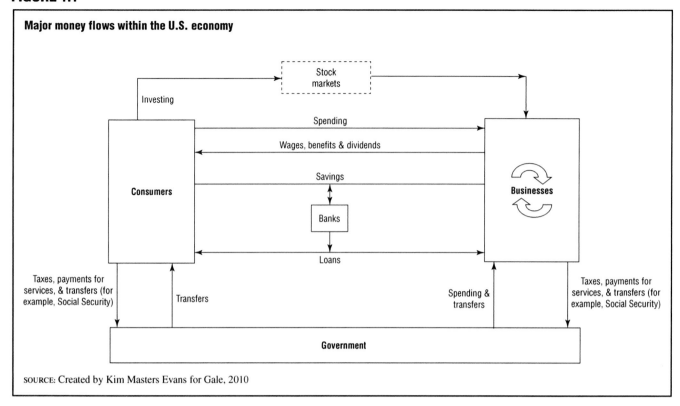

Major money flows within the U.S. economy

SOURCE: Created by Kim Masters Evans for Gale, 2010

that favored a competitive marketplace with little government interference. These principles would dominate the nation's economic policy for more than a century.

During the late 1700s Great Britain and the United States underwent a major social and economic change from agriculture to industry. The Industrial Revolution saw the introduction of the steam engine, the cotton gin, and other machines that were capable of increasing production while decreasing human labor. Farming, in particular, became much less labor intensive, freeing up people to pursue other forms of employment. Over the next century the United States changed from an agrarian-based nation to one in which the majority of income was generated by manufacturing, trade, and business that provided services to consumers.

The 1800s were a period of enormous growth for the United States in terms of territory, population, and economic might. Deep divisions arose between factions in the North and South on the morality of slavery and associated political and economic issues, which led to the devastating American Civil War in 1861. By the time the war ended in 1865, factories in the Northeast had become extremely important in fueling the U.S. economy. The decades following the Civil War were characterized by scandals involving high-level politicians making money from crooked business deals and by an unprecedented boom in business. The resulting social atmosphere was one of decadence among the upper

classes contrasted with poverty and labor unrest among the lower classes.

The U.S. government had a hands-off approach to business regulation, a tactic described by the French term *laissez faire* (leave alone or "do as you please"). It was generally believed that the government should not interfere in economic affairs but should instead allow supply and demand and competition to operate unfettered, resulting in a free market.

Panics and Depressions

In economic terms a panic is a widespread occurrence of public anxiety about financial affairs. People lose confidence in banks and investments and want to hold onto their money instead of spending it. This can lead to a severe downturn, or depression, in the economic condition of a nation. The U.S. economy suffered from panics and depressions even during the booming growth of the 1800s. Economists argue about the exact definitions of panics and depressions, but in general it is agreed that panics and/or depressions occurred in the United States in 1819, 1837, 1857, 1869, 1873, and 1893.

The crises were triggered by a variety of factors. Common problems included too much borrowing and speculation by investors and poor oversight of banks by the federal government. Speculation is the buying of assets on the hope that they will greatly increase in value in the future. During the 1800s many speculators borrowed money from banks to buy land. Huge demand caused land prices to increase dramatically, often above what the land was actually worth in the market. Poorly regulated banks extended too much credit to speculators and to each other. When a large bank failed, there was a domino effect through the industry, which caused other banks and businesses to fail.

A panic or depression results in a downward economic spiral in which individuals and businesses are afraid to make new investments. People rush to withdraw their money from banks. As panic spreads, banks demand that borrowers pay back money, but borrowers may lack the funds to do so. Consumers are reluctant to spend money, which negatively affects businesses. Demand for products goes down, and prices must be lowered to move merchandise off of shelves. This means less profit for business owners. To reduce their costs, businesses begin laying off employees and do not hire new employees. As more people become unemployed or fearful about their jobs, there is even less spending in the marketplace, which leads to more business cutbacks and so forth. The cycle continues until some compelling change takes place to nudge the economy back into a positive direction.

THE EARLY 20TH CENTURY

The early 20th century was a time of social and political change in the United States. Public disgust at the corruption and greed of the late 1800s encouraged the movement called progressivism. Progressives promoted civic responsibility, workers' rights, consumer protection, political and tax reform, "trust busting," and strong government action to achieve social improvements. The Progressive Era greatly affected the U.S. economy because of its focus on improving working conditions for average Americans. Successes for the progressives included child labor restrictions, improved working conditions in factories, compensation funds for injured workers, a growth surge in labor unions, federal regulation of food and drug industries, and the formation of the Federal Trade Commission to oversee business practices.

Despite its laissez-faire attitude, the federal government took two actions in 1913 that had long-lasting effects on the U.S. economy:

- Establishment of the Federal Reserve System to serve as the nation's central bank, furnish currency, and supervise banking

- Ratification of the 16th Amendment to the U.S. Constitution authorizing the collection of income taxes

World War I and Inflation

World War I erupted in Europe in August 1914. The United States entered the conflict in April 1917 and was engaged until the war ended in November 1918. Even though the nation spent only 19 months at war, the U.S. economy underwent major changes during this period.

It is sometimes said that "war is good for the economy" because during a major war the federal government spends large amounts of money on weapons and machinery through contracts with private industries. These industries hire more employees, which reduces unemployment and puts more money into the hands of consumers to spend in the marketplace. This increase in production and hiring also benefits other businesses that are not directly involved in the war effort. On the surface, these economic effects appear positive. However, major wars almost always result in high inflation rates.

Inflation is an economic condition in which the purchasing power of money goes down because of price increases in goods and services. For example, if a nation experiences an inflation rate of 3% in a year, an item that cost $1.00 at the beginning of the year will cost $1.03 at the end of the year. Inflation causes the "value" of a dollar to go down over the course of the year. In general, small increases in inflation occur over time in a healthy growing economy because demand slightly outpaces supply. Economists consider an inflation rate of 3% or less per year to be tolerable. During a major war the supply and demand ratio becomes distorted. This occurs when the nation produces huge amounts of war goods and far fewer consumer goods, such as food, clothing, and cars. This lack of supply and anxiety about the future drive up the prices of consumer goods, making it difficult for people to afford things they need or want.

Even though the government tried to impose some level of price control in the food and fuel industries, inflation still occurred. Figure 1.2 shows the average annual inflation rate between 1914 and 1924. The inflation rate was unusually high between 1916 and 1920, peaking at 18% in 1918. Wartime inflation was particularly hard on nonworking citizens, such as the elderly and the sick, because there were no large government programs in place at that time to assist needy people.

A lasting legacy of World War I was the assumption of large amounts of debt by the federal government to fund the war effort. Figure 1.3 shows the enormous differences that occurred between government spending and revenues (receipts) during the war years. In 1919 government spending peaked at nearly $19 billion, whereas revenues for that year were just over $5 billion. The government made up the difference by borrowing money. One method used was the selling of Liberty bonds. Bonds are a type of financial asset—an IOU (an abbreviation for "I Owe yoU") that promises to pay back at some future date the original purchase price plus interest.

FIGURE 1.2

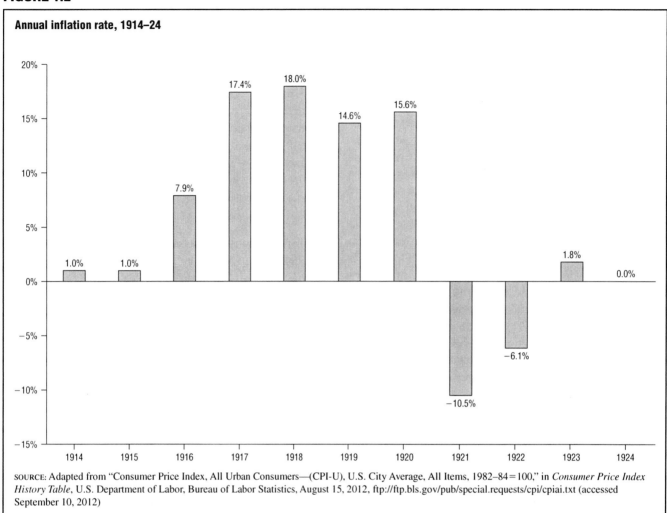

Annual inflation rate, 1914–24

SOURCE: Adapted from "Consumer Price Index, All Urban Consumers—(CPI-U), U.S. City Average, All Items, 1982–84=100," in *Consumer Price Index History Table*, U.S. Department of Labor, Bureau of Labor Statistics, August 15, 2012, ftp://ftp.bls.gov/pub/special.requests/cpi/cpiai.txt (accessed September 10, 2012)

THE ROARING TWENTIES AND THE GREAT DEPRESSION

The Roaring Twenties featured several years of robust economic growth that were characterized by increases in mass production, the availability of electricity, consumer demand for goods, and consumer usage of credit to fund purchases. However, the prosperity of the 1920s was not shared by all Americans. Financial problems rocked the agricultural sector, and there were economic downturns in the coal mining and railroad industries.

The Stock Market Crash

During the late 1920s the stock market became a major factor in the U.S. economy as businesses sold stock (i.e., ownership shares) in their companies. Investors were richly rewarded when their stocks increased dramatically in value. Many people took out loans from banks to pay for stock or purchased stock by "buying on margin." In this arrangement an investor would make a small down payment (as little as 10%) on a stock purchase. The remainder of the balance would be paid (in theory) by

the future increase in the stock value. Buying on margin was extremely risky, but was widely practiced by investors of the time. Over optimism caused stock prices to rise higher than the actual worth of companies. During the fall of 1929 investors began to get nervous and there were selling frenzies as people tried to get rid of stocks they thought might be overvalued. On Tuesday, October 29 ("Black Tuesday"), panic selling took place all day. Stock values dropped dramatically. By the end of the day many margin buyers had lost their life savings and their stock. Those who managed to hold on to their stock found it was worth only a fraction of its former value.

According to Harold Bierman Jr. of Cornell University, in "The 1929 Stock Market Crash" (February 5, 2010, http://eh.net/encyclopedia/article/Bierman .Crash), the U.S. stock market lost 90% of its value between 1929 and 1932.

The Great Depression

The U.S. economy suffered a devastating downturn following the stock market crash. The depression was so deep and lasted so long—more than a decade—that it is

FIGURE 1.3

Government receipts and spending, 1901–29

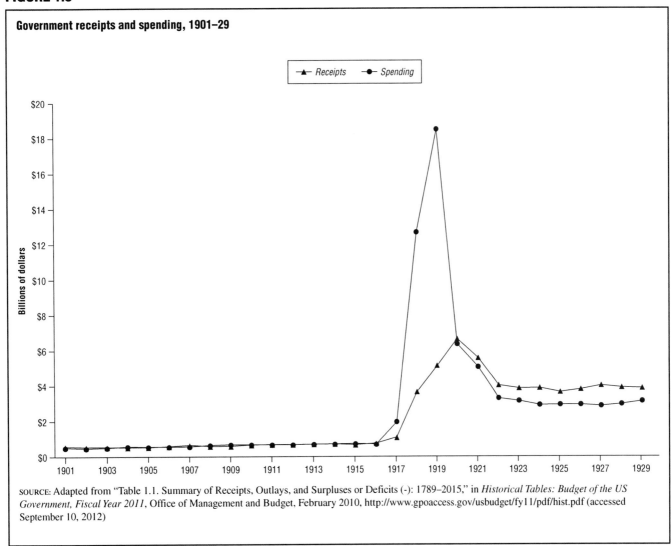

SOURCE: Adapted from "Table 1.1. Summary of Receipts, Outlays, and Surpluses or Deficits (-): 1789–2015," in *Historical Tables: Budget of the US Government, Fiscal Year 2011*, Office of Management and Budget, February 2010, http://www.gpoaccess.gov/usbudget/fy11/pdf/hist.pdf (accessed September 10, 2012)

called the Great Depression. It brought long-term unemployment and hardship to millions of people. The unemployment rate soared from 3.2% in 1929 to 24.9% in 1933. (See Figure 1.4.) It remained more than 10% throughout the 1930s. The public lost confidence in the stock market, the banking system, and big business and at the same time was saddled with large amounts of debt that had been taken on during the 1920s.

The Great Depression was aggravated by a crisis in the banking industry. Some banks had invested heavily in the stock market using their depositors' money or lent large amounts of money to stock market investors. These banks failed after the crash, and the depositors lost their savings. Fear of further failures caused so-called bank runs, in which large numbers of depositors rushed to withdraw their money at the same time. This caused more bank failures, which perpetuated the cycle. In addition, some economists believe that the banking market became oversaturated during the 1920s with underfunded and loosely regulated banks that lent money too easily. These

institutions were already financially troubled before the crash and could not survive the stress.

When the Great Depression began, the laissez-faire attitude still dominated political opinion. However, in 1933 newly elected President Franklin D. Roosevelt (1882–1945) instituted what he called "a New Deal" for the nation. His administration acted aggressively in economic affairs by creating work programs, trying to revive farming and business, and spearheading laws that were designed to reform the stock market and banking industry. After nearly 80 years, economists still argue about whether the New Deal was actually "a good deal" for the nation. They all agree, however, that it was a turning point in U.S. economic history.

Perhaps the greatest legacy of Roosevelt's New Deal was the new role of the federal government as a manipulator of economic forces and a provider of benefits to the needy. In U.S. history the New Deal is considered to be the birth of big government.

FIGURE 1.4

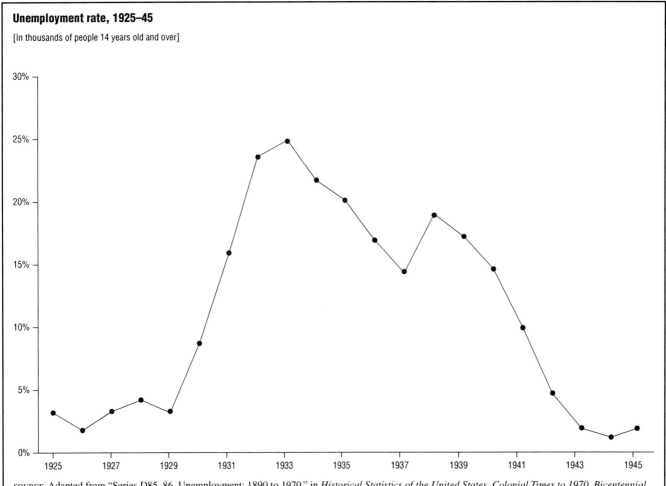

Unemployment rate, 1925–45

[In thousands of people 14 years old and over]

SOURCE: Adapted from "Series D85–86. Unemployment: 1890 to 1970," in *Historical Statistics of the United States, Colonial Times to 1970, Bicentennial Edition, Part 1*, U.S. Department of Commerce, U.S. Census Bureau, September 1975, http://www2.census.gov/prod2/statcomp/documents/CT1970p1-05 .pdf (accessed September 10, 2012)

By 1940 the unemployment rate was 14.6%. (See Figure 1.4.) Even though the rate was down from a peak of 24.9% in 1933, it was still high by historical standards. The hardship suffered by many Americans had been softened by nearly a decade of New Deal programs, but the country was still gripped by the Great Depression. It was going to take a war to bring an end to the Depression.

WORLD WAR II AND THE COLD WAR

The United States was involved in World War II from 1941 to 1945. During the war the federal government established agencies to oversee wartime production, labor relations, and prices. Efforts were made to avoid the huge inflation increase that had occurred during World War I. Rationing (tight controls over how much of an item a person can use or consume in a certain amount of time) was instituted on some goods to prevent dramatic price increases. Overall, these efforts were successful. Figure 1.5 shows the annual rates of inflation that were experienced in the United States between 1940 and 1950.

Inflation spiked during the early years of the war and immediately after but was not consistently high over the decade.

Businesses rushed to increase production and hire workers to produce the goods needed for the war effort. Unemployment dropped dramatically and wages went up, particularly for workers in low-skilled factory jobs. Laborers found themselves in high demand and joined labor unions in record numbers to consolidate their power and seek better working conditions.

Government Actions

World War II was an expensive endeavor for the United States. However, it was believed that the stakes were so high that the war had to be won at any cost. As shown in Figure 1.6, government spending during the war far outpaced revenues. By 1945 the government was spending around $90 billion per year and taking in revenues around half this amount. Once again, the difference was made up by borrowing.

FIGURE 1.5

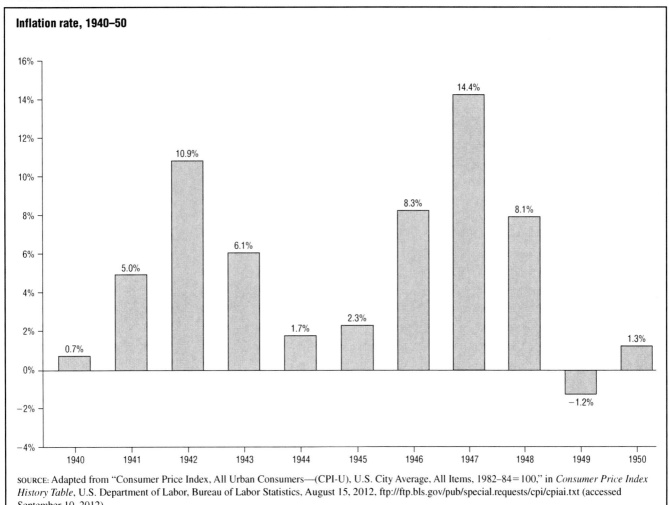

Inflation rate, 1940–50

SOURCE: Adapted from "Consumer Price Index, All Urban Consumers—(CPI-U), U.S. City Average, All Items, 1982–84=100," in *Consumer Price Index History Table*, U.S. Department of Labor, Bureau of Labor Statistics, August 15, 2012, ftp://ftp.bls.gov/pub/special.requests/cpi/cpiai.txt (accessed September 10, 2012)

Following World War II it appeared obvious that huge government spending had helped fuel recovery from the Great Depression. General belief in the laissez-faire approach to economics gave way to a new approach that was advocated by the economist John Maynard Keynes (1883–1946). Keynesian economics stresses strong government intervention in the economy and became the operating principle of the U.S. government during the post–World War II era. Even though Keynes had his critics, and his methods have been revised over time, he is considered by many to be the father of the mixed economy system that is still being used in the United States.

Another innovation of this era was the compilation by the federal government of economic data on the nation's inputs and outputs, such as labor and production of goods and services. Researchers at the National Bureau of Economic Research (NBER) at the University of New York began estimating national income (e.g., wages, profits, and rent) as part of a program called the National Income and Product Accounts (NIPAs). Development was overseen by the U.S. Department of Commerce's Division of Economic Research, which evolved into the modern Bureau of Economic Analysis.

During World War II the federal government began compiling another economic measure called the gross national product (GNP). The GNP is the amount in dollars of the value of final goods and services that are produced by Americans over a particular time period. It is calculated by summing consumer and government spending, business and residential investments, and the net value of U.S. exports (exports minus imports).

The GNP provides a valuable tool for tracking national productivity over time. The NIPAs and GNP became important economic indicators of the state of the economy as a whole—that is, the macroeconomy.

Uneven Prosperity

The decades following World War II were generally prosperous times for the U.S. economy as the nation continued to grow industrially. Figure 1.7 shows the national income that was produced by the business sector between 1953 and 1957. Manufacturing accounted for

FIGURE 1.6

Government receipts and spending, 1930–50

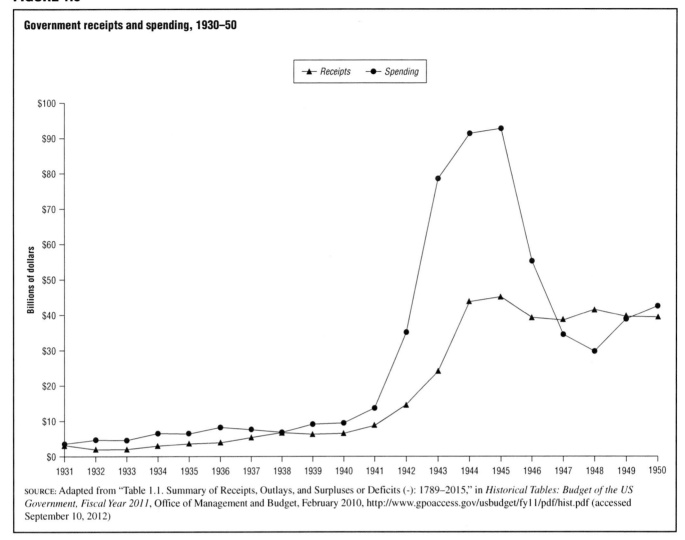

SOURCE: Adapted from "Table 1.1. Summary of Receipts, Outlays, and Surpluses or Deficits (-): 1789–2015," in *Historical Tables: Budget of the US Government, Fiscal Year 2011*, Office of Management and Budget, February 2010, http://www.gpoaccess.gov/usbudget/fy11/pdf/hist.pdf (accessed September 10, 2012)

31% of the national income during this period. Postwar euphoria drove a spending spree by consumers and a baby boom.

Dwight D. Eisenhower (1890–1969) was president from 1953 to 1961. His administration is associated with low inflation rates and general prosperity. However, the prosperity was not shared equally in American society. An oversupply of agricultural goods meant lower prices for consumers, but lower profits for farmers. Agriculture became increasingly an industry in which large factory farms run by corporations were able to survive, whereas many smaller farmers could not compete.

Minority populations (largely African-American) also suffered financial hardship during this era. Figure 1.8 shows the dramatic difference between the unemployment rates for whites and minorities during the postwar decades. By the mid-1950s unemployment among minorities was twice as high as it was among white workers, a disparity that lingered well into the 1960s. It was in this atmosphere that the civil rights movement gained strength and

urgency. In 1954 segregation was ruled unconstitutional by the U.S. Supreme Court. The following year the African-American seamstress and activist Rosa Parks (1913–2005) was arrested in Alabama for refusing to move from the "white" section of a public bus. This incident spurred a bus boycott and ultimately brought Martin Luther King Jr. (1929–1968) and other leaders of the movement to national prominence.

The Cold War, Korea, and Vietnam

The United States left World War II in sound economic shape. By contrast, all other industrialized nations had suffered great losses in their infrastructure, financial stability, and populations. As a result, the United States was able to invest heavily in the postwar economies of Western Europe and Japan, with the hope of instilling an atmosphere that was conducive to peace and the spread of capitalism. U.S. barriers to foreign trade were relaxed to build new markets for U.S. exports and to allow some war-ravaged nations to make money selling goods to American consumers.

FIGURE 1.7

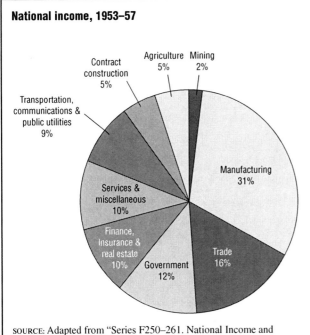

National income, 1953–57

Contract construction 5%

Transportation, communications & public utilities 9%

Agriculture 5% Mining 2%

Manufacturing 31%

Services & miscellaneous 10%

Finance, insurance & real estate 10%

Government 12%

Trade 16%

SOURCE: Adapted from "Series F250–261. National Income and Persons Engaged in Production, by Industry Divisions: 1869 to 1970," in *Historical Statistics of the United States, Colonial Times to 1970, Bicentennial Edition, Part 1*, U.S. Department of Commerce, U.S. Census Bureau, September 1975, http://www2.census.gov/prod2/statcomp/documents/CT1970p1-07.pdf (accessed September 10, 2012)

The Soviet Union had been a wartime ally of the United States, but relations became strained after the war. The Soviet Union had adopted communism following a period of revolution and civil war from 1917 to the early 1920s. During World War II the Soviet Union "liberated" a large part of eastern Europe from Nazi occupation. Through various means the Union of Soviet Socialist Republics (USSR) assumed political control over these nations. The USSR had been largely industrialized before World War II and quickly regained its industrial capabilities. It soon took a major role in international affairs, placing it in direct conflict with the only other superpower of the time: the United States. A cold war began between the two rich and powerful nations that had completely different political, economic, and social goals for the world. Unlike a "hot war" or direct and large-scale military conflict, the conflict between the United States and the Soviet Union was called a "cold war" because it was fought mostly by politicians and diplomats.

A direct and large-scale military conflict between U.S. and Soviet forces never occurred. Regardless, an expensive arms race began in which both sides produced and stockpiled large amounts of weaponry as a show of force to deter a first strike by the enemy. In addition, both sides provided financial and military support to countries around the world in an attempt to influence the political leanings of those populations. Communist China joined

the Cold War during the 1950s and often partnered with the USSR against U.S. interests.

By the 1950s the United States was embroiled in two Asian conflicts over communism: the Korean War (1950–1953) and the Vietnam War (1954–1975). In both wars the United States chose to fight in a limited manner without using its arsenal of nuclear weapons or engaging Chinese or Soviet troops directly for fear of sparking another world war. Unlike World War II, full-scale mobilization of U.S. industries was not required for these wars. Instead, a defense industry developed during the Cold War to supply the U.S. military on a continuous basis with the arms and matériel it needed.

Figure 1.9 shows the percentage of the national budget that was devoted to national defense between 1940 and 1970. Spending on national defense soared during World War II and then declined dramatically following the war's end. However, military spending quickly climbed again as the Cold War intensified during the early 1950s and remained above 40% for nearly two decades.

THE 1960s: SOCIAL UPHEAVAL AND ECONOMIC GROWTH

The 1960s were a time of social and economic change for the United States. The decade began with the election of President John F. Kennedy (1917–1963), who promised to ensure economic growth and address growing social problems within the United States. In 1963 Kennedy's efforts were cut short by his assassination. Lyndon B. Johnson (1908–1973) took over as president and dramatically enlarged the federal government and its role in socioeconomic affairs. Johnson's administration initiated large-scale programs for the needy, including the health care programs Medicare (for the elderly and people with disabilities) and Medicaid (for the poor), jobs programs, federal aid to schools, and food stamps for low-income Americans. The so-called War on Poverty and the escalating war in Vietnam proved to be extremely expensive. At the same time, the United States was pursuing a costly (but ultimately successful) endeavor to land astronauts on the moon before the end of the decade.

Consumer and government spending drove the nation's GNP during the 1960s. However, inflation became a problem (as it often does in a fast-growing economy) during the late 1960s. At the macroeconomic level, there was too much money in the hands of consumers, which resulted in consumer demand that was higher than supply. In *Consumer Price Index* (October 16, 2012, ftp://ftp.bls.gov/pub/special.requests/cpi/cpiai .txt), the U.S. Bureau of Labor Statistics (BLS) notes that by 1970 the inflation rate had reached 5.7%.

FIGURE 1.8

Unemployment rate by race, 1948–70

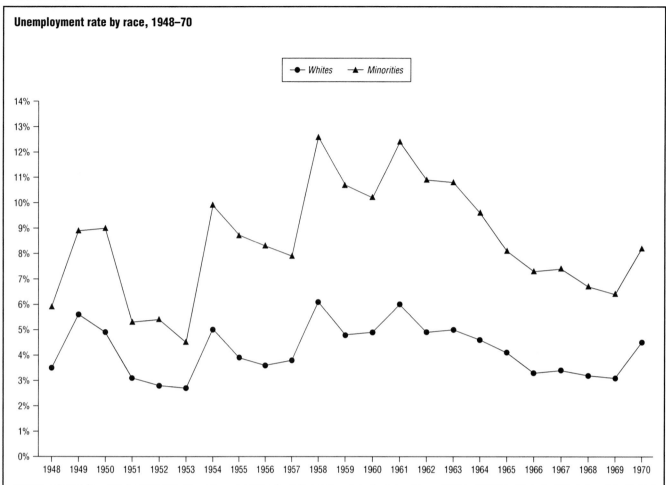

SOURCE: Adapted from "Series D87–101. Unemployment Rates for Selected Groups in the Labor Force: 1947 to 1970," in *Historical Statistics of the United States, Colonial Times to 1970, Bicentennial Edition, Part 1*, U.S. Department of Commerce, U.S. Census Bureau, September 1975, http://www2.census .gov/prod2/statcomp/documents/CT1970p1-05.pdf (accessed September 10, 2012)

FIGURE 1.9

National defense spending as percentage of total federal spending, 1940–70

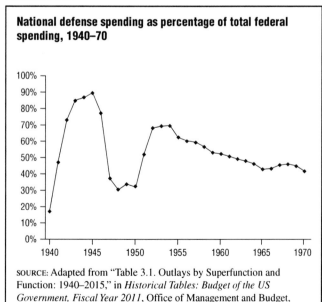

SOURCE: Adapted from "Table 3.1. Outlays by Superfunction and Function: 1940–2015," in *Historical Tables: Budget of the US Government, Fiscal Year 2011*, Office of Management and Budget, February 2010, http://www.gpoaccess.gov/usbudget/fy11/pdf/hist.pdf (accessed September 10, 2012)

According to the NBER, in "US Business Cycle Expansions and Contractions" (November 2012, http:// www.nber.org/cycles.html), the United States left the 1960s having experienced the longest continuous stretch of positive GNP growth in history—from the first quarter of 1961 to the last quarter of 1969. However, high inflation was about to become a major problem.

THE 1970s: STAGFLATION AND ENERGY CRISES

The term *stagflation* was coined during the 1970s to describe an economy suffering stagnant growth, high inflation, and high unemployment all at the same time. This combination of economic problems was unprecedented in U.S. history. Previously, high inflation had occurred when the economy was growing quickly, such as during World War II, and high production had meant high employment levels. By contrast, economic downturns were associated with higher unemployment but lower inflation (and even deflation). These relationships had been considered natural and certain.

FIGURE 1.10

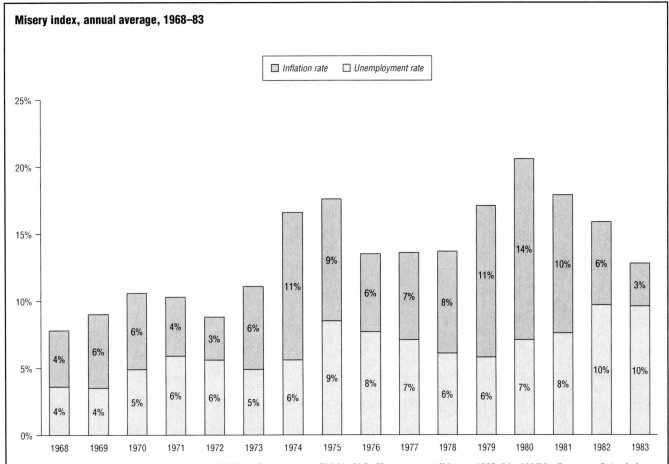

Misery index, annual average, 1968–83

SOURCE: Adapted from "Consumer Price Index, All Urban Consumers—(CPI-U), U.S. City Average, All Items, 1982–84=100," in *Consumer Price Index History Table*, U.S. Department of Labor, Bureau of Labor Statistics, August 15, 2012, ftp://ftp.bls.gov/pub/special.requests/cpi/cpiai.txt (accessed September 10, 2012); and "1. Employment Status of the Civilian Noninstitutional Population, 1941 to Date," in *Labor Force Statistics from the Current Population Survey*, U.S. Department of Labor, Bureau of Labor Statistics, March 9, 2012, http://www.bls.gov/cps/cpsaat01.pdf (accessed September 10, 2012)

The 1970s were unique because both unemployment and inflation were high, by historical standards. The economist Arthur Okun (1928–1980) created the term *discomfort factor* to describe this condition. His discomfort factor, which became popularly known as the Misery index, is computed by summing the unemployment rate and the inflation rate. Figure 1.10 shows the annual Misery index calculated between 1968 and 1983. Beginning in 1974 each rate exceeded 5%.

There were three presidents during the 1970s: Richard M. Nixon (1913–1994), Gerald R. Ford (1913–2006), and Jimmy Carter (1924–). Even though they tried a variety of measures to stem stagflation, their efforts were considered to be ineffective. By 1980 the Misery index had climbed to 21%. (See Figure 1.10.)

Foreign Oil and Competition

The United States' economic problems were aggravated by its dependence on foreign oil and competition from foreign industries. In 1973 the Middle Eastern members of the Organization of the Petroleum Exporting Countries halted oil exports to the United States in retaliation for U.S. support of Israel. The oil embargo lasted five months. When shipments resumed, the price of oil had dramatically increased. Americans faced high prices, long lines, and shortages at the gas pumps. Figure 1.11 shows that the average retail price of gasoline surged from $0.36 per gallon in 1972 to $1.35 per gallon in 1981. During the late 1970s a revolution in oil-rich Iran brought a second wave of shortages to U.S. energy supplies.

The energy crisis of the 1970s had a ripple effect throughout the U.S. economy, causing the prices of other goods and services to increase. Lower profits and uncertainty about the future caused businesses to slow down and reduce their workforces. At the same time, U.S. industries in steel, automobiles, and electronics endured stiff foreign competition, particularly from Japan. Small fuel-efficient Japanese cars became popular in the United States. By 1980 gasoline cost nearly $1.25 per gallon, which was three and a half times the price in 1972. (See Figure 1.11.) U.S. carmakers struggled to compete, having always relied on consumer

FIGURE 1.11

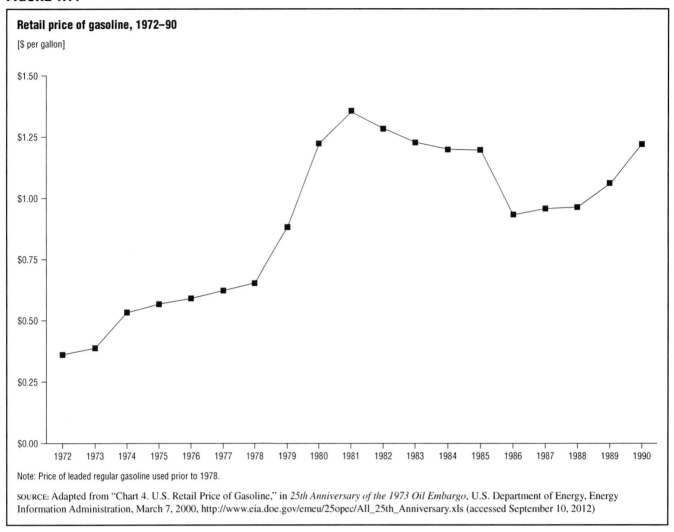

Retail price of gasoline, 1972–90

[$ per gallon]

Note: Price of leaded regular gasoline used prior to 1978.

SOURCE: Adapted from "Chart 4. U.S. Retail Price of Gasoline," in *25th Anniversary of the 1973 Oil Embargo*, U.S. Department of Energy, Energy Information Administration, March 7, 2000, http://www.eia.doe.gov/emeu/25opec/All_25th_Anniversary.xls (accessed September 10, 2012)

demand for large automobiles—which were now considered to be "gas guzzlers."

Deregulation

One of the measures that President Carter used to combat stagflation was deregulation. For decades, certain U.S. industries had been given government immunity from market supply and demand factors. The railroad, trucking, and airline industries were prime examples. Companies in these industries were guaranteed rates and routes and were allowed to operate contrary to antitrust laws. In 1978 the airline industry was deregulated. The result was that airlines began competing with each other over fares and routes, and new companies entered the industry. Some of the large, well-established companies were unable to compete in the new environment and went out of business. However, demand increased as prices came down and flying became available to many more Americans. By 1980 deregulation had been completed or was under way for the railroad, trucking, energy, financial services, and telecommunications industries.

THE 1980s: RECESSION AND REAGANOMICS

In November 1980 the American people elected Ronald Reagan (1911–2004) as the new president. Inflation was at 14% that year, which was incredibly high for a peacetime economy. (See Figure 1.10.) Unemployment was at 7%, meaning that millions of people were unemployed and faced with rapidly increasing prices in the marketplace. The economic situation was dire, and drastic measures were required to turn the economy around.

Slaying the Inflationary Dragon

In late 1979 President Carter had appointed a new chair of the Federal Reserve board of governors, Paul A. Volcker (1927–), who promised to "slay the inflationary dragon." Volcker began by tightening the nation's money supply. This had the effect of making credit more difficult to obtain, which drove up interest rates. The government knew that rising interest rates would probably trigger a production slowdown (a recession) that would push unemployment even higher. It was a trade-off that policy makers during the previous decade had been unwilling to accept.

FIGURE 1.12

Bank prime loan rate, August 1955–September 2012

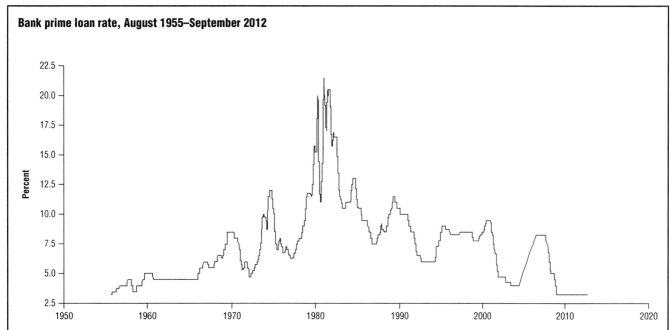

SOURCE: "Graph: Bank Prime Loan Rate (WPRIME)," in *FRED®Economic Data*, Federal Reserve Bank of St. Louis, 2012, http://research.stlouisfed.org/ fred2/graph/fredgraph.pdf?&chart_type=line&graph_id=&category_id=&recession_bars=Off&width=630&height=378&bgcolor=%23b3cde7&graph_ bgcolor=%23ffffff&txtcolor=%23000000&ts=8&preserve_ratio=true&fo=ve&id=WPRIME&transformation=lin&scale=Left&range=Max&cosd=1955- 08-10&coed=2012-09-05&line_color=%230000ff&link_values=&mark_type=NONE&mw=4&line_style=Solid&lw=1&vintage_date=2012-09- 10&revision_date=2012-09-10&mma=0&nd=&ost=&oet=&fml=a&fq=Weekly%2C%20Ending%20Wednesday&fam=avg&fgst=lin (accessed September 10, 2012)

Volcker forged ahead with his policies, and by the early 1980s interest rates had reached historical highs. Figure 1.12 shows that the prime loan rate (the interest rate that banks charge their best customers) peaked at 21.5% in December 1980. According to the Federal Home Loan Mortgage Corporation, in "30-Year Conventional Mortgage Rate" (October 1, 2012, http://research.stlouis fed.org/fred2/data/MORTG.txt), in 1981 the average inter- est rate for a conventional 30-year mortgage soared to nearly 18.5%, the highest rate ever recorded.

The lack of credit caused a business slowdown—a reduction in GNP growth (or recession). As expected, the recession put more people out of work. Unemployment climbed at first, averaging 10% in 1982 and 1983, but then began to decline. (See Figure 1.10.) By the end of the decade it was down around 5%. According to the BLS, in *Consumer Price Index*, the inflation rate dropped from a high of 13.5% in 1980 to 4.8% by 1989. Even though the spike in unemployment had been painful for Americans, the inflationary dragon was finally dead.

Reaganomics

When Reagan took office in 1981, he brought a new approach to curing the nation's financial woes: supply- side economics. Traditionally, the government had focused on the demand side—the role of consumers in stimulating businesses to produce more. Reagan pre- ferred economic policies that directly helped producers.

In "Supply Side Economics" (2005, http://www.aubur n.edu/~johnspm/gloss/supply_side), Paul M. Johnson of Auburn University describes the philosophy this way: "Supply-side policy analysts focus on barriers to higher productivity—identifying ways in which the government can promote faster economic growth over the long haul by removing impediments to the supply of, and efficient use of, the factors of production."

One of the cornerstones of supply-side economics is reducing taxes so that people and businesses have more money to invest in private enterprise. Reagan enacted tax cuts through two pieces of legislation: the Economic Recovery Tax Act of 1981 and the Tax Reform Act of 1986. The result was a much lower number of tax brack- ets (the various rates at which individuals are taxed based on their income), a broader tax base (wealth within a jurisdiction that is liable to taxation), and reduced tax rates on income and capital gains (the profit made from selling an investment, such as land).

At the same time, Reagan pushed for greater national defense spending as part of his "peace through strength" approach to the Soviet Union and for selective cuts in social services spending. However, no cuts were made to the largest and most expensive programs within the social services budget. The combination of all these factors resulted in high federal deficits during the 1980s. In other words, the federal government was spending more than it

FIGURE 1.13

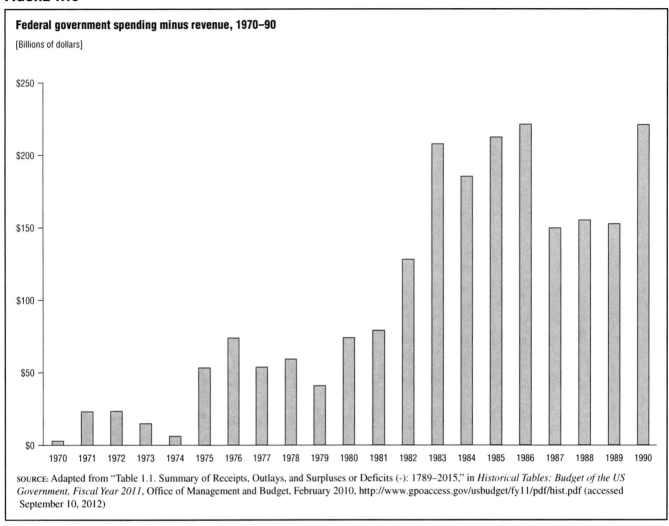

Federal government spending minus revenue, 1970–90

[Billions of dollars]

SOURCE: Adapted from "Table 1.1. Summary of Receipts, Outlays, and Surpluses or Deficits (-): 1789–2015," in *Historical Tables: Budget of the US Government, Fiscal Year 2011*, Office of Management and Budget, February 2010, http://www.gpoaccess.gov/usbudget/fy11/pdf/hist.pdf (accessed September 10, 2012)

was making each year. As shown in Figure 1.13, the federal deficits of the mid-1980s were more than three times what they had been during the mid-1970s. According to the article "U.S. Debt Past $1 Trillion" (*New York Times*, October 23, 1981), the national debt (the sum of all accumulated federal deficits since the nation began) reached $1 trillion in 1981.

THE 1990s: SPARKLING ECONOMIC PERFORMANCE

The 1990s were a time of phenomenal economic growth for the United States. President George H. W. Bush (1924–) took office in 1989 and served until 1993. Bush had been elected in large part because of his promise not to raise taxes. During his presidential campaign he famously said, "Read my lips: No new taxes." However, the promise was not one he could keep, given the economic realities of the time. During the late 1980s there had been a severe financial crisis in the savings and loan industry, which had been recently deregulated. A series of unwise loans and poor business decisions left most of the industry in shambles and necessitated a government

bailout. At the same time, the government faced rapidly rising expenditures on health care programs for the elderly (Medicare) and the needy (Medicaid). Bush reluctantly agreed to a tax increase, a move that was politically damaging. In 1992 he lost his reelection bid to the Arkansas governor Bill Clinton (1946–), who was reelected in 1996.

Joseph Tracy, Henry Schneider, and Sewin Chan indicate in "Are Stocks Overtaking Real Estate in Household Portfolios?" (*Current Issues in Economics and Finance*, vol. 5, no. 5, April 1999) that, overall, the 1990s were a period of peace and prosperity for the United States: the Cold War ended when the Soviet Union disintegrated into individual republics; technological innovations, particularly in the computer industry, helped push the economy to new heights; and sterling business success led to robust investor confidence in the stock markets. Figure 1.14 shows the portion of household assets that were invested in corporate equity (stocks) and real estate between 1945 and 1998. Even though real estate was the preferred investment through nearly all of this period, the 1990s witnessed tremendous increases in

FIGURE 1.14

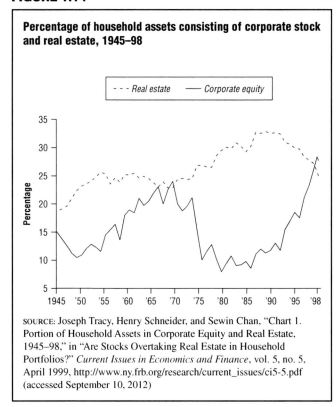

Percentage of household assets consisting of corporate stock and real estate, 1945–98

- - - Real estate   —— Corporate equity

SOURCE: Joseph Tracy, Henry Schneider, and Sewin Chan, "Chart 1. Portion of Household Assets in Corporate Equity and Real Estate, 1945–98," in "Are Stocks Overtaking Real Estate in Household Portfolios?" *Current Issues in Economics and Finance*, vol. 5, no. 5, April 1999, http://www.ny.frb.org/research/current_issues/ci5-5.pdf (accessed September 10, 2012)

the holdings of corporate equity by the average American. During the mid-1980s the average household had only 10% of its assets in corporate equity. By 1998 this percentage had reached nearly 30%, roughly equal to the percentage held in real estate. The Dow Jones Industrial Average is a stock market index—a measure used by economists to gauge the value (and performance) of the stock of 30 large companies. Between the late 1970s and the late 1990s the index soared from around 1,000 points to 11,000 points—reflecting the tremendous value gained by these companies during this period.

The combination of low interest rates, low unemployment, and high investment rates and business growth combined to greatly expand the U.S. economy. According to the article "Excerpts from Federal Reserve Chairman's Testimony" (*New York Times*, January 21, 1999), Alan Greenspan (1926–), the chair of the Federal Reserve board of governors, described this expansion as "America's sparkling economic performance."

THE EARLY 21ST CENTURY

During the early years of the first decade of the 21st century the United States endured the September 11, 2001, terrorist attacks, the outbreak of wars in Afghanistan and Iraq, and devastating hurricanes. Nevertheless, the overall economy was robust at first. As the decade progressed, the nation's economic soundness began to unravel, culminating into problems of historic proportion.

The Internet Bubble Bursts

During the late 1990s the stock market witnessed tremendous growth, driven in large part by investor enthusiasm for Internet-related businesses. Access to the Internet became widespread in the United States and in much of the developed world, which created many new market opportunities for entrepreneurs. Investors enthusiastically poured money into the stock of these new businesses. The National Association of Securities Dealers Automated Quotation System (NASDAQ) is a U.S.-based stock market on which the stock of many technology companies is traded. The NASDAQ composite index is a measure of the performance of many of the stocks on NASDAQ. In 1990 the index was less than 500. In early 2000 it peaked above 4,000 during the height of the Internet stock craze. Many of the stocks had become overvalued, and their high prices could not be sustained based on the actual financial results that the companies were producing. What followed was a sharp market correction, as investors sold off many Internet-based stocks and prices plummeted. By late 2002 the NASDAQ composite index was around 1,200, from which it slowly began to climb again.

In economics a bubble is a phenomenon in which investors overzealously invest (speculate) in a particular commodity or market sector that becomes overvalued. Excitement about possible gains overrules frank analysis of the underlying financial factors. What frustrates investors and analysts alike is that the very existence of a bubble is not evident until after the fact, when the bubble has burst and much value has been lost in the investments and the businesses involved.

The Great Recession

Overall, the U.S. economy prospered through the early part of the first decade of the 21st century. This soundness was evidenced by relatively low unemployment rates, moderate rates of inflation, and growth in the nation's production. National production is tracked through a numerical measure called the gross domestic product (GDP). The GDP is similar to the GNP described earlier, but the GNP includes production of U.S. companies outside the United States, whereas the GDP considers only production of U.S. companies within the United States.

The nation's GDP is considered to be a key measure (or metric) of how the economy is doing. The GDP is expected to increase over time, for example, from quarter to quarter. If the GDP stagnates or declines, then the economy is ailing. Declining GDP means that businesses are producing less. Because they need fewer workers, unemployment rises. As noted earlier, the term *recession* refers to a national production slowdown.

In "Determination of the December 2007 Peak in Economic Activity" (December 11, 2008, http://www

.nber.org/cycles/dec2008.html), the NBER officially defines a recession as "a significant decline in economic activity spread across the economy, lasting more than a few months, normally visible in production, employment, real income, and other indicators. A recession begins when the economy reaches a peak of activity and ends when the economy reaches its trough [lowest point]." According to the NBER, the U.S. economy reached a peak in December 2007 and then went into a recession.

The NBER (September 20, 2010, http://www.nber .org/cycles/sept2010.pdf) notes that its analysis of national economic data indicates that the recession ended in June 2009. In total, the recession spanned a total of 18 months, making it the longest lasting recession since World War II. The NBER also points out that the recession's end does not mean that "the economy has returned to operating at normal capacity," only that a recovery began to occur. In fact, the organization notes that "economic activity is typically below normal in the early stages of an expansion, and it sometimes remains so well into the expansion."

There have been many recessions in U.S. history; most were short and unremarkable. The exception is, of course, the Great Depression. The economic downturn that occurred from December 2007 to June 2009 was so deep and so damaging that many economists have dubbed it "the Great Recession." Its contributing factors and consequences are described briefly here and in detail in the following chapters.

THE HOUSING MARKET COLLAPSES. The root cause of the Great Recession was a bursting bubble—this time in the housing industry. As shown in Figure 1.12, the United States experienced historically low interest rates during the early years of the first decade of the 21st century. This spurred demand throughout the housing industry, which pushed housing prices upward. Homes in many areas of the country began to appreciate (rise in value) at an unprecedented rate. Investors eagerly bought houses and sold them a short time later for a higher price. Many banks and financial institutions became caught up in the frenzy and lowered their normally strict loan standards. They introduced new types of mortgages in which payments were low at first and then quickly rose over a certain period. Eager home buyers, especially first-time buyers, entered into these agreements without adequately considering the consequences to their personal finances.

In late 2005 and early 2006 the housing bubble burst. Overspeculation had pushed home prices above sustainable levels. Demand suddenly plummeted and homes depreciated (lost value) in many areas of the country. Homeowners began defaulting (ceasing making payments) on their loans, which put extreme pressure on mortgage lenders. The lenders were forced to foreclose (take legal possession of) on the homes that had been defaulted and then sell them at a loss. The construction industry, which had rushed to build new homes in response to the high demand, was economically devastated by the sudden collapse. The bursting housing bubble was bad enough on its own, but the problem was aggravated by certain actions taken by the financial industry.

THE FINANCIAL INDUSTRY FALTERS. Mortgages are an asset (something with value) to the company that holds them. Oftentimes, companies will bundle mortgages together and sell these bundles to investors. During the late 1990s and the early years of the first decade of the 21st century large investment companies came up with new and riskier ways to trade bundled mortgages. For one thing they invented a type of insurance contract called the credit default swap. The traditional insurance industry is heavily regulated by the U.S. government. Companies that insure assets against loss must prove that they have sufficient collateral (typically cash or other assets with immediately obtainable and verifiable worth) to cover any losses that do occur. Credit default swaps were not regulated because they were not insurance policies in the traditional sense. As a result, financial corporations were using swaps they owned as "collateral" for swaps they were issuing to each other and to investors.

As noted earlier, many mortgage lenders lowered their standards during the boom in the housing market. This greatly increased the risk that the mortgage holders would default. The investors who bought these bundled mortgages were either unaware or overlooked the risk they were assuming by buying the investments. When the housing bubble burst, mortgage defaults quickly soared and the value of the bundled mortgages plummeted. Panicked investors tried to redeem their credit default swaps, but the swaps were not backed by enough real currency and proved nearly worthless. Major banks and investment corporations, which are the backbone of the U.S. financial industry, suffered huge losses. Some failed, whereas others were rescued by enormous inflows of cash from the U.S. government.

Government Intervention

The Great Recession officially began during the second administration of President George W. Bush (1946–) and ended during the first administration of President Barack Obama (1961–). Bush was a Republican conservative and thus generally favored a laissez-faire attitude toward the economy. However, the extreme depth of the recession prompted Bush and Congress to take action. Congress passed the Emergency Economic Stabilization Act of 2008, which Bush signed in October 2008. The law created the Troubled Asset Relief Program (TARP) and authorized the U.S. Department of the Treasury to spend up to $700 billion to purchase or insure "troubled assets."

The Congressional Budget Office explains in *The Troubled Asset Relief Program: Report on Transactions Through December 31, 2008* (January 2009, http://www.cbo.gov/sites/default/files/cbofiles/ftpdocs/99xx/doc9961/01-16-tarp.pdf) that troubled assets included residential and commercial mortgages and related securities and financial instruments that originated or were issued on or before March 14, 2008. TARP allowed the U.S. secretary of the treasury to purchase these assets if doing so "promote[d] financial market stability." In addition, the secretary of the treasury, in consultation with the chair of the Federal Reserve board of governors, could purchase other financial instruments for the same reason so long as the decision was communicated to Congress.

It should be noted that the law authorizing TARP included provisions for "recoupment," that is, the replenishment of the dispersed funds either through the government's sale of purchased assets or by repayment from the companies receiving the money. Even though the fund caps were later adjusted, as will be explained in Chapter 6, by early 2012 TARP had disseminated more than $400 billion to troubled companies in the financial, insurance, and automotive industries and to struggling homeowners with mortgage difficulties.

The bailout of big businesses proved extremely unpopular politically, but the policy was continued by Obama when he assumed the presidency in 2009. In addition, Obama spearheaded passage of the American Recovery and Reinvestment Act (ARRA) of 2009, a multibillion-dollar stimulus package that was designed to revive the economy. In "The Recovery Act" (2012, http://www.recovery.gov/About/Pages/The_Act.aspx), the Recovery Accountability and Transparency Board notes that ARRA funding has totaled around $800 billion and has been directed toward tax cuts and benefits for families and businesses; funding for entitlement programs, such as extending unemployment benefits for unemployed workers; and funding federal contracts, grants, and loans for the private sector.

The Great Recession officially ended in June 2009 as the economy began to recover. Much like how analysts disagree about whether the government's intervention tactics during the 1930s to overcome the Great Depression were beneficial for the nation, analysts are uncertain whether the government's actions during and after 2008 alleviated or aggravated the Great Recession. Republicans have generally criticized Obama's Keynesian actions, whereas some Democrats have complained that the federal government should inject even more money into the economy. Despite these disagreements, Obama secured another presidential term during the November 2012 general election.

What Lies Ahead?

In one sense the U.S. economy is a machine, as depicted in Figure 1.1. Money is the fuel for the machine because it flows from one component to another and keeps the machine operating. However, in reality the U.S. economy is driven by hope, faith, and confidence. When businesses and consumers are worried about the future, they hold onto their money rather than spend or invest it. Businesses hire fewer people and lay off employees, and consumers do not buy as much, which hurts business profitability. Two of these problems—high unemployment and continuing fallout from the housing bubble burst—were particularly troublesome for the American people. Likewise, consumers' uncertainty was slow to change in the years following the recession. Thus, the damaging effects of the recession were still being felt in late 2012; however, there was cautious, but growing, optimism about the financial future of the nation.

CHAPTER 2
ECONOMIC INDICATORS AND PUBLIC PERCEPTIONS

The U.S. economy is extremely large and complex, with many different interacting factors at play. Macroeconomics is the study of the overall condition of an economy—that is, the big picture. By contrast, microeconomics is the study of one or more small pieces of an economy, for example, how a particular industry or region is performing. Government agencies and private organizations collect voluminous amounts of data on many different aspects of the U.S. economy. Some of these data are aggregated (combined for consideration as a whole) so that the macroeconomic condition of the country can be analyzed and tracked over time. The most common economic indicators are widely broadcast in the media and are the subject of much analysis by leaders in government, industry, and the financial markets. The American public consists of hundreds of millions of individuals experiencing and interpreting various microeconomies and the national macroeconomy. Public opinion polls aggregate data reflecting these individual economic experiences and expectations to provide a picture of the national economic mood of the populace.

CATEGORIZING ECONOMIC INDICATORS

Economic indicators can be broadly categorized by the type of organization that compiles them (e.g., government or private), the economic sectors that are represented by the indicators (i.e., business, personal, or government), and the timing of the indicators relative to the business cycle.

Types of Indicator Compilers

There are many government and private organizations that regularly compile economic indicators. In general, economic data collected about individual businesses and people are aggregated (combined to represent the whole). Many government-compiled indicators are published openly. Even though some nongovernmental entities also publicly disseminate economic data, they more commonly publish only summaries or select portions of the data and charge membership or subscription fees for full access to the data.

The federal government is unarguably the chief collector and compiler of economic data, which it uses to prepare the national economic accounts—that is, accounts that indicate the economic condition of the nation as a whole. Some of the key agencies and bureaus involved in this effort are the U.S. Department of Commerce's Bureau of Economic Analysis (BEA), the U.S. Department of Labor's Bureau of Labor Statistics (BLS), the U.S. Department of the Treasury's Internal Revenue Service (IRS), the U.S. Census Bureau, and the Federal Reserve Board. In *Concepts and Methods of the U.S. National Income and Product Accounts* (November 2011, http://www.bea.gov/national/pdf/NIPAchapters1-9.pdf), the BEA notes that the national economic accounts include three main components:

- National Income and Product Accounts (NIPAs)—data compiled by the BEA showing "the value and composition of national output and the distribution of incomes generated in its production." Perhaps the most well-known NIPA component is the gross domestic product (GDP), which is a measure of the total value of goods and services that are newly produced or newly provided during a given period. The derivation of the GDP is described in detail later in this chapter.

- Industry Accounts—data compiled by the BEA that trace "the flow of goods and services among industries in the production process and which show the value added by each industry and the detailed commodity composition of national output, and the gross domestic product (GDP) by industry accounts, which measure the contribution of each private industry and of government to GDP."

- Flow of Funds—data compiled by the Federal Reserve Board that "record the acquisition of nonfinancial and financial assets (and the incurrence of liabilities) throughout the U.S. economy, the sources of the funds used to acquire those assets, and the value of assets held and of liabilities owed."

The federal government collects data from many different sources, both public and private, to prepare the national economic accounts. Many of the account components, particularly the NIPAs, are examined in detail in this book.

State government organizations (e.g., public colleges) also compile economic indicators, often in concert with private businesses. For example, the University of Michigan collaborates with the media company Thomson Reuters to conduct the Surveys of Consumers (http://www.press.sca.isr.umich.edu/), a series of panel surveys that quiz U.S. consumers about their economic conditions and expectations. The results are published as monthly indexes.

Other major compilers of economic indicators include businesses such as the Dow Jones & Company (http://www.dowjones.com/), which publishes stock market indexes (e.g., the Dow Jones Industrial Average) that track the stock market performance of groups of companies. Many other businesses engaged in the financial services industry also compile stock market indexes; NASDAQ and Standard & Poor's are well-known names in this field.

The Conference Board (2012, http://www.conference-board.org/about/index.cfm?id=1980) is another private compiler of economic indicators. The nonprofit company bills itself as "a global, independent business membership and research association working in the public interest." The Conference Board publishes various indexes that summarize economic data collected from numerous sources, both government and private. One of the Conference Board's most cited indicators is the Consumer Confidence Index, an index that is based on public surveys. The board, like many non-governmental compilers, releases limited data for public review and reserves detailed data and analyses for paying members or subscribers.

Indicators by Economic Sector

Economic indicators can also be broadly categorized by the economic sectors that they represent: business, personal, or government.

BUSINESS SECTOR. The U.S. business sector is extremely diverse with businesses ranging in size from large corporations to small home-based companies. Businesses may be publicly held (meaning that at least some of their ownership shares have been sold to the public) or privately held

(meaning that none of their ownership shares have been sold to the public). This distinction is important because publicly held companies are required by federal law to report certain operating data, such as earnings, to the government and to stockholders. This is a key source of information for entities that compile economic data. In addition, businesses of all sizes and types are required to file tax returns with the IRS and meet other government reporting requirements, particularly if the businesses have employees. The data contained in these documents may or may not be available to the public, but are accessible by government agencies, such as the BEA. Industry organizations and trade associations are also key sources of economic data about business activities.

Economic indicators for the business sector track expenses, profits, sales, prices, taxes, assets, numbers of establishments and employees, wages and salaries, product inventories, capacity, productivity, and other financial factors. Besides the stock market indexes described earlier, some of the most often cited economic indicators for the business sector are:

- Corporate Profits—compiled by the BEA for the NIPAs, this indicator tracks the profits (i.e., pre-tax income or receipts minus expenses) of corporations. In *Concepts and Methods of the U.S. National Income and Product Accounts*, the BEA explains that, for purposes of the NIPAs, corporations are defined as businesses that are required to file federal corporate tax returns. Corporate profits data are examined in detail in Chapter 6.

- Industrial Production and Capacity Utilization—the Federal Reserve compiles this indicator, which includes a monthly index of industrial production and associated capacity indexes and capacity utilization rates for manufacturing and mining companies and electric and gas utilities. According to the Federal Reserve (October 16, 2012, http://www.federalreserve.gov/releases/g17/current/table0.htm), the manufacturing industry includes companies traditionally considered to manufacture goods, plus logging companies and companies that are engaged in publishing newspapers, periodicals, books, and directories.

- Producer Price Index—compiled by the BLS, this is actually a group of indexes that measure the average change over time in the prices received by U.S. producers for their goods and services. The BLS (May 24, 2011, http://www.bls.gov/ppi/ppifaq.htm) notes that more than 10,000 individual products and product groups are covered by the indexes, which account for the output of all U.S. goods-producing industries and companies engaged in mining, agriculture, fishing, forestry, natural gas, construction, and waste and scrap materials. In addition, the indexes cover approximately three-fourths of the U.S. service providing industries.

- Housing Starts—compiled by the Census Bureau in concert with the U.S. Department of Housing and Urban Development, this indicator uses data from the Survey of Construction to estimate the number of new privately owned housing units that begin construction each month. Historical data are provided in Chapter 4.

- Retail Trade—the Census Bureau surveys selected U.S. businesses that are engaged in retail trade to compile national figures for retail sales (including sales over the Internet), inventories, operating expenses, and the number of retail establishments. According to the Census Bureau, in "Monthly & Annual Retail Trade" (2012, http://www.census.gov/retail/index.html), data are collected on a monthly, quarterly, annual, and five-year timetable; however, not all data categories are covered in each survey period.

PERSONAL SECTOR. As of 2012, the population of the United States exceeded 300 million people. For almost their entire lives people earn, spend, save, and invest money. These personal financial activities have an enormous impact on the U.S. economy. In fact, as will be explained later in this chapter, the nation's GDP is hugely dependent on personal consumption expenditures (PCE), that is, consumer spending as measured by the BEA. Two other key economic indicators for the personal sector are the inflation rate (as measured by the BLS using the consumer price index) and the unemployment rate, which is calculated by the BLS. Both economic indicators are examined in detail later in this chapter.

Surveys are widely used to obtain economic data from individual households; the data are then aggregated to represent the entire nation. It should be noted that federal government agencies often lump together individuals and nonprofit organizations in their economic indicators. For example, the BEA considers nonprofit institutions serving households (NPISHs) as people, rather than as businesses. Thus, spending by individuals and NPISHs is included in PCE values.

Indicators of particular interest for the personal sector include income, assets, spending, saving, investing, debts, bankruptcy filings, and attitudes and expectations about the economy. Besides the PCE and the inflation and unemployment rates, some of the most often cited economic indicators for the personal sector are:

- Personal income and disposable personal income (DPI)—the BEA collects data on personal income for tabulation of the NIPAs. As will be explained in Chapter 7, personal income includes employee compensation (e.g., wages and salaries) and income from unincorporated businesses, rental properties, royalties, interest, dividends, and government transfers (e.g., Social Security payments to individuals). The DPI is calculated by subtracting tax payments from personal income and provides an estimate of the amount of money that the personal sector has available to spend, save, or invest.

- Net worth—compiled by the Federal Reserve, this indicator tracks personal assets (e.g., real estate, cash, consumer goods, and certain securities, such as mutual fund shares) minus personal liabilities (i.e., debts). The Federal Reserve lumps together households and nonprofit organizations in its calculations of net worth for the personal sector.

- Consumer credit—the Federal Reserve tracks the amount of credit (excluding loans secured by real estate) that is extended to individuals by banks, credit unions, other financial institutions, and the government. Components of this indicator include credit card debt and loans for vehicles, boats, vacations, educational expenses, and other purposes.

- Debt ratios—government and private entities compile various debt ratios to provide insight of the extent to which the personal sector is leveraged (i.e., relies on credit). Example indicators include the household debt service ratio (the ratio of household debt payments to the DPI), the consumer leverage ratio (the ratio of total household debt to the DPI), and the ratio of consumer debt to total household debt.

- Consumer confidence index—this survey-based indicator is compiled by the Conference Board to track consumer sentiments regarding the economy. It is described in detail later in this chapter.

- Nonbusiness bankruptcy filings—U.S. Courts publishes data on the number and types of nonbusiness (i.e., personal) bankruptcy cases that are filed each year. Bankruptcy is a state of financial ruin. People who declare bankruptcy typically have considerable debt that cannot be repaid. Chapter 4 examines bankruptcy statistics and the benefits and consequences of filing for bankruptcy.

GOVERNMENT SECTOR. The local, state, and federal governments engage in economic activities with far-reaching effects on the nation's business and personal sectors. The indicators of interest for the government sector include revenues (particularly taxes), expenditures, budget surpluses and deficits, and the national debt. All of these indicators are described in detail in Chapter 9.

Timing Relative to the Business Cycle

In a "perfect" economy all economic indicators would be at optimum levels, for example, the employment and productivity rates would constantly be at 100% and the GDP would always grow at a healthy rate. In reality, the economy surges and falls over time. It expands for a while and then contracts, and then recovers and begins to expand again. This is known as the business cycle. Note that the word *cycle* is rather misleading, because the expansions and contractions do not happen on a set time table; they occur irregularly.

As explained in Chapter 1, the National Bureau of Economic Research (NBER) at the University of New York designates the starting and ending dates of recessions. In "Determination of the December 2007 Peak in Economic Activity" (December 11, 2008, http://www.nber.org/cycles/dec2008.html), the NBER officially defines a recession as "a significant decline in economic activity spread across the economy, lasting more than a few months, normally visible in production, employment, real income, and other indicators. A recession begins when the economy reaches a peak of activity and ends when the economy reaches its trough [lowest point]."

Figure 2.1 is a graph of employment in the private sector (i.e., not including government workers) covering several decades. Even though employment shows a general upward trend over time, there are several noticeable peaks and troughs along the way. Comparison of the employment cycle with the list of NBER-declared recessions (http://www.nber.org/cycles/cyclesmain.html) indicates that the employment peaks and troughs shown in Figure 2.1 often occurred near the times of the peaks and troughs in the overall business cycle. Thus, there appears to be a timing relationship between the employment cycle and the business cycle. In fact, such a relationship exists for many economic indicators.

The Conference Board indicates in *Business Cycle Indicators Handbook* (2000, http://www.conference-board.org/pdf_free/economics/bci/BCI-Handbook.pdf) that economists divide some economic indicators into three categories, depending on the timing relationship between the indicators and the business cycle:

- Leading indicators—tend to show peaks and troughs soon before the peaks and troughs that occur in the business cycle

- Coincident indicators—tend to show peaks and troughs that coincide with the peaks and troughs that occur in the business cycle

- Lagging indicators—tend to show peaks and troughs soon after the peaks and troughs that occur in the business cycle

It should be noted that the word *soon* in this context is not time measured in days or weeks, but in months or quarters. For example, a leading indicator might peak three to six months before the business cycle does; likewise, a lagging indicator might peak up to a year or two after the business cycle does.

The Conference Board compiles an index for each of the three types of indicators. For example, the Conference Board Leading Economic Index (http://www.conference-board.org/data/bcicountry.cfm?cid=1) includes 10 components that are economic indicators compiled regularly by government and private sources. One of the components is the average weekly hours of employees in the manufacturing sector, an indicator that is compiled by the BLS. The Conference Board notes "this component tends to lead the business cycle because employers usually adjust work hours before increasing or decreasing their workforce."

FIGURE 2.1

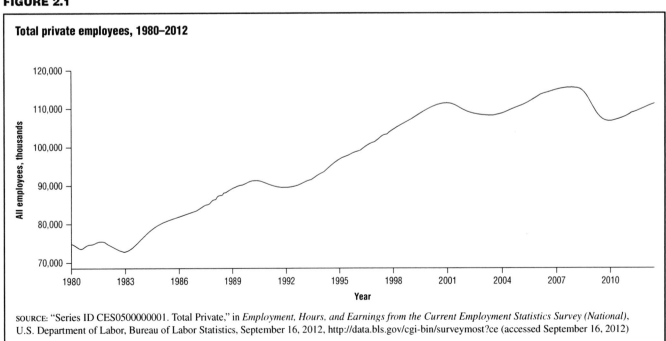

Total private employees, 1980–2012

SOURCE: "Series ID CES0500000001. Total Private," in *Employment, Hours, and Earnings from the Current Employment Statistics Survey (National)*, U.S. Department of Labor, Bureau of Labor Statistics, September 16, 2012, http://data.bls.gov/cgi-bin/surveymost?ce (accessed September 16, 2012)

Leading indicators are closely watched because of their predictive nature—that is, they provide clues about what lies ahead for the economy at large. Investors, in particular, monitor leading indicators to help them make decisions about how best to invest their money for maximum profit. However, leading indicator clues can be difficult to decipher. Sometimes components of the index move in opposite directions. Also, it is impossible to know until after the fact that a certain indicator has definitely peaked or troughed because indicators fluctuate over the short term.

Coincident and lagging indicators coincide with and lag the business cycle, respectively. Thus, they have no predictive nature and receive far less attention than the leading indicators. However, coincident indicators help economists confirm the timing of expansions and contractions in the overall economy. Example coincident indicators include employment and personal income. Both factors tend to change in concert with the business cycle. An example of a lagging indicator is the ratio of consumer debt to personal income. As the Conference Board indicates, "This ratio usually shows a trough many months after the recession ends, because consumers tend to initially hold off personal borrowing until personal income has risen substantially." Another example of a lagging indicator is the duration of unemployment. The board notes that this indicator is low during expansions and rises during recessions; however, it is slow to recover even after recessions end because employers tend to wait for recoveries to show staying power before they begin hiring again.

KEY ECONOMIC INDICATORS

Three key economic indicators will be examined in depth in this chapter because they are so widely reported, closely watched, and provide a good big-picture view of how the U.S. economy is doing. They are the gross domestic product, the consumer price index, and the unemployment rate.

Gross Domestic Product

The gross domestic product (GDP) measures in dollars the total value of U.S. goods and services that are newly produced or newly provided during a given period. It is calculated and published by the BEA and is one of the most important and accurate ways the government tracks the health of the economy. The GDP can be calculated in different ways. One method is the expenditure approach. It sums all the spending that takes place during a specified period on final goods and services that are newly produced or newly provided. The components of this calculation are:

- Consumption—the amount spent by consumers on final goods and services. This includes food, clothing, household appliances, and so on, and payments for medical care, haircuts, dry cleaning, and other types of services. One major item not included in this category is the purchase of residential housing, which is considered to be an investment, rather than a consumption expense.

- Investment—this category has three components. One is the amount spent by businesses on assets they will use to provide goods and services (e.g., new machines and equipment, warehouses, software, and company vehicles). Also included are changes in the value of business inventories. This amount can be positive or negative. Residential housing is the third component of the investment category.

- Government expenditures—the amount spent by the government (local, state, and federal) on final goods and services. This category does not include transfer payments to the public (such as Social Security and unemployment compensation) because these expenditures do not represent goods or services purchased.

- Net exports—the difference between the value of U.S. exports and imports. In other words, net exports equal the amount that foreigners paid for American goods minus the amount that Americans spent on foreign goods. If the United States exports more than it imports, this value will be positive. If the country imports more than it exports, this value will be negative.

It should be noted that the GDP counts only the final value paid for goods and services, not the value of intermediate transactions. For example, the value of steel sold by a steel company to an automaker is not counted. The value of the car made from the steel is counted when the car is sold in the marketplace. As mentioned earlier, to be counted in the GDP, a product must be new; thus, the sales of used items are not included in the GDP.

COMPARISON WITH THE GROSS NATIONAL PRODUCT. Before 1991 the U.S. government relied on an economic indicator called the gross national product (GNP) to measure U.S. productivity. The GNP is calculated the same way that the GDP is calculated, except that the GNP includes the contribution of U.S. production in foreign countries (e.g., an American-owned factory in Mexico). The GDP includes only production that occurs within the boundaries of the United States.

NOMINAL VERSUS REAL GDP. Economists refer to GDP values as being nominal (based on current dollar values) or real (based on inflation-adjusted dollar values). Consider a simple example in which a nation's only production is 1,000 identical new cars produced and sold each year. Assume this nation suffers from inflation, meaning that the price charged and paid for each car increases each year. A graph of this nation's GDP would go upward, indicating that production increases each year, while actually it is just the price of the cars that is increasing.

FIGURE 2.2

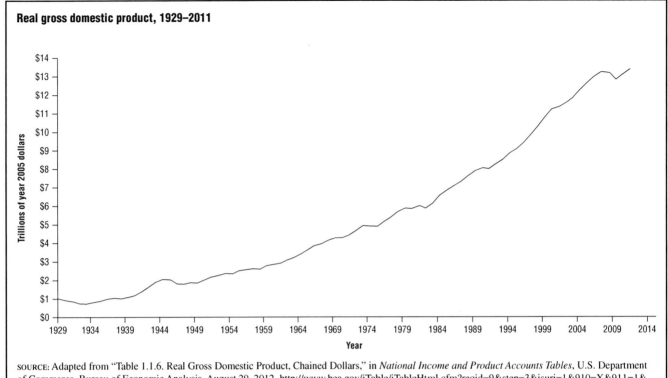

Real gross domestic product, 1929–2011

SOURCE: Adapted from "Table 1.1.6. Real Gross Domestic Product, Chained Dollars," in *National Income and Product Accounts Tables*, U.S. Department of Commerce, Bureau of Economic Analysis, August 29, 2012, http://www.bea.gov/iTable/iTableHtml.cfm?reqid=9&step=3&isuri=1&910=X&911=1& 903=6&904=2010&905=2012&9

FIGURE 2.3

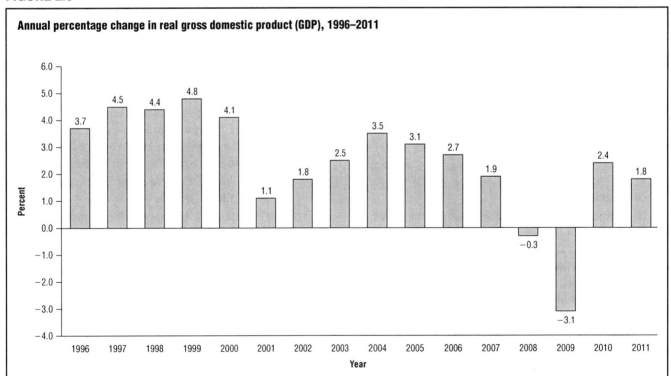

Annual percentage change in real gross domestic product (GDP), 1996–2011

Note: Based on chained (2005) dollars.

SOURCE: Adapted from "Table 7. Real Gross Domestic Product: Percent Change from Preceding Year," in *News Release: Gross Domestic Product: Second Quarter 2012 (Second Estimate); Corporate Profits: Second Quarter 2012 (Preliminary)*, U.S. Department of Commerce, Bureau of Economic Analysis, August 29, 2012, http://www.bea.gov/newsreleases/national/gdp/2012/pdf/gdp2q12_2nd.pdf (accessed September 10, 2012)

To remedy this problem, economists adjust the actual GDP values (nominal values) to account for inflation. The adjusted values are called the real GDP values. They are useful for comparing GDP changes over time. Figure 2.2 shows the real GDP values for the U.S. economy between 1929 and 2011. These values were calculated assuming that a dollar had the exact same value over time—the value it had in 2005.

Figure 2.3 shows the annual percentage change in the real GDP between 1996 and 2011. In general, GDP growth of 2% to 4% per year is considered to be optimal for the U.S. economy. The real GDP experienced negative growth between 2007 and 2008 (−0.3%) and between 2008 and 2009 (−3.1%), reflecting the poor state of the economy. Between 2009 and 2010 the GDP began growing again and was up by 2.4% overall. Likewise, between 2010 and 2011 the GDP grew by 1.8%.

Consumer Price Index

The consumer price index (CPI) provides a measure of price changes in consumer goods and services over a specific period. Each month the BLS calculates the purchase price of a fixed "basket" of thousands of goods and services that are commonly purchased for consumption by U.S. households. These purchases are divided into eight major categories:

- Food and beverages—at-home and away-from-home consumption

- Housing—includes rent of primary residence or owners' equivalent rent

- Apparel

- Transportation—includes insurance payments

- Medical care

- Recreation—includes pet expenses

- Education and communication—includes computer software

- Other goods and services—haircuts, cigarettes, funeral expenses, and so on

The basket price includes sales and excise taxes paid on goods that are purchased. Payments for income taxes and investments, such as stocks and bonds, are not included.

An index is a useful tool for comparing changes over time. The index for the basket price for a selected period is arbitrarily set to 100. This is the reference index. All other basket prices are compared with the reference index using this equation: index = (basket price/reference basket price) × 100. Therefore, a graph of CPI data over time does not show the actual prices paid for the baskets but a series of index numbers that are useful for determining price changes. Figure 2.4 shows the average annual CPI between 1913 and 2011. It uses the period of 1982 to 1984 as the reference period for which the CPI value is arbitrarily set to 100.

FIGURE 2.4

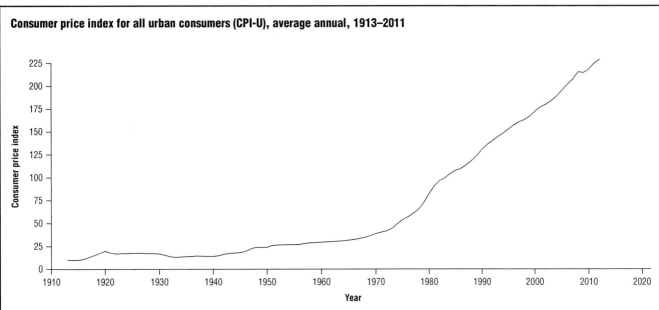

Consumer price index for all urban consumers (CPI-U), average annual, 1913–2011

Note: Reference: 1982–1984 = 100.

SOURCE: Adapted from "Consumer Price Index, All Urban Consumers—(CPI-U), U.S. City Average, All Items, 1982–84=100," in *Consumer Price Index History Table*, U.S. Department of Labor, Bureau of Labor Statistics, August 15, 2012, ftp://ftp.bls.gov/pub/special.requests/cpi/cpiai.txt (accessed September 11, 2012)

Percent changes in price between two years can be determined based on the difference in index values. For example, according to the BLS, in "Consumer Price Index" (October 16, 2012, ftp://ftp.bls.gov/pub/special.requests/cpi/cpiai.txt), the average CPI was 136.2 in 1991. By 2011 it had risen to 224.9—a difference of 88.7 index points. Dividing 88.7 by 136.2 and multiplying by 100 provides a percentage difference of 65%. On average, prices increased by 65% during this 20-year period.

The data presented in Figure 2.4 are for urban households. According to the BLS, in "Frequently Asked Questions (FAQ)" (October 19, 2011, http://www.bls.gov/cpi/cpifaq.htm), the urban CPI (CPI-U) represents the buying habits of approximately 87% of the U.S. population. The BLS also calculates a CPI for urban dwellers employed in clerical or wage occupations, which are a subset of people included in the CPI-U. This subset represents approximately 32% of the U.S. population. Besides the national average, the BLS publishes CPI data for specific regions of the United States and for dozens of metropolitan areas.

CALCULATING AVERAGE ANNUAL INFLATION RATES FROM THE CPI. Price inflation can be defined as the increase in price over time of a fixed basket of goods and services. Thus, the CPI provides economists with a tool for quantifying inflation rates. The percent change in CPI from year to year is the inflation rate for that year. Figure 2.5 shows the average annual inflation rate for the U.S. economy for each year between 1915 and 2011 based on CPI-U data. In "Consumer Price Index," the BLS states that the average CPI-U for 2010 was 218.1 and for 2011 was 224.9. The inflation rate was ([224.9 − 218.1]/218.1) × 100 = 3.2%. This means

that, on average, the price of consumer goods and services increased by 3.1% between 2010 and 2011. It also means that the purchasing power of a dollar decreased during this period. For example, an item that cost $1.00 in 2010 cost just over $1.03 in 2011.

In general, annual inflation rates of 2% to 3% are considered to be signs of a healthy growing economy where demand slightly outpaces supply. Larger inflation rates can be worrisome. The U.S. economy has suffered from double-digit inflation rates due to the effects of the world wars and during the 1970s and early 1980s.

Unemployment Rate

The U.S. government calculates the nation's unemployment rate for a given period by dividing the number of unemployed people by the total labor force (unemployed plus employed people). The employment status of people is determined based on responses by the public to a monthly government survey called the Current Population Survey (CPS). The CPS is administered by the Census Bureau for the BLS. According to the BLS, in "How the Government Measures Unemployment" (October 16, 2009, http://www.bls.gov/cps/cps_htgm.htm), the survey is administered to approximately 60,000 households per month.

The BLS counts people as being unemployed if they meet all the following criteria:

- They do not have a job

- They have actively looked for work in the previous four weeks

- They are currently available for work

FIGURE 2.5

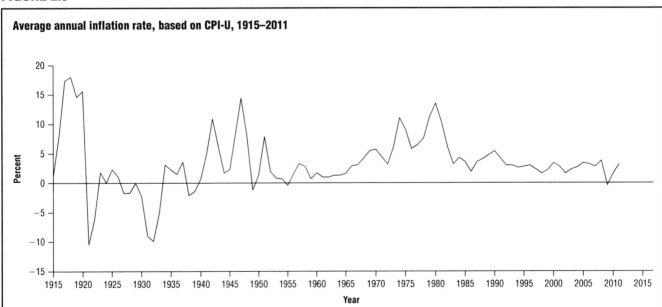

Average annual inflation rate, based on CPI-U, 1915–2011

SOURCE: Adapted from "Consumer Price Index, All Urban Consumers—(CPI-U), U.S. City Average, All Items, 1982–84=100," in *Consumer Price Index History Table*, U.S. Department of Labor, Bureau of Labor Statistics, August 15, 2012, ftp://ftp.bls.gov/pub/special.requests/cpi/cpiai.txt (accessed September 11, 2012)

FIGURE 2.6

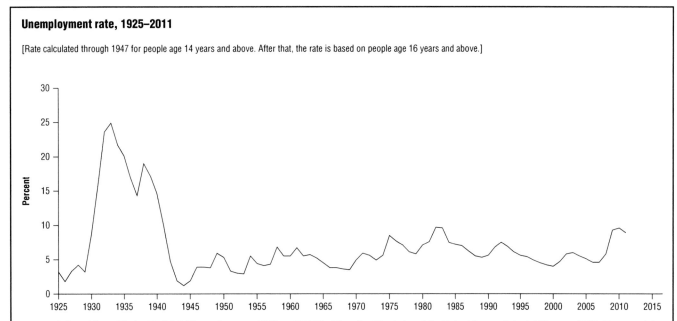

Unemployment rate, 1925–2011

[Rate calculated through 1947 for people age 14 years and above. After that, the rate is based on people age 16 years and above.]

SOURCE: Adapted from "Series D85–86. Unemployment: 1890 to 1970," in *Historical Statistics of the United States, Colonial Times to 1970, Bicentennial Edition, Part 1*, U.S. Department of Commerce, U.S. Census Bureau, September 1975, http://www2.census.gov/prod2/statcomp/documents/CT1970p1-05 .pdf (accessed September 10, 2012), and "1. Employment Status of the Civilian Noninstitutional Population, 1941 to Date," in *Labor Force Statistics from the Current Population Survey*, U.S. Department of Labor, Bureau of Labor Statistics, March 9, 2012, http://www.bls.gov/cps/cpsaat01.pdf (accessed September 10, 2012)

The BLS does not consider active-duty military personnel or institutionalized workers (such as prison inmates) to be in the labor force. In addition, some Americans are neither employed nor unemployed under the BLS definitions and thus are not in the labor force. The most obvious examples are patients in long-term care facilities and retirees. Many students and stay-at-home parents also fall into this category.

Figure 2.6 shows the annual U.S. unemployment rate between 1925 and 2011. For years through 1947, the rate is calculated based on people aged 14 years and older. Because of the passage of child labor laws, the unemployment rate for years following 1947 includes only people aged 16 years and older. The unemployment rate soared during the Great Depression (1929–1939), reaching nearly 25% in 1933. More typically, it has ranged between 3% and 8%. During the early 1980s the unemployment rate was nearly 10%, its highest rate since the 1930s. From the mid-1990s to 2008 it hovered between 4% and 6%, which is generally considered to be a reasonable range for a healthy economy. Between 2008 and 2009 the unemployment rate increased sharply from 5.8% to 9.3%. The BLS (February 28, 2012, http://www.bls.gov/cps/cpsa2011.pdf) indicates that this was the highest value in more than two decades. However, the following year would prove to be even worse; the average unemployment rate rose to 9.6% for 2010. There was a slight improvement in 2011 as the rate declined to 8.9% for the year as a whole.

Critics believe the BLS data are not representative of the nation's actual unemployment rate because the data do not include people who become discouraged and quit actively looking for work. This controversy is discussed at length in Chapter 5.

THE NUMERICAL STATE OF THE U.S. ECONOMY

Government and industry statistics on the state of the U.S. economy are released with varying frequency. Some economic indicators are published monthly, whereas others are published quarterly. Two government agencies—the BLS and the BEA—publish regularly updated economic indicators that provide a good big-picture view of how the economy is doing.

The BLS: Unemployment, Wages, and Prices

The BLS publishes *U.S. Economy at a Glance* (http://data.bls.gov/eag/eag.us.htm), which includes statistics gathered by the agency on unemployment, wages, prices, and other economic factors. Table 2.1 shows data that were available at the end of September 2012.

The unemployment rate in August 2012 was 8.1%. (See Table 2.1.) The rate was virtually unchanged from the previous five months. Comparison with the historical unemployment chart in Figure 2.6 shows that the rates from March to August 2012 are high rates for postdepression America.

TABLE 2.1

U.S. Department of Labor economic indicators, by month and by quarter, March–August 2012

United States—Monthly data	Mar 2012	Apr 2012	May 2012	June 2012	July 2012	Aug 2012
Data series						
Unemployment rate[a]	8.2	8.1	8.2	8.2	8.3	8.1
Change in payroll employment[b]	143	68	87	45	(P) 141	(P) 96
Average hourly earnings[c]	23.37	23.40	23.43	23.50	(P) 23.53	(P) 23.52
Consumer price index[d]	0.3	0.0	−0.3	0.0	0.0	0.6
Producer price index[e]	−0.2	−0.3	(P) −0.9	(P) 0.1	(P) 0.3	(P) 1.7
U.S. import price index[f]	1.4	−0.1	−1.5	(R) −2.3	(R) −0.7	0.7

[a]In percent, seasonally adjusted.
[b]Number of jobs, in thousands, seasonally adjusted.
[c]Average hourly earnings for all employees on private nonfarm payrolls.
[d]All items, U.S. city average, all urban consumers, 1982–84=100, 1-month percent change, seasonally adjusted.
[e]Finished goods, 1982=100, 1-month percent change, seasonally adjusted.
[f]All imports, 1-month percent change, not seasonally adjusted.
(R) Revised
(P) Preliminary

United States—Quarterly data	2nd quarter 2011	3rd quarter 2011	4th quarter 2011	1st quarter 2012	2nd quarter 2012
Data series					
Employment cost index[a]	0.6	0.3	0.5	0.4	0.5
Productivity[b]	1.2	0.6	2.8	−0.5	(R) 2.2

[a]Compensation, all civilian workers, quarterly data, 3-month percent change, seasonally adjusted.
[b]Output per hour, nonfarm business, quarterly data, percent change from previous quarter at annual rate, seasonally adjusted.
(R) Revised

SOURCE: Adapted from "United States," in *Economy at a Glance*, U.S. Department of Labor, Bureau of Labor Statistics, September 20, 2012, http://data.bls.gov/eag/eag.us.htm (accessed September 20, 2012)

The BLS (October 2012, http://www.bls.gov/ces/) also tracks changes in nonfarm payroll employment and average hourly earnings. These data are based on monthly surveys that are administered to approximately 140,000 businesses and government agencies as part of the bureau's Current Employment Statistics program. About 96,000 jobs were added in August 2012. (See Table 2.1.) Overall, more than half a million jobs were added between March 2010 and August 2012. The average hourly wage for employees on private nonfarm payrolls was $23.52 in August 2012, up slightly from $23.37 in March. Note that some data in Table 2.1 are considered to be preliminary and may change after further analysis by the BLS.

The CPI-U increased by 0.6% between July and August 2012. (See Table 2.1.) Monthly movements in the CPI-U for the previous five months ranged from −0.3% to 0.3% per month.

There are three other indexes reported by the BLS:

• Producer price index (PPI)—a family of indexes that measure changes over time in the selling prices received by the makers and providers of goods and services. The PPI has risen dramatically from its reference value of 100 in 1982. (See Figure 2.7.) The PPI had a dramatic downturn in 2008, but then it began to rise again. As shown in Table 2.1, the PPI increased by 1.7% between July and August 2012. PPI values for the previous five months varied from −0.9% to 0.3%. PPI values can differ from CPI values because of factors such as taxes and distribution costs.

• U.S. import price index (MPI)—indicates monthly changes in the prices of nonmilitary goods and services that are imported to the United States from the rest of the world. The MPI increased by 0.7% between July and August 2012. (See Table 2.1.) The BLS also tracks an export price index as part of its International Price Program.

• Employment cost index (ECI)—tracks quarterly changes in nonfarm civilian business labor costs based on a national compensation survey. It includes wages, salaries, and employer costs for employee benefits. The ECI increased by 0.5% from the first quarter of 2012 to the second quarter of 2012. (See Table 2.1.)

Finally, the BLS includes in *U.S. Economy at a Glance* a measure of national productivity (or efficiency). This number is a quarterly estimate of the change in output per hour of nonfarm businesses. It is calculated by comparing the amount of goods and services produced with the inputs that were used to produce them. According to the BLS, productivity increased by 2.2% from the first quarter of 2012 to the second quarter of 2012. (See Table 2.1.)

The BEA: The GDP in Detail

The BEA publishes monthly detailed data about the nation's GDP. It should be noted that until they are dubbed "final," these statistics are estimates and are frequently revised by the BEA as new data become available.

REAL GDP. Figure 2.8 shows the quarterly changes in the real GDP for the third quarter of 2008 to the second quarter of 2012. The real GDP declined between 0.3% and 8.9% per quarter through the second quarter of 2009.

FIGURE 2.7

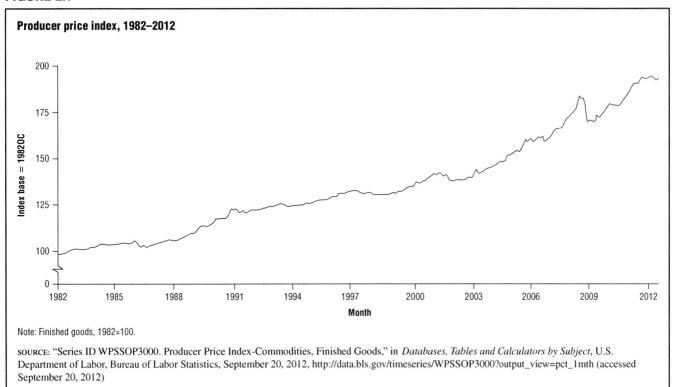

Producer price index, 1982–2012

Note: Finished goods, 1982=100.

SOURCE: "Series ID WPSSOP3000. Producer Price Index-Commodities, Finished Goods," in *Databases, Tables and Calculators by Subject*, U.S. Department of Labor, Bureau of Labor Statistics, September 20, 2012, http://data.bls.gov/timeseries/WPSSOP3000?output_view=pct_1mth (accessed September 20, 2012)

FIGURE 2.8

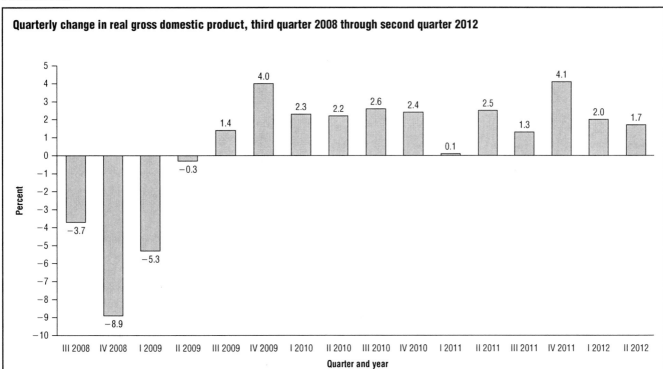

Quarterly change in real gross domestic product, third quarter 2008 through second quarter 2012

Note: Based on chained (2005) dollars.

SOURCE: Adapted from "Table 1. Real Gross Domestic Product and Related Measures: Percent Change from Preceding Period," in *News Release: Gross Domestic Product: Second Quarter 2012 (Second Estimate); Corporate Profits: Second Quarter 2012 (Preliminary)*, U.S. Department of Commerce, Bureau of Economic Analysis, August 29, 2012, http://www.bea.gov/newsreleases/national/gdp/2012/pdf/gdp2q12_2nd.pdf (accessed September 10, 2012)

TABLE 2.2

Components of gross domestic product (GDP), 2011

[Billions of current dollars]

	2011
Gross domestic product	**15,075.7**
Personal consumption expenditures	10,729.0
Goods	3,624.8
Durable goods	1,146.4
Motor vehicles and parts	373.6
Furnishings and durable household equipment	251.7
Recreational goods and vehicles	340.1
Other durable goods	181.0
Nondurable goods	2,478.4
Food and beverages purchased for off-premises consumption	810.2
Clothing and footwear	349.2
Gasoline and other energy goods	428.3
Other nondurable goods	890.7
Services	7,104.2
Household consumption expenditures (for services)	6,812.3
Housing and utilities	1,929.9
Health care	1,751.6
Transportation services	302.0
Recreation services	394.5
Food services and accommodations	670.9
Financial services and insurance	807.1
Other services	956.2
Final consumption expenditures of nonprofit institutions serving households	291.9
Gross output of nonprofit institutions	1,164.5
Less: Receipts from sales of goods and services by nonprofit institutions	872.5
Gross private domestic investment	1,854.9
Fixed investment	1,818.3
Nonresidential	1,479.6
Structures	404.8
Equipment and software	1,074.7
Information processing equipment and software	539.6
Computers and peripheral equipment	78.3
Software	278.7
Other	182.6
Industrial equipment	181.2
Transportation equipment	164.7
Other equipment	189.2
Residential	338.7
Change in private inventories	36.6
Farm	−6.1
Nonfarm	42.7
Net exports of goods and services	−568.1
Exports	2,094.2
Goods	1,474.5
Services	619.7
Imports	2,662.3
Goods	2,229.2
Services	433.0
Government consumption expenditures and gross investment	3,059.8
Federal	1,222.1
National defense	820.8
Consumption expenditures	712.1
Gross investment	108.7
Nondefense	401.3
Consumption expenditures	349.4
Gross investment	51.8
State and local	1,837.7
Consumption expenditures	1,518.0
Gross investment	319.7
Residual	
Addenda:	
Final sales of domestic product	15,039.0

These values represent a substantial downturn from past performance. The worst showing was in the fourth quarter of 2008, when the real GDP declined by 8.9% from the previous quarter. In the press release "Gross

TABLE 2.2

Components of gross domestic product (GDP), 2011 [CONTINUED]

[Billions of current dollars]

	2011
Gross domestic purchases	**15,643.7**
Final sales to domestic purchasers	15,607.1
Gross domestic product	15,075.7
Plus: Income receipts from the rest of the world	783.7
Less: Income payments to the rest of the world	31.8
Equals: Gross national product	15,327.5
Net domestic product	13,138.9

Note: Users are cautioned that particularly for components that exhibit rapid change in prices relative to other prices in the economy, the chained-dollar estimates should not be used to measure the component's relative importance or its contribution to the growth rate of more aggregate series.

SOURCE: Adapted from "Table 3. Gross Domestic Product and Related Measures: Level and Change from Preceding Period," in *News Release: Gross Domestic Product: Second Quarter 2012 (Second Estimate); Corporate Profits: Second Quarter 2012 (Preliminary)*, U.S. Department of Commerce, Bureau of Economic Analysis, August 29, 2012, http://www.bea .gov/newsreleases/national/gdp/2012/pdf/gdp2q12_2nd.pdf (accessed September 10, 2012)

Domestic Product: Fourth Quarter 2008 (Final)" (March 26, 2009, http://www.bea.gov/newsreleases/national/gdp/ 2009/pdf/gdp408f.pdf), the BEA reports that the real GDP for that quarter was negatively affected by sharp decreases in consumer spending, exports, business spending on equipment and software, and residential investment in housing.

During the third quarter of 2009 the real GDP slowly rebounded by showing an increase of 1.4% from the previous quarter. (See Figure 2.8.) The fourth quarter of 2009 was especially robust with a 4% increase. However, growth slowed over subsequent quarters ranging from 2.2% to 2.4% per quarter throughout 2010. The real GDP had only a 0.1% gain in the first quarter of 2011, but then rebounded to 2.5% for the following quarter. This was followed by 1.3% growth for the third quarter of 2011 and an impressive 4.1% growth for the last quarter of the year. As of November 2012, GDP growth for the first two quarters of 2012 was 2% and 1.7%, respectively.

NOMINAL GDP. The BEA reports that the nominal GDP (GDP in current dollars) was $15.1 trillion in 2011. A breakdown by component is detailed in Table 2.2. Personal consumption expenditures (PCE) accounted for $10.7 trillion of the GDP in 2011. This is consumer spending on goods and services. Services accounted for less than one-third of the PCE, totaling close to $7.1 trillion. Housing and utilities was the largest single service component, accounting for just over $1.9 trillion of the total. Health care costs were the second-largest component, at nearly $1.8 trillion. Spending on nondurable goods amounted to nearly $2.5 trillion. Expenditures for durable goods totaled more than $1.1 trillion. The BEA explains in *A Guide to the National Income* *and Product Accounts of the United States* (September 2006, http://www.bea.gov/national/pdf/nipaguid.pdf) that durable goods are "tangible commodities that can be stored or inventoried and that have an average life of at least 3 years." Nondurable goods are classified as "all other tangible commodities that can be stored or inventoried."

Gross private domestic investments totaled nearly $1.9 trillion in 2011. (See Table 2.2.) The vast majority of this total ($1.5 trillion) was devoted to nonresidential (business) investments in structures, equipment, and software. Residential fixed investment totaled $338.7 billion. The contribution from the change in private inventories was $36.6 billion.

Government spending and investment amounted to nearly $3.1 trillion. (See Table 2.2.) State and local governments accounted for more than half of this total. Net exports were a negative contributor to the GDP in 2011 because the value of imports ($2.7 trillion) was greater than the value of exports ($2.1 trillion).

PUBLIC PERCEPTION OF THE ECONOMY

The government's various economic indicators provide a picture of the overall condition of the U.S. economy. In reality, the state of the nation's economy is a reflection of the financial condition of the hundreds of millions of individuals and businesses that contribute to it. Thus, economic conditions at the national level can be quite different from those experienced by people at the regional and local levels.

Regional and Local Economies

Part of microeconomics study (an analysis of the behavior of economic units such as companies, industries, or households) involves the economic health of various geographical regions and communities. A regional economy can be an area as small as a neighborhood or as large as a group of states with climate, geography, industry, or culture in common. The relative strength of a regional economy reflects broader national trends. For example, during the late 19th and early 20th centuries—with the economy of the American South in shambles after the Civil War (1861–1865)—northern cities attracted millions of workers to their rapidly growing industrial centers, such as the steel mills of Pittsburgh, Pennsylvania, and the car factories of Detroit, Michigan. Later, as the population migrated elsewhere, this region became known as the Rust Belt. Similarly, during the late 20th century western states experienced substantial growth with the rise of the computer industry, thanks in large part to Microsoft, which is headquartered in Seattle, Washington, and the dot-com companies centered in California's Silicon Valley. Other major economic regions of the United States include the Farm Belt of the Great Plains and the Sun Belt states of the South and Southwest, with warm climates that make them popular tourist destinations and strong agricultural regions.

When a region or community experiences a serious economic downturn—such as in the upper Midwest, when the auto and steel manufacturers starting losing ground to foreign competitors, or in the Farm Belt, with the rise of agribusiness and the subsequent demise of the small family farm—its citizens often fall into a cycle of unemployment and poverty, leading federal and local governments and private nonprofit organizations to step in to offer assistance.

The Role of the Individual in the Economy

Almost every aspect of American life is influenced by, and further influences, the economy. Whether a person drives or flies during his or her next vacation, how he or she will pay for college and save for retirement, what advertisements he or she sees, what movies he or she watches, and what magazines he or she reads all involve making economic decisions, which then affect the way the economy functions. If a person works or plans to work, that person is a small but important part of the economy. Likewise, every time an individual buys goods or saves money, he or she is participating in economic activity.

Economists maintain that the better off the economy is, the better its participants will be. In a healthy economy people tend to have more job security, earn more money, and are able to increase opportunities for themselves and their family—thus improving their overall quality of life. By contrast, in an unstable, bad economy—such as during the Great Depression and during recessions—people are less certain of the future, face increasing pressures at work and may lose their job, and have less flexibility in being able to pay for goods and services, which in turn affects trends in employment, interest rates, the cost of living, the money supply, and all other aspects of the economy, on both the macro and micro levels.

Public Opinion about the Economy

PROBLEMS FACING THE COUNTRY. The Gallup Organization is a U.S.-based firm that conducts frequent public opinion polls to gauge the mood and attitudes of the American people on a variety of subjects. In August 2012 Gallup asked Americans to name "the most important problem facing this country today." The responses receiving the most mentions during the poll are listed in Table 2.3. "Economy in general" was the top response, cited by 31% of respondents. Unemployment/jobs was mentioned by 23% of respondents. Other economically related problems that were cited include health care (8% of respondents) and the federal budget deficit (7%).

THE PUBLIC RATES THE ECONOMY. Since 1992 the Gallup Organization has asked poll participants to provide their assessment of the overall economic condition of the country by rating it as "excellent," "good," "only fair," or "poor." In addition, respondents are asked if the economy

TABLE 2.3

Public opinion about the most important problem facing the United States, May–August 2012

WHAT DO YOU THINK IS THE MOST IMPORTANT PROBLEM FACING THIS COUNTRY TODAY?

Recent trend

	May 2012	June 2012	July 2012	August 2012
	%	%	%	%
Economy in general	31	31	29	31
Unemployment/jobs	22	25	28	23
Dissatisfaction with government	14	12	13	15
Healthcare	8	6	7	8
Federal budget deficit	9	11	7	7
Moral/ethical decline	4	4	4	5
Education	4	4	4	4
Immigration	3	2	3	4

SOURCE: Jeffrey M. Jones, "What do you think is the most important problem facing this country today?" in *U.S. Satisfaction Levels Remain Depressed*, The Gallup Organization, August 15, 2012, http://www.gallup.com/poll/156686/Satisfaction-Levels-Remain-Depressed.aspx (accessed September 11, 2012). Copyright © 2012 by Gallup, Inc. All rights reserved. The content is used with permission; however, Gallup retains all rights of republication.

is "getting better" or "getting worse." In *Gallup Economy* (September 2012, http://www.gallup.com/poll/151139/Economic-Outlook-Monthly.aspx), Gallup lists the results for the latter question dating from January 2008 to August 2012. Pessimism about the economy was high throughout 2008, with roughly 75% to 85% of those asked saying the economy was worsening. The percentages dropped closer to 55% to 65% through the middle of 2011. After a huge spike in pessimism during the summer of 2011, the country's economic expectations improved

somewhat throughout early 2012. In August 2012, 60% of those asked said the economy was getting worse, whereas 35% said it was getting better.

Gallup has historically used the responses to these two questions to calculate its own economic indicator called the Gallup Economic Confidence Index (GECI). As shown in Figure 2.9, the GECI for the week ending September 9, 2012, was −18. Figure 2.9 shows weekly aggregates of the GECI based on Gallup polls dating back to 2008. The results indicate that the GECI reached its lowest level (−65) in late 2008, and plummeted to −54 in mid- to late 2011.

Another respected indicator of the nation's economic mood is the Consumer Confidence Index (CCI), which is maintained by the Conference Board Inc., a nonprofit business organization that was founded in 1916. The CCI is calculated from the responses to monthly surveys of 5,000 U.S. households. The respondents are asked to rate the state of the existing economy and its likely direction over the next six months. In "The Conference Board Consumer Confidence Index Increases in September" (September 25, 2012, http://www.conference-board.org/data/consumerconfidence.cfm), the Conference Board reports that the CCI was 70.3 in September 2012, up from 61.3 the previous month. An arbitrary baseline value of 100 is assigned to the year 1985. According to Jason Bram and Sydney Ludvigson of the Federal Reserve Bank of New York, in "Does Consumer Confidence Forecast Household Expenditure? A Sentiment Index Horse Race" (*Economic Policy Review*, vol. 4, no. 2, June 1998), the CCI ranged between 95 and 130 during the late 1990s, a time of strong economic performance. In "Consumer Confidence Plummets" (CNN.com, February 24,

FIGURE 2.9

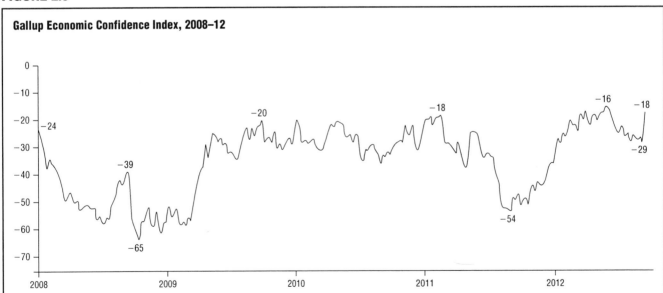

SOURCE: Lydia Saad, "Gallup Economic Confidence Index—Weekly Averages," in *U.S. Economic Confidence Surged 11 Points Last Week*, The Gallup Organization, September 11, 2012, http://www.gallup.com/poll/157385/economic-confidence-surged-points-last-week.aspx (accessed September 11, 2012). Copyright © 2012 by Gallup, Inc. All rights reserved. The content is used with permission; however, Gallup retains all rights of republication.

2009), Ben Rooney notes that the CCI fell to 25 in early 2009, the lowest point ever recorded.

Thomson Reuters and the University of Michigan provide economic indicators based on their monthly Survey of Consumers. In "Confidence Posts Significant Gain" (September 28, 2012, http://thomsonreuters.com/content/financial/pdf/i_and_a/438965/2012_09_28_confidence_posts_significant_gain.pdf), Richard T. Curtin, the director of the program, reports that the Index of Consumer Sentiment was 78.3 in September 2012, up slightly from 74.3 in August 2012 and up by nearly a third (31.6%) from September 2011. The computed index is compared with a benchmark level of 100 arbitrarily set for the first quarter of 1996. According to Curtin, the index was only in the 50s during much of 2008 and early 2009 and for a brief time in late 2011.

PERSONAL FINANCIAL SITUATION. In April 2012 Gallup asked poll participants to name "the most important financial problem facing your family today." The results are reported in *Gallup Poll Social Series: Economy and Personal Finance* (April 2012, http://www.gallup.com/file/poll/154115/Enough_Money_to_Live_Comfortably_Biggest_Financial_Concern_120425.pdf). The problem receiving the most mentions was lack of money/low wages (18%), followed by health care costs (12%), the cost of owning/renting a home (12%), the high cost of living/inflation (11%), energy costs/oil and gas prices (11%), and too much debt/not enough money to pay debts (9%).

Gallup pollsters have also asked Americans if they are "financially better off," "financially worse off," or financially about the same since the previous year. As shown in Figure 2.10, 37% said they were financially better off in 2012 than they were in 2011. A greater percentage (42%) said they were financially worse off in 2012, compared with the year before. Another 20% indicated that their financial situation was virtually unchanged. During the same poll the participants were asked to gauge their financial condition in the coming year. (See Figure 2.11.) Nearly two-thirds (63%) said they expect to be financially better off in 2013, whereas 18% indicated they expect their financial situation to be worse in 2013. Another 15% said they expect to be in about the same financial condition in 2013 as they were in 2012.

Economic Forecasting

The vast complexities of the macroeconomy make it difficult for forecasters to make predictions about future business cycles. Nonetheless, government and private sources do conduct economic forecasting, primarily with regards to individual economic indicators, such as the GDP or unemployment rates. The Congressional Budget Office (CBO) explains in "Overview" (2012, http://www.cbo.gov/about/overview) that it produces "independent,

FIGURE 2.10

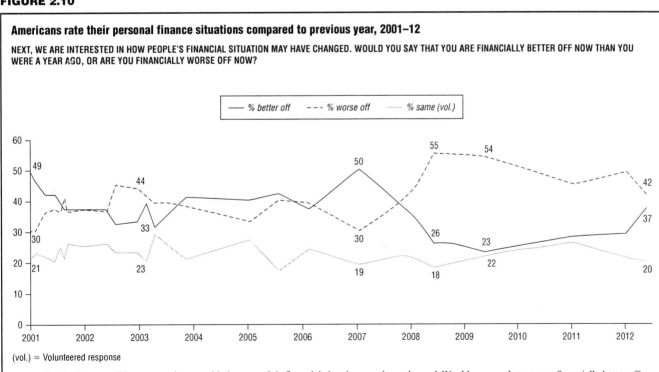

Americans rate their personal finance situations compared to previous year, 2001–12

NEXT, WE ARE INTERESTED IN HOW PEOPLE'S FINANCIAL SITUATION MAY HAVE CHANGED. WOULD YOU SAY THAT YOU ARE FINANCIALLY BETTER OFF NOW THAN YOU WERE A YEAR AGO, OR ARE YOU FINANCIALLY WORSE OFF NOW?

(vol.) = Volunteered response

SOURCE: Frank Newport, "Next, we are interested in how people's financial situation may have changed. Would you say that you are financially better off now than you were a year ago, or are you financially worse off now?" in *Americans' Optimism about Their Financial Future Recovers*, The Gallup Organization, May 16, 2012, http://www.gallup.com/poll/154688/Americans-Optimism-Financial-Future-Recovers.aspx (accessed September 11, 2012). Copyright © 2012 by Gallup, Inc. All rights reserved. The content is used with permission; however, Gallup retains all rights of republication.

FIGURE 2.11

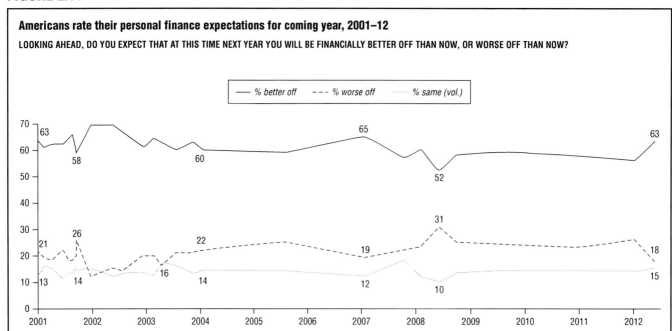

Americans rate their personal finance expectations for coming year, 2001–12

LOOKING AHEAD, DO YOU EXPECT THAT AT THIS TIME NEXT YEAR YOU WILL BE FINANCIALLY BETTER OFF THAN NOW, OR WORSE OFF THAN NOW?

SOURCE: Frank Newport, "Looking ahead, do you expect that at this time next year you will be financially better off than now, or worse off than now?" in *Americans' Optimism About Their Financial Future Recovers*, The Gallup Organization, May 16, 2012, http://www.gallup.com/poll/154688/Americans-Optimism-Financial-Future-Recovers.aspx (accessed September 11, 2012). Copyright © 2012 by Gallup, Inc. All rights reserved. The content is used with permission; however, Gallup retains all rights of republication.

nonpartisan, timely analysis of economic and budgetary issues to support the Congressional budget process." The CBO publishes annual budget outlooks that are updated as needed to reflect changing economic conditions. As of November 2012, the most recent annual outlook, *The Budget and Economic Outlook: Fiscal Years 2012 to 2022* (http://www.cbo.gov/sites/default/files/cbofiles/attach ments/01-31-2012_Outlook.pdf), was published in January 2012. In August 2012 the CBO updated its projections in *An Update to the Budget and Economic Outlook: Fiscal Years 2012 to 2022* (http://www.cbo.gov/sites/default/fil es/cbofiles/attachments/08-22-2012-Update_to_Outlook .pdf). The reports include baseline projections that assume

that current laws will remain in place and an alternative fiscal scenario based on alternative policy assumptions. As will be explained in Chapter 9, future federal budgets were very uncertain as of November 2012 due to political wrangling over spending priorities and the national debt. Even though the CBO reports include projections through 2022 for economic indicators, such as the GDP and unemployment rates, the organization (2012, http://www.cbo .gov/publication/42905) warns that the projections are highly speculative and "are not a forecast of future events; rather, they are intended to provide a benchmark against which potential policy changes can be measured."

CHAPTER 3
THE AMERICAN CONSUMER

The use of money is all the advantage there is in having money.

—Benjamin Franklin, *Poor Richard's Almanack* (1737)

Americans love to spend money, and their aggressive spending helps fuel both the U.S. and global economies, as imported goods are widely available and popular in the U.S. market. The federal government measures consumer spending by summing what it calls personal consumption expenditures (PCE). The PCE is the largest contributing factor, by far, to the nation's gross domestic product (GDP; the total market value of final goods and services that are produced within an economy in a given year). As shown in Table 2.2 in Chapter 2, the GDP was nearly $15.1 trillion in 2011. The PCE totaled $10.7 trillion, or 71% of the GDP. Thus, consumer spending is the most important factor in the nation's GDP.

Consumer spending has a ripple effect that spreads throughout the economy. When consumers spend more money, businesses can earn more profits, which they can use to hire more workers and/or raise worker wages. This, in turn, gives consumers more money to spend. It is a circular process that in good economic times pushes the nation's GDP ever higher. However, the reverse is also true. When consumers spend less money, businesses earn less profits and may lay off workers, freeze hiring, and/or cut wages. These actions give consumers less money to spend—a downward spiral that is reflected in poor GDP performance.

The relationship between employment and consumer spending seems clear-cut on the surface, but there is a complicating factor: debt. Consumer spending funded largely by borrowed money can provide a temporary "false positive" (that is, such spending seems good but, in reality, it is not) in the GDP. The GDP rises, as does employment, because consumer spending is rising. However, at some point the consumers who took on debt must pay it back. This may cut so deeply into their incomes that they reduce their spending. Another factor that affects spending is consumer confidence. People who are optimistic about their future economic conditions tend to spend more freely. Uncertainty and fear about the future have the opposite effect. They spur people to hang on to their money, to save it rather than spend it.

All of these complicating and interrelated factors have been in evidence in the past 20 years. The U.S. economy underwent stunning growth during the late 1990s. However, 10 years later the nation was mired in the so-called Great Recession, a financial mess of historic proportions. The aftereffects of this downslide were still apparent in late 2012 and highlighted the tremendous importance that consumer spending plays in the overall economy.

TRACKING CONSUMER SPENDING

The U.S. government tracks consumer spending and publishes the results in different formats. PCE data are compiled by the U.S. Department of Commerce's Bureau of Economic Analysis (BEA) for the National Income and Product Accounts. In *Concepts and Methods of the U.S. National Income and Product Accounts* (November 2011, http://www.bea.gov/national/pdf/NIPAchapters1-9.pdf), the BEA notes that data used to calculate the PCE are collected from numerous sources, including government agencies and trade associations. Primary sources include the U.S. Census Bureau and the U.S. Bureau of Labor Statistics (BLS). The PCE is based on aggregate data (data summed to represent the entire population).

In addition, the BLS publishes the annual Consumer Expenditure Survey (CE) that estimates the consumer spending of an average U.S. household during a given year. The PCE and the CE are examined in this chapter.

Personal Consumption Expenditures

In *Concepts and Methods of the U.S. National Income and Product Accounts*, the BEA explains that the PCE "measures the goods and services purchased by 'persons'—that is, by households and by nonprofit institutions serving households (NPISHs)—who are resident in the United States." However, the PCE also includes purchases by U.S. government civilian and military personnel who are stationed outside the United States and purchases made by other U.S. residents who are abroad for up to one year.

The PCE primarily covers purchases by households of new goods and services provided by private businesses. However, the following components are also included in the PCE:

- Purchases of new goods and of services by households from government and government enterprises
- Costs incurred by NPISHs in providing services on behalf of households
- Net purchases of used goods by households
- Purchases abroad of goods and services by U.S. residents traveling, working, or attending school in foreign countries
- Expenditures financed by third-party payers on behalf of households, such as employer-paid health insurance and medical care financed through government programs
- Expenses associated with life insurance and with private and government employee pension plans
- Imputed purchases that keep PCE invariant to changes in the way that certain activities are carried out—for example, whether housing is rented or owned or whether employees are paid in cash or in kind

The last item requires some explanation. To "impute" means to attribute. In this context the BEA assigns market values to activities that are not actually market transactions. A simple example given by the BEA concerns a free meal that an employer provides to an employee. The BEA would estimate the market value of the meal to the employee and include it in the PCE as an imputed purchase. In a much more complicated calculation the agency also imputes the "space rent of nonfarm owner-occupied housing." This basically means that the BEA estimates how much in rent would have been paid by a homeowner-occupier to rent space of similar type and size to the owned home. The values of numerous other nonmarket transactions are also imputed by the BEA.

In 2011 the nation's PCE totaled $10.7 trillion. (See Table 3.1.) Major PCE categories include durable goods, nondurable goods, and services. In *Concepts and*

Methods of the U.S. National Income and Product Accounts, the BEA defines goods as "tangible commodities that can be stored or inventoried." Durable goods are goods that have an "average useful life" of at least three years. Thus, nondurable goods are goods with an "average usual life" of less than three years. Services are defined as "commodities that cannot be stored or inventoried and that are usually consumed at the place and time of purchase." Note that housing is listed under services. This category includes rent paid by renters and the imputed cost for homeowners-occupiers.

Services accounted for the largest major component of the PCE in 2011, totaling just over $7.1 trillion. (See Table 3.1.) Housing and utilities ($1.9 trillion) and health care ($1.8 trillion) were the two largest components of services spending. Americans spent nearly $2.5 trillion on nondurable goods in 2011. Nearly one-third ($810 billion) of this amount was devoted to food and beverages purchased for consumption elsewhere.

TABLE 3.1

Personal consumption expenditures, by major type of good and service, 2011

[Billions of dollars]

	2011
Personal consumption expenditures (PCE)	**10,729.0**
Goods	**3,624.8**
Durable goods	1,146.4
Motor vehicles and parts	373.6
Furnishings and durable household equipment	251.7
Recreational goods and vehicles	340.1
Other durable goods	181.0
Nondurable goods	2,478.4
Food and beverages purchased for off-premises consumption	810.2
Clothing and footwear	349.2
Gasoline and other energy goods	428.3
Other nondurable goods	890.7
Services	**7,104.2**
Household consumption expenditures (for services)	6,812.3
Housing and utilities	1,929.9
Health care	1,751.6
Transportation services	302.0
Recreation services	394.5
Food services and accommodations	670.9
Financial services and insurance	807.1
Other services	956.2
Final consumption expenditures of nonprofit institutions serving households (NPISHs)[1]	291.9
Gross output of nonprofit institutions[2]	1,164.5
Less: Receipts from sales of goods and services by nonprofit institutions[3]	872.5
Addenda:	
PCE excluding food and energy[4]	9,271.1
Energy goods and services[5]	647.7
Market-based PCE[6]	9,454.8
Market-based PCE excluding food and energy[6]	7,997.2

SOURCE: "Table 2.3.5. Personal Consumption Expenditures by Major Type of Product," in *National Income and Product Accounts Tables*, U.S. Department of Commerce, Bureau of Economic Analysis, August 29, 2012, http://www.bea.gov/ iTable/iTableHtml.cfm?reqid=9&step=3&isuri=1&910=X&911=0 &903=65&904=2011&905=2011&906=A (accessed September 12, 2012)

Another $1.1 trillion was spent on durable goods, such as motor vehicles and furniture. Note that many PCE values are based on industry information. In other words, the BLS estimates consumer spending by calculating the final value of goods and services sold by businesses.

Consumer Expenditure Survey

Consumer Expenditure Survey (CE) data are compiled by the government based on consumer-supplied information. Purchase diaries are sent to sample households around the country. Participants record their everyday purchases and expenses in the diaries. Periodic interviews are conducted to collect diary information and quiz participants about their finances and spending habits. CE data are collected from households (called "consumer units") that are representative of the civilian noninstitutional population of the United States (i.e., people not in the military and not in institutions, such as prisons or long-term care facilities).

According to the BLS, the average U.S. household spent $49,705 in 2011. (See Table 3.2.) The largest components were housing ($16,803), transportation ($8,293), and food ($6,458). It should be noted that the housing component does not include mortgage principal payments, because they are considered to be repayment of a loan, rather than a consumer expense. Thus, CE data underreport the true cost of housing for Americans with mortgages.

The BLS notes that the average consumer unit in 2011 included 2.5 people and had a pretax annual income of $63,685. (See Table 3.2.) Most (65%) of the consumer units owned their home.

The CE results provide detailed data on American spending habits. For example, participants break down food purchases as to meal location (at home or away from home). The 2011 survey indicates that the average household spent $3,838 on food at home and $2,620 eating out. (See Table 3.2.) Each household averaged $115 per year for reading materials and $1,051 per year for educational expenses. Another $456 per year was spent on alcohol and $351 per year on tobacco products and smoking supplies. The average U.S. household reported spending $3,313 on health care and donating $1,721 in cash to charitable causes.

HISTORICAL TRENDS IN CONSUMER SPENDING

The difference between nominal and real economic data was explained in Chapter 2. In brief, nominal data are based on current dollar values, whereas real data are based on inflation-adjusted dollars. When tracking historical trends, real data are used to provide a consistent comparison over time.

TABLE 3.2

Consumer expenditure survey results, 2011

Item	2011
Number of consumer units (in thousands)	122,287
Consumer unit characteristics:	
Income before taxes[a]	$63,685
Income after taxes[a]	61,673
Age of reference person	49.7
Average number in consumer unit:	
Persons	2.5
Children under 18	0.6
Persons 65 and over	0.3
Earners	1.3
Vehicles	1.9
Percent distribution:	
Sex of reference person:	
Male	47
Female	53
Housing tenure:	
Homeowner	65
With mortgage	40
Without mortgage	25
Renter	35
Race of reference person:	
Black	12
White, Asian, and all other races	88
Hispanic or Latino origin of reference person:	
Hispanic or Latino	12
Not Hispanic or Latino	88
Education of reference person:	
Elementary (1–8)	5
High school (9–12)	34
College	62
Never attended and other	0
At least one vehicle owned or leased	88
Average annual expenditures:	**$49,705**
Food	6,458
Food at home	3,838
Cereals and bakery products	531
Cereals and cereal products	175
Bakery products	356
Meats, poultry, fish, and eggs	832
Beef	223
Pork	162
Other meats	123
Poultry	154
Fish and seafood	121
Eggs	50
Dairy products	407
Fresh milk and cream	150
Other dairy products	257
Fruits and vegetables	715
Fresh fruits	247
Fresh vegetables	224
Processed fruits	116
Processed vegetables	128
Other food at home	1,353
Sugar and other sweets	144
Fats and oils	110
Miscellaneous foods	690
Nonalcoholic beverages	361
Food prep by cu, out-of-town trips	48
Food away from home	2,620

The nation's inflation rate is calculated using the consumer price index (CPI), which was described in Chapter 2. Table 3.3 lists the annual percent change in the urban CPI (CPI-U) for all items and specific categories of items between 2004 and 2011 on a December-to-December basis.

TABLE 3.2

Consumer expenditure survey results, 2011 [CONTINUED]

Item	2011
Alcoholic beverages	456
Housing	16,803
Shelter	9,825
Owned dwellings	6,148
Mortgage interest and charges	3,184
Property taxes	1,845
Maintenance, repairs, insurance, other expenses	1,120
Rented dwellings	3,029
Other lodging	648
Utilities, fuels, and public services	3,727
Natural gas	420
Electricity	1,423
Fuel oil and other fuels	157
Telephone	1,226
Water and other public services	501
Household operations	1,122
Personal services	398
Other household expenses	724
Housekeeping supplies	615
Laundry and cleaning supplies	145
Other household products	340
Postage and stationery	130
Household furnishings and equipment	1,514
Household textiles	109
Furniture	358
Floor coverings	20
Major appliances	194
Small appliances, miscellaneous housewares	89
Miscellaneous household equipment	744
Apparel and services	1,740
Men and boys	404
Men, 16 and over	324
Boys, 2 to 15	80
Women and girls	721
Women, 16 and over	604
Girls, 2 to 15	117
Children under 2	68
Footwear	321
Other apparel products and services	226
Transportation	8,293
Vehicle purchases (net outlay)	2,669
Cars and trucks, new	1,265
Cars and trucks, used	1,339
Other vehicles	64
Gasoline and motor oil	2,655
Other vehicle expenses	2,454
Vehicle finance charges	233
Maintenance and repairs	805
Vehicle insurance	983
Vehicle rental, leases, licenses, other charges	433
Public and other transportation	516
Health care	3,313
Health insurance	1,922
Medical services	768
Drugs	489
Medical supplies	134
Entertainment	2,572
Fees and admissions	594
Audio and visual equipment and services[b]	977
Pets, toys, hobbies and playground Equipment	631
Other supplies, equipment, and services	370
Personal care products and services	634
Reading	115
Education	1,051
Tobacco products and smoking supplies	351
Miscellaneous	775

These numbers represent annual inflation rates. As noted in Chapter 2, small increases in inflation (up to 3% per year)

TABLE 3.2

Consumer expenditure survey results, 2011 [CONTINUED]

Item	2011
Cash contributions	1,721
Personal insurance and pensions	5,424
Life and other personal insurance	317
Pensions and Social Security	5,106
Sources of income and taxes:	
Money income before taxes[a]	63,685
Wages and salaries	49,805
Self-employment income	3,269
Social Security, private and government retirement	7,648
Interest, dividends, rental income, other property income	1,281
Unemployment and workers' compensation, veterans' benefit	579
Public assistance, supplemental security income, food stamps	520
Regular contributions for support	364
Other income	218
Personal taxes (missing values not imputed)[a]	2,012
Federal income taxes	1,370
2008 Tax stimulus (thru Q20091)	n.a.
State and local income taxes	505
Other taxes	136
Income after taxes[a]	61,673
Addenda:	
Net change in total assets and Liabilities	−1,826
Net change in total assets	6,836
Net change in total liabilities	8,662
Other financial information	
Other money receipts	729
Mortgage principal paid, owned property	−2,008
Estimated market value of owned home	151,165
Est monthly rental value owned home	849
Gifts of goods and services	1037
Food	84
Alcoholic beverages[c]	17
Housing	194
Housekeeping supplies	25
Household textiles	11
Appliances and miscellaneous housewares	18
Major appliances	7
Small appliances, miscellaneous housewares	11
Miscellaneous household equipment	45
Other housing	96
Apparel and services	205
Males, 2 and over	53
Females, 2 and over	77
Children under 2	22
Other apparel products and services	52
Jewelry and watches	18
All other apparel products and services	34
Transportation	90
Health care	30
Entertainment	93
Toys, games, hobbies, and tricycles	26
Other entertainment	67
Personal care products and services[c]	15
Reading[c]	2
Education	216
All other gifts[c]	91

are considered to be a sign of a healthy growing economy in which demand slightly outpaces supply. The overall inflation rate of 3% in 2011 for all items was exceeded by the inflation rates for transportation (5.2%), apparel (4.6%), food and beverages (4.5%), and medical care (3.5%). In addition, the increase of 6.6% in the special aggregate index for energy was more than twice the overall inflation rate. According to the BLS, in "How BLS Measures Price Change for Household Fuels in the Consumer Price Index"

TABLE 3.2

[a]Components of income and taxes are derived from "complete income reporters" only through 2003.
Beginning in 2004 income imputation was implemented. As a result, all consumer units are considered to be complete income reporters.
[b]Prior to 2005, the title of Audio and visual equipment and services was Televisions, radio, sound equipment.
[c]Prior to 2000, gifts of Alcoholic beverages, Personal care products and services, and Reading materials were included in "All other gifts".
Note: All values have been rounded, and as a result some cell values have been rounded to zero. This is particularly evident in the characteristic section. When data are not reported or are not applicable (i.e., missing values), tabulated cell values have been set to zero.

SOURCE: Adapted from "Average Annual Expenditures and Characteristics of All Consumer Units, Consumer Expenditure Survey, 2006–2011," in *Consumer Expenditure Survey: CE Tables: Most Recent Multiyear Table*, U.S. Department of Labor, Bureau of Labor Statistics, September 28, 2012, http://www.bls.gov/cex/2011/standard/multiyr.pdf (accessed October 8, 2012)

(August 19, 2009, http://www.bls.gov/cpi/cpifachf.htm), the energy index includes fuel and utility costs that fall under the housing category and motor fuel costs that fall under the transportation category.

Components of the CPI-U that experienced lower rates of inflation than the overall rate of 3% in 2011 were services (2.2%), housing (1.9%), education and communication (1.7%), other goods and services (1.7%), and recreation (1%). (See Table 3.3.) Likewise, the special

aggregate index for all items less food and energy showed a 2.2% increase between December 2010 and December 2011.

Figure 3.1 shows 12-month changes in the CPI-U for all items and for all items less food and energy between July 2002 and July 2012. The inflation rate peaked at around 5.5% in July 2008. This means that, on average, prices for all items increased by 5.5% between July 2007 and July 2008. However, the inflation rate for all items less food and energy for this period was closer to 2%. This indicates that food and energy were the primary culprits in price volatility between 2007 and 2008. In general, this also holds true on a historical basis. Figure 3.1 shows that the inflation rates for all items less food and energy fluctuated much less than the rates for all items between July 2002 and July 2012. This fluctuation can also be seen in Table 3.3, which indicates significant volatility on an annual average basis for energy items (particularly energy commodities) compared with food and beverages.

As shown in Figure 3.1, throughout much of 2009 the inflation rate for all items less food and energy was actually negative—a condition known as deflation. The purchasing power of money went up because of price decreases in goods and services (excluding food and energy).

TABLE 3.3

Percentage change in the urban Consumer Price Index (CPI-U) for selected expenditure categories, December to December, 2004–11, December 2011–August 2012

	Percent change from previous December								
	December								August 2012
Item and group	2004	2005	2006	2007	2008	2009	2010	2011	
Expenditure category									
All items	3.3	3.4	2.5	4.1	0.1	2.7	1.5	3.0	2.1
Food and beverages	2.6	2.3	2.2	4.8	5.8	−0.4	1.5	4.5	1.2
Housing	3.0	4.0	3.3	3.0	2.4	−0.3	0.3	1.9	1.6
Apparel	−0.2	−1.1	0.9	−0.3	−1.0	1.9	−1.1	4.6	0.1
Transportation	6.5	4.8	1.6	8.3	−13.3	14.4	5.3	5.2	5.0
Medical care	4.2	4.3	3.6	5.2	2.6	3.4	3.3	3.5	2.8
Recreation*	0.7	1.1	1.0	0.8	1.8	−0.4	−0.8	1.0	1.3
Education and communication*	1.5	2.4	2.3	3.0	3.6	2.4	1.3	1.7	1.0
Other goods and services	2.5	3.1	3.0	3.3	3.4	8.0	1.9	1.7	1.3
Special aggregate indexes									
Commodities	3.6	2.7	1.3	5.2	−4.1	5.5	2.0	4.2	2.5
Services	3.1	3.8	3.4	3.3	3.0	0.9	1.2	2.2	1.8
Energy	16.6	17.1	2.9	17.4	−21.3	18.2	7.7	6.6	7.8
All items less energy	2.2	2.2	2.5	2.8	2.4	1.4	0.9	2.6	1.5
All items less food and energy	2.2	2.2	2.6	2.4	1.8	1.8	0.8	2.2	1.5
Energy commodities	26.7	16.7	6.1	29.4	−40.5	46.5	13.9	10.6	11.4
Services less energy services	2.8	2.9	3.7	3.3	2.7	1.4	1.3	2.3	1.8

*Indexes on a December 1997=100 base.
Note: Index applies to a month as a whole, not to any specific date.

SOURCE: Adapted from Malik Crawford, Jonathan Church, and Darren Rippy, eds., "Table 26. Historical Consumer Price Index for All Urban Consumers (CPI-U): U.S. City Average, by Commodity and Service Group and Detailed Expenditure Categories," in *CPI Detailed Report, Data for August 2012*, U.S. Department of Labor, Bureau of Labor Statistics, September 14, 2012, http://www.bls.gov/cpi/cpid1208.pdf (accessed September 20, 2012)

FIGURE 3.1

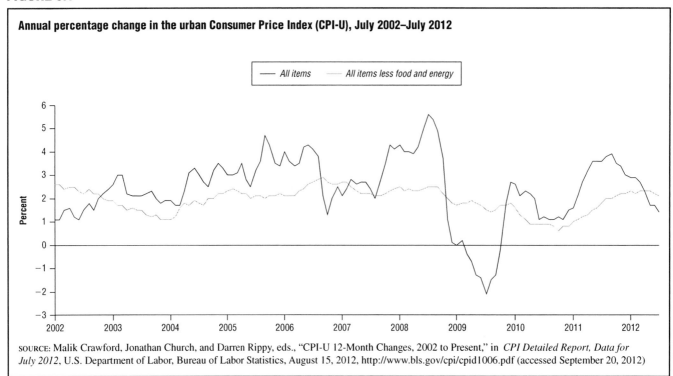

Annual percentage change in the urban Consumer Price Index (CPI-U), July 2002–July 2012

— All items   ⋯⋯ All items less food and energy

SOURCE: Malik Crawford, Jonathan Church, and Darren Rippy, eds., "CPI-U 12-Month Changes, 2002 to Present," in *CPI Detailed Report, Data for July 2012*, U.S. Department of Labor, Bureau of Labor Statistics, August 15, 2012, http://www.bls.gov/cpi/cpid1006.pdf (accessed September 20, 2012)

The Great Recession

As noted earlier, consumer spending underwent a tremendous change between the late 1990s and the latter half of the first decade of the 21st century. In the press release "Gross Domestic Product: Second Quarter 2012 (Third Estimate), Corporate Profits: Second Quarter 2012 (Revised Estimate)" (September 27, 2012, http://www.bea.gov/newsreleases/national/gdp/2012/pdf/gdp2q12_3rd.pdf), the BEA reports that annual real PCE values changed by the following percentages from the year before:

- 1996—up 3.5%
- 1997—up 3.7%
- 1998—up 5.2%
- 1999—up 5.5%
- 2000—up 5.1%
- 2001—up 2.7%
- 2002—up 2.7%
- 2003—up 2.8%
- 2004—up 3.3%
- 2005—up 3.4%
- 2006—up 2.9%
- 2007—up 2.3%
- 2008—down 0.6%
- 2009—down 1.9%
- 2010—up 1.8%
- 2011—up 2.5%

The PCE increased by more than 5% annually from 1998 through 2000 and then slowed considerably. Between 2001 and 2007 PCE growth ranged from 2.3% to 3.4% per year. Then from 2007 to 2008 the PCE decreased by 0.6%. As noted in Chapter 1, the National Bureau of Economic Research reports that the U.S. economy reached a peak of activity in December 2007 and then went into a recession that lasted through June 2009. The Great Recession was historically long and deep. In 2009 the PCE declined by 1.9% from the year before, demonstrating a steep drop in consumer spending. In 2010 spending began to increase; the PCE grew by 1.8% from 2009 to 2010 and by 2.5% from 2010 to 2011. Thus, Americans were beginning to return to their prerecession spending habits.

On a macroeconomic scale, it is interesting to see how expenditures for some components making up the PCE have changed over several decades. Figure 3.2 shows spending on durable goods, nondurable goods, housing and utilities, and health care as a percentage of the total PCE for 1970, 1980, 1990, 2000, and 2011. These categories have historically been the four largest components of the PCE.

The data show that the percentage of the PCE dedicated to housing and utilities remained relatively steady between 1970 and 2011. (See Figure 3.2.) A slight downward trend is evident in the percentage spent on durable goods over time. A much more dramatic decrease is seen

FIGURE 3.2

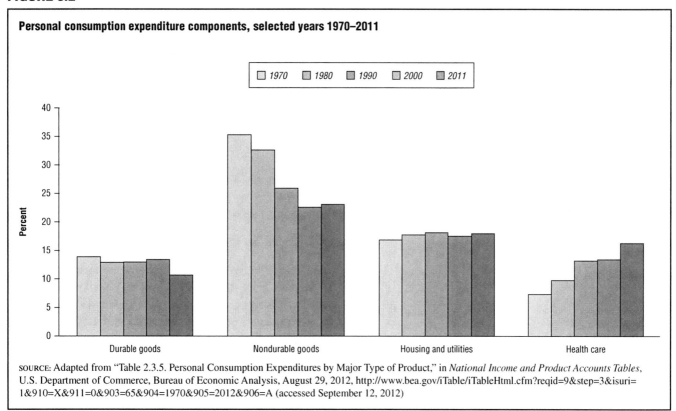

Personal consumption expenditure components, selected years 1970–2011

SOURCE: Adapted from "Table 2.3.5. Personal Consumption Expenditures by Major Type of Product," in *National Income and Product Accounts Tables,* U.S. Department of Commerce, Bureau of Economic Analysis, August 29, 2012, http://www.bea.gov/iTable/iTableHtml.cfm?reqid=9&step=3&isuri= 1&910=X&911=0&903=65&904=1970&905=2012&906=A (accessed September 12, 2012)

in the percentage of the PCE devoted to nondurable goods—from 35% in 1970 to 23% in 2011. A percentage decrease in one component making up the PCE means a percentage increase in one or more of the other components. For example, the percentage of the PCE devoted to health care more than doubled from around 7% in 1970 to 16% in 2011.

Food and Energy Price Volatility

Over the short term, food and energy prices can vary tremendously. Food prices are dependent on a variety of factors, including weather conditions (which affect growing costs), transportation and processing costs, and subsidies paid to farmers by the government that influence supply and demand ratios. Energy prices, particularly for oil, are affected by political and economic factors in the Middle East. Because of the volatile nature of food and energy prices, these costs are not included in the economic indicator called the core inflation.

FOOD PRICES. One component of the PCE that has historically become more affordable over time is food. The U.S. Department of Agriculture (USDA; October 1, 2012, http://www.ers.usda.gov/datafiles/Food_Expenditures/ Food_Expenditures/table8.xls) has calculated food prices as a percentage of personal disposable income on an annual basis since 1929. Personal disposable income is also known as after-tax income or take-home pay. In 1929 the average U.S. household spent nearly a quarter of its disposable

income on food. By the 1960s the percentage had fallen to around 15%. In 2011 U.S. consumers spent approximately 11.3% of their disposable income on food. Enormous gains in agricultural productivity and crop yields have been responsible for decreasing the price of food.

In *CPI Detailed Report, Data for August 2012* (September 18, 2012, http://www.bls.gov/cpi/cpid1208.pdf), the BLS shows CPI-U values for food on a December-to-December basis between 2004 and 2011. From 2004 to 2006 food inflation averaged 2.1% to 2.7% per year. The CPI-U values for 2007 and 2008 were historically high. Ronald Trostle of the USDA's Economic Research Service reports in *Fluctuating Food Commodity Prices: A Complex Issue with No Easy Answers* (November 2008, http://webarchives.cdlib.org/sw1vh5dg3r/http://ers.usda.gov/ AmberWaves/November08/Features/FoodPrices.htm) that the higher food prices were due to a variety of factors, including rising costs for food commodities (such as grains and vegetable oils), fluctuating oil prices, demand for biofuels (such as corn-based ethanol), and increasing demand for food in developing countries.

In 2009 the CPI-U for food plummeted to −0.5%. According to the Economic Research Service, in "Food Price Outlook, 2010"(August 25, 2010, http://www.ers .usda.gov/data-products/food-price-outlook.aspx), lower prices in 2009 were primarily the result of decreased demand during the Great Recession. By 2010 the inflation rate for food was positive again at 1.5%. It rose to 4.5% in 2011;

however, as shown in Table 3.3, the food inflation rate as of August 2012 was much lower, at 1.2%.

ENERGY EXPENDITURES AND PRICES. Nondurable energy goods accounted for $428.3 billion of the PCE in 2011. (See Table 3.1.) This category does not include electricity and gas for household operation, which fall under services. Nondurable energy goods include products such as gasoline, other motor fuels, and lubricants. The BLS indicates in *CPI Detailed Report, Data for August 2012* that the CPI-U values for motor fuels (including gasoline) fluctuated wildly between 2004 and 2011. The values on a December-to-December basis are as follows:

- 2004—26.1%
- 2005—16.2%
- 2006—6.4%
- 2007—29.5%
- 2008——42.2%
- 2009—50.7%
- 2010—13.9%
- 2011—10.3%

GASOLINE PRICES. Figure 3.3 graphs the weekly average retail price of a gallon of regular gasoline in the United States between August 1990 and August 2012. The price hovered between $1.00 and $1.50 per gallon from 1990 to about 2003 and then began to

increase dramatically. In mid-2008 consumers paid around $4.00 per gallon—the highest price on record. By the end of 2008 the price was back down to around $1.65 per gallon. It began to rise again, and as of late August 2012, the price was near $3.70 per gallon.

Figure 3.4 illustrates that the average retail price of $3.85 for a gallon of regular-grade gasoline in the United States in September 2012 had four contributing components:

- Crude oil price—62%
- Refining costs—18%
- Taxes—11%
- Distribution and marketing costs—9%

Thus, the cost of crude oil accounts for nearly two-thirds of the retail price of gasoline. Crude oil is sold by the barrel, with each barrel containing 42 U.S. gallons (158.9 L). It is then refined and otherwise processed into usable products, such as gasoline. Even though there are many different measures of crude oil prices, one measure is called the refiner acquisition cost and represents the amount paid by U.S. refiners for each barrel of crude oil. In *Annual Energy Review 2011* (September 2012, http://www.eia.gov/total energy/data/annual/pdf/aer.pdf), the U.S. Department of Energy's Energy Information Administration (EIA) indicates that during the 1990s the average refiner acquisition cost for crude oil was around $20 per barrel. In mid-2008 the cost peaked near $100 per barrel. By mid- to late 2009 the

FIGURE 3.3

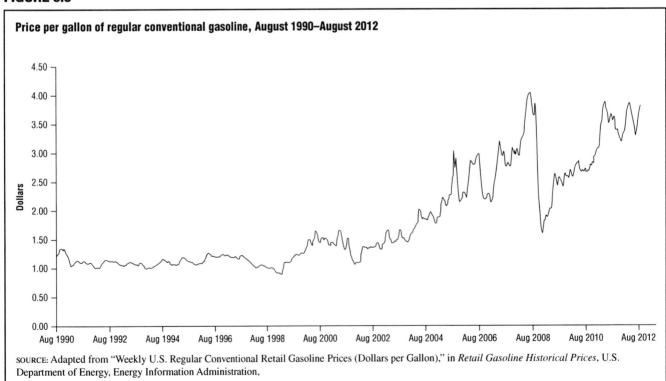

Price per gallon of regular conventional gasoline, August 1990–August 2012

SOURCE: Adapted from "Weekly U.S. Regular Conventional Retail Gasoline Prices (Dollars per Gallon)," in *Retail Gasoline Historical Prices*, U.S. Department of Energy, Energy Information Administration,

FIGURE 3.4

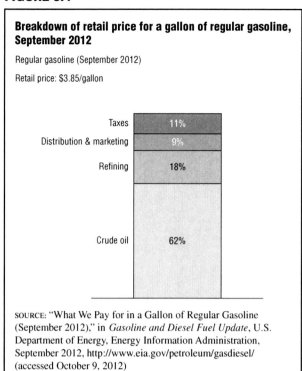

Breakdown of retail price for a gallon of regular gasoline, September 2012

Regular gasoline (September 2012)

Retail price: $3.85/gallon

SOURCE: "What We Pay for in a Gallon of Regular Gasoline (September 2012)," in *Gasoline and Diesel Fuel Update*, U.S. Department of Energy, Energy Information Administration, September 2012, http://www.eia.gov/petroleum/gasdiesel/ (accessed October 9, 2012)

price had declined to close to $60 per barrel, which was an unprecedented drop. Through the remainder of 2009 and through 2011 the price climbed back up to around $100 per barrel. The EIA notes in *Short Term Energy Outlook* (October 2012, http://www.eia.gov/forecasts/steo/pdf/steo_full.pdf) that the refiner acquisition cost for the first and second quarters of 2012 averaged $107.62 and $101.45 per barrel, respectively.

THE COST OF MEDICAL CARE

As noted earlier, the PCE proportion devoted to health care more than doubled from 7% in 1970 to 16% in 2011. (See Figure 3.2.) Health care expenses accounted for nearly $1.8 trillion of the PCE in 2011. (See Table 3.1.)

Table 3.4 shows the CPI-U for medical care on a December-to-December basis between 2004 and 2011 and between December 2011 and August 2012. Overall, medical care prices increased by 2.6% to 5.2% per year during this period. The CPI-U for medical care in 2011 was 3.5%, slightly higher than the overall inflation rate of 3%. (See Table 3.3.) Health care inflation during 2011 was driven largely by price increases in health insurance (6.1%), hospital and related services (5.3%), and prescription drugs (4.1%). (See Table 3.4.) The lowest inflation rates were seen in costs for medical equipment and supplies (−0.4%), nonprescription drugs (0.1%), and eyeglasses and eye care (0.7%).

Comparison of the medical care CPI-U values in Table 3.4 with the CPI-U values for all items in

Table 3.3 between 2004 and 2011 reveals that medical care inflation outpaced overall inflation in each of these years. In other words, medical care prices have been increasing at a faster pace than overall prices in the economy. Medical inflation is blamed, in part, on technological advances in medicine that have increased expenses associated with the diagnosis and treatment of patients.

Analysts often talk about health care expenditures as a percentage of the GDP. According to the Federal Reserve Bank of New York (July 2012, http://www.newyorkfed.org/research/directors_charts/ireg_40.pdf), during the late 1990s U.S. medical care expenditures accounted for approximately 11% of the GDP. By 2011 the percentage had increased to close to 14%.

Health Insurance Coverage

The Agency for Healthcare Research and Quality (AHRQ) is a division of the U.S. Department of Health and Human Services. The AHRQ conducts large-scale surveys of medical care recipients and providers as part of its Medical Expenditure Panel Survey (MEPS; http://www.meps.ahrq.gov/), which provides detailed data and reports on medical utilization and expenditures. As of November 2012, comprehensive MEPS data were available for the first half of 2011. The data cover the noninstitutionalized civilian population of the United States, that is, people not institutionalized in prisons, nursing homes, and so on, or members of the military.

As shown in Table 3.5, the AHRQ estimates that 21.1%, or 56.1 million people of the 266 million noninstitutionalized civilian population under the age of 65 years, did not have health insurance coverage during the first half of 2011. Note that data are not included for people aged 65 years and older, because this age group is widely covered by Medicare (a federal health insurance program for people aged 65 years and older and people with disabilities).

Table 3.5 provides detailed information from the AHRQ study about the uninsured population under the age of 65 years during the first half of 2011. The age group with the highest percent uninsured was young adults aged 19 to 24 years (34.9%). Other substantial proportions included adults aged 25 to 29 years (33.7%) uninsured and adults aged 30 to 34 years (28.6%) uninsured. Overall, more of the uninsured population was male (53.9%) than female (46.1%).

The AHRQ also assesses insurance coverage by racial and ethnic identity. Slightly less than half (48.4%) of the uninsured population during the first half of 2011 was white. (See Table 3.5.) Hispanics or Latinos accounted for the next-largest contingent, at 30.2%. African-Americans made up 14.3% and Asians and Pacific Islanders accounted for 4.9% of the uninsured population in early 2011.

TABLE 3.4

Percentage change in the urban Consumer Price Index (CPI-U) for medical care expenditure categories, December to December, 2004–11, December 2011–August 2012

	Percent change from previous December								August 2012
	December								
Item and group	2004	2005	2006	2007	2008	2009	2010	2011	
Expenditure category									
Medical care	4.2	4.3	3.6	5.2	2.6	3.4	3.3	3.5	2.8
Medical care commodities	2.2	3.7	1.8	2.7	1.6	3.3	2.9	3.2	2.7
Medicinal drugs[e]	—	—	—	—	—	—	3.1	3.4	2.8
Prescription drugs	3.5	4.4	1.9	3.3	1.5	4.4	4.1	4.1	3.3
Nonprescription drugs[e]	—	—	—	—	—	—	−1.0	0.1	0.7
Medical equipment and supplies[e]	—	—	—	—	—	—	−0.1	−0.4	0.5
Medical care services	4.9	4.5	4.1	5.9	3.0	3.4	3.4	3.6	2.9
Professional services	4.0	3.8	2.6	4.2	3.0	2.5	2.7	2.2	1.7
Physicians' services[c]	4.0	3.1	1.7	4.1	2.9	2.5	3.4	2.7	1.9
Dental services[c]	4.9	5.7	5.0	5.8	3.7	3.2	2.7	2.2	1.8
Eyeglasses and eye care[d]	2.9	3.1	2.0	1.5	0.3	1.7	0.3	0.7	1.1
Services by other medical professionals[c, d]	2.5	2.5	3.1	3.1	3.8	1.8	1.8	1.3	0.9
Hospital and related services	5.2	5.1	6.1	8.1	5.4	7.1	6.7	5.3	2.8
Hospital services[c, f]	5.2	5.2	6.2	8.3	5.9	7.7	7.6	5.8	2.8
Inpatient hospital services[a, c, f]	5.6	5.3	6.8	7.6	5.7	7.7	9.2	6.2	2.7
Outpatient hospital services[a, c, d]	4.5	5.0	5.2	9.9	5.6	8.2	5.1	5.0	2.8
Nursing homes and adult day services[c, f]	3.5	3.5	5.0	4.8	3.2	3.6	3.1	2.9	3.2
Care of invalids and elderly at home[b]	—	—	3.1	3.4	1.6	1.6	1.5	1.9	0.9
Health insurance[b]	—	—	6.4	8.8	−3.5	−3.0	−4.0	6.1	9.0

—Data not available.
Note: Index applies to a month as a whole, not to any specific date.
[a]Special index based on a substantially smaller sample.
[b]Indexes on a December 2005=100 base.
[c]This index series was calculated using a Laspeyres estimator.
[d]Indexes on a December 1986=100 base.
[e]Indexes on a December 2009=100 base.
[f]Indexes on a December 1996=100 base.
All other item stratum index series were calculated using a geometric means estimator.

SOURCE: Adapted from Malik Crawford, Jonathan Church, and Darren Rippy, eds., "Table 26. Historical Consumer Price Index for All Urban Consumers (CPI-U): U.S. City Average, by Commodity and Service Group and Detailed Expenditure Categories," in *CPI Detailed Report, Data for August 2012*, U.S. Department of Labor, Bureau of Labor Statistics, September 14, 2012, http://www.bls.gov/cpi/cpid1208.pdf (accessed September 20, 2012)

Combining the racial, ethnic, and sex characteristics indicates the following three largest groups among the uninsured:

- White males—26.3%
- White females—22.1%
- Hispanic or Latino males—16.8%

Among people aged 16 to 64 years, those who had never been married (40.2%) were more likely to be uninsured than those who were married (32.3%), divorced (11.4%), separated (3.1%), or widowed (1.5%). (See Table 3.5.) The South had, by far, the largest percentage (44.7%) of the uninsured, whereas the Northeast had the lowest percentage (13.9%). The vast majority (87%) of the uninsured population reported their health status to be excellent (30.2%), very good (29.3%), or good (27.5%). Another 10.3% reported their health to be fair, and 2.6% said their health was poor.

THE COST OF LIVING

The nontechnical term *cost of living* refers to the cost of basic necessities to U.S. households, such as food,

clothing, and shelter. Even though many factors affect the prices of these commodities, one economic factor has played a major role in recent decades: inflation. Because of inflation, the cost of living increases each year as the prices of necessities become more expensive. The CPI is the economic indicator commonly used to gauge changes in inflation and the cost of living.

A cost of living adjustment (COLA) is an adjustment made to wages or benefits to compensate consumers for the effects of inflation. Historically, the government has applied annual COLAs to increase the amounts paid out to recipients of certain benefits, such as Social Security and food stamps. These increases are designed to help people keep up with the rising cost of living due to inflation.

The COLA for Social Security recipients is calculated on the CPI for urban wage earners and clerical workers (CPI-W) from the third quarter of one year to the third quarter of the next year. In "Prior Cost-of-Living Adjustments" (October 16, 2012, http://www.ssa.gov/cola/facts/index.htm), the Social Security Administration notes that there was no COLA made during 2010 and 2011, because the CPI-W did not rise above the level recorded for the

TABLE 3.5

Characteristics of uninsured persons under age 65, as of first half of 2011

Population characteristics	Total population in thousands	Percent distribution of population	Percent uninsured	Percent distribution of uninsured population
Total[a]	266,004	100.0	21.1	100.0
Age in years				
Under 4	16,746	6.3	8.3	2.5
4–6	12,773	4.8	8.9	2.0
7–12	24,847	9.3	10.7	4.7
13–17	20,696	7.8	12.6	4.7
Total under 18	75,062	28.2	10.4	13.9
18	4,222	1.6	20.2	1.5
19–24	25,099	9.4	34.9	15.6
25–29	21,173	8.0	33.7	12.7
30–34	20,145	7.6	28.6	10.3
35–54	83,381	31.3	22.6	33.7
55–64	36,921	13.9	18.7	12.3
Sex				
Male	132,744	49.9	22.8	53.9
Female	133,260	50.1	19.4	46.1
Race/ethnicity				
Total Hispanic or Latino	47,024	17.7	36.0	30.2
Total black, single race	33,702	12.7	23.8	14.3
Total white, single race	165,237	62.1	16.4	48.4
Total Asian/Pacific Islander, single race	13,797	5.2	20.0	4.9
Total other races/multiple races	6,244	2.3	19.4	2.2
Race/ethnicity and sex				
Hispanic or Latino male	24,417	9.2	38.6	16.8
Black male, single race	15,915	6.0	26.2	7.4
White male, single race	82,691	31.1	17.9	26.3
Asian/Pacific Islander male, single race	6,664	2.5	19.4	2.3
Other races/multiple race male	3,057	1.1	18.9	1.0
Hispanic or Latino female	22,607	8.5	33.1	13.4
Black female, single race	17,787	6.7	21.7	6.9
White female, single race	82,546	31.0	15.0	22.1
Asian/Pacific Islander female, single race	7,133	2.7	20.5	2.6
Other races/multiple race female	3,187	1.2	20.0	1.1
Marital status[b]				
Married	99,099	37.3	18.3	32.3
Widowed	3,050	1.1	27.1	1.5
Divorced	21,780	8.2	29.4	11.4
Separated	5,263	2.0	33.2	3.1
Never married	70,552	26.5	31.9	40.2
Census region				
Northeast	46,991	17.7	16.6	13.9
Midwest	57,454	21.6	15.8	16.1
South	98,310	37.0	25.5	44.7
West	63,249	23.8	22.3	25.2
Perceived health status, under age 65				
Excellent	98,065	36.9	17.3	30.2
Very good	82,535	31.0	19.9	29.3
Good	59,602	22.4	25.8	27.5
Fair	19,312	7.3	29.9	10.3
Poor	6,330	2.4	22.8	2.6

[a]Total includes persons with unknown perceived health status and marital status.
[b]For individuals age 16 and over. Excludes unknown marital status. As a result, percents do not sum to 100.
Note: Percent distributions may not add to 100 because of rounding.

SOURCE: "Table 4. Total Population and Uninsured Persons under Age 65: Percent by Selected Population Characteristics, United States, First Half of 2011," in *Medical Expenditure Panel Survey*, U.S. Department of Health and Human Services, Centers for Medicare and Medicaid Services, Agency for Healthcare Research and Quality, 2012, http://meps.ahrq.gov/mepsweb/data_stats/summ_tables/hc/hlth_insr/2011/alltables.pdf (accessed September 13, 2012)

third quarter of 2008. As a result, monthly Social Security benefits payable during 2010 and 2011 did not increase. However, there was a 3.6% COLA increase in Social Security payments during 2012. Likewise, the Social Security Administration indicates that there will be a 1.7% COLA increase during 2013.

PUBLIC OPINION ON CONSUMER ISSUES

The Gallup Organization conducts many polls that question Americans about their consumer habits and concerns. In April 2012 pollsters asked Americans about their financial comfort. As shown in Figure 3.5, 60% of those asked said they "have enough money to live comfortably," whereas

FIGURE 3.5

Poll respondents rate their financial comfort, April 2002–12

RIGHT NOW, DO YOU HAVE ENOUGH MONEY TO LIVE COMFORTABLY, OR NOT?

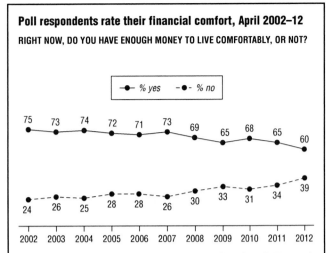

SOURCE: Lydia Saad, "Americans' Financial Comfort," in *U.S. Financial Comfort Falls to New Low*, The Gallup Organization, April 25, 2012, http://www.gallup.com/poll/154106/Financial-Comfort-Falls-New-Low.aspx (accessed September 13, 2012). Copyright © 2012 by Gallup, Inc. All rights reserved. The content is used with permission; however, Gallup retains all rights of republication.

TABLE 3.6

Poll respondents' most important financial problems, April 2012

Based on national adults, and by perception of having enough money to live comfortably

	National adults	Have enough	Don't have enough
	%	%	%
Lack of money/low wages	18	13	25
Healthcare costs	12	11	13
Cost of owning/renting a home	12	11	13
High cost of living/inflation	11	9	15
Energy costs/oil and gas prices	11	11	10
Too much debt/can't pay debts	9	7	12
Unemployment/loss of job	9	6	13
College expenses	7	9	3
Taxes	5	6	3
Retirement savings	4	5	1
Other	12	12	9
None	11	14	5
No opinion	4	3	4

Totals add to more than 100% due to multiple responses.

SOURCE: Lydia Saad, "What is the most important financial problem facing your family today?" in *U.S. Financial Comfort Falls to New Low*, The Gallup Organization, April 25, 2012, http://www.gallup.com/poll/154106/Financial-Comfort-Falls-New-Low.aspx (accessed September 13, 2012). Copyright © 2012 by Gallup, Inc. All rights reserved. The content is used with permission; however, Gallup retains all rights of republication.

39% said they did not enjoy that kind of financial comfort. Since Gallup first asked this question in 2002, the proportion of Americans stating they have sufficient money to live comfortably has fallen by 15 percentage points, from 75% in 2002 to 60% in 2012. Table 3.6 lists the "most important financial problem" named by the respondents. Overall, 18% of those asked named lack of money/low wages as their most important problem. Five consumer spending answers

were also given: health care costs (12%), the cost of owning/renting a home (12%), the high cost of living/inflation (11%), energy costs/oil and gas prices (11%), and college expenses (7%).

The Gallup Organization finds that concern about medical costs is extremely high. In a May 2012 poll participants were asked to rank 10 economic issues in terms of their importance to the country. (See Table 3.7.) Forty percent of those asked ranked the cost of health care as "extremely important," the most for any single issue. Another 44% rated the issue as "very important." Overall, 84% of the respondents said the cost of health care was an "extremely important" or "very important" economic issue facing the country. College education was another consumer spending issue that was ranked high. More than three-fourths (78%) of the respondents rated this issue as "extremely important" or "very important."

CONSUMER SPENDING, JOB CREATION, AND INTEREST RATES

Consumer spending is essential to economic growth in the United States and, as noted earlier, is greatly affected by employment. When people have steady and dependable work, they are more likely to spend money, which also adds jobs to the economy. Spending is also related to interest rates. Historically, when interest rates have been lower, people have spent more money, which has in turn stimulated the job market.

TABLE 3.7

Public opinion on the importance of various economic issues, May 2012

IN YOUR VIEW, HOW IMPORTANT ARE EACH OF THE FOLLOWING ECONOMIC ISSUES FACING THE COUNTRY TODAY—EXTREMELY IMPORTANT, VERY IMPORTANT, SOMEWHAT IMPORTANT, OR NOT IMPORTANT?

	Extremely important	Very important	Extremely/ very important
	%	%	%
The cost of healthcare	40	44	84
Unemployment	36	46	82
The federal budget deficit and debt	41	41	82
Weak economic growth	32	47	79
The cost of a college education	35	43	78
The financial performance of Americans' savings and retirement investments	34	44	78
Home values, foreclosures, and mortgages	31	43	74
Living standards for the poorest Americans	28	41	69
Too much wealth controlled by too few Americans	26	28	54
Government regulations on private enterprise	19	32	51

SOURCE: Lydia Saad, "Importance of 10 Economic Issues," in *Obama, Romney Each Has Economic Strengths with Americans*, The Gallup Organization, May 21, 2012, http://www.gallup.com/poll/154727/Obama-Romney-Economic-Strengths-Americans.aspx (accessed September 13, 2012). Copyright © 2012 by Gallup, Inc. All rights reserved. The content is used with permission; however, Gallup retains all rights of republication.

Consumer buying choices can also stimulate—and even shift—job growth among industries. The higher the demand is for certain products and services, the more growth those industries will experience. The goods and services that are purchased by the consumer are called final goods; those that are used in the production of final goods are called intermediate goods. Demand for both final and intermediate goods leads to expansion in their respective industries, which in turn adds jobs to the economy.

Interest Rates and Spending

Interest rates are determined by the Board of Governors of the Federal Reserve System, which is the central bank of the United States. The Federal Reserve sets the federal funds rate (the interest rate banks charge for overnight loans to each other), which then influences the prime rate (the rate that banks charge their best customers; the prime rate is usually set at about three percentage points above the federal funds rate). From there, creditors set competitive rates for lending money to consumers. When interest rates are high, consumer spending (particularly for high-priced items such as cars and houses) tends to slow down because the cost of borrowing money is higher. Lower interest rates stimulate the economy because consumers can afford to borrow more at lower rates. This is particularly true for housing. As noted in Chapter 1, interest rates on home mortgages were historically low during the 1990s and the early years of the first decade of the 21st century.

In economics, to liquefy an asset means to exchange it for cash or to extract cash out of it. The cash is then available to spend or save. For many American families their most valuable asset is their home. People liquefy their home wealth by turning the equity they have built up in their homes into cash. Equity is the proportion of a home's mortgage value that a homeowner has paid off and actually owns. A cash down payment can be one component of equity. In addition, there are the monthly mortgage payments, which include both an interest payment and a principal payment. The interest payments represent a bonus or profit for the lender. Over the life of the mortgage the principal payments pay off the original mortgage amount. They also are a major component of the equity that accrues (builds up over time). Another way that equity increases is through appreciation (increase in value). Traditionally, homes have been considered a good investment because they appreciate over time.

There are two primary ways in which homeowners liquefy their home wealth. First, homeowners who sell their home for more than they paid for it reap a cash profit. They can then use that money toward the purchase of another home, spend it in other ways, or save or invest it. Second,

homeowners can borrow the equity they have built up in their home. These loans are called second mortgages, refinances, or home equity loans, and they become very popular when interest rates are low. During the 1990s and the early years of the first decade of the 21st century U.S. homeowners took advantage of rising property values and low interest rates by liquefying billions of dollars in equity from their homes. Economists believe that some of this money was pumped back into the economy in the form of consumer spending (i.e., consumption of goods and services).

Alan Greenspan and James Kennedy explain in *Sources and Uses of Equity Extracted from Homes* (March 2007, http://www.federalreserve.gov/pubs/feds/2007/200720/2007 20pap.pdf) that "there is broad agreement in the literature that housing wealth supports consumption; however, there is considerable disagreement as to the magnitude of the effect." They calculate that the cash extracted from home equity between 1991 and 2005 averaged $530 billion per year. The majority of this cash (approximately two-thirds) was from sales of existing homes. The remaining one-third was from equity-based loans. The researchers rely on respected surveys conducted by the University of Michigan and by industry groups, such as the National Association of Realtors and the American Bankers Association, to determine how the liquefied equity was used by homeowners. They point out that these data are self-reported by survey participants and are only available for certain transactions. Greenspan and Kennedy estimate that Americans who liquefied their equity by selling their home and then purchased another home used their equity as follows:

- Applied the equity to the next home purchase—87% of the total cash

- Spent the equity on PCE—7% of the total cash

- Invested the equity or otherwise used it—6% of the total cash

In regard to equity-based loans transacted between 1991 and 2005, Greenspan and Kennedy estimate that approximately one-third of the cash was used by homeowners to pay nonmortgage debt (e.g., credit card debt). Another one-third of the cash likely went toward home improvements. Approximately one-fourth of the liquefied equity is believed to have been spent on PCE. The remainder was used for investment purposes or for other uses.

Thus, low interest rates spur consumer spending, which helps drive up the nation's GDP. However, low interest rates are not always good for individual finances or the economy because they lead to more debt in the form of home equity loans, car loans, and credit cards. The problems associated with this debt will be discussed in detail in Chapter 4.

CHAPTER 4
PERSONAL DEBT

Beautiful credit! The foundation of modern society.

—Mark Twain and Charles Dudley Warner, *The Gilded Age: A Tale of To-day* (1873)

He who goes a borrowing, goes a sorrowing.

—Benjamin Franklin, *Poor Richard's Almanack* (1757)

Personal debt has both good and bad effects on the U.S. economy. Americans borrow money to buy houses, cars, and other consumer goods. They also take out loans to pay for vacations, investments, and educational expenses. All of this spending helps businesses and boosts the nation's gross domestic product (the total market value of final goods and services that are produced within an economy in a given year). As long as debt is handled prudently, it can be a positive economic force. However, some Americans take on too much debt and get into financial difficulties. Debt becomes a problem on a macroeconomic scale when people must devote large amounts of their disposable income (after-tax income or take-home pay) to repaying loans instead of spending or investing their money.

During the late 1990s and the first half of the first decade of the 21st century Americans took on massive amounts of mortgage debt as a housing boom swept the nation. When the boom ended, many people found themselves unable (or unwilling) to repay their loans. This produced a widespread financial crisis that affected the economy as a whole. The United States sank into the so-called Great Recession, an economic slowdown that officially lasted from December 2007 to June 2009. The latter month represents the time when the economy quit contracting and began expanding (recovering). Americans' debt declined dramatically during the Great Recession and continued to decrease through mid-2012. As of November 2012, it was unclear whether this trend would continue once the economy fully recovered or whether Americans would return to their pre-recession borrowing habits.

CATEGORIES OF DEBT

Economists divide personal debt into two broad categories: investment debt and consumer debt. Money that is borrowed to buy houses and real estate is considered to be investment debt. Because most property appreciates (increases in value) over time, the debt that is assumed to finance its purchase will likely be a wise investment. Likewise, money that is borrowed to start a business or pay for a college education can bring financial benefits. All of this assumes that the investment was a wise one and that the short-term costs of the debt can be borne. By contrast, consumer debt is assumed purely for consumption purposes. The money is spent to gain immediate access to goods and services that will not appreciate in value (and will likely lose value) over time to help offset the costs of the debt.

Credit falls into two other categories: nonrevolving credit and revolving credit. Nonrevolving loans require regular payments of amounts that will ensure that the original debt (the principal) plus interest will be paid off in a particular amount of time. They are also known as closed-end loans and are commonly used to finance the purchase of real estate, cars, and boats or to pay for educational expenses. Nonrevolving loans feature predictable payment amounts and schedules that are laid out in amortization tables. The term *amortize* is derived from the Latin term *mort*, which means "to kill or deaden." An amortization schedule details how a loan will be gradually eliminated (killed off) over a set period. Revolving debt is a different kind of arrangement in which the debtor is allowed to borrow against a predetermined total amount of credit and is billed for the outstanding principal plus interest. The loans typically require regularly scheduled minimum payments, but not a set time period for repaying the entire amount due. Credit card loans are the primary example of revolving debt.

Loans can also be secured or unsecured. A secured loan is one in which the borrower puts up an asset called collateral to lessen the financial risk of the lender. If the borrower

TABLE 4.1

Household debt, 2006 through the second quarter of 2012

[Billions of dollars. Amounts outstanding end of period, not seasonally adjusted.]

	2006	2007	2008	2009	2010	2011 Q1	2011 Q2	2011 Q3	2011 Q4	2012 Q1	2012 Q2
Total liabilities	13354.5	14263.0	14111.3	13888.3	13714.5	13641.0	13556.7	13474.9	13484.7	13441.2	13458.5
Credit market instruments	12839.7	13699.1	13682.7	13410.5	13137.5	13020.9	12935.6	12912.6	12933.7	12857.5	12895.5
Home mortgages[a]	9879.2	10566.9	10514.7	10369.2	9950.9	9884.7	9826.5	9773.7	9721.6	9640.0	9589.1
Consumer credit	2385.0	2528.8	2548.9	2438.8	2545.3	2512.3	2534.2	2578.6	2631.7	2619.0	2661.1
Municipal securities	230.1	250.7	258.7	264.6	262.3	261.9	260.7	256.1	254.4	252.3	247.6
Depository institution loans n.e.c.[b]	30.9	21.8	26.4	10.2	61.0	45.3	−1.0	−9.8	12.4	34.8	88.5
Other loans and advances	123.8	127.0	133.2	133.7	136.1	136.4	136.9	137.8	138.1	137.8	137.6
Commercial mortgages	190.7	204.0	200.9	194.0	181.9	180.3	178.3	176.2	175.5	173.7	171.6
Security credit	292.1	325.5	164.8	203.0	278.2	315.7	312.8	251.9	238.5	267.7	244.5
Trade payables	199.9	214.5	236.7	252.7	274.1	279.1	282.6	286.0	288.2	289.8	290.5
Deferred and unpaid life insurance premiums	22.8	23.9	27.0	22.1	24.7	25.2	25.6	24.4	24.3	26.2	28.0

[a]Includes loans made under home equity lines of credit and home equity loans secured by junior liens.
[b]Includes loans extended by the Federal Reserve to financial institutions such as domestic hedge funds through the Term Asset-Backed Securities Loan Facility (TALF).

SOURCE: Adapted from "L.100. Households and Nonprofit Organizations," in *Flow of Funds Accounts of the United States; Flows and Outstandings Second Quarter 2012*, Board of Governors of the Federal Reserve System, September 20, 2012, http://www.federalreserve.gov/Releases/Z1/Current/z1.pdf (accessed September 20, 2012)

defaults (fails to pay back the loan), the lender can seize the collateral and sell it to recoup some or all of the money that was lent. Mortgages on homes and property and loans on cars, boats, motor homes, and other goods of high value are typically secured loans. In all these cases the collateral can be legally repossessed by the lenders. Unsecured loans are not backed by collateral. They are granted solely on the good financial reputation of the borrower. Credit card debts and debts owed to medical practitioners and hospitals are the major types of unsecured debts.

HOUSEHOLD DEBT SERVICE

The Federal Reserve System, the national bank of the United States, compiles several economic indicators related to debt. One indicator is called total liabilities and includes both households and nonprofit organizations. As shown in Table 4.1, total liabilities were nearly $13.5 trillion at the end of the second quarter of 2012. This value was down from nearly $14.3 trillion at the end of 2007. Almost all ($12.9 trillion, or 96% of the total) of the total liabilities held at the end of the second quarter of 2012 were in the form of credit market instruments, mainly mortgages ($9.6 trillion) and consumer credit ($2.7 trillion). Consumer credit includes nonmortgage loans, such as credit cards and auto loans.

Table 4.2 shows the percent change in credit market debt for households and nonprofit organizations from 1992 through the second quarter of 2012. The highest growth year overall was 2003, when total credit market debt grew by 11.8% from the year before. The growth slowed considerably over subsequent years and went negative from 2008 through the first quarter of 2012. During the second quarter of 2012 total credit market debt increased by 1.2%. The breakdown by debt type in Table 4.2 shows that home

TABLE 4.2

Household debt growth in percent, 1992 through the second quarter of 2012

	Domestic nonfinancial sectors		
	Total	Households home mortgage	Consumer credit
1992	5.4	6.5	1.1
1993	6.0	5.5	7.4
1994	7.7	5.6	15.2
1995	7.0	4.9	14.4
1996	6.7	6.2	9.0
1997	5.9	6.1	5.5
1998	7.6	8.0	7.2
1999	8.0	9.4	7.8
2000	9.0	8.7	11.4
2001	9.6	10.5	8.6
2002	10.6	13.2	5.6
2003	11.8	14.5	5.3
2004	11.1	13.5	5.6
2005	11.1	13.2	4.5
2006	9.8	11.1	5.0
2007	6.7	7.0	5.9
2008	−0.2	−0.5	0.8
2009	−1.7	−1.4	−4.5
2010	−2.2	−2.9	−1.3
2011	−1.6	−2.3	3.4
2012–Q1	−0.9	−3.3	5.7
Q2	1.2	−2.1	6.2

Note: Data shown are on an end-of-period basis.

SOURCE: Adapted from "D.1. Credit Market Debt Growth by Sector," in *Flow of Funds Accounts of the United States; Flows and Outstandings Second Quarter 2012*, Board of Governors of the Federal Reserve System, September 20, 2012, http://www.federalreserve.gov/Releases/Z1/Current/z1.pdf (accessed September 20, 2012)

mortgage debt decreased each period from 2008 through the second quarter of 2012, while consumer credit was much more variable. After declining in 2009 and 2010 consumer

FIGURE 4.1

Household debt service ratio, 1st quarter 1980 through 1st quarter 2012

SOURCE: Adapted from "Household Debt Service Payments and Financial Obligations As a Percentage of Disposable Personal Income; Seasonally Adjusted," in *Household Debt Service and Financial Obligations Ratios*, The Federal Reserve, June 22, 2012, http://www.federalreserve.gov/releases/housedebt/default.htm (accessed September 13, 2012)

credit grew 3.4% in 2011, 5.7% during the first quarter of 2012, and 6.2% during the second quarter of 2012.

Another economic indicator compiled by the Federal Reserve is the household debt service ratio (DSR). The DSR is the ratio of household debt payments to disposable personal income. It indicates the estimated fraction of disposable income that is devoted to payments on outstanding mortgage and consumer debt.

As shown in Figure 4.1, the DSR steadily increased between 1994 and 2007. It peaked at nearly 14% in late 2007 and then declined dramatically. By the first quarter of 2010 the DSR was around 12.5%. At the end of the second quarter of 2012 Americans as a whole were spending 10.7% of their disposable income on their debt.

INTEREST RATES

One of the chief factors affecting the amount of debt that people assume is the amount of interest charged on loans. Banks and other financial institutions charge interest to make money on lending money. The interest rate charged must be low enough to tempt potential borrowers, but high enough to make a profit for lenders. In general, commercial lenders base their interest rates on the rates that are charged by the Federal Reserve. Lower interest rates encourage consumers to borrow money.

The Federal Reserve makes short-term loans to banks at an interest rate called the discount rate. If the Federal Reserve raises or lowers the discount rate, then banks adjust the federal funds rate, which is the rate they charge each other for loans. This affects the prime rate, the interest rate banks charge their best customers (typically large corporations), which in turn affects the rates on other loans. Figure 1.12 in Chapter 1 shows the bank prime loan rate from August 1955 to September 2012. The rate varied widely

over time from less than 5% in 1955 to more than 20% during the early to mid-1980s. Since 1990 the prime rate has consistently remained below 10% and has dipped below 5%. From December 2008 through September 2012 the rate was stationary at 3.3%

When a loan is granted, the creditor sets terms that specify whether the interest rate to be paid will be fixed or variable. A fixed interest rate remains constant throughout the life of the loan. A variable rate changes and is typically tied to a publicly published interest rate, such as the prime rate. For example, a loan can be made with the stipulation that the interest rate charged each month will be one percentage point higher than the prime rate. As the prime rate changes, so will the interest rate on the loan and the borrower's monthly payments.

Table 4.3 shows the tremendous difference between loans with differing interest rates and repayment periods. A $100,000 mortgage with a 30-year fixed interest rate of 5% will result in $193,300 being paid over the lifetime of the loan. The same $100,000 loan at 10% interest will cost $315,900. Loans for new cars typically have a repayment period of three to five years. A 7% fixed interest car loan for $20,000 paid over three years results in a total payment of $22,200. The same loan spread over five years will end up costing $23,800. Thus, the shorter loan period results in a much lower overall payout for the car. However, the trade-off to the borrower for a shorter loan period will be higher monthly payments. Borrowers must consider the financial consequences of monthly payments and interest rates to get a loan they can afford in the short and long term.

MORTGAGES

For most Americans a mortgage is the largest personal debt they will ever incur. In 2011 the outstanding

TABLE 4.3

Interest payments for particular loans

Interest rate	Years of loan	Amount borrowed (principal)	Total interest paid*	Total principal + interest paid*
5%	30	$100,000	$93,300	$193,300
10%	30	$100,000	$215,900	$315,900
15%	30	$100,000	$355,200	$455,200
5%	15	$100,000	$42,300	$142,300
10%	15	$100,000	$93,400	$193,400
15%	15	$100,000	$151,900	$251,900
7%	3	$20,000	$2,200	$22,200
7%	4	$20,000	$3,000	$23,000
7%	5	$20,000	$3,800	$23,800

*Rounded to nearest $100

SOURCE: Created by Kim Masters Evans for Gale, 2010

TABLE 4.4

Household home mortgage debt outstanding, 1978–2012

[Billions of dollars. Quarterly figures are seasonally adjusted.]

		Domestic nonfinancial sectors		
	Total	Total	Households home mortgage	Consumer credit
1978		1111.2	708.6	311.3
1979		1278.5	826.7	354.6
1980		1396.0	926.5	358.0
1981		1505.9	998.2	377.9
1982		1575.8	1031.1	396.7
1983		1731.1	1116.2	444.9
1984		1943.1	1242.8	526.6
1985		2277.7	1449.6	610.6
1986		2534.2	1648.3	666.4
1987		2752.5	1827.9	698.6
1988		3039.8	2054.2	745.2
1989		3309.2	2259.5	809.3
1990		3571.6	2488.8	824.4
1991		3758.5	2667.0	815.6
1992		3961.7	2840.0	824.8
1993		4203.5	2998.7	886.2
1994		4527.0	3165.3	1021.2
1995		4846.1	3318.9	1168.2
1996		5183.8	3537.0	1273.9
1997		5489.4	3752.9	1344.2
1998		5902.9	4054.0	1441.3
1999		6377.6	4430.8	1553.6
2000		6963.5	4814.0	1741.3
2001		7627.8	5320.9	1891.8
2002		8439.1	6025.6	1997.0
2003		9462.0	6907.0	2102.9
2004		10534.9	7855.8	2220.1
2005		11704.9	8894.5	2320.6
2006		12839.7	9879.2	2385.0
2007		13699.1	10566.9	2528.8
2008		13682.7	10514.7	2548.9
2009		13410.5	10369.2	2438.8
2010		13137.5	9950.9	2545.3
2011		12933.7	9721.6	2631.7
2012–Q1	38576.6	12905.7	9640.7	2668.9
Q2	39063.1	12945.1	9589.5	2708.5

Note: Data shown are on an end-of-period basis.

SOURCE: Adapted from "D.3 Credit Market Debt Outstanding by Sector," in *Flow of Funds Accounts of the United States; Flows and Outstandings Second Quarter 2012*, Board of Governors of the Federal Reserve System, September 20, 2012, http://www.federalreserve.gov/Releases/Z1/Current/z1.pdf (accessed September 20, 2012)

household home mortgage debt totaled $9.7 trillion. (See Table 4.4.) Mortgage debt is a form of investment debt because real estate usually increases in value. Thus, assuming mortgage debt is generally considered to be a sensible economic move, as long as the payments are well matched to the borrower's income and ability to pay. During the second half of the first decade of the 21st century the U.S. housing market suffered a deep financial crisis. In many cases real estate did not appreciate in value, but depreciated (decreased in value). The causes and consequences of this crisis will be explained later in the chapter. First, it is necessary to understand some basic information about mortgages and how the mortgage market operates.

A mortgage represents a lien, or binding charge, against a piece of property for the payment of a debt. In other words, the loan is granted on the condition that the property can be claimed by the lender (creditor) in the event the borrower defaults. If the loan is satisfactorily paid, full ownership of the property is granted to the borrower. Lenders use a process called underwriting to assess the creditworthiness of potential mortgage borrowers.

Mortgage Underwriting Standards

A home mortgage is a very large loan, usually totaling $100,000 or more, for which the repayment period may be several decades. Mortgage agreements are complex legal documents that bind lenders and borrowers to do certain things. Lenders typically charge borrowers fees (e.g., application fees, home appraisal fees, and so on) to originate a mortgage. In addition, lenders that hold the mortgages they originate will earn money from the interest payments that the borrowers make each month.

If a borrower quits paying on a mortgage, the lender can take possession of the home through a legal process called foreclosure and resell the home to someone else. However, this requires a significant investment of time and resources by the lender. In addition, foreclosed homes are typically sold at a loss. Thus, it is in a lender's best interest to issue mortgages to borrowers who are highly likely to repay the loans. As a result, lenders use specific underwriting standards to screen potential borrowers. There are four important factors that lenders take into consideration: documentation of the borrower's income and assets, the borrower's credit score, the borrower's debt ratio, and the loan-to-value ratio of the mortgage.

DOCUMENTATION OF INCOME AND ASSETS. Lenders typically require mortgage applicants to provide documentation of their income and assets. Many workers receive regular paychecks from their employer. These applicants provide the lender with paperwork showing the amount and timing of their salary or wages. The length of time the applicant has had the same job is also important to the lender. Some people are self-employed. They typically have to provide the lender with copies of their income tax returns or other documents for proof of income.

Borrowers must also supply written documentation of their assets. These assets usually include cash in bank accounts, savings bonds, stocks or other investments with value, and real estate or vehicles for which the loans have already been paid off.

CREDIT SCORE. A credit score is a numerical rating of a person's creditworthiness based on his or her past history of managing credit. According to Malgorzata Wozniacka and Snigdha Sen, in "Credit Scores: What You Should Know about Your Own" (November 23, 2004, http://www.pbs.org/wgbh/pages/frontline/shows/credit/more/scores.html), credit scoring began during the late 1950s with companies called credit bureaus that collected information about the credit history and general reputation of individuals. In 1971 Congress passed the Fair Credit Reporting Act. Wozniacka and Sen note that the law "established a framework for fair information practices to protect privacy and promote accuracy in credit reporting."

As of November 2012, there were several companies that compiled credit scores. The three major U.S. credit bureaus are Experian, TransUnion, and Equifax. Each company has its own scoring system and maintains a record called a credit report for each individual in its database. Anyone who has ever taken out a loan of any type (including credit cards) from a commercial entity, such as a bank, department store, or auto dealership, most likely has a credit report on file. Lenders regularly update the credit bureaus about the loan payment histories of borrowers, such as whether or not the borrowers make their loan payments on time and in full. Other sources that can influence credit scores are utilities, medical service providers, landlords and leasing agents, and companies with which consumers establish contracts to pay for goods or services, such as cell phone companies.

Fair Isaac Company (now known as FICO) is a financial company that was founded during the 1950s. Over the decades it has developed statistical models that are widely used by the credit bureaus to determine credit scores. A credit score calculated using FICO software is called a FICO score. The FICO method is highly regarded in the credit industry. Thus, FICO scores are relied on by many major financial institutions as reliable measures of the creditworthiness of customers. According to FICO, in "What's in Your FICO Score" (2012, http://www.myfico.com/CreditEducation/WhatsInYourScore.aspx), a FICO score generally depends on the following elements:

- Payment history—35%

- Amounts owed—30%

- Length of credit history—15%

- New credit (i.e., recently opened accounts)—10%

- Types of credit used—10%

In "What's Not in Your FICO Score" (2012, http://www.myfico.com/CreditEducation/WhatsNotInYourScore.aspx), FICO notes that federal law prohibits the use of information on a person's race, religion, color, national origin, sex, marital status, or age in credit scores.

There are some general guidelines about what FICO scores mean to lenders. In "FICO Credit Scoring" (2012, http://www.mbda.gov/blogger/financial-education/fico-credit-scoring), the U.S. Department of Commerce's Minority Business Development Agency indicates that FICO scores range from 375 to 900 points, with higher scores indicating better creditworthiness. People with higher scores are more likely to be granted credit and to receive better credit terms (e.g., lower interest rates) than people with lower scores. Typically, a score of at least 680 is required to get the best (or prime) credit terms. People with scores lower than about 620 are said to have "subprime" (less than prime) creditworthiness. If they are granted credit, they may be charged a high interest rate by the lender because they are "risky" borrowers who are less likely than "prime" borrowers to repay a loan.

BORROWER'S DEBT RATIO. A borrower's debt ratio can be calculated in different ways. One ratio results from dividing total assets (or total income) by total debt. Another example is a ratio of monthly debt payments to all monthly obligations. For example, a borrower's monthly obligations might include utility payments, car and student loan payments, and contract payments, such as for cell phone service. A borrower who already has substantial monthly obligations will find it difficult to also make mortgage payments.

LOAN-TO-VALUE RATIO. A loan-to-value (LTV) ratio is calculated by dividing the amount of a mortgage loan by the value of the home to be purchased. For example, a borrower seeking an $80,000 mortgage to buy a $100,000 home would have an LTV ratio of 0.8. The borrower would have to pay in cash the difference between the purchase price and the mortgage amount—in this case $20,000. This is called a down payment on the home purchase. Historically, mortgage lenders have been reluctant to lend the full purchase price of a home. A borrower who defaults on a mortgage and loses the home through foreclosure also loses the down payment that he or she made when the home was purchased. Thus, a down payment has long been considered by lenders to be a good sign that the borrower will faithfully make the mortgage payments.

Risk Classifications

Lenders use the results of the underwriting process to classify mortgages into different risk categories, depending on the creditworthiness of the borrower and the likelihood that the person will repay the loan.

As noted earlier, prime loans feature better (lower) interest rates than subprime loans. Nonprime loans are for people who do not qualify for prime mortgages for various reasons—poor or short credit history, lack of assets, low income or inability to prove income, and so on. Nonprime loan holders are more likely than prime loan holders to default on their loans. As a result, lenders charge higher interest rates on nonprime loans because of the greater risk that is associated with them.

Some lenders further classify nonprime loans as near-prime or subprime. In *The Rise in Mortgage Defaults* (November 2008, http://www.federalreserve.gov/pubs/feds/2008/200859/200859pap.pdf), Christopher J. Mayer, Karen M. Pence, and Shane M. Sherlund point out that these classifications are not strictly or uniformly defined in the mortgage industry. However, near-prime mortgages are generally for borrowers with "minor credit quality issues" or those "who are unable or unwilling to provide full documentation of assets or income." People buying a home as an investment, rather than to live in, might also be considered near-prime borrowers because investors are more likely than owner-occupiers to default on mortgage loans. (Investors buy homes with the expectation that the properties will appreciate in value. If this happens, they can resell the homes in a relatively short period for more than they originally paid and make a profit.) Subprime mortgages are for borrowers posing the greatest risk of nonpayment. This classification is typically assigned due to lender concerns about the borrower's credit history, income, assets, debt ratios, and/or lack of documentation.

Mortgage Interest Rates: Fixed and Adjustable

A fixed-rate mortgage charges a set interest rate over the entire lifetime of the loan, typically 30 years. Figure 4.2 shows the average annual interest rate charged on a 30-year fixed mortgage from April 1971 to August 2012, when the rate was 3.6%. Comparison to Figure 1.12 in Chapter 1 shows that fixed mortgage rates mirror the ups and downs of the prime rate. One feature of a fixed-rate mortgage is that the monthly payment remains the same throughout the lifetime of the loan.

Creative financing terms introduced by creditors since the late 1990s have led to many alternatives to the conventional 30-year fixed-rate mortgage. One alternative is a shorter loan period, for example, 15 years instead of 30 years. Another option is an adjustable-rate mortgage (ARM). ARMs feature variable interest rates (and consequently variable monthly payments) over the lifetime of the loan. An ARM rate is typically tied to a published benchmark rate called an index rate. Low index rates during the first half of the first decade of the 21st century enticed many home buyers to take on ARMs instead of fixed-rate mortgages. Lenders may offer discount (or teaser) rates that are even lower than the index rate during the early months or years of the ARM repayment period. This translates into extra low monthly payments for an initial period, followed by much higher payments as the ARM matures.

Some creditors offer mortgages that allow homeowners to make interest-only payments for a short initial portion of the loan period. This is followed by a longer

FIGURE 4.2

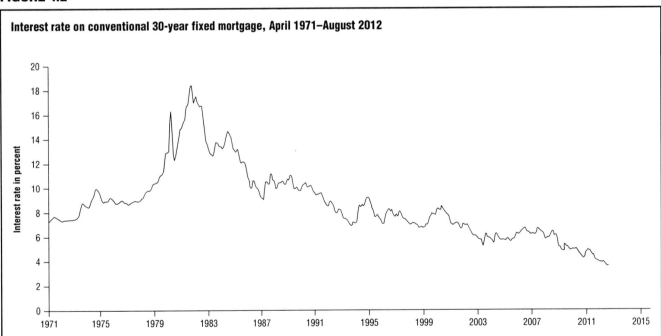

Interest rate on conventional 30-year fixed mortgage, April 1971–August 2012

SOURCE: Adapted from "Contract Rate on 30-Year, Fixed-Rate Conventional Home Mortgage Commitments," in *Federal Reserve Statistical Release: H.15. Selected Interest Rates—Historical Data*, The Federal Reserve, 2012, http://www.federalreserve.gov/datadownload/Output.aspx?rel=H15&series=4c9742f6cd2efded850db98de3f2c75d&lastObs=&from=&to=&filetype=csv&label=include&layout=seriescolumn (accessed September 14, 2012)

period of much higher monthly payments. A similar product is the payment-option mortgage, which allows homeowners to make small minimum payments for an initial short period. Short-term payment schedules requiring one large balloon payment are also offered in some mortgage products.

Mortgage arrangements with changeable monthly payments and balloon payments can pose a financial problem for homeowners who overestimate their ability to meet the costs of the mortgage. Figure 4.3 illustrates how monthly payments can vary significantly between different types of mortgages on a $200,000 home. The buyer assuming a fixed-rate 30-year mortgage at 6% interest pays $1,199.10 per month for the entire lifetime of the loan. The 5/1 ARM is a common ARM arrangement in which the initial interest rate remains fixed for five years and then begins to fluctuate with the index rate. In this example, the buyer pays a discounted rate of 4% during the first five years of the ARM. This translates to a monthly mortgage payment of $954.83. In year six the monthly payment is tied to a 6% ARM rate, and the monthly payment jumps to $1,165.51. In year seven the ARM rate increases to 7%; consequently, the monthly payment increases to $1,389.51. Two other types of mortgages depicted in Figure 4.3—a 5/1 ARM with interest-only payments and a payment-option mortgage—both feature large increases in monthly payments after the initial low-rate period.

FIGURE 4.3

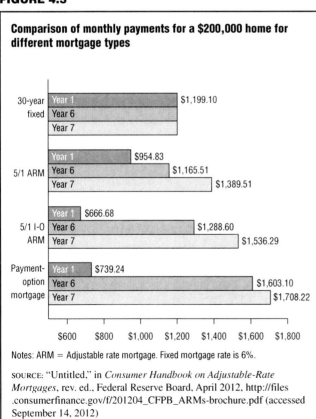

Comparison of monthly payments for a $200,000 home for different mortgage types

Notes: ARM = Adjustable rate mortgage. Fixed mortgage rate is 6%.

SOURCE: "Untitled," in *Consumer Handbook on Adjustable-Rate Mortgages*, rev. ed., Federal Reserve Board, April 2012, http://files .consumerfinance.gov/f/201204_CFPB_ARMs-brochure.pdf (accessed September 14, 2012)

Refinancing Mortgages

Most home mortgages cover long periods—up to 30 years. Interest rates, however, can change dramatically in the short term, rising and falling in response to macroeconomic factors. Home buyers who assume mortgages during times of high interest rates can ask creditors to refinance (adjust the mortgage terms) when interest rates go down. Basically, refinancing entails drawing up a new mortgage contract on a property. Because mortgage contracts are complicated legal documents, creditors usually charge fees to refinance mortgages. Thus, homeowners must weigh the long-term benefits of a reduced interest rate against the expense of refinancing fees.

During the first decade of the 21st century interest rates trended downward, making mortgage refinancing popular. This was particularly true for consumers who had purchased homes during the 1980s, when interest rates were extremely high by historical standards.

Refinancing frequently results in lower monthly payments for the homeowner because of the lower interest rate and because refinancing is commonly performed after several years of payments have been made on the original loan. This frees up the borrowers' money for consumer spending, investing, or saving. However, refinances that are conducted with a long payment period will keep the homeowner in mortgage debt for a longer period than originally anticipated. Some homeowners opt for a shorter loan payback period when they refinance. For example, consider a homeowner who has been paying for five years on a fixed-rate 30-year mortgage. There are 25 years left in the repayment period. Refinancing at a much lower interest rate with a new 15-year payback period may not decrease the monthly payment, but it will reduce by 10 years the amount of time the homeowner will be in mortgage debt.

Home Equity Loans

Real estate tends to appreciate in value. Thus, a property can increase in value above the amount that was originally borrowed to pay for it. For example, imagine a homeowner who bought a house in 2000 for $100,000 with a 30-year fixed-rate mortgage. After making mortgage payments for several years, the homeowner discovers that the principal due on the loan has dropped to $90,000, but the property has increased in value to $140,000. The difference between the amount of principal owed (the outstanding loan balance) and the value of the property is $50,000 and is called home equity. Home equity is an asset that can be borrowed against. Basically, homeowners can liquefy (turn into cash) the equity they have built up in their homes.

As noted in Chapter 3, during the 1990s and the first half of the first decade of the 21st century U.S. homeowners took advantage of rising property values and low interest rates to liquefy billions of dollars in equity from their homes. Alan Greenspan and James Kennedy calculate in *Sources and Uses of Equity Extracted from Homes* (March 2007, http://www.federalreserve.gov/pubs/feds/2007/200720/200720pap.pdf) that the cash extracted from home equity between 1991 and 2005 averaged $530 billion per year. Approximately two-thirds of this total was from sales of existing homes. The remaining one-third was due to equity-based loans. Greenspan and Kennedy estimate that the vast majority (87%) of the liquefied equity from home sales was used by Americans toward the purchase of their next home. The remaining 13% was spent or invested. They believe that one-third of the cash from equity-based loans was applied toward nonmortgage debt (e.g., credit card debt). Another one-third was likely spent on home improvements, and the remainder was spent on other purchases or invested.

Economists generally approve of the use of home equity loans for home improvements. This type of spending is considered to be an investment because it adds value to the home. Many homeowners choose to use home equity loans to repay other debt. Because mortgage loans typically have lower interest rates than other loans, this exchange is beneficial. In addition, the interest paid on mortgage loans is tax deductible for most Americans, whereas interest paid on other types of loans is not deductible. Thus, conversion of "bad" types of debt (such as credit cards) to mortgage debt has favorable consequences.

However, some economists worry that homeowners who use home equity loans to pay off bad kinds of debt may succumb to temptation and run up bad debt again. This could put them in a dire financial situation. They will no longer have their home equity to fall back on if their new debts become more than they can afford, and they might have to default on their loans. Home equity loans, like all mortgage loans, are secured by property. Thus, defaulting on a home equity loan can result in the loss of the home by the owner.

Foreclosures, Defaults, and Delinquencies

Foreclosure is a legal process in which a lender takes possession of the collateral (i.e., the home) of a borrower who has stopped paying on a mortgage loan. The borrower is said to be in default, meaning that the borrower has failed to abide by the legally binding mortgage agreement. Typically, lenders grant borrowers up to 90 days to "catch up" on late mortgage payments. After that 90-day period, the foreclosure process begins. Mortgage loans on which borrowers have not made a payment for at least 90 days are said to be "seriously delinquent."

The Secondary Market for Mortgages

Mortgage loans represent an investment for lenders. Mortgages will provide income well into the future as the loan payments (including interest) are paid by the borrowers. As a result, mortgages are commodities that are purchased by investors. This is known as the secondary mortgage market. In general, individual mortgages are bundled together and sold on the stock market. This process is called securitization. The packages are known as mortgage-backed securities or mortgage-based securities. Both are abbreviated MBS.

The original lenders are often eager to sell mortgages on the secondary market to obtain cash that they can use to make new loans. Companies purchase MBS products because mortgages have historically been considered relatively safe investments that will provide regular income in the future. Of course, the secondary buyers are trusting that the original lenders used good underwriting practices and lent money only to people who are very likely to keep making their mortgage payments. If borrowers default on mortgages that are within MBS packages, the MBS investors suffer a financial loss.

The Federal Government's Role in Mortgages

There are two types of mortgages in common use: conventional mortgages and government-underwritten mortgages. Conventional mortgages are loans made by nongovernmental businesses, such as banks and finance companies. Government-underwritten mortgages are insured by a federal, state, or local government agency.

Because high rates of homeownership are considered to be good for the U.S. economy, the government has taken an active role in the mortgage market. Mortgage terms have changed dramatically since the early 1930s. At that time home buyers could borrow only up to half of a property's market value (i.e., an LTV ratio of 0.5). A typical repayment plan included three to five years of regular payments and then one large balloon payment of the remaining balance. According to the Federal Housing Administration (FHA; 2012, http://www.hud.gov/offices/hsg/fhahistory.cfm), these terms discouraged many potential homeowners. As a result, the homeownership rate stood at around 40%.

During the 1930s the federal government introduced a variety of initiatives to boost a housing industry that was devastated by the Great Depression (1929–1939) and increase homeownership. These efforts were focused on encouraging the supply side of the mortgage industry. They benefited consumers by enhancing the availability and flexibility of home mortgages. For example, amortization schedules covering 15 years or more became common and balloon payments were eliminated—both of these changes made it much easier for consumers to afford houses. Following World War II (1939–1945) the Veteran's Administration (VA; now known as the U.S. Department of Veterans Affairs) began offering mortgages with favorable terms to returning veterans. Postwar economic prosperity and relatively low interest rates led to a housing boom. According to the U.S. Census Bureau, in "Residential Vacancies and Homeownership in the Second Quarter 2010" (July 27,

FIGURE 4.4

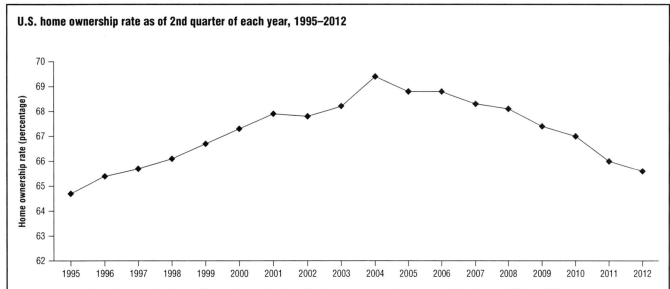

U.S. home ownership rate as of 2nd quarter of each year, 1995–2012

SOURCE: Adapted from Robert R. Callis and Melissa Kresin, "Table 4SA. Homeownership Rates for the United States: 1995 to 2012, Seasonally Adjusted (in Percent)," in *Residential Vacancies and Homeownership in the Second Quarter 2012*, U.S. Department of Commerce, U.S. Census Bureau, July 27, 2012, http://www.census.gov/hhes/www/housing/hvs/qtr212/files/q212press.pdf (accessed September 14, 2012)

2010, http://www.census.gov/hhes/www/housing/hvs/qtr210/files/q210press.pdf), the nation's homeownership rate was 64% during the mid-1980s. It climbed to a record high of 69.4% in 2004 and then began to decline. (See Figure 4.4.) As of the second quarter of 2012, the homeownership rate was 65.6%.

Besides the VA, there are several other agencies and organizations that operate under government control or mandate to increase homeownership among Americans, including the FHA, the Federal National Mortgage Association, and the Federal Home Loan Mortgage Corporation.

FEDERAL HOUSING ADMINISTRATION. The FHA was created in 1934 and later placed under the oversight of the U.S. Department of Housing and Urban Development. The FHA provides mortgage insurance on loans that are made by FHA-approved lenders to buyers of single- and multi-family homes. FHA-insured loans require less cash down payment from the home buyer than most conventional loans. The insurance provides assurances to lenders that the government will cover losses resulting from homeowners who default on their loans.

FEDERAL NATIONAL MORTGAGE ASSOCIATION. The Federal National Mortgage Association (Fannie Mae) was created in 1938. Fannie Mae began buying FHA-insured mortgages from banks and other lenders. It then bundled the mortgages together and sold the mortgage packages as investments on the stock market. In essence, Fannie Mae created the secondary market for home mortgages. Lenders benefit because they receive immediate money that can be lent to new customers, and home buyers benefit from the increased availability of mort-

gage loans. The mortgage packages are attractive to investors because the mortgages are backed by FHA insurance. In 1968 Fannie Mae became a private organization and expanded its portfolio beyond FHA-insured mortgages to private-label MBS (i.e., MBS products securitized by nongovernmental businesses, such as banks and financial institutions).

FEDERAL HOME LOAN MORTGAGE CORPORATION. The Federal Home Loan Mortgage Corporation (Freddie Mac) was created by the federal government in 1970 to prevent Fannie Mae's monopolization of the mortgage market. Like Fannie Mae, Freddie Mac is a private organization operating under a government charter and buys and sells home mortgages on the secondary market. Both Fannie Mae and Freddie Mac are shareholder-owned corporations.

The Housing Market Booms and Busts

As noted in Chapter 1, markets sometimes boom (become overly inflated in value) and then bust (lose value suddenly and dramatically). What frustrates investors and analysts alike is that the evidence of a boom is not obvious until after a bust occurs. In other words, most people do not see a bust coming because they are caught up in the excitement of making money and expect the financial windfall to continue indefinitely.

The historically low interest rates during the first half of the first decade of the 21st century spurred demand in the real estate market. For example, sales of newly built single-family homes increased steadily from the late 1990s to 2005, when a record of 1.4 million units were sold. (See Figure 4.5.)

FIGURE 4.5

Number of new single-family homes sold, January 1963–July 2012

SOURCE: Adapted from "New One Family Houses Sold: United States (HSN1F)," in *FRED® Economic Data*, Federal Reserve Bank of St. Louis, August 23, 2012, http://research.stlouisfed.org/fred2/series/HSN1F (accessed September 14, 2012)

FIGURE 4.6

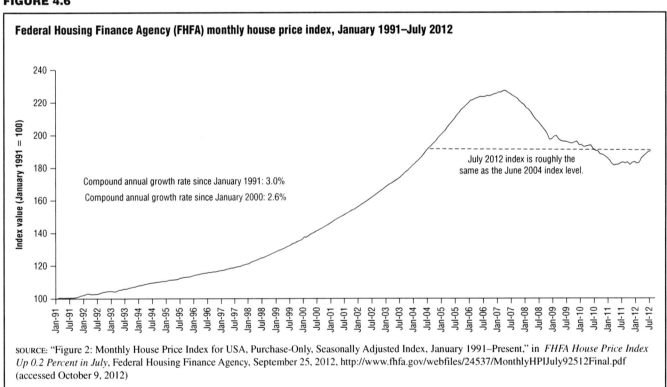

Federal Housing Finance Agency (FHFA) monthly house price index, January 1991–July 2012

Compound annual growth rate since January 1991: 3.0%
Compound annual growth rate since January 2000: 2.6%

July 2012 index is roughly the same as the June 2004 index level.

SOURCE: "Figure 2: Monthly House Price Index for USA, Purchase-Only, Seasonally Adjusted Index, January 1991–Present," in *FHFA House Price Index Up 0.2 Percent in July*, Federal Housing Finance Agency, September 25, 2012, http://www.fhfa.gov/webfiles/24537/MonthlyHPIJuly92512Final.pdf (accessed October 9, 2012)

High demand pushes prices upward. The Federal Housing Finance Agency uses an index called the house price index (HPI) to track home prices for mortgages that are acquired by Fannie Mae and Freddie Mac. (It should be noted that the HPI covers purchase-only mortgages and not refinanced loans.) The HPI for January 1991 is arbitrarily set at 100. According to Figure 4.6, the HPI increased dramatically through mid-2007, when it peaked above 220. Figure 4.7 shows the quarterly change and four-quarter change in the HPI from the first quarter of

1992 to the second quarter of 2012. The HPI grew by 1% to 2% per quarter from the late 1990s to the end of the fourth quarter of 2004. By the second quarter of 2005 the HPI had increased (appreciated) by 10.5% compared with the year before. (See Figure 4.8.)

The financial company Standard & Poor's (S&P) maintains home price indexes known as the S&P/Case-Shiller indexes. They are named after the economists Karl E. Case and Robert J. Shiller. One of the indexes—

FIGURE 4.7

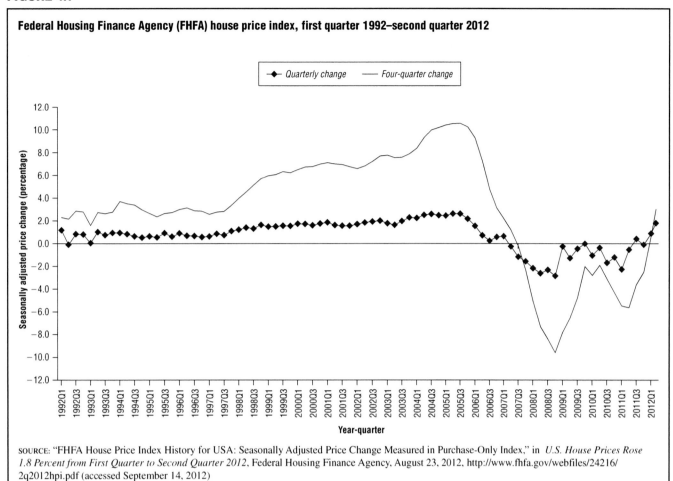

Federal Housing Finance Agency (FHFA) house price index, first quarter 1992–second quarter 2012

SOURCE: "FHFA House Price Index History for USA: Seasonally Adjusted Price Change Measured in Purchase-Only Index," in *U.S. House Prices Rose 1.8 Percent from First Quarter to Second Quarter 2012*, Federal Housing Finance Agency, August 23, 2012, http://www.fhfa.gov/webfiles/24216/ 2q2012hpi.pdf (accessed September 14, 2012)

the 20-city composite—measures home price changes by compiling and weighting data for 20 major metropolitan areas:

- Atlanta, Georgia

- Boston, Massachusetts

- Charlotte, North Carolina

- Chicago, Illinois

- Cleveland, Ohio

- Dallas, Texas

- Denver, Colorado

- Detroit, Michigan

- Las Vegas, Nevada

- Los Angeles, California

- Miami, Florida

- Minneapolis, Minnesota

- New York City, New York

- Phoenix, Arizona

- Portland, Oregon

- San Diego, California

- San Francisco, California

- Seattle, Washington

- Tampa, Florida

- Washington, D.C.

In the press release "For the Past Year Home Prices Have Generally Moved Sideways According to the S&P/ Case-Shiller Home Price Indices" (July 27, 2010, http:// www.standardandpoors.com/), S&P reports that the 20-city composite index reached its highest point—just over 200—in 2006. The index is benchmarked to a value of 100 that is assigned to January 2000. Thus, the index more than doubled between 2000 and 2006.

During the first half of the first decade of the 21st century homeowner-occupiers and investors became excited about appreciating home prices. The homeowner-occupiers saw their homes quickly increase in value, allowing them to borrow against the rising equity. Investors reaped handsome profits by selling homes relatively

FIGURE 4.8

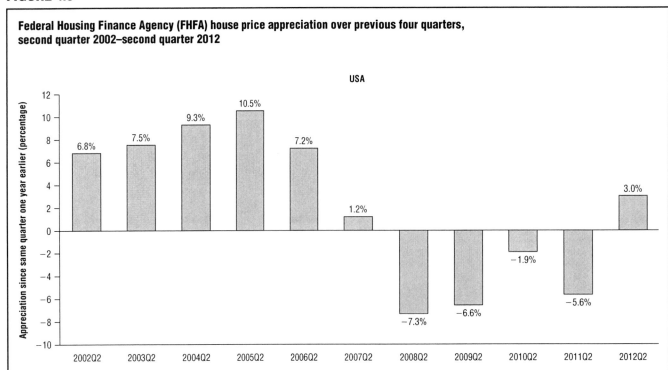

Federal Housing Finance Agency (FHFA) house price appreciation over previous four quarters, second quarter 2002–second quarter 2012

SOURCE: "FHFA Price Appreciation over Previous Four Quarters (Seasonally Adjusted, Purchase-Only Index)," in *U.S. House Prices Rose 1.8 Percent From First Quarter to Second Quarter 2012*, Federal Housing Finance Agency, August 23, 2012, http://www.fhfa.gov/webfiles/24216/2q2012hpi.pdf (accessed September 14, 2012)

quickly for more than what they paid for them. This process became known as "flipping houses."

Huge demand from potential homeowner-occupiers and investors prompted many lenders to relax their underwriting standards and extend loans to borrowers they might have previously rejected. In addition, many lenders greatly expanded their use of creative financing terms, such as ARMs that featured low initial monthly payments. Subprime ARMs became particularly popular. Eric Petroff indicates in "Who Is to Blame for the Subprime Crisis?" (September 5, 2007, http://www.investopedia.com/articles/07/subprime-blame.asp) that only $35 billion in subprime mortgage loans were initiated in 1994. By 2002 that number had risen to $213 billion. Over the next three years the subprime market skyrocketed. In 2005 subprime lenders originated $665 billion of the risky mortgage loans. The White House notes in *Economic Report of the President* (February 2008, http://www.gpoaccess.gov/eop/2008/2008_erp.pdf) that the percentage of mortgage originations that were subprime increased from 5% in 2001 to over 20% in 2006.

Mortgage originators also greatly relaxed their LTV standards during the housing boom. As noted earlier, a low LTV ratio (e.g., less than 0.8 to 0.9) has historically been associated with buyers who are more invested in their properties and less likely to default. Mayer, Pence, and Sherlund find that the median LTV ratio (half of the

LTV ratios were higher and half were lower) for subprime mortgages actually increased from 90% in 2003 to 100% in 2005. In other words, many subprime borrowers made no down payment when they purchased their home. In addition, subprime borrowers were regularly put into nontraditional mortgage arrangements, such as ARMs and loans that offered interest-only payments for a short period. These loans featured balloon payments and/or sharp increases in monthly payments at some point during the loan period. The variable interest rates were often tied to economic indexes that can change suddenly and drastically. Mayer, Pence, and Sherlund conclude that "the riskiest borrowers were matched with the most complicated products."

Both the borrowers and lenders of subprime loans expected homes to keep appreciating in value. For homeowners, this appreciation would allow them to refinance their loan and tap into home equity to offset the financial burden of the coming higher monthly payments. Likewise, lenders believed that home appreciation would offset the risk they were taking in lending money to people with poor credit histories or other financial problems. Thus, like all booms, the housing boom was driven by high expectations that future events would take a favorable path.

Investment companies also drove the housing boom by enthusiastically buying mortgage products on the secondary market. This provided cash to lending companies

FIGURE 4.9

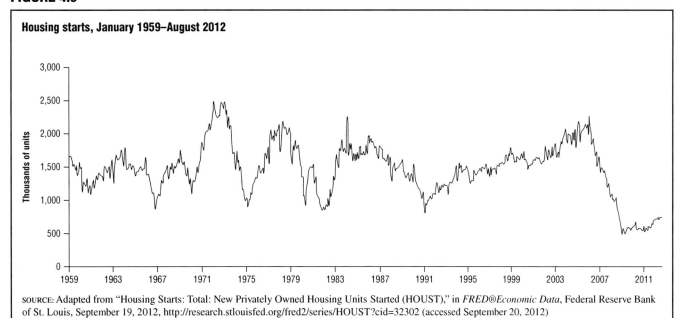

Housing starts, January 1959–August 2012

SOURCE: Adapted from "Housing Starts: Total: New Privately Owned Housing Units Started (HOUST)," in *FRED®Economic Data*, Federal Reserve Bank of St. Louis, September 19, 2012, http://research.stlouisfed.org/fred2/series/HOUST?cid=32302 (accessed September 20, 2012)

FIGURE 4.10

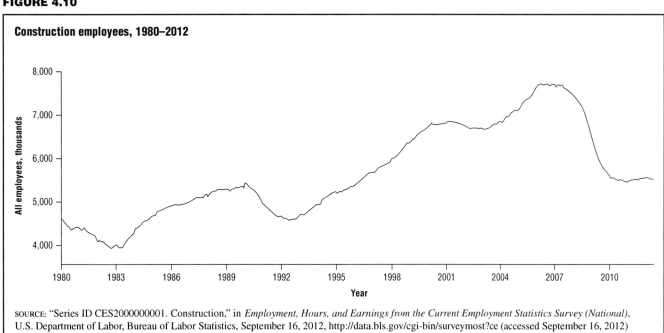

Construction employees, 1980–2012

SOURCE: "Series ID CES2000000001. Construction," in *Employment, Hours, and Earnings from the Current Employment Statistics Survey (National)*, U.S. Department of Labor, Bureau of Labor Statistics, September 16, 2012, http://data.bls.gov/cgi-bin/surveymost?ce (accessed September 16, 2012)

to underwrite more mortgages. Meanwhile, the stock of banks and other financial institutions providing mortgages greatly rose in value, as investors became excited about the increasing loan portfolios. Construction companies also responded to high housing demand by building more houses. Figure 4.9 shows the number of housing starts in the United States from January 1959 to August 2012. Housing starts is the number of new housing units (or homes) on which construction has begun. The number of housing starts for single-family homes topped 2.2 million units in 2005 and early 2006.

This construction boom resulted in incredibly high employment in the industry. The U.S. Bureau of Labor

Statistics indicates that the number of workers employed in construction grew dramatically, from 4.6 million workers in 1992 to 7.7 million workers in late 2006 and early 2007. (See Figure 4.10.)

DEFAULTING BEGINS TO GROW. According to Mayer, Pence, and Sherlund, the mortgage market first showed signs of trouble in mid-2005, when large lenders noticed a troubling increase in the percentage of their subprime loans that had become "seriously delinquent." Between 2000 and 2004 an average of 1.5% of subprime loans were in default only one year after the loans were originated. In other words, the borrowers stopped making their mortgage payments within months of taking out the loans. Analysts refer to these events as "early payment defaults." By the end of 2005 early payment defaults for subprime loans had climbed to 2.5% and continued to grow, reaching 5% at year-end 2006 and 8% at year-end 2007.

Early payment defaults are particularly troubling because they happen only months after underwriting occurs. Mayer, Pence, and Sherlund note that these loans "may have been underwritten so poorly that borrowers were unable to afford the monthly payments almost from the moment of origination." They also point to evidence suggesting "fraudulent practices by both borrowers and mortgage brokers." These practices may have kept buyers on the secondary mortgage market from realizing the actual riskiness of the investments they were buying. Regardless, Mayer, Pence, and Sherlund maintain that "some of the deterioration in underwriting characteristics should have been apparent to investors in mortgage-backed securities."

In *Economic Report of the President*, the White House notes that between 2004 and 2006 the default rate among homeowners with subprime ARMs was around 6%. By late 2007 the rate had skyrocketed to more than 15%. The default rate for prime mortgage loans also increased during this period, from around 1% to nearly 4%.

Maura Reynolds reports in "Loan Troubles Hit New Heights" (*Los Angeles Times*, March 7, 2008) that the national average foreclosure rate at the end of the fourth quarter of 2007 was the highest in recorded history. Just over 2% of mortgages were in foreclosure at that time. The foreclosure rate was highest in states that had experienced the greatest housing boom (and hence the greatest housing bust): Arizona, California, Florida, and Nevada.

THE ECONOMY SUFFERS. The unusually high default rates caused mounting financial losses for original lenders and MBS investors. The White House states in *Economic Report of the President* that "there were significant disruptions in [the] financial markets in the summer of 2007." In fact, it was the beginning of a vicious downward spiral. As banks, financial institutions, and investment companies reported huge losses, their stock plummeted in value. Some of the companies failed, and many others were in danger of failing.

By this time many banks and financial institutions had stopped originating new mortgages because they were fearful of experiencing more losses. Meanwhile, the demand for new houses was decreasing rapidly. (See Figure 4.9.) As a result, employment in the construction industry declined. (See Figure 4.10.) Sales of newly built single-family homes also dropped considerably. (See Figure 4.5.) Figure 4.11 shows the median and average sales price of new homes sold in the United States on an annual basis between 1980 and July 2012. In March 2007 the median price peaked at $262,600, whereas the average price of a new home peaked at $329,400. By 2009 these values had dropped to around $214,500 and $268,233, respectively. As shown in Figure 4.7 and Figure 4.8, home

FIGURE 4.11

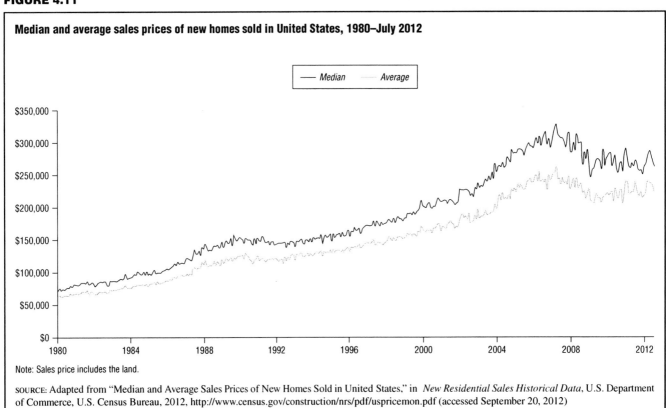

Median and average sales prices of new homes sold in United States, 1980–July 2012

Note: Sales price includes the land.

SOURCE: Adapted from "Median and Average Sales Prices of New Homes Sold in United States," in *New Residential Sales Historical Data*, U.S. Department of Commerce, U.S. Census Bureau, 2012, http://www.census.gov/construction/nrs/pdf/uspricemon.pdf (accessed September 20, 2012)

prices declined at a record pace. Second quarter home price appreciation was 1.2% in 2007, −7.3% in 2008, and −6.6% in 2009.

The decline in housing values left many homeowners owing more on their mortgages than their homes were worth in the marketplace. This is called being "upside down" or "underwater" in one's mortgage. Mayer, Pence, and Sherlund report that by mid-2008 more than half of the borrowers in Arizona, California, Florida, and Nevada had negative equity (i.e., they were upside down in their mortgages). More than one-third of borrowers in Indiana, Michigan, and Ohio and approximately 10% of borrowers in the rest of the country were upside down in their mortgages.

TROUBLE FOR FANNIE MAE AND FREDDIE MAC. The housing market bust put tremendous financial pressure on Fannie Mae and Freddie Mac. Like many other MBS holders, the two companies suffered huge financial losses due to defaulted loans. By mid-2008 investors were concerned that Fannie Mae and Freddie Mac would be unable to raise sufficient money to cover these losses.

Katie Benner reports in "The $5 Trillion Mess" (CNNMoney.com, July 14, 2008) that shares in Fannie Mae and Freddie Mac dropped in value by 65% and 75%, respectively, during the first half of 2008. At that time the two companies held or guaranteed approximately $5 trillion in mortgage loans.

In July 2008 Congress passed the Housing and Economic Recovery Act (HERA). The act created the Federal Housing Finance Agency (FHFA) and gave it the power to put Fannie Mae and/or Freddie Mac into conservatorship. Mark Jickling of the Congressional Research Service explains in "Fannie Mae and Freddie Mac in Conservatorship" (September 15, 2008, http://fpc.state.gov/documents/organization/110097.pdf) that the FHFA was given "full powers to control the assets and operations of the firms." A conservatorship for both companies was officially established in September 2008.

Jickling notes that the U.S. Department of the Treasury began investing money into the firms by buying shares of their stock and "newly issued" Fannie Mae and Freddie Mac MBS packages. In addition, the two firms were allowed to get short-term loans from the Treasury Department using MBS as collateral.

Under the HERA, the FHFA must submit an annual report to Congress about the status and financial soundness of Fannie Mae and Freddie Mac. In *Report to Congress, 2009* (May 25, 2010, http://www.fhfa.gov/webfiles/15784/FHFAReportToCongress52510.pdf), the FHFA notes that the main reason the companies were put into conservatorship was because of their investments in private-label MBS. The market value of these investments had declined sharply between 2007 and 2008.

According to the FHFA, Fannie Mae's annual net income was positive in 2005 and 2006. In 2007 the company suffered a loss of around $2 billion. In 2008 and 2009 its annual losses skyrocketed between $60 billion and $70 billion per year. Freddie Mac's financial performance followed a similar pattern. The company had positive net income in 2005 and 2006 and then reported losses of $2 billion in 2007, $50 billion in 2008, and $22 billion in 2009. At year-end 2009 Fannie Mae and Freddie Mac held or guaranteed nearly half (47%) of the country's outstanding residential mortgage debt.

In *Report to Congress, 2011* (June 13, 2012, http://www.fhfa.gov/webfiles/24009/FHFA_RepTo Congr11_6_14_508.pdf), the FHFA reports that the companies have taken a variety of actions since being put into conservatorship to conserve their assets and prevent future losses. These safeguards include higher FICO credit scores for potential borrowers than were required before 2008 and lower average LTV ratios for newly issued mortgages. In addition, the FHFA notes that the companies have "completed more than two million foreclosure prevention actions, including more than one million loan modifications."

Nevertheless, as of June 2012 the FHFA believed that Fannie Mae and Freddie Mac faced "significant risks" as both companies were expected to continue to suffer losses from mortgages that had been originated before they went into conservatorship.

GOVERNMENT PROGRAMS. The HERA is only one of many actions that have been taken by the federal government to try to boost the ailing housing market. After taking office in January 2009, President Barack Obama (1961–) pushed for major reforms of the financial markets and set up programs that were specifically designed to address the housing market crisis. The Making Home Affordable (MHA) program (http://www.makinghomeaffordable.gov/) helps individual homeowners restructure their mortgages, while the Hardest Hit Fund (2012, http://www.treasury.gov/initiatives/financial-stability/TARP-Programs/housing/hhf/Pages/Program-Purpose-and-Overview.aspx) funnels money to state housing finance agencies "to develop locally-tailored foreclosure prevention solutions in areas that have been hard hit by home price declines and high unemployment." Both programs were established by the Treasury Department's Office of Financial Stability under the Troubled Asset Relief Program (TARP), a broad-scaled financial program that was started during the administration of President George W. Bush (1946–) and authorized by Congress through the Emergency Economic Stabilization Act of 2008. The TARP program is described in detail in Chapter 6.

MHA program components include the Home Affordable Modification Program (HAMP), which allows homeowners who are struggling to make their monthly payments and who face foreseeable and/or imminent default to have their mortgages restructured to be more affordable. Another component is the Home Affordable Refinance Program (HARP), which provides homeowners with mortgages that are owned or guaranteed by Fannie Mae or Freddie Mac an opportunity to refinance the loans to make the monthly payments more affordable.

Though highly touted, the MHA program has had limited success. In *The Obama Administration's Efforts to Stabilize the Housing Market and Help American Homeowners* (June 2010, http://portal.hud.gov/hudportal/documents/huddoc?id=Jun_score.pdf), the Departments of Housing and Urban Development and the Treasury indicate disappointing progress for HAMP. The agencies note that between April 2009 and June 2010 only 346,800 people achieved permanent mortgage modifications through HAMP, out of the nearly 1.2 million people who applied. The article "Obama Administration to Extend and Expand Foreclosure Relief Program" (Associated Press, January 27, 2012) indicates that as of January 2012 approximately $29 billion had been spent on the program, but just over 900,000 applicants had gotten their mortgages permanently lowered. The article notes that "homeowners have complained that they were disqualified after banks lost their documents and failed to return phone calls. Banks have blamed homeowners for failing to submit needed paperwork." According to the article, the Treasury Department has chastised some large lenders, such as Bank of America, "for not doing enough to help Americans avoid foreclosures." In February 2012 the Obama administration expanded HAMP to offer more incentives to increase the number lenders and extended the program through the end of 2013.

Also in February 2012 President Obama proposed a new program to help homeowners, a program that would require congressional approval to be implemented. In "Obama Proposes New Home Loan Refinancing Plan" (CNNMoney.com, February 1, 2012), Les Christie explains that the new program would allow homeowners who are current on their payments to refinance into low-interest loans that are backed by the FHFA. The $10 billion program would be funded by fees that are imposed on "large banks." According to Christie, Congress has considered and rejected previous plans that were based on imposing new fees or taxes on the financial industry. Indeed, as of November 2012, no bills had been passed by Congress that implemented the plan laid out by Obama.

Federal and state officials announced in February 2012 that a $25 billion settlement had been reached with five large home lenders—Ally Financial, Bank of America, Citigroup, JPMorgan Chase, and Wells Fargo—that had been accused of engaging in improper foreclosure procedures. At the center of the case was a practice called "robo-signing," in which loan servicers allegedly signed

documents that authorized foreclosures to proceed without checking to see if all the proper paperwork (i.e., proof of ownership changes) had been filed as mortgages were sold between companies and bundled into securities. Chris Isidore and Jennifer Liberto note in "Mortgage Deal Could Bring Billions in Relief" (CNNMoney.com, February 15, 2012) that most of the settlement money was slated to help homeowners who were underwater in their mortgages. The deal covered all states, except Oklahoma, which negotiated a separate $18.6 billion settlement for its residents who were allegedly victims of improper foreclosures.

THE HOUSING MARKET SLOWLY RECOVERS. Figure 4.9 shows that the number of housing starts bottomed out in early 2009 at around 500,000 units per month. Thereafter, housing starts began to climb, reaching around 750,000 units per month by August 2012. Sales of new homes have also slowly recovered, from less than 300,000 units per month in mid-2009 to around 370,000 units per month in July 2012. (See Figure 4.5.)

House prices have also been creeping upward. As shown in Figure 4.7, the FHFA HPI was negative from early 2007 through late 2011. During the second quarter of 2012 the HPI was up around 2% compared with the quarter before. Table 4.5 provides a breakdown by state for home appreciation rates as of June 30, 2012. The national five-year average was −17.43%. Nevada, Arizona, Florida, and California suffered the highest five-year depreciation in home values. These four states had appreciation rates ranging from −55.15% to −40.09%, which were considerably worse than the national average. However, as shown in Table 4.5 the one-year and one-quarter rates had improved, with nearly all states reporting positive values. The national one-year average was 3.03%.

According to S&P, in "For the Past Year Home Prices Have Generally Moved Sideways According to the S&P/Case-Shiller Home Price Indices," the 20-city composite S&P/Case-Shiller Home Price Index plunged below 140 in 2009 (from its record-high value above 200 in late 2006). The index showed only slight improvement over subsequent years and was hovering just below 150 in mid-2012.

Figure 4.12 shows the vacancy rates for rental units and owned homes from the first quarter of 1995 to the second quarter of 2012. The rental vacancy rate peaked above 11% in mid-2009 and then declined dramatically. It was at 8.6% for the second quarter of 2012. The homeowner vacancy rate rose to its highest level (nearly 3%) in 2008 and then slowly declined. It stood at 2.1% in the second quarter of 2012.

Meanwhile, delinquency and foreclosure data show some improvements in the housing market. The Mortgage Bankers Association (MBA) provides regular reports on delinquency and foreclosure rates based on surveys it conducts. In "National Delinquency Survey Q1 2010: Data as of

TABLE 4.5

Federal Housing Finance Agency (FHFA) house price appreciation, by state, period ending June 30, 2012

[Estimates use FHFA's seasonally adjusted, purchase -only House Price Index]

State	Rank*	1-Yr.	Qtr.	5-Yr.
Arizona (AZ)	1	12.93	5.95	−41.89
Idaho (ID)	2	8.67	3.89	−25.51
Florida (FL)	3	7.44	3.25	−40.29
Michigan (MI)	4	7.25	3.50	−20.47
Arkansas (AR)	5	7.18	1.87	−5.00
Utah (UT)	6	7.13	2.52	−20.58
North Dakota (ND)	7	6.27	1.81	17.68
Hawaii (HI)	8	6.16	2.89	−14.48
Colorado (CO)	9	4.83	4.04	−3.24
California (CA)	10	4.13	3.54	−40.09
Texas (TX)	11	4.09	1.29	3.83
Alabama (AL)	12	4.03	1.16	−10.75
South Dakota (SD)	13	3.99	2.64	4.98
Georgia (GA)	14	3.98	2.62	−24.41
West Virginia (WV)	15	3.89	−3.66	−0.57
Missouri (MO)	16	3.74	0.79	−10.84
Tennessee (TN)	17	3.55	1.79	−8.83
Oregon (OR)	18	3.51	1.98	−25.63
South Carolina (SC)	19	3.44	1.92	−10.90
Maryland (MD)	20	3.42	4.69	−21.72
Minnesota (MN)	21	3.26	1.80	−18.98
District of Columbia (DC)	22	3.24	−0.10	1.07
Kentucky (KY)	23	3.24	1.80	−1.19
Nebraska (NE)	24	3.21	0.75	−2.57
USA		**3.03**	**1.80**	**−17.43**
New Mexico (NM)	25	2.91	3.16	−13.78
Iowa (IA)	26	2.68	−1.08	−0.72
Nevada (NV)	27	2.48	4.80	−55.15
Ohio (OH)	28	2.26	0.95	−11.61
Vermont (VT)	29	2.09	−0.90	−4.23
Virginia (VA)	30	2.03	0.81	−15.04
Kansas (KS)	31	1.97	0.31	−4.16
Wyoming (WY)	32	1.95	1.66	−4.61
New Hampshire (NH)	33	1.66	1.38	−16.77
Indiana (IN)	34	1.32	0.65	−5.76
Louisiana (LA)	35	1.09	1.69	−2.51
Washington (WA)	36	1.07	3.57	−23.68
Montana (MT)	37	1.06	0.55	−7.23
Wisconsin (WI)	38	1.04	0.78	−11.43
Alaska (AK)	39	1.00	4.55	0.85
Mississippi (MS)	40	0.87	−1.60	−9.90
North Carolina (NC)	41	0.62	0.23	−10.91
Maine (ME)	42	0.47	0.39	−9.07
Illinois (IL)	43	0.27	1.65	−19.25
Pennsylvania (PA)	44	−0.34	0.60	−8.00
Oklahoma (OK)	45	−0.35	0.25	2.56
New Jersey (NJ)	46	−0.76	1.63	−18.20
New York (NY)	47	−0.80	0.06	−7.74
Rhode Island (RI)	48	−1.03	−0.68	−21.70
Massachusetts (MA)	49	−1.14	0.48	−11.49
Delaware (DE)	50	−3.40	−0.60	−22.68
Connecticut (CT)	51	−4.69	−1.36	−18.04

*Ranking based on one-year appreciation.

SOURCE: Adapted from "House Price Appreciation by State; Percent Change in House Prices Period Ended June 30, 2012," in *U.S. House Prices Rose 1.8 Percent From First Quarter to Second Quarter 2012*, Federal Housing Finance Agency, August 23, 2012, http://www.fhfa.gov/webfiles/24216/2q2012hpi.pdf (accessed September 14, 2012).

March 31, 2010" (May 2010, http://www.mortgagebankers .org/files/Research/NDSQ110flyer.pdf), the MBA reports that 10.1% of all mortgage loans on one-to-four-unit residential properties were past due on payments at the end of the first quarter of 2010. The past due rates by type of loan were: subprime (27.2%—the highest level on record), FHA

(13.2%), VA loans (7.9%), and prime loans (7.3%). Remember that prime loans are made to people who are considered very creditworthy. The past due rate for prime loans was only 2% to 3% from 2000 to the second quarter of 2007. However, between the third quarter of 2007 and the first quarter of 2010 the rate more than doubled, from 3.1% to 7.3%.

According to the MBA, 4.6% of all loans were in foreclosure at the end of the first quarter of 2010. The rates varied from only 2.6% for VA loans to 15.4% for subprime loans.

Over the following two years the delinquency and foreclosure rates improved. The MBA notes in the press release "Mortgage Delinquencies Increase in Latest MBA Survey" (August 9, 2012, http://www.mbaa.org/NewsandMedia/PressCenter/81589.htm) that 7.6% of all mortgage loans on one-to-four-unit residential properties were past due on payments at the end of the second quarter of 2012. This was down from 10.1% at the end of the first quarter of 2010. Likewise, 4.3% of loans were in the foreclosure process at the end of the second quarter of 2012, down from 4.6% at the end of the first quarter of 2010. The highest foreclosure rates at the end of the second quarter of 2012 were in Florida (13.7%), New Jersey (7.7%), and Illinois (7.1%).

CONSUMER CREDIT

The Federal Reserve defines the term *consumer credit* as credit extended to individuals that does not include loans secured by real estate. In other words, mortgages are excluded from consumer credit.

Figure 4.13 shows that the amount of outstanding consumer credit grew relatively slowly during the 1970s and 1980s and then skyrocketed during the 1990s and the first half of the first decade of the 21st century. Consumer credit peaked at nearly $2.6 trillion in mid-2008 and then declined to less than $2.3 trillion in mid-2010. At first, this drop was hailed as proof that Americans had retreated from the heavy reliance on credit that characterized the years leading up to the Great Recession. However, the change was short lived. As shown in Figure 4.13, the amount of consumer credit began rising again, reaching $2.7 trillion in July 2012.

Consumer credit during the 1970s and 1980s consisted almost entirely of nonrevolving debt, which includes loans for vehicles, boats, vacations, and student loans. During the 1990s the breakdown began to change with revolving debt accounting for an ever-increasing proportion of consumer debt. Revolving debt consists almost entirely of credit card debt. Of the $2.7 trillion in consumer debt in July 2012, nonrevolving debt accounted for $1.8 trillion (69% of the total) and revolving debt accounted for $815.4 billion (31% of the total). (See Table 4.6.)

FIGURE 4.12

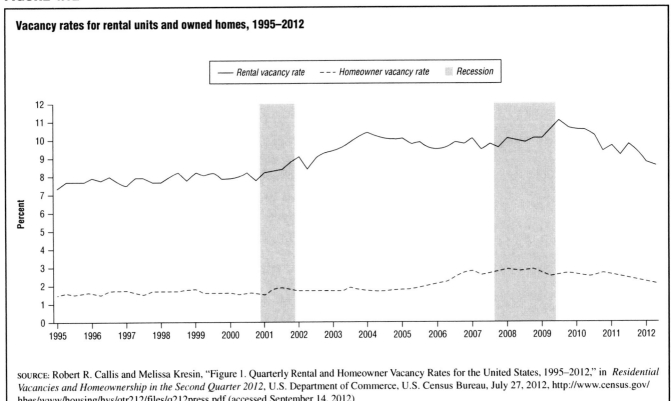

Vacancy rates for rental units and owned homes, 1995–2012

SOURCE: Robert R. Callis and Melissa Kresin, "Figure 1. Quarterly Rental and Homeowner Vacancy Rates for the United States, 1995–2012," in *Residential Vacancies and Homeownership in the Second Quarter 2012*, U.S. Department of Commerce, U.S. Census Bureau, July 27, 2012, http://www.census.gov/hhes/www/housing/hvs/qtr212/files/q212press.pdf (accessed September 14, 2012)

FIGURE 4.13

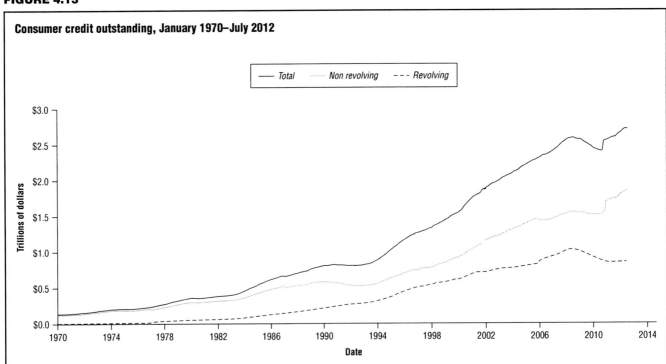

Consumer credit outstanding, January 1970–July 2012

SOURCE: Adapted from "Consumer Credit Outstanding (Levels) (Millions of Dollars; Seasonally adjusted)," in *Consumer Credit—G.19 Historical Data*, Board of Governors of the Federal Reserve System, September 10, 2012, http://www.federalreserve.gov/releases/G19/HIST/cc_hist_sa_levels.html (accessed

TABLE 4.6

Consumer credit outstanding, by major holders and major types of credit, July 2012

[Billions of dollars]
Not seasonally adjusted

	July[p]
Total	**2,664.4**
Major holders	
Depository institutions	1,176.2
Finance companies	676.7
Credit unions	233.1
Federal government[a]	471.8
Nonfinancial business	51.8
Pools of securitized assets[b, c]	54.9
Major types of credit, by holder	
Revolving	815.4
Depository institutions	645.6
Finance companies	72.4
Credit unions	37.4
Federal government[a]	—
Nonfinancial business	31.6
Pools of securitized assets[b, c]	28.5
Nonrevolving	1,849.0
Depository institutions	530.6
Finance companies	604.3
Credit unions	195.7
Federal government[a]	471.8
Nonfinancial business	20.3
Pools of securitized assets[b, c]	26.4

[a]Consumer loans held by the federal government include loans originated by the Department of Education under the Federal Direct Loan Program, as well as Federal Family Education Program loans that the government purchased from depository institutions and finance companies.
[b]Outstanding balances of pools upon which securities have been issued; these balances are no longer carried on the balance sheets of the loan originators.
[c]The shift of consumer credit from pools of securitized assets to other categories is largely due to financial institutions' implementation of the FAS 166/167 accounting rules.
p = preliminary.

SOURCE: Adapted from "Consumer Credit Outstanding (Levels) (Billions of dollars), Not Seasonally Adjusted," in *Federal Reserve Statistical Release G.19 Consumer Credit*, Board of Governors of the Federal Reserve System, September 10, 2012, http://www.federalreserve.gov/releases/G19/Current/g19.pdf (accessed September 20, 2012)

Table 4.6 also provides a detailed breakdown of outstanding consumer debt by creditor as of July 2012. Depository institutions, such as commercial banks, held nearly $1.2 trillion (44% of the total), finance companies held $676.7 billion (25% of the total), and the federal government held $471.8 billion (18% of the total). The remaining balance was held by credit unions, nonfinancial businesses, and pools of securitized assets (bundled debts sold as securities on the stock markets).

Interest Rates on Consumer Loans

Consumer loans are not secured by real estate. Because they have a higher risk of default, consumer loans generally have a higher interest rate than mortgage loans. Table 4.7 lists the average interest rates that were charged on various kinds of consumer loans from 2007 to the second quarter of 2012. It should be noted that borrowers with good credit histories would have likely received lower interest rates than these averages and that borrowers with poor credit histories would have been charged higher rates.

New Car Loans

Loans for the purchase of new cars (and other types of vehicles) are secured by the vehicle being purchased. In other words, the creditor can repossess the vehicle if the loan is in default. As a result of this collateral, the interest rates on new vehicle loans tend to be lower than on other types of consumer loans.

In the second quarter of 2012 the average interest rate on a 48-month (four-year) loan from a commercial bank for the purchase of a new car was 4.9%. (See Table 4.7.) This was down from an average rate of 7.8% in 2007. The interest rates charged by auto finance companies for a new car loan during 2012 were not available at the time Table 4.7 was published. However, in 2011 the rate was 4.7%. According to the Federal Reserve, the interest rate charged by auto finance companies is based on the rates charged by the finance companies of the three major U.S. automobile manufacturers. These companies are General Motors Corporation, Ford Motor Company, and Chrysler Group.

The typical loan period reported by the auto finance companies during 2011 was 62.3 months (just over five years). (See Table 4.7.) This is much longer than the three-year loan period that was common for new car loans during the mid-1970s. Longer loan periods reflect longer car lifetimes. The average LTV ratio reported by the auto finance companies for 2011 was 80%. This means that the average new car buyer borrowed 80% of the value of the new car being purchased. The remaining 20% was a down payment paid by the buyer in cash or via trade-in of another vehicle. The average amount financed during 2011 for a new car purchase was $26,673.

Personal Loans

Personal loans are generally unsecured loans based on the creditworthiness of the borrower. A lack of collateral makes personal loans more risky from the lenders' viewpoint; thus, interest rates are higher for personal loans than for car loans. In the second quarter of 2012 the average interest rate charged by commercial banks for a 24-month personal loan was 10.9%. (See Table 4.7.) The rate varied from 10.9% to 12.4% between 2007 and 2011.

Credit Cards

Credit cards have the highest average interest rates of all types of consumer loans. Most credit card loans are unsecured and are granted based on the creditworthiness of the borrower. The higher risk factor for the creditor and the huge demand for credit cards contribute to the high interest rates that are charged.

TABLE 4.7

Terms of credit at commercial banks and finance companies, 2007–second quarter 2012

Not seasonally adjusted. Percent except as noted.

	2007	2008	2009	2010ʳ	2011ʳ	2011 Q2ʳ	2011 Q3ʳ	2011 Q4ʳ	2012 Q1ʳ	2012 Q2ʳ
Commercial banks										
Interest rates										
48-mo. new car	7.77	7.02	6.72	6.21	5.73	5.79	5.89	5.40	5.07	4.87
24-mo. personal	12.38	11.37	11.10	10.87	10.88	11.37	10.80	10.36	10.88	10.94
Credit card plans										
All accounts	13.30	12.08	13.40	13.78	12.74	12.89	12.28	12.36	12.34	12.06
Accounts assessed interest	14.68	13.57	14.31	14.26	13.09	13.06	13.08	12.78	13.04	12.76
Finance companies (new car loans)*										
Interest rates	4.87	5.52	3.82	4.26	4.73	n.a.	n.a.	n.a.	n.a.	n.a.
Maturity (months)	62.0	63.4	62.0	63.0	62.3	n.a.	n.a.	n.a.	n.a.	n.a.
Loan-to-value ratio	95	91	90	86	80	n.a.	n.a.	n.a.	n.a.	n.a.
Amount financed (dollars)	28,287	26,178	28,272	27,959	26,673	n.a.	n.a.	n.a.	n.a.	n.a.

ʳRevised.

n.a. = not available.

Notes: Interest rates are annual percentage rates (APR) as specified by the Federal Reserve's Regulation Z. Interest rates for new-car loans and personal loans at commercial banks are simple unweighted averages of each bank's most common rate charged during the first calendar week of the middle month of each quarter. For credit card accounts, the rate for all accounts is the stated APR averaged across all credit card accounts at all reporting banks. The rate for accounts assessed interest is the annualized ratio of total finance charges at all reporting banks to the total average daily balances against which the finance charges were assessed (excludes accounts for which no finance charges were assessed).

*The statistical foundation for these series has deteriorated. Therefore, publication of these series is temporarily being suspended. The statistical foundation is in the process of being improved, and publication will resume as soon as possible

SOURCE: Adapted from "Terms of Credit, Not Seasonally Adjusted. Percent except as Noted," in *Federal Reserve Statistical Release: G.19. Consumer Credit*, Board of Governors of the Federal Reserve System, September 10, 2012, http://www.federalreserve.gov/releases/G19/Current/g19.pdf (accessed September 20, 2012)

The average interest rate charged by commercial banks on credit card loans was 12.1% in the second quarter of 2012. (See Table 4.7.) The rate varied from 12.1% to 13.8% between 2007 and 2011.

REVOLVING CREDIT AND MINIMUM PAYMENTS. Credit card debt is an example of revolving debt, a type of debt that is not amortized. There is no preset schedule of payments that will eliminate the debt within a particular time frame. The creditor grants the borrower a total amount of credit at a particular interest rate. Even though the interest rate may be fixed for a short introductory period, in general, credit card interest rates are variable.

Each month the borrower is billed for the outstanding balance on the credit card, which includes principal plus interest. The borrower can pay off the entire balance or a lesser amount down to the minimum payment required by the credit card issuer. Payment of any amount less than the minimum required will result in additional finance charges on the remaining balance. This is an example of compound interest (interest charged on an amount that already includes built-up interest charges).

When credit cards were first introduced, it was common for creditors to require 5% or more of the balance as a minimum monthly payment. Minimum payment requirements were gradually reduced to 2% by most credit card issuers. Low required minimum payments, high interest rates, and the effect of compounding interest make it difficult for many consumers to pay off credit card debt. The Bankruptcy

Abuse Prevention and Consumer Protection Act of 2005 requires creditors to tell borrowers how long it will take to pay off their credit card debt if only minimum payments are made. The Credit CARD Act of 2009 puts limits on when credit card issuers can raise interest rates and bans "unfair or deceptive" billing procedures.

Student Loans

Student loans are loans obtained to pay for educational expenses, primarily at the college level. Even though they are technically consumer loans, student loans are not for consumption purposes. They fund the advancement of skill and knowledge in individuals, likely increasing the potential for higher future income. Thus, student loans are considered to be a type of "human investment." Because the federal government encourages secondary education, it plays a major role in ensuring that student loans are available. As shown in Table 4.6, the federal government held $471.8 billion in consumer credit in July 2012. According to the Federal Reserve, this credit consisted of loans that were originated by the U.S. Department of Education under the William D. Ford Federal Direct Loan Program as well as by the Federal Family Education Loan program, which consisted of loans that the government purchased from depository institutions and finance companies. Student loans are also available through the private sector, such as from commercial banks.

The Federal Reserve Bank of New York (FRBNY) tracks student loan debt and other forms of debt that are held by U.S. households (excluding nonprofit organizations). In *Quarterly Report on Household Debt and Credit* (August 2012, http://www.newyorkfed.org/research/national _economy/householdcredit/DistrictReport_Q22012.pdf), the FRBNY indicates that it performs its analyses by examining the credit reports for a nationally representative sample of individuals and households. The data are then aggregated to represent the nation as a whole. According to FRBNY, the nation's total debt balance in the first quarter of 2012 was $11.4 trillion. This value was down from the peak in total debt of over $12 trillion recorded by the organization in the third quarter of 2008.

The FRBNY indicates that only student loan debt increased between 2008 and 2012; all other forms of debt decreased. Student loan debt was an estimated $914 billion in the second quarter of 2012, up $303 billion since the third quarter of 2008. The FRBNY also finds that 8.9% of student loan balances were 90 or more days delinquent as of June 30, 2012. However, the organization believes that this rate vastly underreports the true level of delinquency because the rate only covers loans in repayment. The Department of Education explains in "Deferment and Forbearance" (2012, http://studentaid.ed.gov/repay-loans/ deferment-forbearance) that federal student loan payments can be temporarily postponed through conditions known as deferment and forbearance. For example, students who are enrolled at least part time in college can postpone making their loan payments. The FRBNY suggests that if student loans in deferment and forbearance were included in the delinquency rate, then the rate for the second quarter of 2012 would be "roughly twice as high" (i.e., around 19%).

Concern about student loan delinquency rates has been building for years. In fact, some analysts believe that student loan debt constitutes an economic "bubble" that will burst, much as the housing loan bubble burst. Of course, outstanding mortgage debt has been and continues to be vastly greater than outstanding student loan debt. For example, the FRBNY estimates that mortgage debt totaled around $8.2 trillion in the second quarter of 2012, as compared with $914 billion in student loan debt. Nonetheless, the so-called student loan bubble is a concern because of the devastating financial effects of loan defaults on the individuals involved and the financial burden that would fall on the federal government (and hence U.S. taxpayers) in the event of massive defaults.

In August 2012 the Consumer Financial Protection Bureau (CFPB) released *Private Student Loans* (http:// files.consumerfinance.gov/f/201207_cfpb_Reports_Private-Student-Loans.pdf), a report developed for congressional committees that are devoted to educational and financial concerns. The CFPB summarizes the lengthy report in the press release "Consumer Financial Protection Bureau

and U.S. Department of Education Joint Report Finds a Cycle of Boom and Bust in Private Student Loan Market" (July 19, 2012, http://www.consumerfinance .gov/). According to the CFPB, the total outstanding student loan debt was just over $1 trillion in 2011, including $864 billion in federal loans and approximately $150 billion in private loans.

The CFPB is highly critical of private student loans, noting that they typically feature variable interest rates and "lack repayment flexibility," for example, by not offering postponement options. In addition, private student loan servicers are accused of relaxing their underwriting standards during the overall credit boom that characterized the first decade of the 21st century until the recession began in late 2007. The CFPB quotes Arne Duncan (1964–), the U.S. secretary of education, as saying: "Subprime-style lending went to college and now students are paying the price." (As discussed earlier in this chapter, subprime mortgage lending is blamed in large part for precipitating the bust of the housing market and the subsequent recession.) According to the CFPB, more than $8.1 billion in private student loans were in default as of mid-2012. This represented around 5.4% of the estimated $150 billion total in private student loans outstanding at that time.

The Department of Education tracks default rates on certain federal student loans using what it calls cohort default rates (CDRs). In "Two-Year Official Cohort Default Rates for Schools" (September 28, 2012, http:// www2.ed.gov/offices/OSFAP/defaultmanagement/ cdr2yr.html), the Department of Education notes that two-year CDRs measure the percentage of a school's borrowers who begin repaying certain federal loans during a particular fiscal year and either default or "meet other specified conditions" before the end of the next fiscal year. (A federal fiscal year covers October 1 through September 30.) A historical graph of two-year CDRs (2012, http:// www2.ed.gov/offices/OSFAP/defaultmanagement/ defaultrates.html) shows rates in excess of 15% during the late 1980s and early 1990s. Then rates began a long tumble that bottomed out at 4.5% in 2003. Thereafter, the rates rose to 7% in 2008, to 8.8% in 2009, and to 9.1% in 2010. The CDRs are for loans that were made as part of the Federal Family Education Loan (FFEL) program and the William D. Ford Federal Direct Loan Program (also known as the Direct Loan Program). The FFEL program featured loans that were guaranteed by the federal government, but were made by private companies that received subsidies (government payments) for the loans they made. In April 2009 President Obama (http://www.whitehouse.gov/ the_press_office/Remarks-by-the-President-on-Higher-Education/) announced his decision to end the FFEL program to save taxpayers' money and eliminate the government's role as a so-called middleman. All federal student loans were shifted to the Direct Loan Program, in which money is lent directly to students or their parents from the federal government.

Another student loan program highly touted by the Obama administration is the Income-Based Repayment (IBR) program. This program actually originated during the Bush administration as part of the College Cost Reduction and Access Act of 2007. The IBR program went into effect on July 1, 2009, and allows student loan borrowers to cap their loan payments based on their income and other factors. In addition, borrowers who work in public service, such as public school teachers, can have all or some portion of their federal student loan debts forgiven through the Public Service Loan Forgiveness program. The website StudentLoans.gov provides information about these programs and other federal government student loan programs.

PERSONAL BANKRUPTCIES

The word *bankrupt* is derived from the Italian phrase *banca rotta*, which means "bench broken," referring to the benches or tables that were used by merchants in outdoor markets in 16th-century Italy. Bankruptcy is a state of financial ruin. Under U.S. law people with more debts than they can reasonably hope to repay can file for personal bankruptcy. This results in a legally binding agreement between debtors and the federal government worked out in a federal bankruptcy court. The agreement calls for the debtors to pay as much as they can with whatever assets they have, and after a predetermined amount of time—usually a number of years—the debtors begin again with new credit. Depending on state law, certain belongings may be kept through the bankruptcy.

The American Bankruptcy Institute explains in "Frequently Asked Questions" (2012, http://consumer.abi.org/consumers/faq) that an official declaration of bankruptcy benefits individuals in the short term because it puts a stop to all collection efforts by creditors. An "automatic stay" goes into effect that prevents creditors from calling, writing, or suing debtors who are covered by a bankruptcy plan.

Figure 4.14 shows the number of nonbusiness (personal) bankruptcy cases per 12-month period ending June 30 of each year between 2004 and 2012. For the 12-month period ending June 30, 2012, there were nearly 1.3 million personal bankruptcy filings. This value was down from the previous three years, but higher than levels reported for 2007 and 2008.

There are three types (or chapters) of personal bankruptcy under which individuals may file:

- Chapter 7—a liquidation plan is developed in which the debtor turns over certain assets that are sold and used to pay creditors.

- Chapter 13—a payment plan is developed under which debtors receiving regular income repay their creditors. Liquidation of assets is not required in most cases.

- Chapter 11—while similar to Chapter 13, Chapter 11 is reserved for individuals with substantial debts and assets.

FIGURE 4.14

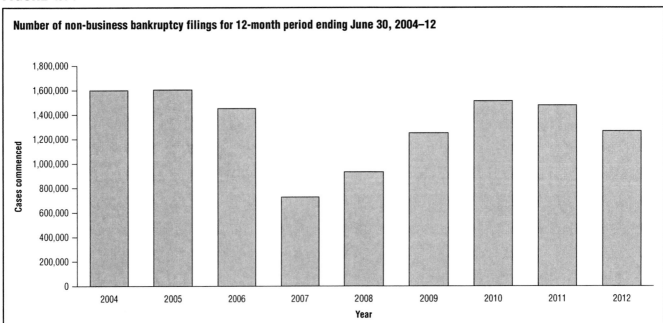

Number of non-business bankruptcy filings for 12-month period ending June 30, 2004–12

SOURCE: Adapted from "Table F-2. U.S. Bankruptcy Courts—Business and Nonbusiness Cases Commenced, by Chapter of the Bankruptcy Code, during the 12 Month Period Ending June 30, 2012," in *Bankruptcy Statistics: 12 Month Period Ending June 30, 2012*, The U.S. Courts, 2012, http://www.uscourts.gov/Statistics/BankruptcyStatistics/12-month-period-ending-june.aspx (accessed September 20, 2012)

According to the U.S. Courts (2012, http://www.us courts.gov/Statistics/BankruptcyStatistics/12-month-period-ending-june.aspx), 914,015 personal bankruptcy cases were filed under Chapter 7 during the 12-month period ending June 30, 2012. This represented 70% of the total 1.3 million personal bankruptcy filings. Another 385,949 (29%) filings were under Chapter 13 and the remaining 10,921 (0.8%) were under Chapter 11.

CHAPTER 5

THE AMERICAN WORKER

When we are all in the business working together, we all ought to have some share in the profits—by way of a good wage, or salary, or added compensation.

—Henry Ford, *My Life and Work* (1922)

The American workforce plays a major role in the U.S. economy. Workers produce goods and provide services, the consumption of which drives the nation's gross domestic product (the total market value of final goods and services that are produced within an economy in a given year) growth. However, there is an age-old struggle between employers and employees over compensation. Businesses must compensate workers with pay and benefits that are high enough to attract and keep motivated employees, but not so high as to damage the profitability and growth of the business itself. On a macroeconomic scale, gainful employment of large numbers of workers is important to the overall health of the U.S. economy. As noted in Chapter 2, the so-called Great Recession (which lasted from December 2007 to June 2009) led to a huge increase in the nation's unemployment rate. High unemployment lingered even after the recession ended and still plagued the country as of November 2012. Unemployment was one of the most devastating effects of the recession on the economic well-being of the American people.

THE EMPLOYMENT SITUATION

The U.S. Bureau of Labor Statistics (BLS) publishes the monthly news release "The Employment Situation," which the media commonly calls the "monthly jobs report." The BLS tracks employment and unemployment using two surveys. The Current Employment Statistics (CES) program includes monthly surveys of approximately 141,000 nonfarm businesses and government agencies with around 486,000 worksites around the country to obtain detailed information on employment, work hours, and payroll. The BLS refers to these data as "establishment data." The agency tracks the number of unemployed using data collected by the U.S. Census Bureau from approximately 60,000 households as part of the Current Population Survey (CPS). The BLS refers to these data as "household data."

The BLS defines the civilian labor force as including all civilian noninstitutionalized people (i.e., people not in the military and not in institutions, such as prisons or long-term care facilities) aged 16 years and older who have a job or are actively looking for a job. People are considered to be employed during a given week if they meet any of the following criteria:

- They performed any work that week for pay or profit

- They worked without pay for at least 15 hours that week in a family operated enterprise

- They had a job but could not work that week due to illness, vacation, personal obligations, leave of absence, bad weather, or labor disputes

People considered not to be in the labor force are those who do not have a job and are not looking for a job. This category includes many students, retirees, stay-at-home parents, the mentally and physically challenged, and people in prison and other institutions, as well as those who are not employed but have become discouraged from looking for work. The unemployed are counted as those who do not have a job but have actively looked for a job during the previous four weeks and are available for work. Also included are people who did not work during a given week due to temporary layoffs.

Employment and Unemployment

As shown in Table 5.1, the civilian labor force consisted of 154.6 million people in August 2012. Another 88.9 million people were considered to not be in the labor force. The BLS estimates that this number included 844,000 "discouraged workers."

TABLE 5.1

Employment and unemployment data, August 2012

[Numbers in thousands]

Category	Aug. 2012
Employment status	
Civilian noninstitutional population	243,566
Civilian labor force	154,645
Participation rate	63.7
Employed	142,101
Employment-population ratio	58.4
Unemployed	12,544
Unemployment rate	8.3
Not in labor force	88,921
Reason for unemployment	
Job losers and persons who completed	7,003
temporary jobs	
Job leavers	878
Reentrants	3,318
New entrants	1,277
Duration of unemployment	
Less than 5 weeks	2,844
5 to 14 weeks	2,868
15 to 26 weeks	1,845
27 weeks and over	5,033
Employed persons at work part time	
Part time for economic reasons	8,031
Slack work or business conditions	5,217
Could only find part-time work	2,507
Part time for noneconomic reasons	18,996
Persons not in the labor force (not seasonally adjusted)	
Marginally attached to the labor force	2,561
Discouraged workers	844

Note: Persons whose ethnicity is identified as Hispanic or Latino may be of any race. Detail for the seasonally adjusted data shown in this table will not necessarily add to totals because of the independent seasonal adjustment of the various series. Updated population controls are introduced annually with the release of January data.

SOURCE: Adapted from "Summary Table A. Household Data, Seasonally Adjusted," in *The Employment Situation—August 2012*, U.S. Department of Labor, Bureau of Labor Statistics, September 7, 2012, http://www.bls.gov/news.release/archives/empsit_09072012.pdf (accessed September 15, 2012)

Figure 5.1 shows monthly changes in nonfarm payroll employment between August 2010 and August 2012. In August and September 2010 nonfarm payrolls were losing tens of thousands of workers per month, which was a lingering effect of the Great Recession. According to the BLS (November 1, 2012, http://data.bls.gov/timeseries/CES0000000001?output_view=net_1mth), between 200,000 and 800,000 payroll jobs per month were lost from mid-2008 through late 2009, which was a severe blow to the nation's employment. However, from late 2010 to August 2012 nonfarm payrolls were adding a few hundred thousand workers per month. (See Figure 5.1.)

Table 5.1 indicates that the breakdown for the civilian labor force in August 2012 was 142.1 million employed and 12.5 million unemployed, giving an overall unemployment rate of 8.3%. This rate was down from October 2009, when it peaked at 10%. (See Figure 5.2.) However, the unemployment rate in August 2012 was high by historical standards. Figure 2.6 in Chapter 2 shows annual unemployment rates dating back to 1925. Rates above 8% have been uncommon since the 1930s, during the height of the Great Depression (1929–1939).

The unemployment rate in August 2012 varied widely according to certain demographic factors. Teenagers aged 16 to 19 years were unemployed at a rate of 24.6%. (See Figure 5.3.) Racial and ethnic differences were also significant; African-American workers had an unemployment rate of 14.1% and Hispanic workers had a rate of 10.2%. These values were higher than the 7.2% unemployment rate reported for white workers. However, the rate for Asian-American workers was only 5.9%. There was a small

FIGURE 5.1

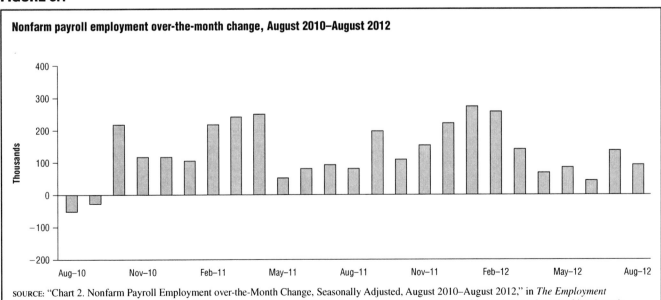

Nonfarm payroll employment over-the-month change, August 2010–August 2012

SOURCE: "Chart 2. Nonfarm Payroll Employment over-the-Month Change, Seasonally Adjusted, August 2010–August 2012," in *The Employment Situation—August 2012*, U.S. Department of Labor, Bureau of Labor Statistics, September 7, 2012, http://www.bls.gov/news.release/archives/empsit_09072012.pdf (accessed September 15, 2012)

FIGURE 5.2

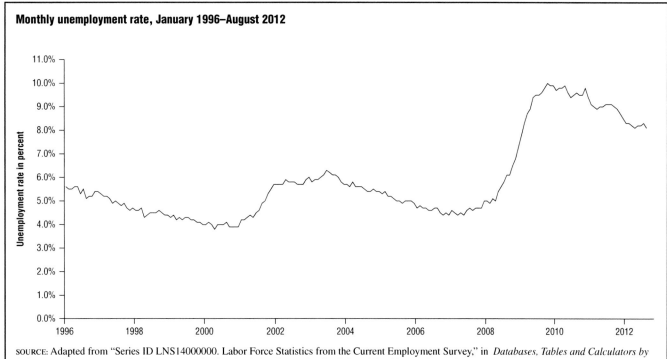

Monthly unemployment rate, January 1996–August 2012

SOURCE: Adapted from "Series ID LNS14000000. Labor Force Statistics from the Current Employment Survey," in *Databases, Tables and Calculators by Subject*, U.S. Department of Labor, Bureau of Labor Statistics, September 2012, http://data.bls.gov/timeseries/LNS14000000 (accessed September 16, 2012)

FIGURE 5.3

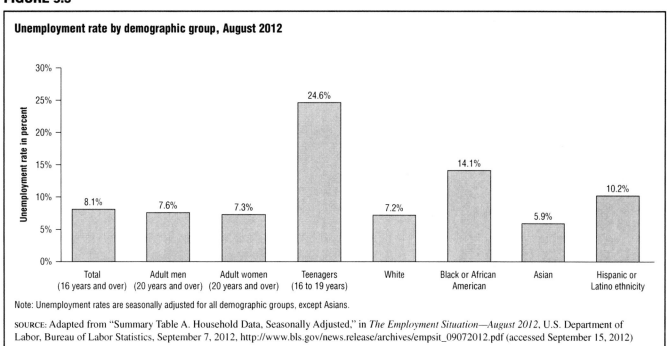

Unemployment rate by demographic group, August 2012

Note: Unemployment rates are seasonally adjusted for all demographic groups, except Asians.

SOURCE: Adapted from "Summary Table A. Household Data, Seasonally Adjusted," in *The Employment Situation—August 2012*, U.S. Department of Labor, Bureau of Labor Statistics, September 7, 2012, http://www.bls.gov/news.release/archives/empsit_09072012.pdf (accessed September 15, 2012)

difference in rates by sex among adults; for adult men the rate was 7.6% and for adult women it was 7.3%.

Educational attainment played a major role in unemployment rates in August 2012. (See Figure 5.4.) The rate for all workers aged 25 years and older was 6.8%. Among those with less than a high school diploma the rate was much higher, at 12%. High school graduates with no college had

an unemployment rate of 8.8%. Workers who had taken some college courses or who had earned an associate's degree had a rate of 6.6%. Those with a bachelor's degree or higher had the lowest unemployment rate, at 4.1%.

Figure 5.5 provides a breakdown on the duration of unemployment as of August 2012. Forty percent of the unemployed had been unemployed for 27 weeks or more

FIGURE 5.4

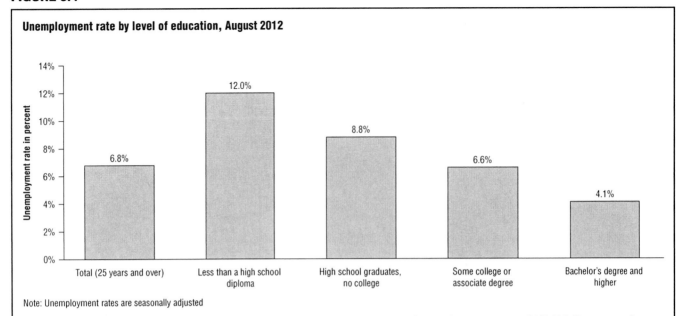

Unemployment rate by level of education, August 2012

Note: Unemployment rates are seasonally adjusted

SOURCE: Adapted from "Summary Table A. Household Data, Seasonally Adjusted," in *The Employment Situation—August 2012*, U.S. Department of Labor, Bureau of Labor Statistics, September 7, 2012, http://www.bls.gov/news.release/archives/empsit_09072012.pdf (accessed September 15, 2012)

FIGURE 5.5

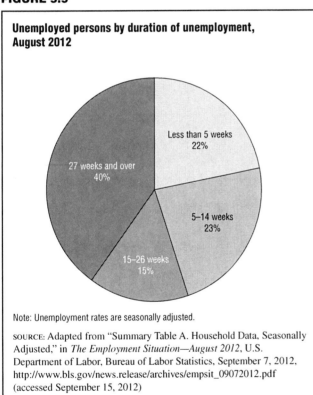

Unemployed persons by duration of unemployment, August 2012

Note: Unemployment rates are seasonally adjusted.

SOURCE: Adapted from "Summary Table A. Household Data, Seasonally Adjusted," in *The Employment Situation—August 2012*, U.S. Department of Labor, Bureau of Labor Statistics, September 7, 2012, http://www.bls.gov/news.release/archives/empsit_09072012.pdf (accessed September 15, 2012)

(i.e., roughly six months or more). Another 15% had been unemployed for 15 to 26 weeks, and 23% had been employed for five to 14 weeks. The remaining 22% of the unemployed had been unemployed for less than five weeks.

The Gallup Organization conducts regular polls that question Americans about their perceptions of the job situation. In *U.S. Optimism about Quality Jobs Rises* (March 16, 2012, http://www.gallup.com/poll/153287/Optimism-Quality-Jobs-Rises.aspx), Dennis Jacobe of the Gallup Organization finds that in March 2012, 78% of those asked thought it was a "bad time" to find a quality job. Only 19% said it was a "good time" to find a quality job. (See Figure 5.6.) This number was down significantly from early 2007, when nearly half of those asked said it was a "good time" to find a quality job.

The Unemployment Rate Controversy

As noted earlier, the BLS tracks the number of unemployed using survey data that are collected by the Census Bureau through the CPS, which covers approximately 60,000 households in the United States. The BLS uses the data to estimate the total number of unemployed in the United States. Then, the agency calculates various unemployment rates. For example, the rate that is highlighted in "The Employment Situation" and reported by the media is the number of unemployed as a percent of the civilian labor force. This is the official unemployment rate or the U-3 rate.

As shown in Table 5.2, the BLS also calculates other unemployment rates (U-1, U-2, U-4, U-5, and U-6) using different population subsets. Some critics argue that the U-4 rate is actually more demonstrative than the U-3 rate of overall unemployment because the U-4 rate includes discouraged workers. As noted earlier, discouraged workers are not employed, but have become discouraged from looking for work. The U-4 unemployment rate in August 2012 was 8.6%, which was half a percentage point higher than the official unemployment rate of 8.1%. Table 5.3

FIGURE 5.6

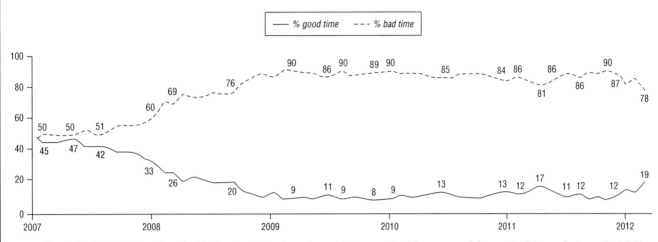

Public opinion about the job situation, 2007–12

THINKING ABOUT THE JOB SITUATION IN AMERICA TODAY, WOULD YOU SAY THAT IT IS NOW A GOOD TIME OR A BAD TIME TO FIND A QUALITY JOB?

— % good time   - - - % bad time

TABLE 5.2

Alternative measures of labor underutilization, August 2012

[Percent]

Measure	Not seasonally adjusted Aug. 2012	Seasonally adjusted Aug. 2012
U-1 Persons unemployed 15 weeks or longer, as a percent of the civilian labor force	4.3	4.4
U-2 Job losers and persons who completed temporary jobs, as a percent of the civilian labor force	4.4	4.5
U-3 Total unemployed, as a percent of the civilian labor force (official unemployment rate)	8.2	8.1
U-4 Total unemployed plus discouraged workers, as a percent of the civilian labor force plus discouraged workers	8.7	8.6
U-5 Total unemployed, plus discouraged workers, plus all other persons marginally attached to the labor force, as a percent of the civilian labor force plus all persons marginally attached to the labor force	9.7	9.6
U-6 Total unemployed, plus all persons marginally attached to the labor force, plus total employed part time for economic reasons, as a percent of the civilian labor force plus all persons marginally attached to the labor force	14.6	14.7

Note: Persons marginally attached to the labor force are those who currently are neither working nor looking for work but indicate that they want and are available for a job and have looked for work sometime in the past 12 months. Discouraged workers, a subset of the marginally attached, have given a job-market related reason for not currently looking for work. Persons employed part time for economic reasons are those who want and are available for full-time work but have had to settle for a part-time schedule. Updated population controls are introduced annually with the release of January data.

TABLE 5.3

Discouraged workers, 1996–2012

Year	Annual
1996	397
1997	343
1998	331
1999	273
2000	262
2001	321
2002	369
2003	457
2004	466
2005	436
2006	381
2007	369
2008	462
2009	778
2010	1173
2011	989
2012	906

Note: Annual total for 2012 is through August 2012. Data are in thousands.

shows the numbers of discouraged workers counted by the BLS on an annual average basis from 1996 through August 2012. From 1996 to 2008 discouraged workers numbered between 262,000 and 466,000 per year. However, the value jumped to 778,000 in 2009 and to nearly 1.2 million in 2010. It then fell to 989,000 in 2011 and to 906,000 from January to August 2012. These historically high values have led some to question the BLS's decision to exclude discouraged workers from the calculation of the official unemployment rate.

The U-5 and U-6 unemployment rates are even more inclusive than the U-4 rate. As shown in Table 5.2, the U-5 rate includes "all persons marginally attached to the labor force," which the BLS defines as people who are not currently working or looking for work, but who indicate they want to work and are available for work and have looked for work at some time in the previous 12 months. (Note that discouraged workers are a subset of marginally attached people.) The BLS explains that discouraged workers gave surveyors "a job-market related reason for not currently looking for work." Thus, the remainder of the marginally attached people provided some other reason for not currently looking for work. According to the BLS (October 5, 2012, http://www.bls.gov/web/empsit/cpseea38.htm), these reasons include family responsibilities, school or training, ill health or disability, lack of child care or transportation, and other reasons. The BLS reports that there were nearly 2.6 million marginally attached people in August 2012. (See Table 5.1.) As shown in Table 5.2, including these people in the unemployment rate provides a U-5 unemployment rate of 9.6% for August 2012.

The last category of people not included in the official unemployment rate is "total employed part time for economic reasons." According to the BLS, these are people who want to work full time and are available to work full time, but "have had to settle for a part-time schedule." This component numbered just over 8 million people in August 2012. (See Table 5.1.) Including the marginally attached and the so-called involuntary part-time workers in the unemployment rate provides a U-6 unemployment rate of 14.7%. (See Table 5.2.) This rate is substantially higher than the 8.1% official unemployment rate for August 2012.

Proponents of the U-4, U-5, and/or U-6 unemployment rates argue that the U-3 rate (the official unemployment rate) is too restrictive and does not provide an accurate estimate of the unemployed population. The Great Recession witnessed huge jumps in the numbers of marginally attached people and involuntary part-time workers. Because these people are not considered to be part of the labor force, they are basically ignored by the U-3 unemployment rate. However, it must be acknowledged that at least some of the controversy over the U-3 rate is driven by politics, rather than by concern for accurate data reporting. In "Is the Real Unemployment Rate 40 Percent" (*Huffington Post*, July 6, 2012), Eli Lehrer notes that during the administration of President George W. Bush (1946–), who was a conservative, liberal commentators used alternative unemployment rates to "cast doubt on his economic policies." Lehrer points out that the same thing was happening in mid-2012, with conservative commentators using the broader unemployment rates, such as the U-6 rate,

to argue that the economic policies of President Barack Obama (1961–), a liberal, were failing.

Unemployment Insurance Claims

Another indicator used to measure unemployment in the country is derived from the government's unemployment insurance (UI) program. Every state operates a UI trust fund that is managed in concert with the federal government. The UI trust funds are funded by taxes levied on employers and in some states on employees. Payments from the UI trust funds are made temporarily, typically up to 26 weeks, to unemployed people who meet specific criteria set by each state. The U.S. Department of Labor explains in "State Unemployment Insurance Benefits" (January 13, 2010, http://workforcesecurity.doleta.gov/unemploy/uifactsheet.asp) that workers are eligible to receive UI benefits (i.e., UI trust fund payments) if they become unemployed "through no fault of their own" and meet other state-defined criteria for time worked and wages earned before becoming unemployed.

Figure 5.7 shows the number of new state UI claims filed by applicants on a weekly basis from January 1, 2005, to September 15, 2012. The number peaked around 670,000 in early 2009. Initial UI claims then fell over subsequent years, dropping to below 400,000 claims per week in mid-September 2012.

INDUSTRIES AND JOBS

The federal government broadly characterizes jobs as being in the goods-providing or service-providing categories. Goods-providing industries include businesses engaged in manufacturing, construction, mining, and natural resources. Service-providing industries include businesses whose main function is to provide a professional or trade service, rather than a product. Service-providing industries are extremely diverse and include businesses involved in retail and wholesale trade, professional and business services, education and health services, leisure and hospitality, government, and many other services.

Since the mid-20th century the service-providing industries have grown to dominate the U.S. economy. As shown in Figure 5.8, in 1980 goods-producing industries employed nearly 25 million people. This value rose and fell over the following two decades, but declined sharply during the first decade of the 21st century. By 2006 approximately 22.5 million people were employed in goods-producing industries. However, the Great Recession was associated with deep employment losses in these industries. Employment plummeted to around 17.5 million in 2010 before beginning to rise. It was at 18.3 million as of August 2012. By comparison, the number of people employed in service-providing industries (private and government) has skyrocketed. Figure 5.9 shows that private service-providing employment rose from around 50 million in 1980 to

FIGURE 5.7

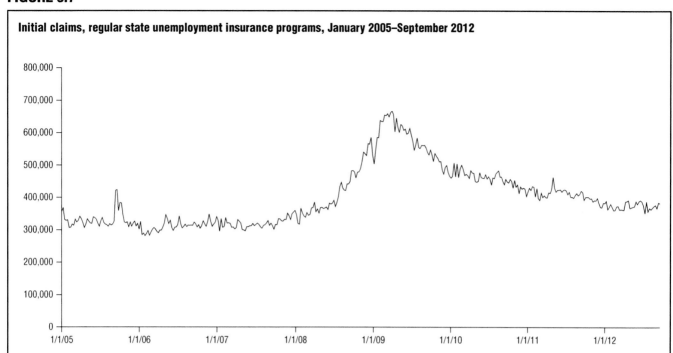

Initial claims, regular state unemployment insurance programs, January 2005–September 2012

SOURCE: Adapted from "Unemployment Insurance Weekly Claims Data—Report r539cy," in *Unemployment Insurance Weekly Claims Data*, U.S. Department of Labor, Employment and Training Administration, September 20, 2012, http://www.ows.doleta.gov/unemploy/claims.asp (accessed September 20, 2012); and "Unemployment Insurance Data for Regular State Programs," in *Unemployment Insurance Weekly Claims Report*, U.S. Department of Labor, Employment and Training Administration, September 20, 2012, http://www.dol.gov/opa/media/press/eta/ui/current.htm (accessed September 20, 2012)

FIGURE 5.8

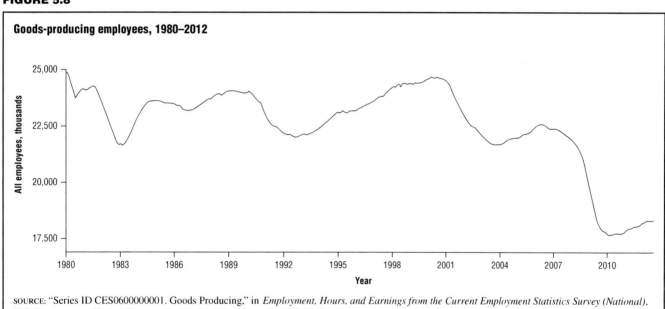

Goods-producing employees, 1980–2012

SOURCE: "Series ID CES0600000001. Goods Producing," in *Employment, Hours, and Earnings from the Current Employment Statistics Survey (National)*, U.S. Department of Labor, Bureau of Labor Statistics, September 16, 2012, http://data.bls.gov/cgi-bin/surveymost?ce (accessed September 16, 2012)

nearly 94 million in early 2008. After a slight decline to just under 90 million in 2009, employment rebounded to around 93.1 million in August 2012. As shown in Table 5.4, government service-providing employees numbered 21.9 million as of August 2012. Historical government employment will be discussed in detail later in this chapter.

Industry Supersectors

The government categorizes jobs by using the North American Industry Classification System (NAICS). Adopted in 1997, the NAICS was devised by the U.S. Economic Classification Policy Committee in conjunction with Statistics Canada and the Instituto Nacional de

FIGURE 5.9

Private service-providing employees, 1980–2012

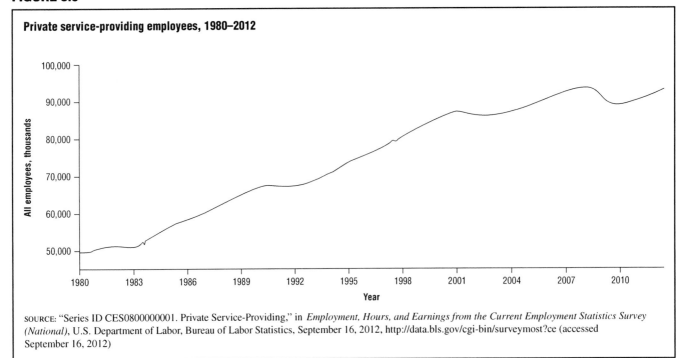

SOURCE: "Series ID CES0800000001. Private Service-Providing," in *Employment, Hours, and Earnings from the Current Employment Statistics Survey (National)*, U.S. Department of Labor, Bureau of Labor Statistics, September 16, 2012, http://data.bls.gov/cgi-bin/surveymost?ce (accessed September 16, 2012)

Estadística, Geografia e Informática of Mexico and is the standard classification system for businesses throughout North America. There are 11 major so-called supersectors tracked by the BLS that encompass all public and private jobs within the United States and businesses owned by U.S.-based companies operating in other countries.

The 11 supersectors are:

- Construction
- Education and health services
- Financial activities
- Government
- Information
- Leisure and hospitality
- Manufacturing
- Natural resources and mining
- Other services
- Professional and business services
- Trade, transportation, and utilities

Virtually every job can be placed into one of these categories. It should be noted that industry tracking focuses on the core mission of the business rather than on the particular tasks performed by employees. For example, jobs in public schools and government-owned hospitals are considered to be part of the government supersector rather than part of the education and health services supersector.

Table 5.4 itemizes the number of employees by industry sector as of August 2012. Approximately 133.3 million workers were on nonfarm payrolls that month. As shown in Figure 5.10, the number of employees on nonfarm payrolls has grown dramatically since the 1980s. The value peaked between 2007 and 2008 at about 137 million employees, and then declined as the Great Recession progressed. The number began to grow again in early 2010. As of August 2012, the vast majority (111.4 million employees) of nonfarm employees were in the private (nongovernmental) sector.

Table 5.5 shows the numbers of unemployed people and the unemployment rates in August 2012 for each supersector and for agricultural and self-employed workers. The highest unemployment rate was 11.3% for construction workers. As described in Chapter 4, the housing industry underwent a sharp downturn during the second half of the first decade of the 21st century, leaving millions of construction workers unemployed. Other industries with relatively high unemployment rates in August 2012 were leisure and hospitality (10.1%), professional and business services (8.9%), wholesale and retail trade (8.3%), and agriculture (8.1%). The lowest unemployment rates were associated with government workers (5.1%), self-employed and unpaid family workers (5.3%), financial activities workers (5.3%), and mining, quarrying, and oil and gas extraction workers (5.8%).

General industry information in the following sections was obtained from the BLS sources *Occupational Outlook Handbook* (2012, http://www.bls.gov/ooh/home.htm) and *Industries at a Glance* (2012, http://stats.bls.gov/iag/iaghome.htm), which profiles U.S. businesses.

TABLE 5.4

Employees on nonfarm payrolls by industry sector, August 2012

[In thousands]

Industry	Seasonally adjusted Aug. 2012ᵖ
Total nonfarm	**133,300**
Total private	111,400
Goods-producing	18,323
Mining and logging	838
Logging	49.3
Mining	789.1
Construction	5,515
Manufacturing	11,970
Durable goods	7,489
Nondurable goods	4,481
Private service-providing	93,077
Trade, transportation, and utilities	25,350
Wholesale trade	5,646.7
Durable goods	2,800.9
Nondurable goods	1,978.8
Retail trade	14,751.3
Transportation and warehousing	4,385.4
Utilities	566.5
Information	2,640
Financial activities	7,742
Professional and business services	17,958
Education and health services	20,354
Educational services	3,330.8
Health care and social assistance	17,023.6
Health careᵇ	14,382.7
Social assistanceᵃ	2,640.9
Leisure and hospitality	13,659
Arts, entertainment, and recreation	1,921.6
Accommodation and food services	11,737.6
Other services	5,374
Repair and maintenance	1,160.8
Personal and laundry services	1,299.0
Membership associations and organizations	2,914.6
Government	21,900
Federal	2,804.0
State government	5,040.0
Local government	14,056.0

ᵃIncludes other industries, not shown separately.
ᵇIncludes ambulatory health care services, hospitals, and nursing and residential care facilities.
p = Preliminary

SOURCE: Adapted from "Table B-1. Employees on Nonfarm Payrolls by Industry Sector and Selected Industry Detail," in *The Employment Situation—August 2012*, U.S. Department of Labor, Bureau of Labor Statistics, September 7, 2012, http://www.bls.gov/news.release/archives/empsit_09072012.pdf (accessed September 15, 2012)

CONSTRUCTION. The construction supersector includes all businesses that contribute to the development of land, roads, utilities, buildings and houses, and structures such as bridges and dams. Included are firms that build new projects and those that provide maintenance, repairs, and alterations to existing structures. For the most part, such enterprises are managed from a central location with work performed elsewhere. Construction employment often fluctuates throughout the year, especially in areas of the country that experience severe winter weather.

Figure 4.10 in Chapter 4 shows employment in the construction industry between 1980 and 2012. Employment peaked at around 7.7 million workers between 2006 and 2007 and then plummeted due to the housing market bust. In August 2012 the industry employed around 5.5 million workers. (See Table 5.4.) As noted earlier, the unemployment rate that month for construction workers was 11.3%. (See Table 5.5.) According to the BLS (November 1, 2012, http://data.bls.gov/timeseries/LNU04032231), the unemployment rate for this sector from 2002 and 2008 was between 5% and 15%. It peaked above 27% in February 2010 and then began falling.

In February 2012 the BLS published employment projections, by industry, through 2020 using employment data from 2010. The BLS predicts modest growth for the construction supersector through 2020. Employment is projected to increase by 2.9% annually. (See Table 5.6.) This is higher than the 1.3% growth rate expected for employment overall.

EDUCATION AND HEALTH SERVICES. The education and health services supersector includes all instructional and training facilities, including private schools and universities, that are not funded by the government. Non-governmental organizations that provide child day care, medical care, and social assistance are also included. Businesses of this type that are government owned (e.g., public schools and hospitals) are considered to be part of the government supersector.

In August 2012 employment in this supersector was 20.4 million, including 17 million in health care and social assistance and 3.3 million in educational services. (See Table 5.4.) The BLS provides in "Employment Situation—August 2012" (September 7, 2012, http://www.bls.gov/news.release/archives/empsit_09072012.pdf) the numbers of employees in selected health care and social assistance fields as follows:

- Health care: Total—14.4 million workers

- Health care: Offices of physicians—2.4 million workers

- Health care: Outpatient care centers—665,000 workers

- Health care: Home health care services—1.2 million workers

- Health care: Hospitals—4.8 million workers

- Health care: Nursing and residential care facilities—3.2 million workers

- Social assistance: Total—2.6 million workers

- Social assistance: Child day care services—835,800 workers

The unemployment rate for this supersector was 6.2% in August 2012. (See Table 5.5.) This value was up substantially from the early part of the decade. According to the BLS (November 1, 2012, http://data.bls.gov/timeseries/LNU04032240), from 2002 to 2008 the average annual unemployment rate varied between 3% and 3.6%. From 2009 to 2011 the average annual rate was between 5.3% to 5.8%.

FIGURE 5.10

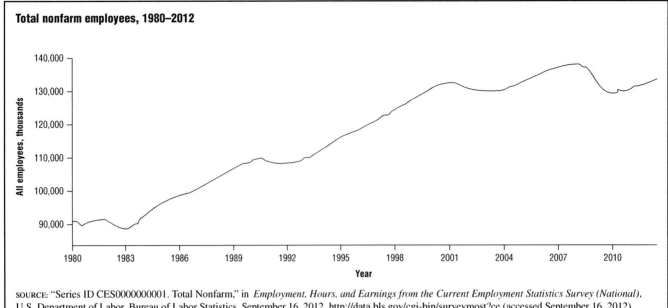

Total nonfarm employees, 1980–2012

SOURCE: "Series ID CES0000000001. Total Nonfarm," in *Employment, Hours, and Earnings from the Current Employment Statistics Survey (National)*, U.S. Department of Labor, Bureau of Labor Statistics, September 16, 2012, http://data.bls.gov/cgi-bin/surveymost?ce (accessed September 16, 2012)

TABLE 5.5

Unemployment by industry and class of worker, August 2012

Industry and class of worker	Number of unemployed persons (in thousands) Aug. 2012	Unemployment rates Aug. 2012
Total, 16 years and over*	12,696	8.2
Nonagricultural private wage and salary workers	9,552	7.9
Mining, quarrying, and oil and gas extraction	61	5.8
Construction	923	11.3
Manufacturing	1,136	7.3
Durable goods	698	7.2
Nondurable goods	437	7.6
Wholesale and retail trade	1,723	8.3
Transportation and utilities	424	7.1
Information	211	7.3
Financial activities	469	5.3
Professional and business services	1,377	8.9
Education and health services	1,369	6.2
Leisure and hospitality	1,416	10.1
Other services	443	6.7
Agriculture and related private wage and salary workers	125	8.1
Government workers	1,059	5.1
Self-employed workers, unincorporated, and unpaid family workers	548	5.3

*Persons with no previous work experience and persons whose last job was in the U.S. Armed Forces are included in the unemployed total.
Note: Updated population controls are introduced annually with the release of January data.

SOURCE: Adapted from "Table A-14. Unemployed Persons by Industry and Class of Worker, Not Seasonally Adjusted," in *The Employment Situation—August 2012*, U.S. Department of Labor, Bureau of Labor Statistics, September 7, 2012, http://www.bls.gov/news.release/archives/empsit_09072012.pdf (accessed September 15, 2012)

As shown in Table 5.6, the BLS projections for employment growth in this supersector are good. Employment in health care and social assistance is expected to grow at an average annual rate of 3% (the highest of any industry sector) through 2020. Likewise, educational services employment is projected to increase by 2.3% annually through 2020. Both values are well above the annual average growth rate of 1.3% forecast for overall employment.

FINANCIAL ACTIVITIES. The financial activities supersector includes the banking, insurance, and real estate industries, including businesses that, according to the BLS in *Industries at a Glance* (November 1, 2012, http://stats.bls.gov/iag/tgs/iag52.htm), facilitate "transactions involving the creation, liquidation, or change in ownership of financial assets." The real estate sector includes businesses that manage properties for others, appraise real estate, and facilitate property buying, selling, and leasing.

As shown in Table 5.4, the financial activities supersector employed 7.7 million workers in August 2012. In "Employment Situation—August 2012," the BLS notes that 5.8 million of these employees worked in finance and insurance. The remaining 1.9 million were in real estate or rental and leasing services.

The unemployment rate for this supersector was 5.3% in August 2012, the lowest of any private supersector. (See Table 5.5.) According to the BLS (November 1, 2012, http://data.bls.gov/timeseries/LNU04032238), from 2002 to 2008 the annual average unemployment rate for the financial activities supersector was low, averaging between 2.7% and 3.9%. The housing market boom buoyed the economic performance of the financial industry. However, the resulting bust and associated mortgage crisis brought instability to many financial institutions. From 2009 to 2011 the annual average rate was between 6.4% and 6.9%.

TABLE 5.6

Employment by major industry sector, 2010 and projected for 2020

[In thousands]

Industry sector	Employment		Change	Percent distribution		Annual growth rate (percent)
	2010	2020	2010–20	2010	2020	2010–20
Total[a]	143,068.2	163,537.1	20,468.9	100.0	100.0	1.3
Nonagriculture wage and salary[b]	130,435.6	150,176.8	19,741.2	91.2	91.8	1.4
Goods-producing, excluding agriculture	17,705.5	19,496.8	1,791.3	12.4	11.9	1.0
Mining	655.9	680.7	24.8	0.5	0.4	0.4
Construction	5,525.6	7,365.1	1,839.5	3.9	4.5	2.9
Manufacturing	11,524.0	11,450.9	−73.1	8.1	7.0	−0.1
Services-providing	112,730.1	130,680.1	17,950.0	78.8	79.9	1.5
Utilities	551.8	516.1	−35.7	0.4	0.3	−0.7
Wholesale trade	5,456.1	6,200.2	744.1	3.8	3.8	1.3
Retail trade	14,413.7	16,182.2	1,768.5	10.1	9.9	1.2
Transportation and warehousing	4,183.3	5,036.2	852.9	2.9	3.1	1.9
Information	2,710.9	2,851.2	140.3	1.9	1.7	0.5
Financial activities	7,630.2	8,410.6	780.4	5.3	5.1	1.0
Professional and business services	16,688.0	20,497.0	3,809.0	11.7	12.5	2.1
Educational services	3,149.6	3,968.8	819.2	2.2	2.4	2.3
Health care and social assistance	16,414.5	22,053.9	5,639.4	11.5	13.5	3.0
Leisure and hospitality	13,019.6	14,362.3	1,342.7	9.1	8.8	1.0
Other services	6,031.3	6,850.7	819.4	4.2	4.2	1.3
Federal government	2,968.0	2,596.0	−372.0	2.1	1.6	−1.3
State and local government	19,513.1	21,154.8	1,641.7	13.6	12.9	0.8
Agriculture, forestry, fishing, and hunting[c]	2,135.5	2,005.3	−130.2	1.5	1.2	−0.6
Agriculture wage and salary	1,282.1	1,236.1	−46.0	0.9	0.8	−0.4
Agriculture self-employed and unpaid family workers	853.4	769.3	−84.1	0.6	0.5	−1.0
Nonagriculture self-employed and unpaid family worker	8,943.8	9,720.6	776.8	6.3	5.9	0.8
Secondary wage and salary jobs in agriculture and private household industries[d, e]	111.6	112.7	1.1	0.1	0.1	0.1
Secondary jobs as a self-employed or unpaid family worker[d, f]	1,441.7	1,521.7	80.0	1.0	0.9	0.5

[a]Employment data for wage and salary workers are from the BLS Current Employment Statistics survey, which counts jobs, whereas self-employed, unpaid family workers, and agriculture, forestry, fishing, and hunting are from the Current Population Survey (household survey), which counts workers.
[b]Includes wage and salary data from the Current Employment Statistics survey, except private households, which is from the Current Population Survey. Logging workers are excluded.
[c]Includes agriculture, forestry, fishing, and hunting data from the Current Population Survey, except logging, which is from Current Employment Statistics survey. Government wage and salary workers are excluded.
[d]Due to methodological changes, these data are not comparable to previously published numbers for these categories of secondary workers.
[e]Workers who hold a secondary wage and salary job in agricultural production, forestry, fishing, and private household industries.
[f]Wage and salary workers who hold a secondary job as a self-employed or unpaid family worker.

SOURCE: Adapted from "Table 2. Employment by Major Industry Sector, 2000, 2010, and projected 2020," in *Employment Projections—2010–20*, U.S. Department of Labor, Bureau of Labor Statistics, February 1, 2012, http://www.bls.gov/news.release/pdf/ecopro.pdf (accessed September 16, 2012)

The BLS predicts that employment in the financial activities supersector will increase on average by 1% annually through 2020. (See Table 5.6.) This is slightly less than the 1.3% growth rate expected for employment overall.

GOVERNMENT. The government supersector encompasses all local, state, and federal government agencies as well as public schools and public hospitals. It also includes law enforcement agencies, courts, and legislative assemblies, but, for the purposes of industry tracking, it does not include military personnel.

The government was the largest employer among all the supersectors in August 2012, employing 21.9 million people. (See Table 5.4.) The breakdown by level of government was as follows:

- Local government—14.1 million

- State government—5 million

- Federal government—2.8 million

In "Employment Situation—August 2012," the BLS indicates that more than half (7.8 million) of the local government workers and slightly less than half (2.4 million) of the state government workers were employed in education. The total federal workforce of 2.8 million workers included 610,400 employees of the U.S. Postal Service.

The unemployment rate for government workers was only 5.1% in August 2012, the lowest of all the supersectors. (See Table 5.5.)

As shown in Figure 5.11, the total number of people employed in government grew steadily from around 16.3 million in 1980 to 23.3 million in 2010. There was no decrease in employment between 2008 and 2009 as occurred in other supersectors. However, government employment did decline slightly from 2010 through August 2012. The BLS predicts relatively poor annual growth in government employment through 2020. Employment in the federal government is expected to decrease by 1.3% per year. (See Table 5.6.) State and local

FIGURE 5.11

Government employees, 1980–2012

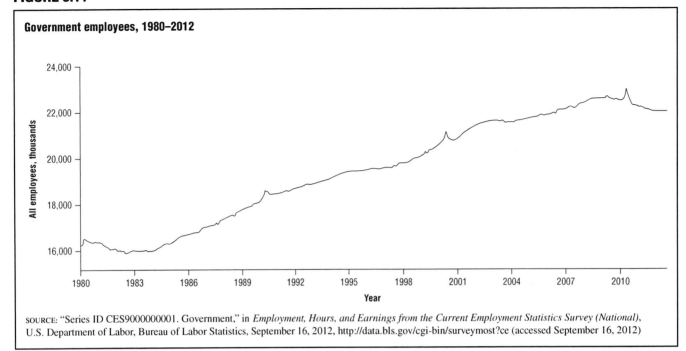

SOURCE: "Series ID CES9000000001. Government," in *Employment, Hours, and Earnings from the Current Employment Statistics Survey (National)*, U.S. Department of Labor, Bureau of Labor Statistics, September 16, 2012, http://data.bls.gov/cgi-bin/surveymost?ce (accessed September 16, 2012)

government employment is expected to grow by only 0.8% through 2020. Both values are less than the 1.3% growth rate expected for employment overall.

INFORMATION. The production and distribution of information falls under the information supersector of the U.S. economy. This supersector includes book and software publishing, Internet service providers, and television broadcasting, as well as the motion picture and sound recording industries.

This supersector employed 2.6 million people in August 2012. (See Table 5.4.) In "Employment Situation—August 2012," the BLS explains that the three largest industries were telecommunications (829,400 workers); publishing, excluding the Internet (740,200 workers); and motion pictures and sound recording (377,100).

As shown in Table 5.5, the unemployment rate for the information supersector was 7.3% in August 2012. According to the BLS (November 1, 2012, http://data.bls.gov/timeseries/LNU04032237), unemployment in this industry fluctuated greatly on a monthly and annual basis over the past decade. The average annual unemployment rate was 6.9% in 2002, but then declined year over year to 3.6% in 2007. It rose modestly to 5% in 2008 and then shot up to 9.2% and 9.7% in 2009 and 2010, respectively. The annual average unemployment rate for 2011 was down to 7.3%.

The BLS expects employment in this supersector to increase by only 0.5% annually through 2020. (See Table 5.6.) This is less than the 1.3% growth rate expected for the employment overall.

LEISURE AND HOSPITALITY. The leisure and hospitality supersector encompasses businesses in the arts, entertainment, recreation, spectator sports, accommodation, and food service industries. It also includes performance venues, gambling outlets, golf courses, amusement parks, arcades, hotels and other lodging sites, food service establishments, and privately funded exhibit spaces and historic sites.

As shown in Table 5.4, nearly 13.7 million people worked in leisure and hospitality in August 2012. The industry with the largest employment, by far, within this supersector was accommodation and food services, with 11.7 million workers. The BLS notes in "Employment Situation—August 2012" that the vast majority of workers within this industry (9.9 million, or 85% of the total) were employed in food services and drinking places. The other 1.8 million workers were employed in accommodations (e.g., motels).

The unemployment rate for this supersector was 10.1% in August 2012, the second-highest unemployment rate for any supersector. (See Table 5.5.) Historical data from the BLS (November 1, 2012, http://data.bls.gov/timeseries/LNU04032241) indicate that this industry experienced relatively high average annual unemployment rates of between 7.3% and 8.7% from 2002 to 2008. These are high rates compared with the other supersectors for the same period. Unemployment in leisure and hospitality rose to 11.7% in 2009 and then peaked at 12.2% in 2010 before declining to 11.6% in 2011.

The BLS projects that employment in the leisure and hospitality supersector will grow by 1% annually through 2020. (See Table 5.6.) This is slightly less than the 1.3% growth rate expected for employment overall.

MANUFACTURING. An organization is considered to be part of the manufacturing supersector if its primary business is to transform raw materials into new products through mechanical, physical, or chemical processes. Manufacturing covers many separate industries and provides products that contribute and support all other economic sectors. The government categorizes manufactured goods as either durable goods or nondurable goods. The BLS (November 1, 2012, http://www.bls.gov/iag/tgs/iag423.htm) defines durable goods as "items generally with a normal life expectancy of three years or more." Thus, it can be inferred that nondurable goods are those with a normal life expectancy of less than three years.

In "Employment Situation—August 2012," the BLS lists the following industry sectors as manufacturing durable goods:

- Wood products
- Nonmetallic mineral products
- Primary metals
- Fabricated metal products
- Machinery
- Computer and electronic products
- Electrical equipment and appliances
- Transportation equipment
- Furniture and related products
- Miscellaneous manufacturing

Likewise, the BLS lists the following industry sectors as manufacturing nondurable goods:

- Food manufacturing
- Beverages and tobacco products
- Textile mills
- Textile product mills
- Apparel
- Leather and allied products
- Paper and paper products
- Printing and related support activities
- Petroleum and coal products
- Chemicals
- Plastics and rubber products

Figure 5.12 shows how employment in the manufacturing supersector declined significantly between 1980 and 2012. In 1980 approximately 19 million people were employed in manufacturing. By early 2010 that number was less than 11.5 million. Employment grew slightly over the following two years. In August 2012 the manufacturing supersector employed almost 12 million workers. (See Table 5.4.) The BLS indicates that nearly 7.5 million workers were in durable goods. The remaining 4.5 million workers produced nondurable goods. The BLS notes in "Employment Situation—August 2012" that the industries with the largest number of employees as of August 2012 were food manufacturing (1.5 million), transportation equipment (1.5 million), and fabricated metal products (1.4 million).

The unemployment rate for the manufacturing supersector was 7.3% in August 2012. (See Table 5.5.)

FIGURE 5.12

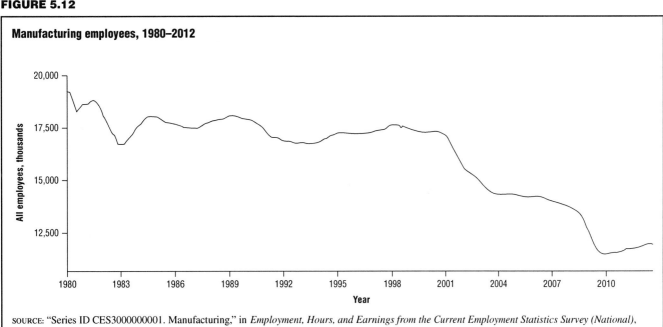

Manufacturing employees, 1980–2012

SOURCE: "Series ID CES3000000001. Manufacturing," in *Employment, Hours, and Earnings from the Current Employment Statistics Survey (National)*, U.S. Department of Labor, Bureau of Labor Statistics, September 16, 2012, http://data.bls.gov/cgi-bin/surveymost?ce (accessed September 16, 2012)

Unemployment was slightly higher in the nondurable goods industries (7.6%) than in the durable goods industries (7.2%).

According to the BLS (November 1, 2012, http://data.bls.gov/timeseries/LNU04032232), the manufacturing supersector had average annual unemployment rates that declined from 6.7% in 2002 to 4.2% in 2006. The rate climbed slightly to 4.3% in 2007 and to 5.8% in 2008 and then more than doubled to 12.1% in 2009 as the supersector was hard hit by the Great Recession. In 2010 the unemployment rate declined to 10.6% and then to 9% in 2011.

The BLS projects that manufacturing employment will decrease by 0.1% annually through 2020. (See Table 5.6.) This is considerably less than the 1.3% growth rate expected for employment overall.

NATURAL RESOURCES AND MINING. The natural resources and mining supersector includes all agriculture, forestry, fishing, hunting, and mining enterprises. Farms engaged in growing crops and raising animals are included in this supersector, as are lumber and fishing operations, coal mining, petroleum and natural gas extraction, and other mining and quarrying activities. This supersector also includes heavy truck and tractor-trailer drivers.

In August 2012 employment in the mining and logging industries was 789,100 and 49,300, respectively. (See Table 5.4.) Employment estimates for the agriculture, forestry, fishing, and hunting industries are not included in Table 5.4. Many people engaged in these activities are self-employed, for example, farmers and ranchers. In *Industries at a Glance* (November 1, 2012, http://stats.bls.gov/iag/tgs/iag11.htm), the BLS reports that these industries employed more than 224,000 people as laborers, farm hands, supervisors, and equipment operators in 2011. Another 12,360 people worked as truck drivers.

As shown in Table 5.5, the unemployment rate for wage and salary workers in the agriculture and related industries was 8.1% in August 2012. The economic performance of the agriculture industry will be examined in more detail in Chapter 6. The unemployment rate in August 2012 for the mining, quarrying, and oil and gas extraction industries was 5.8%. (See Table 5.5.) As shown in Table 5.6, the BLS predicts that employment in the mining industry will grow by only 0.4% annually through 2020. The projections are even worse for workers in the agriculture, forestry, fishing, and hunting industries; employment is expected to decrease by 0.6% through 2020. Employment projections are not provided for other industries within this supersector.

OTHER SERVICES. This supersector includes jobs such as repairing equipment and machinery; promoting or administering religious activities; operating dry cleaning and laundry services; conducting personal care, death care, and pet care services; and supplying photo processing, temporary parking, and dating services. People who work in grant making and advocacy are also included in this category.

Nearly 5.4 million people were employed in the other services supersector in August 2012. (See Table 5.4.) In "Employment Situation—August 2012," the BLS notes that 2.9 million of these workers were employed by membership associations and organizations. Nearly 1.3 million performed personal and laundry services. The remaining 1.2 million worked in repair and maintenance occupations.

The unemployment rate for this supersector was 6.7% in August 2012. (See Table 5.5.) The BLS (November 1, 2012, http://data.bls.gov/timeseries/LNU04032242) reports that the average annual unemployment rates from 2002 to 2008 were relatively low, averaging between 3.9% and 5.7%. In 2009 the rate increased to 7.5%, then to 8.5% in 2010 and 8.8% in 2011.

The BLS projects that employment in the other services supersector will grow by 1.3% annually through 2020. (See Table 5.6.) This is the same growth rate predicted for employment overall.

PROFESSIONAL AND BUSINESS SERVICES. The professional and business services supersector includes legal, accounting, architectural, engineering, advertising, marketing, translation, and veterinary services. This supersector also includes those who manage companies and all the administrative support that is needed for a business to operate. In addition, security, surveillance, cleaning, and waste disposal services are tracked in this category.

This large supersector employed nearly 18 million people in August 2012. (See Table 5.4.) The BLS explains in "Employment Situation—August 2012" that the largest number of employees (8 million) worked in administrative and waste services. Nearly 8 million worked in professional and technical services, such as accounting, legal, architectural, engineering, computer system, and management and technical consulting services. Other industries with large numbers of employees included employment services (3.2 million) and temporary help services (2.5 million).

In August 2012 the unemployment rate for this supersector was relatively high, at 8.9%. (See Table 5.5.) The BLS (November 1, 2012, http://data.bls.gov/timeseries/LNU04032239) indicates that the average annual unemployment rates from 2002 to 2008 varied widely, from a high of 8.2% in 2003 to a low of 5.3% in 2007. The rates in 2009 and 2010 were 10.8% and then declined to 9.7% in 2011.

The BLS predicts that employment in this supersector will increase by 2.1% annually through 2020.

(See Table 5.6.) This is higher than the rate of 1.3% projected for employment overall.

TRANSPORTATION, WAREHOUSING, AND UTILITIES. The transportation, warehousing, and utilities supersector includes businesses that transport passengers or cargo by air, rail, water, road, or pipeline. The sector also includes businesses that provide storage of goods and that support transportation activities. Also tracked in this sector are private enterprises that generate, transmit, or distribute utilities such as electric power, natural gas, and water.

As shown in Table 5.4, nearly 4.4 million people worked in transportation and warehousing in August 2012. The BLS indicates in "Employment Situation—August 2012" that the largest component (1.4 million) was engaged in truck transportation. Another 566,500 people were employed by utilities.

The unemployment rate for this supersector was 7.1% in August 2012. (See Table 5.5.) The BLS (November 1, 2012, http://data.bls.gov/timeseries/LNU04034171) reports that unemployment was extremely low in the utilities industry for most of the decade. From 2002 to 2008 the average annual rate was less than 3.1%. In 2009 the rate increased to 4.8%, which was well below the rates experienced by other industries. The unemployment rate for the utilities industry dropped to 3.4% in 2010, but then rose to 4.9% in 2011. According to the BLS (November 1, 2012, http://data.bls.gov/timeseries/LNU04034168), the transportation and warehousing industry also enjoyed relatively low unemployment rates of between 4.3% and 5.7% from 2000 to 2008. In 2009 the rate grew dramatically to 9.7%. It fell to 9.4% in 2010 and to 8.8% in 2011.

As shown in Table 5.6, employment in transportation and warehousing is expected to increase by an average of 1.9% per year through 2020. This is better than the forecasted rate of 1.3% growth for employment overall. The outlook is not as good for utilities. Employment in this industry is projected to decrease on average by 0.7% annually through 2020.

WHOLESALE AND RETAIL TRADE. The wholesale and retail supersector encompasses private businesses that trade in products that they do not produce. Wholesalers buy large quantities of finished goods from manufacturers and sell the goods in smaller lots to businesses that are engaged in retail trade. Retailers then offer the goods for sale to consumers at an increased price, usually figured as a percentage of the wholesale cost. Even though the traditional notion of a retail establishment includes at least one store location, many retailers in the early 21st century sell their products over the Internet or in catalogs without stores.

As shown in Table 5.4, this supersector employed 14.8 million people in retail trade and 5.6 million people in wholesale trade in August 2012. The BLS explains in "Employment Situation—August 2012" that the largest numbers of retail employees worked in general merchandise stores (3.1 million), food and beverage stores (2.9 million), and motor vehicle and parts dealers (1.7 million).

The overall unemployment rate for this supersector was 8.3% in August 2012. (See Table 5.5.) According to the BLS (November 1, 2012, http://data.bls.gov/timeseries/LNU04034154), the unemployment rates in wholesale trade were relatively low from 2002 to 2008, averaging between 3.2% and 5.1% per year. In 2009 and 2010 the rates climbed to 7.2% and 7.3%, respectively. The rate dropped to 6.9% in 2011. Historically, the unemployment rates in retail have been slightly higher than those in wholesale. The BLS (November 1, 2012, http://data.bls.gov/timeseries/LNU04034163) reports that rates on an average annual basis were between 5.1% and 6.4% from 2000 to 2008. The rates in 2009 and 2010 increased to 9.5% and 10%, respectively, before they declined to 9.4% in 2011.

The BLS predicts that employment in wholesale trade will increase at a rate of 1.3% annually through 2020. (See Table 5.6.) The projected growth for retail trade is almost as strong at 1.2%. (See Table 5.6.) A growth rate of 1.3% is projected for employment overall.

LABOR UNIONS

Even though many historians trace the origins of labor unions to medieval guilds (organized groups of tradespeople and artisans in the Middle Ages), the modern labor movement is more directly linked to the trade unions of the early Industrial Revolution, when working conditions in factories and mines were barely tolerable and employees began joining together to demand reasonable work hours, safe conditions, and decent wages. Since their establishment, unions have had tense relationships with both employers and government; at times, they have been banned altogether, and the struggle between labor and employers has sometimes resulted in violence.

Labor unions have had a significant impact on the U.S. workforce and labor policy. Unions are often able to secure higher wages and increased benefits for their members. The BLS reports in "Union Members—2011" (January 27, 2012, http://www.bls.gov/news.release/union2.nr0.htm) that 14.8 million wage and salary workers were union members in 2011. This represented 11.8% of all wage and salary workers in the United States. The percentage is significantly lower than the rate of 20.1% reported in 1983 (the first year the BLS tracked union membership). According to the BLS, 37% of government workers were unionized in 2011, compared with only 6.9% of private industry workers. Local governments have the most highly unionized employees, particularly teachers, police officers, and firefighters. The highest rates of union membership in the private

FIGURE 5.13

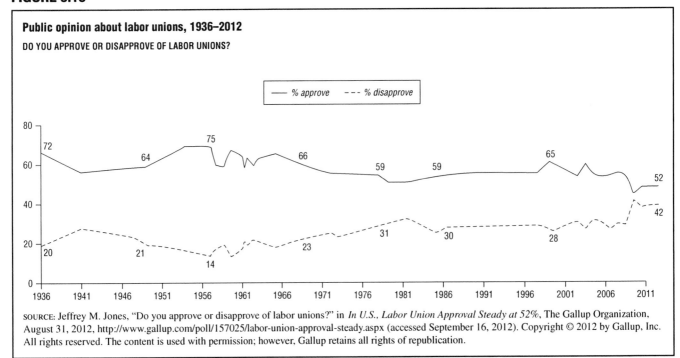

Public opinion about labor unions, 1936–2012

DO YOU APPROVE OR DISAPPROVE OF LABOR UNIONS?

SOURCE: Jeffrey M. Jones, "Do you approve or disapprove of labor unions?" in *In U.S., Labor Union Approval Steady at 52%*, The Gallup Organization, August 31, 2012, http://www.gallup.com/poll/157025/labor-union-approval-steady.aspx (accessed September 16, 2012). Copyright © 2012 by Gallup, Inc. All rights reserved. The content is used with permission; however, Gallup retains all rights of republication.

industries are found in the transportation and construction sectors.

Despite their successes on behalf of American workers, contemporary labor unions continue to face opposition from employers, and often from employees, who question whether the benefits of being associated with a union are worth the cost. Union members are required to go on strike when the union has an unresolved grievance against an employer, and striking union members receive only a fraction of their income in strike pay. Workers who are part of a union may also find themselves facing fines for not abiding by the union bylaws.

For employers, unions can pose other problems. Business operations can be greatly interrupted by unresolved negotiations, whether or not they lead to a strike. Furthermore, because of the increased expenses associated with employing union members, a company's products or services might become less competitively priced in the marketplace. If sales are lost to foreign or nonunion competitors, companies may be forced to lay off employees or even go out of business.

The Gallup Organization has polled Americans regarding their opinions about labor unions since the 1930s. The most recent polls were conducted in August 2012. As shown in Figure 5.13, approval of labor unions reached its lowest point in 2009, when only 48% of respondents said they approve of labor unions. The percentage climbed to 52% in 2012. Historical support for unions was much higher, regularly 60% or greater through 2006. Support was highest during the 1950s, when 75% of those asked approved of unions.

Jeffrey M. Jones of the Gallup Organization notes in *In U.S., Labor Union Approval Steady at 52%* (August 31, 2012, http://www.gallup.com/poll/157025/labor-union-approval-steady.aspx) that in August 2012, 10% of respondents said they belonged to a union. Another 17% of respondents said another household member belonged to a union. Overall, less than one-third (29%) of respondents said labor unions should have "more influence than they have today." About four out of 10 (41%) of those asked said labor unions should have "less influence than they have today." According to Jones, when respondents were asked to predict the future strength of labor unions in the United States, 52% predicted that labor unions will become weaker, whereas 21% said labor unions will become stronger in the future.

COMPENSATION OF AMERICAN WORKERS

As explained in Chapter 2, the U.S. Department of Commerce's Bureau of Economic Analysis tracks personal income, which includes compensation of workers, as part of its compilation of the National Income and Product Accounts. Compensation has two components: pay and benefits. Pay includes wages (which is the term used primarily for pay made on an hourly, weekly, or monthly basis) and salaries (which is pay calculated yearly). Benefits provided by employers include paid time off from work, various insurance and retirement plans, and other programs that are designed to attract and keep employees.

Table 5.7 shows the wage and salary disbursements and supplements paid by employers in 2010 and 2011

TABLE 5.7

Employee compensation, 2010–11, and first and second quarters 2012

[Billions of dollars]

	2010	2011	2012 I*	2012 II*
			Seasonally adjusted at annual rates	
Compensation of employees, received	7,970.0	8,295.2	8,495.7	8,562.9
Wage and salary disbursements	6,404.6	6,661.3	6,825.9	6,882.0
Private industries	5,213.3	5,466.0	5,626.8	5,682.0
Goods-producing industries	1,057.5	1,108.6	1,144.0	1,147.3
Manufacturing	674.1	706.6	723.1	726.2
Services-producing industries	4,155.8	4,357.4	4,482.7	4,534.7
Trade, transportation, and utilities	1,005.5	1,050.1	1,083.3	1,096.0
Other services-producing industries	3,150.3	3,307.3	3,399.4	3,438.7
Government	1,191.3	1,195.3	1,199.1	1,200.0
Supplements to wages and salaries	1,565.4	1,633.9	1,669.8	1,680.9
Employer contributions for employee pension and insurance funds	1,097.3	1,139.0	1,159.6	1,167.7
Employer contributions for government social insurance	468.1	494.9	510.2	513.2

*Revised. Revisions include changes to series affected by the incorporation of revised wage and salary estimates for the first quarter of 2012.

SOURCE: Adapted from "Table 2. Personal Income and Its Disposition (Years and Quarters)," in *Personal Income and Outlays: July 2012*, U.S. Department of Commerce, Bureau of Economic Analysis, August 30, 2012, http://www.bea.gov/newsreleases/national/pi/2012/pdf/pi0712.pdf (accessed September 16, 2012)

and in the first two quarters of 2012. (Note that the quarterly values are seasonally adjusted at annual rates.) Nearly $8.3 trillion was paid out in compensation in 2011, up from less than $8 trillion in 2010. The quarterly values for 2012 indicate that wage and salary disbursements for the year were on track to be higher than the 2010 and 2011 values. In addition, nearly $1.6 trillion in supplements was estimated to be contributed by employers in 2010, primarily for employee pensions and insurance funds. In 2011 supplements to wages and salaries increased to more than $1.6 trillion. The value for the second quarter of 2012, which is seasonally adjusted at annual rates, was nearly $1.7 trillion.

Benefits

To attract and keep the best employees and earn a level of loyalty from them, many U.S. employers offer benefits and incentives. The BLS publishes an annual report on employee benefits. As of November 2012, the most recent report was "Employee Benefits in the United States—March 2012" (July 11, 2012, http://www.bls.gov/news.release/pdf/ebs2.pdf). The BLS notes that as of March 2012, a majority of employees in private industry and in state and local governments had access to retirement benefits (see Table 5.8), medical care benefits (see Table 5.9), life insurance (see Table 5.10), and paid sick leave, paid vacation, and paid holidays (see Table 5.11). Access was greatest for full-time workers, union workers, and those in the highest wage-earning categories. The take-up rates (the number of employees with access divided by the number of employees participating) were highest for life insurance benefits (97% of private industry workers and 98% of state and local government workers).

Figure 5.14 and Figure 5.15 compare benefit availability by establishment size for workers employed in private industry as of March 2012. Across the board, the largest establishments (i.e., those with 500 or more workers) offered greater access to benefits than did smaller establishments. There were significant access differences between the largest and smallest establishments; for example, access to retirement benefits was less than 50% at the smallest establishments (i.e., those with 1 to 99 workers), but greater than 80% at the largest establishments.

MEDICAL INSURANCE. One of the most valued benefits offered by employers is medical insurance. Typically, the total cost of monthly health insurance coverage is split between employers and employees, with employers paying the largest portion. As shown in Table 3.3 in Chapter 3, the price of medical care grew at a faster rate between 2004 and 2011 than the overall rate for the urban consumer price index. Because of rising health care costs, medical insurance has become a costly benefit for both employers and employees.

One of the factors driving up health costs is the overall declining health of Americans. In "Declining Health of U.S. Workers Is Driving up Employer Costs" (April 20, 2011, http://www.shrm.org/hrdisciplines/benefits/Articles/Pages/DecliningHealth.aspx), Stephen Miller describes the Thomson Reuters Workforce Wellness Index, an index that gauges six health-related risk factors that affect the costs of employer-sponsored health insurance. The risk factors include high blood pressure, excessive weight, and alcohol use. According to Miller, the index declined by 2% between 2005 and 2009, reflecting growing problems

TABLE 5.8

Access, participation, and take-up rates in percent for retirement benefits, March 2012

[All workers = 100 percent]

Characteristics	Civilian[a]			Private industry			State and local government		
	Access	Participation	Take-up rate	Access	Participation	Take-up rate	Access	Participation	Take-up rate
All workers	68	54	79	65	48	75	89	84	95
Full time	78	65	83	74	59	80	99	94	95
Part time	38	21	54	38	19	50	39	35	90
Union	95	88	93	92	85	92	97	92	95
Nonunion	64	48	75	62	45	72	83	78	95
Average wage within the following categories:[b]									
Lowest 25 percent	41	21	51	38	17	45	73	69	94
Lowest 10 percent	30	10	33	29	8	28	59	55	93
Second 25 percent	70	52	75	65	46	70	93	88	95
Third 25 percent	79	67	85	75	61	82	94	89	94
Highest 25 percent	88	80	91	85	75	89	98	94	96
Highest 10 percent	90	83	92	86	78	91	98	94	96

Notes: Includes defined benefit pension plans and defined contribution retirement plans. Workers are considered as having access or as participating if they have access to or are participating in at least one of these plan types. The take-up rate is an estimate of the percentage of workers with access to a plan who participate in the plan, rounded for presentation.
[a]Includes workers in the private nonfarm economy except those in private households, and workers in the public sector, except the federal government.
[b]The categories are based on the average wage for each occupation surveyed, which may include workers with earnings both above and below the threshold. The average wages are based on the estimates published in the "National Compensation Survey: Occupational Earnings in the United States, 2010."

SOURCE: Adapted from "Table 1. Retirement Benefits: Access, Participation, and Take-up Rates, National Compensation Survey, March 2012," in *Employee Benefits in the United States—March 2012*, U.S. Department of Labor, Bureau of Labor Statistics, July 11, 2012, http://www.bls.gov/news.release/pdf/ebs2.pdf (accessed September 16, 2012)

TABLE 5.9

Access, participation, and take-up rates in percent for medical care benefits, March 2012

[All workers = 100 percent]

Characteristics	Civilian[a]			Private industry			State and local government		
	Access	Participation	Take-up rate	Access	Participation	Take-up rate	Access	Participation	Take-up rate
All workers	73	54	74	70	51	72	87	73	84
Full time	88	67	76	86	64	74	99	83	84
Part time	24	13	56	24	13	54	24	17	71
Union	95	79	83	94	78	83	95	79	83
Nonunion	69	50	72	67	48	71	80	68	84
Average wage within the following categories:[b]									
Lowest 25 percent	38	22	59	34	19	57	68	55	81
Lowest 10 percent	21	11	51	19	9	50	54	43	79
Second 25 percent	77	55	72	74	51	69	91	78	86
Third 25 percent	87	68	78	86	65	76	93	79	85
Highest 25 percent	93	75	80	92	73	79	97	80	83
Highest 10 percent	95	76	80	93	74	79	97	82	84

[a]Includes workers in the private nonfarm economy except those in private households, and workers in the public sector, except the federal government.
[b]The categories are based on the average wage for each occupation surveyed, which may include workers with earnings both above and below the threshold. The average wages are based on the estimates published in the "National Compensation Survey: Occupational Earnings in the United States, 2010."
Notes: The take-up rate is an estimate of the percentage of workers with access to a plan who participate in the plan, rounded for presentation.

SOURCE: Adapted from "Table 2. Medical Care Benefits: Access, Participation, and Take-up rates, National Compensation Survey, March 2012," in *Employee Benefits in the United States—March 2012*, U.S. Department of Labor, Bureau of Labor Statistics, July 11, 2012, http://www.bls.gov/news.release/pdf/ebs2.pdf (accessed September 16, 2012)

with less than optimal health among the population. This health decline translates to higher health insurance costs for employers—an estimated $670 per employee per year according to index data from March 2011.

As explained in Chapter 3, the Agency for Healthcare Research and Quality (AHRQ), a division of the U.S. Department of Health and Human Services, conducts large-scale surveys of medical care recipients and providers. The AHRQ estimates that 56.1 million (21.1%) people under the age of 65 years did not have health insurance coverage during the first half of 2011. (See Table 3.5 in Chapter 3.) It should be noted that people aged 65 years and older are not counted because this age group is widely covered by

TABLE 5.10

Access, participation, and take-up rates in percent for life insurance benefits, March 2012

[All workers = 100 percent]

Characteristics	Civilian[a]			Private industry			State and local government		
	Access	Participation	Take-up rate	Access	Participation	Take-up rate	Access	Participation	Take-up rate
All workers	61	59	97	57	56	97	79	77	98
Full time	76	74	97	73	71	97	90	88	98
Part time	14	13	92	13	12	92	22	21	95
Union	85	84	98	85	83	98	86	84	98
Nonunion	56	55	97	55	53	97	73	71	97
Average wage within the following categories:[b]									
Lowest 25 percent	26	24	92	22	20	91	62	60	98
Lowest 10 percent	12	11	89	11	10	87	48	46	96
Second 25 percent	63	61	97	60	57	96	83	81	98
Third 25 percent	74	73	98	72	70	98	84	83	98
Highest 25 percent	84	83	99	82	81	99	88	86	97
Highest 10 percent	87	86	99	85	85	99	90	86	96

[a]Includes workers in the private nonfarm economy except those in private households, and workers in the public sector, except the federal government.
[b]The categories are based on the average wage for each occupation surveyed, which may include workers with earnings both above and below the threshold. The average wages are based on the estimates published in the "National Compensation Survey: Occupational Earnings in the United States, 2010."
Notes: The take-up rate is an estimate of the percentage of workers with access to a plan who participate in the plan, rounded for presentation.

SOURCE: Adapted from "Table 5. Life Insurance Benefits: Access, Participation, and Take-up rates, National Compensation Survey, March 2012," in *Employee Benefits in the United States—March 2012*, U.S. Department of Labor, Bureau of Labor Statistics, July 11, 2012, http://www.bls.gov/news.release/pdf/ebs2.pdf (accessed September 16, 2012)

TABLE 5.11

Access, participation, and take-up rates in percent for paid sick leave, vacation, and holidays, March 2012

[All workers = 100 percent]

Characteristics	Civilian[a]			Private industry			State and local government		
	Paid sick leave	Paid vacation	Paid holidays	Paid sick leave	Paid vacation	Paid holidays	Paid sick leave	Paid vacation	Paid holidays
All workers	66	74	76	61	77	77	89	59	67
Full time	79	87	—	75	91	90	98	67	74
Part time	25	34	39	23	35	40	40	20	29
Union	84	75	80	73	91	91	97	57	69
Nonunion	62	74	75	60	75	76	82	62	66
Average wage within the following categories:[b]									
Lowest 25 percent	32	51	52	29	49	50	75	55	62
Lowest 10 percent	20	38	35	18	37	33	62	41	49
Second 25 percent	68	82	84	64	83	84	93	84	87
Third 25 percent	79	89	—	75	90	90	93	69	76
Highest 25 percent	87	79	82	84	90	91	96	36	49
Highest 10 percent	90	76	79	86	90	90	98	34	45

[a]Includes workers in the private nonfarm economy except those in private households, and workers in the public sector, except the federal government.
[b]The categories are based on the average wage for each occupation surveyed, which may include workers with earnings both above and below the threshold. The average wages are based on the estimates published in the "National Compensation Survey: Occupational Earnings in the United States, 2010."
Note: Dash indicates no workers in this category or data did not meet publication criteria.

SOURCE: Adapted from "Table 6. Selected Paid Leave Benefits: Access, National Compensation Survey, March 2012," in *Employee Benefits in the United States—March 2012*, U.S. Department of Labor, Bureau of Labor Statistics, July 11, 2012, http://www.bls.gov/news.release/pdf/ebs2.pdf (accessed September 16, 2012)

Medicare (a federal health insurance program for people aged 65 years and older and people with disabilities).

Concern has been growing for decades about the large number of Americans lacking medical insurance. In 2010 the Obama administration spearheaded the passage of federal legislation—the Patient Protection and Affordable Care Act and the Health Care and Education Reconciliation Act (which are commonly known as the ACA)—that is scheduled to be phased in through 2020 and is intended to reform the nation's health care system to improve availability, affordability, and consumer protections. The ACA includes provisions to make health care insurance available

FIGURE 5.14

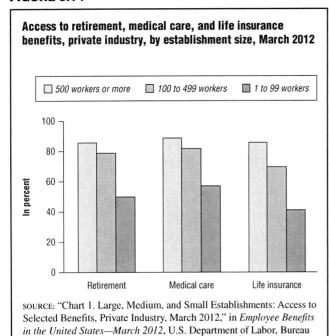

Access to retirement, medical care, and life insurance benefits, private industry, by establishment size, March 2012

SOURCE: "Chart 1. Large, Medium, and Small Establishments: Access to Selected Benefits, Private Industry, March 2012," in *Employee Benefits in the United States—March 2012*, U.S. Department of Labor, Bureau of Labor Statistics, July 11, 2012, http://www.bls.gov/news.release/pdf/ebs2.pdf (accessed September 16, 2012)

FIGURE 5.15

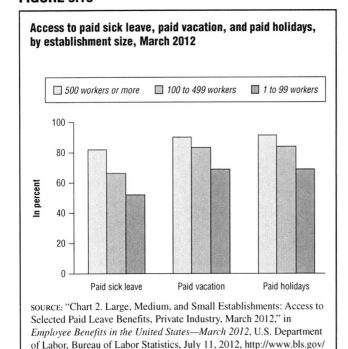

Access to paid sick leave, paid vacation, and paid holidays, by establishment size, March 2012

SOURCE: "Chart 2. Large, Medium, and Small Establishments: Access to Selected Paid Leave Benefits, Private Industry, March 2012," in *Employee Benefits in the United States—March 2012*, U.S. Department of Labor, Bureau of Labor Statistics, July 11, 2012, http://www.bls.gov/news.release/pdf/ebs2.pdf (accessed September 16, 2012)

to millions of uninsured people, including those with preexisting conditions. It also calls for tax credits for small businesses to help them better afford medical insurance for their employees. As of November 2012, only a few of the ACA's provisions had been implemented, so its potential effects on American workers were still uncertain.

NONTRADITIONAL WORK ARRANGEMENTS

Working at Home

With technological advances such as Internet access, e-mail, and teleconferencing, working at home has become a viable option for many types of jobs. As employees conduct much of their daily work from home offices, employers are able to save on operating costs. Many employers will pay for computers, additional telephone lines, and even utilities to allow their employees to work from home offices. This allows them to reduce office space, which is one of the higher costs for an employer, especially in large metropolitan markets.

Self-Employment

Self-employed workers are not on the payroll of a company. They may own or operate small businesses or work under contract arrangements with companies. Detailed information about self-employed business owners is provided in Chapter 6.

FOREIGN WORKERS IN THE UNITED STATES

Relatively high wages and favorable working conditions have attracted workers from around the world to the United States. There are two broad categories of foreign workers: those who have entered the country legally with the proper paperwork to pursue work and those who have entered illegally. Legal workers are tracked by the U.S. Citizenship and Immigration Service, formerly the U.S. Immigration and Naturalization Service.

Legal Foreign Workers

The Department of Labor explains in "Guestworker Programs" (June 30, 2011, http://www.doleta.gov/Business/gw/guestwkr/) that it issues a limited number of certifications to foreign workers to work in the United States on a temporary or permanent basis. According to the Department of Labor, "certification may be obtained in cases where it can be demonstrated that there are insufficient qualified U.S. workers available and willing to perform the work at wages that meet or exceed the prevailing wage paid for that occupation in the area of intended employment."

The U.S. Department of Homeland Security's Office of Immigration Statistics tracks the number of foreign workers entering the United States and publishes related data in annual reports. In *Nonimmigrant Admissions to the United States: 2011* (July 2012, http://www.dhs.gov/xlibrary/assets/statistics/publications/ni_fr_2011.pdf), Randall Monger of the Department of Homeland Security notes that nearly 2.1 million temporary workers and trainees were admitted into the United States in fiscal year 2011 (October 1, 2010, to September 30, 2011). This value was up from 1.7 million the previous fiscal year.

Temporary foreign workers maintain the citizenship of their native country, and after fulfilling their contracts with U.S. employers they typically return to their country. Immigrant workers are people who have come to the United States through legal channels and intend to become citizens. They obtain jobs while waiting for their naturalization (the process of becoming a U.S. citizen) to be finalized.

Illegal Foreign Workers

The issue of illegal immigration has become a heated topic. Much of the debate centers on the economic effect of undocumented workers (foreign workers who have entered the United States illegally). Some people claim that undocumented workers take jobs away from Americans and place a large burden on government-provided social programs. Others believe that undocumented workers are willing to take jobs that Americans do not want—low-paying, labor-intensive jobs with no benefits and little to no chance for advancement.

Employers are required by law to verify that new hires are U.S. citizens or foreigners with legal working status who are eligible to work in the United States. Job applicants have to show identification and documentation, including a Social Security card. However, the authenticity of these documents cannot be verified immediately. Thus, well-meaning businesses may unknowingly hire and train illegal workers who use fake documentation to obtain jobs.

There is little doubt that some businesses purposely hire illegal workers or at least ignore questionable paperwork to get inexpensive labor. Many critics maintain that the federal government's focus on terrorism and national security has diminished attention on issues that are related to undocumented workers. Others believe that businesses willing to hire the workers are to blame. Like many factors in the U.S. economy, the issue of undocumented workers is driven by supply and demand factors.

POLITICAL DEBATE AND PUBLIC PROTEST. Michael Hoefer, Nancy Rytina, and Bryan Baker of the Department of Homeland Security indicate in *Estimates of the Unauthorized Immigrant Population Residing in the United States: January 2011* (March 2012, http://www.dhs.gov/xlibrary/assets/statistics/publications/ois_ill_pe_2011.pdf) that there were around 11.5 million illegal immigrants in the United States in January 2011. This number was down from an estimated 11.6 million in January 2010. Many analysts believe job losses and other economic pressures of the Great Recession are responsible for the decrease.

Illegal immigration has become a politically charged and divisive issue. Some politicians advocate allowing many illegal immigrants already in the country the opportunity to obtain U.S. citizenship under certain conditions.

This is called an amnesty provision by its critics and a conditional pathway to legal status by its supporters. The gist of the concept was advocated by President Bush.

As of November 2012, the White House (http://www.whitehouse.gov/issues/immigration) described President Obama's views on the conditional pathway to legal status as follows: "We can create a pathway for legal status that is fair and reflects our values." During the summer of 2012 Obama took a major step toward pathway creation by establishing a program whereby young illegal immigrants can request temporary relief from deportation proceedings and apply for work authorization. The program is only open to those who came to the United States as children and have a clean criminal record.

The federal government has funded several provisions that are designed to improve security along the U.S.-Mexican border, including building a 700-mile (1,300-km) fence along the border. Even though it is commonly referred to as a fence or wall, the structure includes steel fencing in some areas (primarily urban areas) and concrete barriers in other areas. The structure is not continuous. In addition, border security has been enhanced with larger numbers of border guards and new surveillance equipment. These measures are intended to stem the flow of illegal immigrants across the border and to cut down on the smuggling of illegal drugs and human trafficking.

Many state governments have grown frustrated by what they consider to be the failure of the federal government to stem the flow of illegal immigrants into the United States. Since the 1990s hundreds of laws addressing illegal immigration have been passed by state legislatures. Some of the laws have not survived court challenges. The most controversial of these laws was Arizona's Senate Bill 1070, which was signed into law in April 2010. Among other provisions, the law gives Arizona law enforcement officials the power to detain anyone they suspect of being in the United States illegally. The constitutionality of the law was challenged in court by the federal government and by private organizations. Chau Lam and Ann Morse of the National Conference of State Legislatures report in "U.S. Supreme Court Rules on Arizona's Immigration Enforcement Law" (June 25, 2012, http://www.ncsl.org/issues-research/immig/us-supreme-court-rules-on-arizona-immigration-laws.aspx) that in 2012 the U.S. Supreme Court struck down three sections of the law, but upheld the authority granted law enforcement officers to determine the immigration status of lawfully stopped people. Lam and Morse note that five other states—Alabama, Georgia, Indiana, South Carolina, and Utah—passed similar laws during 2011; however, some or all of the provisions of those laws have not passed court challenges.

U.S. JOBS GOING TO FOREIGN COUNTRIES

One consequence of the globalization of U.S. business has been offshoring (the transfer of jobs from the United States to other countries). This can occur when an entire business establishment, such as a factory or service center, is relocated to another nation or when certain jobs within a business are transferred to a foreign company. The latter is also an example of outsourcing (a business practice in which certain tasks within a company are contracted out to another firm; outsourcing may or may not involve sending work to another country). During the 1990s outsourcing became a popular means of reducing costs for some companies. Non-core functions, such as payroll management or housekeeping, are common examples in which outsourcing can be cost effective. However, offshoring is controversial because jobs move outside of the United States, primarily to developing countries, where labor costs are much cheaper.

Critics suggest that offshoring harms the U.S. economy by putting Americans out of work. Others claim that relocation of some operations to foreign countries has a limited effect on domestic employment. They argue that offshoring leads to lower prices for consumer and investment goods, with the ultimate effect of raising real wages (wages that are adjusted for changes in the price of consumer goods) and living standards in the United States.

PROTECTING AMERICAN WORKERS

The United States has enacted comprehensive labor laws to ensure that workplaces are operated safely and that workers are treated fairly. These include relatively strict laws to protect American workers from discrimination on the basis of gender, age, race, ethnicity, religion, sexual orientation, and other factors.

The Fair Labor Standards Act

The Fair Labor Standards Act (FLSA) offers protection for full- and part-time workers in private and government jobs and covers minimum wages, overtime pay, employer record keeping, and child labor. The FLSA also established the standard 40-hour workweek. Local fire and police employees are typically not covered by the FLSA. It was passed in 1938 and has been amended many times over the years.

THE MINIMUM WAGE. The FLSA established a federal hourly minimum wage that U.S. employers must honor for many nonsupervisory, nonfarm, private-sector, and government employees. Most states have their own minimum wage as well. In states with minimum wages that differ from the federal minimum wage, the employer must pay the higher of the two. As of November 2012, the federal minimum wage was $7.25 per hour, a level maintained since 2009.

There are many exceptions to the minimum wage law. Employers may apply for subminimum wage certificates for disabled workers, full-time students, workers under the age of 20 years who are in their first 90 days of employment, workers who receive tips, and student-learners (usually high school students). Lawmakers reason that exempting employers from paying the minimum wage to certain workers (e.g., the disabled and students) encourages them to hire more of those workers who may otherwise be at a disadvantage. Employers may not, however, displace other workers to hire those subject to the subminimum wage. Other workers exempt from the minimum wage include certain professional and administrative employees, certain workers in the fishing industry, certain seasonal employees, babysitters, and certain farm workers.

The BLS tracks the number of hourly wage earners in the United States based on the results of the CPS. In "Characteristics of Minimum Wage Workers: 2011" (March 2, 2012, http://www.bls.gov/cps/minwage2011.htm), the BLS indicates that there were 1.7 million workers paid the federal minimum wage during 2011. Another 2.2 million workers earned less than the minimum wage. The total number of workers earning minimum wage or less accounted for 5.2% of the 73.9 million people earning hourly wages that year.

The minimum wage policy is not without controversy. Advocates for low-income workers believe the minimum wage should be increased regularly to keep up with the effects of inflation. Opponents of the minimum wage assert that wage levels should be determined by market conditions and supply and demand factors. They argue that forcing businesses to pay a higher minimum wage discourages the hiring of low-income workers.

Occupational Safety and Health Administration

The Occupational Safety and Health Administration (OSHA) was formed in 1971 to institute and monitor safety regulations in the workplace. By focusing mainly on industries with high rates of work-related injuries and illnesses, OSHA works directly with employers and employees to ensure that health and safety standards are followed.

Equal Employment Opportunity Commission

The Equal Employment Opportunity Commission (EEOC) enforces federal workplace discrimination laws. It consists of a general counsel and five commissioners who are appointed by the U.S. president and approved by the U.S. Senate. Besides its enforcement role, the EEOC has a training institute to educate employers on workplace discrimination and help them comply with the laws.

CHAPTER 6
U.S. BUSINESSES

After all, the chief business of the American people is business.

—President Calvin Coolidge, January 17, 1925

Businesses are diverse in the United States. They range in size from the huge multinational corporation employing thousands of people to the self-employed individual. They include large and small businesses, home-based businesses, Internet-based businesses, and corporate and family farms. Businesses are a vital part of the American economic engine. They supply goods and services to the world. The consumption of business output is the primary driver behind the growth of the nation's gross domestic product (GDP; the total market value of final goods and services that are produced within an economy in a given year). Businesses also provide opportunities for employment, wealth-building, and investment.

Capitalism encourages business growth. However, businesses can become so large and powerful that they trigger concern about the lack of competition within an industry. Corporate fraud and accounting scandals have eroded the public's trust in the integrity of "big business." These negative feelings deepened during the latter half of the first decade of the 21st century because many Americans blamed irresponsible behavior by large corporations, particularly those in the financial industry, for causing the so-called Great Recession (which lasted from December 2007 to June 2009).

LEGAL STRUCTURES OF BUSINESSES

For legal and tax purposes, all U.S. businesses must be structured as one of several legally defined forms: sole proprietorships, business partnerships, corporations, or limited liability companies. Each offers both advantages and disadvantages to the business owner.

Sole Proprietorships

In a sole proprietorship one person owns and operates the whole business. Because the business and its owner are considered to be a single entity under the law, the owner assumes all the risk but also reaps all the benefits of the business. If the business fails, the sole proprietor may have to cover the losses from his or her personal assets, but if the business succeeds, he or she keeps all the profits. Sole proprietors typically pay lower taxes than those who head corporations or other forms of small businesses. Still, because almost all credit decisions are based on the owner's assets and credit history, it is often difficult for a business set up under this structure to borrow enough money to expand as rapidly as other kinds of businesses.

Business Partnerships

A business partnership has two or more co-owners. As in a sole proprietorship, members of a business partnership are legally recognized as one and the same with their company, meaning that they are personally responsible for the company's debts and other liabilities. Most partnerships start with the partners signing agreements that specify their duties in the business. Many states allow for silent partners, who invest start-up capital but have little role in the company's day-to-day affairs. (Start-up capital is the money used to start a new business.) A significant drawback to this form of business is that each of the partners is responsible for every other partner's actions. If a partner loses or steals money from the company, the other partners will have a legal responsibility to pay that debt.

There are three kinds of business partnerships: a general partnership is the simplest form, in which profits and liability are equally divided among partners or divided according to the terms of the signed agreement; a limited partnership allows partners to have limited liability for the company but also limited decision-making rights; and a joint venture, which is similar to a general partnership but is used only for single projects or for short periods.

Corporations

A corporation is an entity recognized by the state and federal government as entirely separate from its owner or owners. As such, a corporation can be taxed and sued and can enter into contractual agreements. Because it is an individual legal entity, a corporation allows its owners to have less personal liability for debts and lawsuits than a sole proprietorship or business partnership. Owners of corporations are considered to be shareholders, and they may elect a board of directors to oversee management of the company.

Even though corporations are commonly thought of as large companies with hundreds or thousands of employees and publicly traded stock, this is not always the case. Owners of small businesses frequently incorporate as their business expands. All corporate owners must file "articles of incorporation" with their state government. For smaller businesses these forms are simple to fill out and file. One option is to file with the Internal Revenue Service as a subchapter S corporation. In an S corporation the owner must pay him- or herself wages like any other employee, but the structure also offers substantial tax flexibility. All corporations that are publicly traded have C corporation status. This means they have nearly unrestricted ownership and are subject to corporate taxes, paying at both the corporate and stockholder levels.

Limited Liability Company

The limited liability company is a combination of a corporation and a partnership in which the owners (or shareholders) have less personal liability for the company's debts and legal issues and have the benefit of simpler tax filings and more control over management issues.

EMPLOYERS AND NONEMPLOYERS

The U.S. Census Bureau collects data on U.S. businesses annually and conducts an economic census every five years in which it collects more comprehensive data about American businesses. As of November 2012, the most recent economic census data published were from the 2007 census. The Census Bureau divides businesses into two broad categories: employer firms and nonemployer firms.

Employer Firms

According to the Census Bureau (June 17, 2010, http://www.sba.gov/advo/research/us_07ss.pdf), the 2007 economic census indicated there were just over 6 million employer firms operating in 2007. They had more than 7.7 million establishments (facilities) around the country that employed 120.6 million people. The annual payroll of all the businesses was just over $5 trillion. The agency estimates that employer businesses had receipts of $29.7 trillion in 2007.

TABLE 6.1

Employer firm statistics, 2010

Enterprise employment size	Number of firms	Number of establishments	Employment	Annual payroll ($1,000)
Total	5,734,538	7,396,628	111,970,095	4,940,983,369
0–4	3,575,240	3,582,826	5,926,452	226,541,056
5–9	968,075	982,019	6,358,931	212,039,611
10–19	617,089	652,662	8,288,385	283,246,473
<20	5,160,404	5,217,507	20,573,768	721,827,140
20–99	475,125	648,386	18,554,372	719,061,251
100–499	81,773	354,313	15,868,540	665,644,629
<500	5,717,302	6,220,206	54,996,680	2,106,533,020
500+	17,236	1,176,422	56,973,415	2,834,450,349

Note: An establishment with 0 employment is an establishment with no paid employees in the mid-March pay period but with paid employees at some time during the year.

SOURCE: Adapted from "Number of Firms, Number of Establishments, Employment, and Annual Payroll by Enterprise Employment Size for the United States and States, Totals: 2010," in *Statistics of U.S. Businesses (SUSB) Main: Latest SUSB Annual Data*, U.S. Department of Commerce, U.S. Census Bureau, 2012, http://www2.census.gov/econ/susb/data/2010/us_state_totals_2010.xls (accessed November 2, 2012)

The Census Bureau (http://www.census.gov/econ/susb/) notes that as of November 2012 the 2007 economic census was the most recent source for employer firm receipt data. However, the agency has published more recent data regarding other aspects of employer firms. Table 6.1 shows the number of firms and establishments, employment, and annual payrolls for 2010. More than 5.7 million firms were operating (down from just over 6 million in 2007). In 2010 the firms employed nearly 112 million people and had a total annual payroll of $4.9 trillion.

In 2010 more than 99% of employer firms had less than 500 employees each. (See Table 6.1.) Only 17,236 firms had 500 or more employees each. However, the two size categories employed roughly the same number of workers and had similar annual payrolls.

Nonemployer Firms

In "Nonemployer Statistics: Definitions" (January 9, 2012, http://www.census.gov/econ/nonemployer/definitions.htm), the Census Bureau defines a nonemployer business as a business "that has no paid employees, has annual business receipts of $1,000 or more ($1 or more in the construction industry), and is subject to federal income taxes." The Census Bureau compiles nonemployer statistics using data from the Internal Revenue Service.

The Census Bureau indicates in *American Fact Finder: 2007 Economic Census* (July 2, 2010, http://factfinder2.census.gov/) that the 2007 economic census showed nearly 21.5 million nonemployer establishments in the United States. They had combined sales, shipments, receipts, revenues, or "business done" of more than $981 billion.

TABLE 6.2

Nonemployer firm statistics, 2010

Description	Firms	Receipts ($1,000)
Total for all sectors	**22,110,628**	**$950,813,840**
Agriculture, forestry, fishing and hunting	236,705	$10,115,355
Mining, quarrying, and oil and gas extraction	105,922	$6,922,791
Utilities	16,644	$697,528
Construction	2,424,231	$120,150,896
Manufacturing	318,409	$14,571,621
Wholesale trade	393,408	$34,082,418
Retail trade	1,821,620	$75,719,636
Transportation and warehousing	1,021,217	$60,746,245
Information	311,127	$10,739,102
Finance and insurance	716,815	$50,626,266
Real estate and rental and leasing	2,343,136	$209,549,445
Professional, scientific, and technical services	3,121,404	$130,613,013
Administrative and support and waste management and remediation services	1,937,326	$39,110,676
Educational services	567,274	$7,702,746
Health care and social assistance	1,934,831	$57,686,231
Arts, entertainment, and recreation	1,154,020	$26,755,943
Accommodation and food services	328,796	$14,354,581
Other services (except public administration)	3,357,743	$80,669,347

Note: Nonemployer Statistics originate from tax return information of the Internal Revenue Service. The data are subject to nonsampling error such as errors of self-classification by industry on tax forms, as well as errors of response, nonreporting and coverage. Values provided by each firm are slightly modified to protect the respondent's confidentiality.

SOURCE: Adapted from "2010 Nonemployer Statistics," in *Nonemployer Statistics*, U.S. Department of Commerce, U.S. Census Bureau, 2012, http://censtats.census.gov/cgi-bin/nonemployer/nonsect.pl (accessed November 2, 2012)

Table 6.2 shows nonemployer statistics that were compiled by the Census Bureau for 2010. At that time 22.1 million nonemployer firms were operating and had total receipts of $950.8 billion. As described in Chapter 5, the government categorizes jobs using the North American Industry Classification System (NAICS). The NAICS is the standard classification system for businesses throughout North America. As shown in Table 6.2, the largest numbers of nonemployer firms were in the NAICS categories of other services (except public administration); professional, scientific, and technical services; and construction. The NAICS categories with the largest receipts in 2010 were real estate and rental and leasing ($209.5 billion); professional, scientific, and technical services ($130.6 billion); and construction ($120.2 billion).

As noted earlier, employer firms had an estimated $29.7 trillion in receipts in 2007, while nonemployer firms reported nearly $981 billion in sales, shipments, receipts, revenue, or business done. Thus, nonemployer firms make up a very large fraction of the number of U.S. businesses, but a small fraction of the overall business sales and receipts.

SMALL BUSINESSES

Many people perceive the U.S. economy as being dominated by large businesses, such as McDonald's and Microsoft. Even though it is true that many of the world's largest companies are headquartered in the United States, small businesses exert enormous influence on the U.S. economy.

The U.S. Small Business Administration (SBA) is a federal agency that was created in 1953 with the passage of the Small Business Act. The SBA's purpose is to support small businesses by offering financial and counseling assistance and ensuring that small businesses can compete against large companies in receiving government contracts.

The size of what is considered to be a small business varies by industry, and official size standards are determined by the SBA's Office of Size Standards, which issues standards according to a business's number of employees or its average annual receipts. However, the more generally accepted definition of a small business is one that employs fewer than 500 people at any one time.

Small businesses include both employer and nonemployer firms. As shown in Table 6.1, there were just over 5.7 million employer firms with less than 500 employees each in 2010. These small businesses constituted more than 99% of all employer firms. Small employer firms employed nearly 55 million workers in 2010 and had a total payroll of around $2.1 trillion. Thus, small businesses accounted for roughly half of total employment and payroll for all employer firms.

Nonemployer firms, by definition, are small businesses. As shown in Table 6.2, there were more than 22.1 million nonemployer firms operating in 2010 with total receipts of $950.8 billion.

Every year since 1982 the SBA has prepared a report that summarizes the economic status and impact of small businesses (those with fewer than 500 employees each). As of November 2012, the most recent report was *Small Business Economy 2011* (2012, http://www.sba.gov/sites/default/files/SBE_2011_2.pdf), with data through 2010. In the report the SBA assumes that small businesses account for half of the nation's nonfarm private real GDP. This is based on a 2007 report by Katherine Kobe of the Economic Consulting Services, LLC. In *The Small Business Share of GDP, 1998–2004* (April 2007, http://www.sba.gov/advo/research/rs299tot.pdf), Kobe reports that small businesses were responsible for approximately 48% to 51% of the nation's nonfarm private industry GDP between 1998 and 2004. In addition, the SBA uses Census Bureau data to estimate that in 2009 small businesses accounted for around 43% of the nation's annual payroll and 49% of total nonfarm private employment.

Self-Employment

Self-employed people derive at least part of their income from sources other than employer payrolls. Thus, people who own and operate their own businesses are self-employed. So are people who sell their goods or services directly to customers and clients (i.e., outside of an employer-employee relationship). The self-employed are variously called independent contractors, entrepreneurs, proprietors, and freelancers.

In "Self-Employed Individuals Tax Center" (October 1, 2012, http://www.irs.gov/Businesses/Small-Businesses-&-Self-Employed/Self-Employed-Individuals-Tax-Center), the Internal Revenue Service defines a self-employed person as someone who meets any of the following criteria:

- Carries on a trade or business as a sole proprietor or independent contractor

- Is a member of a partnership that carries on a trade or business

- Is otherwise in business for him- or herself (including a part-time business)

There are various estimates of the number of self-employed people in the United States. As noted earlier, the Census Bureau estimates there were 22.1 million nonemployer firms operating in 2010. (See Table 6.2.) The agency (October 18, 2012, http://www.census.gov/econ/nonemployer/index.html) states that "most nonemployers are self-employed individuals operating unincorporated businesses (known as sole proprietorships), which may or may not be the owner's principal source of income." However, the Census Bureau limits its definition of nonemployers to those with annual business receipts of $1,000 or more ($1 or more in the construction industry). Thus, its count of nonemployer firms does not include self-employed people making less than these amounts. In addition, of the 5.7 million employer firms that were tabulated by the Census Bureau in 2010, there is a possibility that many of the smaller firms were owned and operated by self-employed people. (See Table 6.1; note that smaller firms are more likely than larger firms to be sole proprietorships, partnerships, or limited liability companies.)

BENEFITS AND DRAWBACKS. One of the main benefits of self-employment is the freedom of being one's own boss; that is, setting one's own hours, working conditions, pay rate, and so on. This level of independence is particularly appealing to self-motivated individuals who do not want to depend on an employer for their economic well-being. Of course, self-employed people miss out on coveted employer-supplied benefits, such as employer-subsidized medical insurance, employer contributions to employee retirement plans, and paid time off.

Taxation is another consideration. Employees typically pay most if not all of their income taxes through withdrawals from their paychecks. Likewise, employers deduct from employee paychecks Social Security and Medicare taxes. As will be explained in Chapter 9, these taxes are assessed based on the amounts that employers pay their employees. Half of the amount is paid by employees through paycheck deductions and the other half is paid directly by employers to the government. Because self-employment income is not payroll-based, self-employed people are responsible for remitting directly to the government the income, Social Security, and Medicare taxes that they owe.

Some analysts complain that government programs and policies favor larger businesses, particularly those that are incorporated, over self-employed individuals. In "To Boost the Economy, Help the Self-Employed" (Businessweek.com, August 4, 2011), Richard Greenwald notes that many self-employed people are unable to take advantage of government programs, such as unemployment insurance and workman's compensation. As described in Chapter 5, employers pay money into state unemployment trust funds to provide a source of payments for employees who become unemployed and meet specific criteria. Likewise, the workman's compensation program is a form of insurance that employers purchase to provide payments to employees who become injured on the job.

BIG BUSINESS

As shown in Table 6.1, there were 17,236 firms in 2010 that had 500 or more employees each. These big firms accounted for less than 1% of the total number of firms, but encompassed slightly more than half of employment and total receipts. Many large U.S. firms operate globally with offices, factories, or other establishments in numerous countries.

The business magazine *Forbes* publishes the Global 2000, an annual list of the world's 2,000 largest companies. In "The World's Biggest Public Companies" (April 18, 2012, http://www.forbes.com/global2000/), *Forbes* ranks public companies using a composite score based on sales, assets, profits, and market value. The top-10 companies in the 2012 report and their primary business areas and main locations were:

- Exxon Mobil (oil and gas; United States)

- JPMorgan Chase (banking; United States)

- General Electric (conglomerate; United States)

- Royal Dutch Shell (oil and gas; Netherlands)

- ICBC (banking; China)

- HSBC Holdings (banking; United Kingdom)

- Petro China (oil and gas; China)

- Berkshire Hathaway (conglomerate; United States)

- Wells Fargo (banking; United States)

- Petrobras-Petróleo (oil and gas; Brazil)

Five of the top-10 companies are based in the United States.

BUSINESS AND POLITICS

Large companies often have strong ties to the government. They have the resources to donate millions of dollars to political campaigns to elect sympathetic law-makers and to otherwise encourage the passage of pro-business legislation. Likewise, lawmakers, eager to have companies locate facilities in their constituencies to boost local economies, may support policies that favor business interests to the detriment of other programs. Members of Congress may be more inclined to pass pro-business laws if their region has benefited from a large corporation's presence, or if they have received campaign contributions from such a company. This raises concerns that big businesses may be able to convince the government to favor their interests at the expense of the interests of other businesses, or even the population as a whole.

THE FINANCIAL INDUSTRY FALTERS

The U.S. financial industry consists of companies that are engaged primarily in banking, insurance, and investment. Large corporations, in particular, may be involved in a mixture of these enterprises. However, there is an important distinction between commercial banking and investment banking. John Waggoner and David J. Lynch explain in "Red Flags in Bear Stearns' Collapse" (*USA Today*, March 19, 2008) that commercial banks offer products, such as checking and savings accounts, and make loans. They are heavily regulated by the federal government and in most cases the deposits of the banks' customers are insured by the federal government through the Federal Deposit Insurance Corporation (FDIC). In contrast, investment banks facilitate and finance the buying and selling of investments, including stocks and bonds. Investment products are not FDIC insured. The clients of investment banks are mainly companies and government bodies, such as counties and cities. Waggoner and Lynch point out that investment banks receive much less government scrutiny and regulation than commercial banks.

As noted in Chapter 4, investment companies helped drive the housing boom during the first few years of the first decade of the 21st century by buying mortgage-backed securities (MBS) in the secondary mortgage market. The cash inflow allowed lenders to underwrite even more mortgages. At first, MBS were considered to be a wise investment, and financial institutions saw their stock values rise. However, many of the underlying mortgages were poorly underwritten, meaning that the applicants had not been properly screened by the mortgage companies. In many cases, applicants with poor credit histories were given complex mortgages with fluctuating interest rates and ballooning payments. The result was a recipe for disaster. The housing bubble burst and mortgage default rates skyrocketed. Ever since the bust, economists have argued about whether or not investment companies knew that the products they were buying contained these so-called toxic mortgages.

Credit Default Swaps

Investment always entails a certain amount of risk. The article "Credit Default Swaps" (*New York Times*, March 9, 2012) explains that during the late 1990s the financial industry "invented" a type of insurance contract called the credit default swap (CDS) that was supposed to protect investors "against a default by a particular bond or security." However, CDS products are not technically insurance. The insurance industry is heavily regulated by the federal government. Insurance companies must show that they have the collateral (typically cash or other assets with immediately obtainable and verifiable worth) to cover losses that their clients might suffer.

The *New York Times* article notes that between 2000 and 2008 CDS sales skyrocketed from $900 billion to more than $30 trillion. Unbeknown to the investors, many of these products were "insuring" MBS that contained toxic mortgages. In addition, the swaps were not backed by enough cash collateral. Economists call this being undercapitalized. Some investment companies were even using swaps as collateral for the other swaps they were selling to investors.

In *The U.S. Financial Crisis: The Global Dimension with Implications for U.S. Policy* (January 30, 2009, http://graphics8.nytimes.com/packages/pdf/globaleconcrs.pdf), Dick K. Nanto of the Congressional Research Service examines in detail the role of CDSs in the Great Recession. Nanto points out that investors may have thought that CDSs were safe because the swaps were rated by credit rating firms. Credit rating firms are paid fees to assess the financial soundness of companies and investments. The firms use past historical data and computer models in their assessments. However, Nanto notes that CDSs were relatively new during the first decade of the 21st century. In addition, the credit rating firms used computer models that were supplied by the very companies that were issuing the CDSs. Nanto also suspects that the firms were advising clients "how to structure securities in order to receive higher ratings." Nanto concludes that "the large fees offered to credit rating firms for providing credit ratings were difficult for them to refuse in spite of doubts they might have had about the underlying quality of the securities."

Too Big to Fail?

By 2007 the toxic mortgages that had been initiated during the housing boom were going into default in record high numbers. These defaults devastated the value of the MBS. However, the supposed safety net—the CDSs—were too undercapitalized to cover the losses. The resultant effect was disastrous for the financial industry. Companies, many of them large corporations that had been in business for more than a century and that had weathered the Great Depression (1929–1939), were at the brink of failing. In early 2008 the Federal Reserve System, the national bank of the United States, brokered the sale of the investment bank Bear Stearns to JPMorgan Chase. Waggoner and Lynch note that the Federal Reserve agreed to cover $30 billion in bad assets held by Bear Stearns. The media called it the government's "too big to fail" approach, meaning that some banks are so vital to the overall success of the nation's financial industry that they cannot be allowed to fail. However, Waggoner and Lynch point out that it is more appropriate to say that some banks are "too interconnected to fail." They note that "Bear Stearns had a web of intertwined [investment] agreements with other banks, investment houses and corporations." Thus, the failure of one party in the web could bring down all the others.

Yalman Onaran notes in "Banks' Subprime Losses Top $500 Billion on Writedowns (Update1)" (Bloomberg.com, August 12, 2008) that by August 2008 banks and securities firms around the world had suffered losses totaling more than $500 billion due to declining MBS values. In September 2008 the investment firm Lehman Brothers declared bankruptcy after the government refused to bail out the company. However, later that month the government did intervene to save American International Group (AIG), a giant insurance corporation. Meanwhile, the administration of President George W. Bush (1946–) proposed a $700 billion bailout fund to rescue other struggling companies in the financial and automotive industries. It was called the Troubled Asset Relief Program (TARP) and was very unpopular politically. According to the article "Credit Crisis—The Essentials" (*New York Times*, July 12, 2010), "many Americans were angered by the idea of a proposal that provided billions of dollars in taxpayer money to Wall Street banks, which many believed had caused the crisis in the first place." Nevertheless, Congress approved the bailout measure. In February 2009 newly inaugurated President Barack Obama (1961–) proposed and Congress passed a $787 billion stimulus package that included funds that could be used to buy up toxic assets from troubled companies.

Bailout Update

The Congressional Budget Office (CBO) provides in *Report on the Troubled Asset Relief Program—March 2012* (March 28, 2012, http://www.cbo.gov/sites/default/files/cbofiles/attachments/03-28-2012TARP.pdf) an update on TARP funding as of February 22, 2012. The CBO divides TARP funding into four broad categories:

- Capital purchases and other support for financial institutions—$313 billion had been disbursed to assist over 700 businesses. Of the total, $242 billion had been repaid. AIG was responsible for most ($50 billion) of the $67 billion remaining to be repaid. Another $5 billion

was written off by the government as unrecoverable (e.g., because a company went bankrupt or the stock purchased by the government had to be sold at a loss). The CBO anticipated no additional disbursements under this TARP category.

- Financial assistance to the automotive industry—$80 billion had been disbursed to assist General Motors (GM) and Chrysler and their associated financing businesses. Of the total, $35 billion had been repaid and $7 billion had been written off, leaving approximately $37 billion outstanding. The CBO anticipated no additional disbursements under this TARP category.

- Investment partnerships designed to increase liquidity in securitization markets—more than $18 billion had been disbursed through various public-private partnerships that were designed to encourage private investment in certain financial assets. Of the total, $2 billion had been repaid and no money had been written off, leaving $16 billion outstanding. The CBO anticipated that $4 billion of additional disbursements would take place under this TARP category.

- Mortgage programs—$3 billion had been disbursed to programs such as the Home Affordable Modification Program, which is described in Chapter 4. No money had been repaid or written off. The CBO anticipated that $13 billion of additional disbursements would take place under this TARP category.

Commercial Bank Failures

Commercial banks are heavily regulated by the government. They may be chartered (incorporated and authorized to conduct a certain business) at the state or federal level. The U.S. Department of the Treasury's Office of the Comptroller of the Currency (OCC) explains in "Answers & Solutions for Customers of National Banks" (2012, http://www.helpwithmybank.gov/national_banks/index.html) that two federal agencies—the OCC and the Federal Reserve—are responsible for supervising and regulating all federally chartered banks and credit unions and some state-chartered banks. The FDIC has regulatory authority for state-chartered banks that are not members of the Federal Reserve System. All state-chartered banks are also supervised by state banking regulators.

Federal and state regulators closely monitor commercial financial institutions to ensure that they have enough assets to cover their obligations. The regulators close down banks that are in danger of failing and temporarily take over banks that fail. Following the Great Depression, a number of strict commercial bank regulations were implemented. The direct result was that bank failures became very rare. However, the housing industry bust and the crisis in the financial industry that set off the Great Recession in late 2007 triggered historically high numbers of bank failures. The FDIC reports in "Failed Bank List" (November 2, 2012, http://www.fdic.gov/bank/individual/failed/banklist.html) the following number of bank failures per year:

- 2001—4 failed banks

- 2002—11 failed banks

- 2003—3 failed banks

- 2004—4 failed banks

- 2005—no failed banks

- 2006—no failed banks

- 2007—3 failed banks

- 2008—25 failed banks

- 2009—140 failed banks

- 2010—157 failed banks

- 2011—92 failed banks

In addition, between January and October 2012 another 49 banks had failed.

ECONOMIC PERFORMANCE

U.S. businesses produce goods and provide services that are purchased by consumers. The consumption of business output is the major driving force behind the nation's GDP growth.

The U.S. Department of Commerce's Bureau of Economic Analysis (BEA) compiles data on the contributions that are made to the real GDP by various industries. Figure 6.1 shows the BEA breakdown of real GDP growth per year by private industry category between 2008 and 2011. In 2008 the services-producing sector had 0.2% annual growth in the real GDP, compared with −5.1% for the goods-producing sector. In 2009 both sectors had negative annual growth. The services-producing sector dropped to −3.9%, and the goods-producing sector dropped to −6.4%. Both sectors rebounded in 2010, with 3% growth for the services-producing sector and 5.6% growth for the goods-producing sector. Growth slowed somewhat in 2011, but was still positive at 1.6% for the services-producing sector and 2.5% for the goods-producing sector.

Another measure of business output is called "real value added." This is defined as gross output minus the consumption of intermediate inputs. For example, the real value added to the economy by a manufacturer is calculated using the market value of the goods sold minus the cost of producing the goods. Table 6.3 shows the real value added by private industry group between 2008 and 2011. The best performers in 2011 were durable goods manufacturing (7.9%), mining (6.4%), and information

FIGURE 6.1

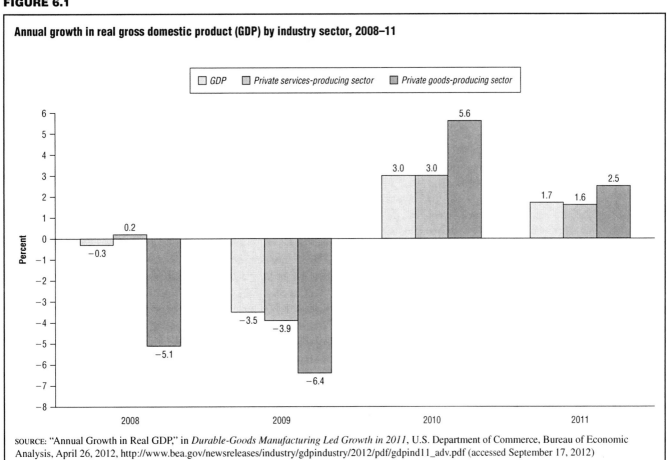

Annual growth in real gross domestic product (GDP) by industry sector, 2008–11

SOURCE: "Annual Growth in Real GDP," in *Durable-Goods Manufacturing Led Growth in 2011*, U.S. Department of Commerce, Bureau of Economic Analysis, April 26, 2012, http://www.bea.gov/newsreleases/industry/gdpindustry/2012/pdf/gdpind11_adv.pdf (accessed September 17, 2012)

TABLE 6.3

Percentage change in real value added by industry group, 2008–11

	2008	2009	2010	2011
Gross domestic product	−0.3	−3.5	3.0	1.7
Private industries	**−1.0**	**−4.4**	**3.6**	**1.8**
Agriculture, forestry, fishing, and hunting	8.7	10.8	−3.1	−12.4
Mining	−3.8	20.9	−6.1	6.4
Utilities	4.6	−11.4	3.3	−6.2
Construction	−6.6	−12.9	−3.2	−0.3
Manufacturing	−5.8	−9.4	11.2	4.3
Durable goods	−1.6	−14.9	17.0	7.9
Nondurable goods	−10.9	−2.7	5.1	0.3
Wholesale trade	−1.1	−13.5	3.9	3.3
Retail trade	−5.7	−2.4	10.1	2.0
Transportation and warehousing	0.9	−12.0	3.5	0.3
Information	1.7	−3.6	3.0	5.1
Finance, insurance, real estate, rental, and leasing	−0.7	1.1	−0.2	−0.8
Finance and insurance	−6.5	6.8	6.6	1.8
Real estate and rental and leasing	2.8	−1.9	−4.4	−2.6
Professional and business services	3.9	−6.9	3.8	4.2
Professional, scientific, and technical services	5.2	−7.0	4.9	4.9
Management of companies and enterprises	2.0	−2.4	−4.4	2.0
Administrative and waste management services	1.7	−9.5	6.4	3.7
Educational services, health care, and social assistance	4.6	1.0	2.8	2.1
Educational services	2.3	0.8	0.2	−0.9
Health care and social assistance	5.0	1.0	3.2	2.6
Arts, entertainment, recreation, accommodation, and food services	−5.1	−7.6	7.8	3.3
Arts, entertainment, and recreation	−5.8	−3.8	6.5	3.3
Accommodation and food services	−4.8	−8.8	8.2	3.3
Other services, except government	−4.2	−5.1	2.1	−0.2
Government	**1.8**	**0.9**	**0.6**	**−0.5**
Federal	2.7	3.7	3.2	0.7
State and local	1.4	−0.4	−0.7	−1.0
Addenda:				
Private goods-producing industries[a]	−5.1	−6.4	5.6	2.5
Private services-producing industries[b]	0.2	−3.9	3.0	1.6
Information-communications-technology-producing industries[c]	6.1	1.7	14.7	6.9

[a]Consists of agriculture, forestry, fishing, and hunting; mining; construction; and manufacturing.

[b]Consists of utilities; wholesale trade; retail trade; transportation and warehousing; information; finance, insurance, real estate, rental, and leasing; professional and business services; educational services, health care, and social assistance; arts, entertainment, recreation, accommodation, and food services; and other services, except government.

[c]Consists of computer and electronic products within durable-goods manufacturing; publishing industries (includes software) and information and data processing services within information; and computer systems design and related services within professional, scientific, and technical services.

SOURCE: "Table 1. Real Value Added by Industry Group," in *Durable-Goods Manufacturing Led Growth in 2011*, U.S. Department of Commerce, Bureau of Economic Analysis, April 26, 2012, http://www.bea.gov/newsreleases/industry/gdpindustry/2012/pdf/gdpind11_adv.pdf (accessed September 17, 2012)

(5.1%). The worst performers were agriculture, forestry, fishing, and hunting (−12.4%); utilities (−6.2%); and real estate and rental and leasing (−2.6%). Overall, the real value added for all private industries in 2011 was 1.8%. This was down from 3.6% in 2010, but up from −1% in 2008 and −4.4% in 2009.

Agriculture

The U.S. Department of Agriculture's National Agricultural Statistics Service (NASS) performs a census of agriculture every five years. As of November 2012, the most recent NASS results available were from the 2007 census. In *2007 Census of Agriculture: Farm Numbers* (February 2009, http://www.agcensus.usda.gov/Publications/2007/Online_Highlights/Fact_Sheets/Farm_Numbers/farm_numbers.pdf), the NASS defines a farm as "any place from which $1,000 or more of agricultural products were, or normally would be, produced and sold during the census year." According to the NASS, there were 2.2 million farms and ranches operating in 2007.

The Department of Agriculture's Economic Research Service provides regularly updated estimates of the farm sector's income and wealth valuation. As shown in Table 6.4, the value of U.S. farm sector production was $418.1 billion in 2011, which included $204.8 billion from crop production, $164.6 billion from livestock production, and $48.6 billion from forestry and services revenues. In 2011 farmers received $10.4 billion in direct government payments. Overall, total production expenses amounted to $310.6 billion and net farm income was $117.9 billion.

Corporate Profits

One of the economic indicators tracked by the BEA is corporate profits. This is a measure of the income generated by corporations from the current production of goods and services. Because only current production

TABLE 6.4

Agricultural sector economic statistics, 2011

Billions of dollars

Year	Value of crop production*	Value of livestock production*	Revenues from forestry & services	Value of farm sector production	Direct government payments	Total production expenses	Net farm income
2011	204.8	164.6	48.6	418.1	10.4	310.6	117.9

*For both crops and livestock, the value of production equates to the sum of cash receipts, home consumption, and the value of the change in inventories. The three components represent a partitioning of the production and the relative shares have no effect on net farm income, thus value of production is the key to understanding the economic forces underlying trends and changes in the farm sector as reflected in the two income measures, net value added and net farm income.

SOURCE: Adapted from "Part 2. Farm Income and Balance Sheet Indicators, 1929–2012F, Expressed in Nominal Dollars," in *U.S. Farm Income and Wealth Statistics*, U.S. Department of Agriculture, Economic Research Service, August 28, 2012, http://www.ers.usda.gov/datafiles/Farm_Income/US_Farm_Income_and_Wealth_Statistics_includes_the_US_Farm_Income_Forecast_2012/Constant-dollar-table.XLS (accessed September 17, 2012)

is counted, corporate profits do not include capital gains, such as inventory profits.

Table 6.5 lists the corporate profits by industry from 2009 to the second quarter of 2012 and the changes per period. Note that quarterly corporate profits are seasonally adjusted at annual rates. Corporate profits totaled $1.8 trillion in 2011, up from $1.7 trillion in 2010 and $1.3 trillion in 2009. In the second quarter of 2012 corporate profits totaled $1.9 trillion. Domestic industries accounted for nearly $1.5 trillion (77%) of the total in the second quarter of 2012. These values included adjustments for inventory valuation and capital consumption.

As shown in Table 6.5, corporate profits with inventory valuation adjustment totaled nearly $2.1 trillion in the second quarter of 2012. Domestic industries accounted for almost $1.7 trillion (79%) of the total. The top-performing domestic nonfinancial industries included nondurable goods manufacturing ($187.1 billion), durable goods manufacturing ($185.7 billion), and wholesale trade ($149.6 billion).

Industry Outlook

Table 6.6 lists the industries that are expected to undergo the greatest growth or decline in output through 2020. This list was compiled by the U.S. Bureau of Labor Statistics (BLS) in January 2012. The BLS expects phenomenal growth (a 14.5% average increase annually) from businesses that are engaged in the manufacture of computers and peripheral equipment. This industry is expected to increase its output by $380.7 billion between 2010 and 2020. Strong performance is also expected from software publishers, with an increase in output of $211.3 billion during this period and an average growth of 8.9% annually. Likewise, businesses engaged in the manufacture of semiconductors and other electronic components are expected to increase output by $146.1 billion during this period and have an average growth of 7.3% annually.

The BLS expects declining output from apparel knitting mills between 2010 and 2020. (See Table 6.6.) Their

output is projected to fall by a total of $7.7 billion, or 7.1% annually on an average basis. Another industry expected to suffer a large decline in output is leather and hide tanning and finishing and other leather and allied product manufacturing. This sector is projected to lose a total of $1.3 billion in output, for an average annual decline of 3.3%. General federal nondefense government compensation, a federal government enterprise, is expected to see its output decrease by a total of $18.3 billion, for an annual average decline of 1.3%.

Table 6.7 lists the industries that the BLS expects will experience the largest average annual growth or decline in wage and salary employment through 2020. Businesses engaged in home health care services are projected to have the greatest annual rate of change (6.1%) by adding a total of 871,800 jobs. Businesses engaged in individual and family services within the health care and social assistance sector are projected to add a total of 851,400 jobs, for an average annual growth rate of 5.5%. Management, scientific, and technical consulting services are projected to add a total of 575,600 jobs, for an average annual growth rate of 4.7%.

According to the BLS, the three most rapidly declining industries in terms of employment are expected to be apparel knitting mills (down an average of 8.3% annually, with 91,600 total jobs lost), leather and hide tanning and finishing and other leather and allied product manufacturing (down an average of 7.6% annually, with 15,100 jobs lost), and the U.S. Postal Service (down an average of 3.2% annually, with 181,800 jobs lost. (See Table 6.7.)

FEDERAL REGULATION OF BUSINESS

Historically, U.S. economic philosophy has been to let the market operate with a minimum of government interference. This does not mean, however, that U.S. businesses go unregulated. Many local, state, and federal laws exist to protect the public and the economy from dangerous, unfair, or fraudulent activities by businesses. Major federal programs that oversee business activities are:

TABLE 6.5

Level of corporate profits and change from preceding period, by industry, 2009–second quarter 2012

[Billions of dollars]

	Level — Seasonally adjusted at annual rates								Change from preceding period						Line
				2011			2012				2011		2012		
	2009	2010	2011	II	III	IV	I	II'	2010	2011	III	IV	I	II'	
Corporate profits with inventory valuation and capital consumption adjustments	1,342.3	1,702.4	1,827.0	1,800.9	1,830.5	1,953.1	1,900.1	1,921.9	360.1	124.6	29.6	122.6	-53.0	21.8	1
Domestic industries	989.5	1,300.9	1,388.1	1,364.7	1,382.7	1,502.2	1,497.2	1,485.3	311.4	87.2	18.0	119.5	-5.0	-11.9	2
Financial	328.9	383.7	381.0	338.3	353.2	441.2	428.9	389.2	54.8	-2.7	14.9	88.0	-12.3	-39.7	3
Nonfinancial	660.6	917.1	1,007.1	1,026.4	1,029.6	1,061.0	1,068.3	1,096.1	256.5	90.0	3.2	31.4	7.3	27.8	4
Rest of the world	352.8	401.6	438.9	436.3	447.8	450.9	402.9	436.5	48.8	37.3	11.5	3.1	-48.0	33.6	5
Receipts from the rest of the world	493.7	584.4	645.2	658.5	650.2	645.2	631.5	641.5	90.7	60.8	-8.3	-5.0	-13.7	10.0	6
Less: Payments to the rest of the world	140.9	182.9	206.3	222.3	202.4	194.2	228.6	205.0	42.0	23.4	-19.9	-8.2	34.4	-23.6	7
Corporate profits with inventory valuation adjustment	1,443.6	1,777.7	1,791.6	1,764.6	1,798.8	1,923.5	2,100.8	2,124.3	334.1	13.9	34.2	124.7	177.3	23.5	8
Domestic industries	1,090.8	1,376.1	1,352.7	1,328.4	1,351.0	1,472.5	1,697.9	1,687.7	285.3	-23.4	22.6	121.5	225.4	-10.2	9
Financial	374.8	424.3	408.3	365.6	380.8	469.1	481.2	441.9	49.5	-16.0	15.2	88.3	12.1	-39.3	10
Federal Reserve banks	47.3	71.6	75.9	79.8	76.6	75.2	74.5	74.2	24.3	4.3	-3.2	-1.4	-0.7	-0.3	11
Other financial	327.5	352.7	332.3	285.8	304.1	393.9	406.6	367.6	25.2	-20.4	18.3	89.8	12.7	-39.0	12
Nonfinancial	716.0	951.8	944.4	962.8	970.2	1,003.4	1,216.8	1,245.8	235.8	-7.4	7.4	33.2	213.4	29.0	13
Utilities	23.1	27.9	17.7	36.5	10.2	15.1	38.3	41.3	4.8	-10.2	-26.3	4.9	23.2	3.0	14
Manufacturing	131.0	233.5	244.9	229.2	248.9	285.9	363.5	372.8	102.5	11.4	19.7	37.0	77.6	9.3	15
Durable goods	21.1	103.1	100.3	87.1	98.6	133.2	174.9	185.7	82.0	-2.8	11.5	34.6	41.7	10.8	16
Fabricated metal products	11.3	15.0	16.4	15.3	16.1	19.4	23.6	24.4	3.7	1.4	0.8	3.3	4.2	0.8	17
Machinery	7.3	17.5	21.5	19.4	22.1	25.6	30.2	33.3	10.2	4.0	2.7	3.5	4.6	3.1	18
Computer and electronic products	19.1	35.2	27.6	25.3	26.4	36.4	42.2	46.2	16.1	-7.6	1.1	10.0	5.8	4.0	19
Electrical equipment, appliances, and components	9.1	7.7	5.1	4.4	4.5	5.4	10.2	7.6	-1.4	-2.6	0.1	0.9	4.8	-2.6	20
Motor vehicles, bodies and trailers, and parts	-49.7	-11.7	-12.7	-14.5	-16.4	-4.8	3.3	5.0	38.0	-1.0	-1.9	11.6	8.1	1.7	21
Other durable goods	24.0	39.3	42.4	37.2	45.9	51.2	65.4	69.2	15.3	3.1	8.7	5.3	14.2	3.8	22
Nondurable goods	109.9	130.4	144.6	142.1	150.3	152.7	188.6	187.1	20.5	14.2	8.2	2.4	35.9	-1.5	23
Food and beverage and tobacco products	43.3	41.2	34.6	34.8	29.4	38.3	47.5	44.8	-2.1	-6.6	-5.4	8.9	9.2	-2.7	24
Petroleum and coal products	11.9	23.5	40.8	48.8	51.8	32.2	45.4	46.2	11.6	17.3	3.0	-19.6	13.2	0.8	25
Chemical products	38.5	45.9	50.1	42.7	51.7	59.1	63.3	65.0	7.4	4.2	9.0	7.4	4.2	1.7	26
Other nondurable goods	16.2	19.8	19.1	15.8	17.3	23.0	32.4	31.1	3.6	-0.7	1.5	5.7	9.4	-1.3	27
Wholesale trade	86.6	98.2	96.3	94.7	105.3	106.0	134.6	149.6	11.6	-1.9	10.6	0.7	28.6	15.0	28
Retail trade	108.0	122.6	108.9	101.9	103.8	120.9	138.6	136.4	14.6	-13.7	1.9	17.1	17.7	-2.2	29
Transportation and warehousing	24.8	48.1	45.5	45.8	45.6	49.5	56.7	55.0	23.3	-2.6	-0.2	3.9	7.2	-1.7	30
Information	72.8	86.0	85.5	90.2	87.5	85.4	109.8	118.6	13.2	-0.5	-2.7	-2.1	24.4	8.8	31
Other nonfinancial	269.7	335.4	345.7	364.5	368.9	340.6	375.3	372.2	65.7	10.3	4.4	-28.3	34.7	-3.1	32
Rest of the world	352.8	401.6	438.9	436.3	447.8	450.9	402.9	436.5	48.8	37.3	11.5	3.1	-48.0	33.6	33

'Revised

Note: Estimates in this table are based on the 2002 North American Industry Classification System (NAICS).

SOURCE: "Table 12. Corporate Profits by Industry: Level and Change From Preceding Period," in *Gross Domestic Product: Second Quarter 2012 (Third Estimate); Corporate Profits: Second Quarter 2012 (Revised Estimate)*, U.S. Department of Commerce, Bureau of Economic Analysis, September 27, 2012, http://www.bea.gov/newsreleases/national/gdp/2012/pdf/gdp2q12_3rd.pdf (accessed October 9, 2012)

TABLE 6.6

Industries with the fastest growing and most rapidly declining output, 2010–20

Industry description	Sector	Billions of chained 2005 dollars		Change, 2010–2020	Annual rate of change, 2010–2020
		2010	2020		
Fastest growing					
Computer and peripheral equipment manufacturing	Manufacturing	132.3	513.0	380.7	14.5
Software publishers	Information	156.9	368.2	211.3	8.9
Semiconductor and other electronic component manufacturing	Manufacturing	143.8	290.0	146.1	7.3
Computer systems design and related services	Professional and business services	258.5	466.5	208.0	6.1
Data processing, hosting, related services, and other information services	Information	168.2	303.2	135.0	6.1
Communications equipment manufacturing	Manufacturing	62.8	105.7	42.8	5.3
Lessors of nonfinancial intangible assets (except copyrighted works)	Financial activities	134.1	219.6	85.5	5.1
Management of companies and enterprises	Professional and business services	318.8	494.7	175.8	4.5
Securities, commodity contracts, and other financial investments and related activities	Financial activities	410.7	636.6	226.0	4.5
Home health care services	Health care and social assistance	48.7	74.4	25.7	4.3
Agriculture, construction, and mining machinery manufacturing	Manufacturing	47.8	72.5	24.7	4.3
Telecommunications	Information	511.3	774.7	263.4	4.2
Manufacturing and reproducing magnetic and optical media	Manufacturing	7.3	11.1	3.7	4.2
Couriers and messengers	Transportation and warehousing	73.9	110.9	37.0	4.1
Commercial and service industry machinery manufacturing	Manufacturing	21.0	31.2	10.1	4.0
Railroad rolling stock manufacturing	Manufacturing	10.6	15.7	5.1	4.0
Outpatient, laboratory, and other ambulatory care services	Health care and social assistance	146.1	215.5	69.4	4.0
Scenic and sightseeing transportation and support activities for transportation	Transportation and warehousing	63.1	93.0	29.9	4.0
Management, scientific, and technical consulting services	Professional and business services	166.7	242.9	76.1	3.8
Employment services	Professional and business services	157.7	229.3	71.6	3.8
Construction	Construction	814.7	1,183.3	368.7	3.8
Automotive equipment rental and leasing	Financial activities	49.7	72.0	22.3	3.8
Other chemical product and preparation manufacturing	Manufacturing	47.3	68.4	21.1	3.8
Most rapidly declining					
Apparel knitting mills	Manufacturing	14.8	7.1	−7.7	−7.1
Leather and hide tanning and finishing, and other leather and allied product manufacturing	Manufacturing	4.4	3.2	−1.3	−3.3
General federal nondefense government compensation	Federal government	147.0	128.7	−18.3	−1.3
General federal nondefense government consumption of fixed capital	Federal government	31.3	27.4	−3.9	−1.3
Fiber, yarn, and thread mills	Manufacturing	44.1	39.9	−4.2	−1.0
General federal nondefense government except compensation and consumption of fixed capital	Federal government	138.5	127.2	−11.3	−0.8
Postal service	Federal government	62.0	57.5	−4.6	−0.8
General federal defense government compensation	Federal government	241.6	225.0	−16.5	−0.7
General federal defense government consumption of fixed capital	Federal government	83.1	77.4	−5.7	−0.7
General federal defense government except compensation and consumption of fixed capital	Federal government	288.6	272.0	−16.6	−0.6
General state government hospitals compensation	State and local government	29.7	28.2	−1.5	−0.5
Tobacco manufacturing	Manufacturing	54.3	52.0	−2.2	−0.4
Fishing, hunting, and trapping	Agriculture, forestry, fishing, and hunting	6.3	6.1	−0.2	−0.3

SOURCE: Adapted from Richard Henderson, "Table 5. Industries with the Fastest Growing and Most Rapidly Declining Output, 2010–2020," in "Employment Outlook: 2010–2020; Industry Employment and Output Projections to 2020," *Monthly Labor Review*, vol. 135, no. 1, January 2012, http://www.bls.gov/opub/mlr/2012/01/art4full.pdf (accessed September 17, 2012)

- Federal Trade Commission (FTC)—created in 1914 with the passage of the Federal Trade Commission Act. Originally intended to combat the rise of business monopolies, the FTC grew to become the U.S. government's consumer protection agency, addressing consumer issues such as identity theft, false advertising, telemarketing and Internet scams, and anticompetition moves by businesses.

- Consumer Product Safety Commission (CPSC)—established in 1973 to protect the American public from unreasonable risks of serious injury or death from consumer products. Through a combination of voluntary and mandatory safety standards, the CPSC tries to prevent dangerous products from entering the market. If a product is found to be dangerous after it has already been sold to consumers, the CPSC has the duty to inform the public and the power to force a recall of the product if it is deemed necessary.

- Equal Employment Opportunity Commission (EEOC)—established in 1965, the EEOC is the primary federal agency responsible for preventing discrimination in the workplace. Its original purpose was to investigate violations of the Civil Rights Act of 1964, which prohibited discrimination in the workplace on the basis of race, color, national origin, sex, and religion. Over the years its powers have been expanded and it has been given responsibility to enforce other antidiscrimination laws.

- Employment Standards Administration (ESA)—one of the largest branches of the U.S. Department of Labor,

TABLE 6.7

Industries with the fastest growing and most rapidly declining wage and salary employment, 2010–20

Industry description	Sector	Thousands of jobs		Change, 2010–2020	Annual rate of change, 2010–2020
		2010	2020		
Fastest growing					
Home health care services	Health care and social assistance	1,080.6	1,952.4	871.8	6.1
Individual and family services	Health care and social assistance	1,215.0	2,066.4	851.4	5.5
Management, scientific, and technical consulting services	Professional and business services	991.4	1,567.0	575.6	4.7
Veneer, plywood, and engineered wood product manufacturing	Manufacturing	64.7	94.9	30.2	3.9
Computer systems design and related services	Professional and business services	1,441.5	2,112.8	671.3	3.9
Cement and concrete product manufacturing	Manufacturing	171.8	236.1	64.3	3.2
Outpatient, laboratory, and other ambulatory care services	Health care and social assistance	1,077.1	1,471.2	394.1	3.2
Offices of health practitioners	Health care and social assistance	3,818.2	5,209.6	1,391.4	3.2
Software publishers	Information	259.8	351.6	91.8	3.1
Construction	Construction	5,525.6	7,365.1	1,839.5	2.9
Commercial and industrial machinery and equipment rental and leasing	Financial activities	113.5	151.2	37.7	2.9
Other professional, scientific, and technical services	Professional and business services	573.1	760.2	187.1	2.9
Facilities support services	Professional and business services	134.0	177.6	43.6	2.9
Community and vocational rehabilitation services	Health care and social assistance	557.5	738.4	180.9	2.9
Lessors of nonfinancial intangible assets (except copyrighted works)	Financial activities	25.2	33.4	8.2	2.9
Other educational services	Educational services	604.2	787.1	182.9	2.7
Automotive repair and maintenance	Leisure and hospitality	799.7	1,037.2	237.5	2.6
Grantmaking and giving services and social advocacy organizations	Other services	394.5	510.7	116.2	2.6
Sawmills and wood preservation	Manufacturing	81.3	105.1	23.8	2.6
Child day care services	Health care and social assistance	851.8	1,101.3	249.5	2.6
Most rapidly declining					
Apparel knitting mills	Manufacturing	157.7	66.1	−91.6	−8.3
Leather and hide tanning and finishing, and other leather and allied product manufacturing	Manufacturing	27.8	12.7	−15.1	−7.6
Postal Service	Federal government	656.4	474.6	−181.8	−3.2
Communications equipment manufacturing	Manufacturing	118.0	85.7	−32.3	−3.1
Computer and peripheral equipment manufacturing	Manufacturing	161.6	117.5	−44.1	−3.1
Pipeline transportation	Transportation and warehousing	42.4	32.6	−9.8	−2.6
Metal ore mining	Mining	36.4	28.1	−8.3	−2.5
Pesticide, fertilizer, and other agricultural chemical manufacturing	Manufacturing	35.3	27.5	−7.8	−2.5
Federal enterprises except the Postal Service and electric utilities	Federal government	76.6	60.2	−16.4	−2.4
Other miscellaneous manufacturing	Manufacturing	266.0	210.3	−55.7	−2.3
Other chemical product and preparation manufacturing	Manufacturing	82.9	68.6	−14.3	−1.9
Metalworking machinery manufacturing	Manufacturing	153.2	130.5	−22.7	−1.6
Glass and glass product manufacturing	Manufacturing	80.7	68.8	−11.9	−1.6
Basic chemical manufacturing	Manufacturing	142.4	121.6	−20.8	−1.6
Electrical equipment manufacturing	Manufacturing	136.3	116.9	−19.4	−1.5
Pulp, paper, and paperboard mills	Manufacturing	112.7	97.4	−15.3	−1.4
Fiber, yarn, and thread mills	Manufacturing	237.8	206.1	−31.7	−1.4
Iron and steel mills and ferroalloy manufacturing	Manufacturing	85.4	74.3	−11.1	−1.4
Petroleum and coal products manufacturing	Manufacturing	114.0	100.0	−14.0	−1.3
Newspaper, periodical, book, and directory publishers	Information	501.3	439.7	−61.6	−1.3

SOURCE: Adapted from Richard Henderson, "Table 3. Industries with the Fastest Growing and Most Rapidly Declining Wage and Salary Employment, 2010–2020," in "Employment Outlook: 2010–2020; Industry Employment and Output Projections to 2020," *Monthly Labor Review*, vol. 135, no. 1, January 2012, http://www.bls.gov/opub/mlr/2012/01/art4full.pdf (accessed September 17, 2012)

the ESA is charged with enforcing a wide variety of labor laws dealing with minimum wage requirements, overtime pay standards, child labor protections, and unpaid leaves of absence. It also provides oversight of federal contractors concerning employment issues.

- U.S. Environmental Protection Agency (EPA)—develops and enforces federal environmental regulations. The EPA keeps track of industrial pollutants and regularly updates its compliance codes for individual sectors and industries.

- U.S. Food and Drug Administration (FDA)—works to ensure that the food, drugs, and cosmetics sold in the United States are safe and effective. It establishes safety and sanitation standards for manufacturers of these goods, as well as quality standards that the goods themselves must meet. The FDA must prove that certain products, especially drugs, are safe and effective before they can be sold in the United States, and it can force products off the market if they are later discovered to be dangerous. In addition, the FDA ensures that the labeling of food, drugs, and cosmetics is complete and truthful.

- Occupational Safety and Health Administration (OSHA)—establishes and enforces workplace safety standards. One or more OSHA standards covers almost every workplace in the United States.

Other Agencies

Besides the previously mentioned agencies, there are a number of other government agencies that regulate specific industries or aspects of the economy. Some of them are well known, whereas many others may be virtually unknown to people outside the fields they regulate. A few examples are:

- Federal Communications Commission—regulates the telecommunications industry, including all television, radio, satellite, cable, and wire services in the United States and its territories

- Federal Energy Regulatory Commission—regulates the national transmission network for oil, natural gas, and electricity

- Federal Maritime Commission—regulates the waterborne foreign commerce of the United States

- National Highway Traffic Safety Administration—regulates automobile design and safety

- Office of Surface Mining—regulates surface coal mining

- U.S. Securities and Exchange Commission—regulates the stock market

Government Regulation and Deregulation

Since the late 1970s the federal and many state governments have lessened their restrictions on certain industries. Called deregulation, this process allows industries to set their own standards and control their own systems of pricing and other business functions. For example, beginning in 1938 the airline industry was regulated by a federal body called the Civil Aeronautics Board, which controlled airlines' schedules, flying routes, and prices. To stimulate competition in the industry, Congress passed the Airline Deregulation Act of 1978. The industry experienced a flood of new airlines that offered low fares to compete with the established airlines. Even though deregulation has actually caused some problems with larger airlines having too much control (or monopolizing) of the industry and with overly crowded flight routes, most economists agree that the result has been a safer, but cheaper, air transportation system. Other industries that have experienced some degree of deregulation include electric utilities, telephone services, trucking, railroads, and banking.

MARKET POWER

One of the foundations of a capitalistic economy is competition. Competition for customers among sellers theoretically ensures that buyers receive the lowest price. Likewise, competition among buyers drives up demand, helping to ensure that sellers have profitable markets for their products. However, sometimes market power becomes concentrated within an industry, for example,

with only one company wielding great control over supply and/or demand factors.

Monopolies

If an industry becomes dominated by one seller, the lack of competition allows that entity to set prices in the marketplace—a situation known as monopolization. The federal government has long fought against monopolization in most private U.S. industries. In 1890 Congress passed the Sherman Antitrust Act to strengthen competitive forces in the economy. Section 2 of the law states: "Every person who shall monopolize, or attempt to monopolize, or combine or conspire with any other person or persons, to monopolize any part of the trade or commerce among the several States, or with foreign nations, shall be deemed guilty of a felony."

However, the law proved difficult to enforce as Congress and the courts argued over its interpretation. In 1911 the U.S. Supreme Court established a historic legal standard in *Standard Oil Co. of New Jersey v. United States* (221 U.S. 1) that the law "prohibits all contracts and combination which amount to an unreasonable or undue restraint of trade in interstate commerce." Mathew Ingram explains in "A Google Monopoly Isn't the Point" (Businessweek.com, September 23, 2011) that "for the purposes of U.S. antitrust law, at least—being a monopoly isn't illegal. What is illegal is either acquiring that monopoly by nefarious or anticompetitive means or using that dominant position in a way that harms the market for those services." Thus, the legal standard focuses on any negative effects on consumers.

It should be noted that the government has allowed monopolies to form in certain industries that are deemed vital to the public interest. Two examples are telephone services and providers of electric power. For nearly 100 years the private company AT&T was allowed to monopolize the telephone services industry in the United States. In 1974 the U.S. Department of Justice filed suit against AT&T, accusing it of using unfair business practices. The suit was finally settled nearly a decade later and resulted in the breakup of the giant company into several smaller business units. Likewise, private utility companies have been permitted by the government to monopolize electric power service in certain geographic areas.

Companies that become hugely successful and powerful in their industry face an increased risk of being accused of using monopolistic practices by their competitors. Dominance also brings more intense scrutiny by federal regulators. This was particularly true for companies that dominated markets in the information technology sector, which came under fire by their competitors and U.S. and foreign governments beginning in the 1990s.

In 1993 the Department of Justice began an investigation of the software giant Microsoft based on allegations that the company was engaging in unfair competition.

Microsoft's Windows program already dominated the operating systems market. By bundling web browsers and other applications with Windows, Microsoft made it difficult for other companies to compete in the market for these other applications. Throughout the 1990s and the first decade of the 21st century Microsoft fought (and mostly lost) antitrust cases that were brought against it in the United States and in other countries. The company paid millions of dollars in fines and agreed to stop bundling other products with Windows.

Google, a major leader in the search engine and Internet advertising markets, came under fire in 2008 when it was accused by competitors of using unfair business practices. James B. Stewart reports in "Few Match Google; Does That Make It a Monopoly?" (*Wall Street Journal*, May 6, 2009) that in 2008 the federal government had threatened four separate times to bring antitrust cases against Google for various company actions. Stewart describes Google as a "natural monopoly," meaning that the company's dominance has resulted from its business skill, rather than from treating competitors unfairly. He calls the company "a victim of its own success" and asks "why would the U.S. government be so eager to punish the country's most successful and innovative start-up in recent memory?" This opinion is broadly shared by free-trade advocates, who argue that government crackdowns on alleged monopolists are bad for business overall.

As Google became increasingly powerful, so did calls for investigation of alleged unfair practices. In July 2010 the French government announced its intentions to investigate Google for alleged unfair practices. In "France Calls Google a Monopoly" (*New York Times*, July 1, 2010), Floyd Norris explains that French regulators accused Google of holding "a dominant position on the advertising market related to online searches." Similar pressures were building in the United States. More than a dozen high-tech companies, including Microsoft, Oracle, Nokia, Trip Advisor, Hotwire, and Expedia, banded together to present their accusations against Google to the public via the website Fairsearch.org. In *Global Scrutiny: Law Enforcement Agencies around the World Are Investigating Google* (August 2012, http://www.fairsearch.org/wp-content/uploads/2012/06/global-scrutiny.pdf), the coalition claims that as of mid-2012 regulators in the United States, South Korea, and France and other European countries were investigating Google for unfair business practices. However, as of November 2012, no formal charges had been filed in these cases.

Monopsonies

A monopsony is a different situation, in which the power lies with one buyer. This arrangement can occur if one company wields enormous power over the suppliers in that industry. The lack of other customers forces the suppliers to meet the price and quota demands of the monopsonist. Monopsony is an obscure economic concept to most Americans. However, during the first few years of the first decade of the 21st century the megaretailer Wal-Mart was widely accused in the media of practicing monopsonism. In general, the accusations were that the company had so much market power that it pressured suppliers to sell their goods to Wal-Mart at extremely low prices, which hurt the profits of the suppliers. As of November 2012, no formal complaints or government actions had been taken against the retail company.

CORPORATE BEHAVIOR AND RESPONSIBILITY

Businesses play a vital role in the economic well-being of the United States. Besides economic performance, Americans also expect businesses to behave in a legally and socially responsible manner. There is no public or political consensus on the exact social responsibilities of businesses. However, it is recognized that the decisions and practices of company officials, particularly of large corporations, affect not only employees and investors but also the communities in which businesses are located. Fraud and corruption at the corporate level can adversely affect large numbers of people. Likewise, poor performance by businesses in meeting environmental, health, or consumer-protection standards has detrimental effects on society at large.

Big Tobacco: An Industry under Attack

During the 1990s several state governments brought lawsuits against the nation's major tobacco firms to recoup taxpayer money that was spent treating sick smokers under state Medicaid programs. In 1998 a settlement was reached in which the companies agreed to pay a total of $246 billion spread among the governments of all 50 states. The payments are to be made over a 25-year period. The settlement also required the tobacco companies to change their advertising methods and to reduce their political lobbying efforts.

In 1999 the federal government filed its own lawsuit, *United States v. Philip Morris Inc.* (116 F. Supp. 2d 131), against the tobacco companies, alleging that the defendants had engaged in a decades-long scheme to "defraud the American public" regarding the safety of cigarette smoking. The case centered on internal documents obtained from tobacco companies that seemed to demonstrate that the companies were well aware that nicotine was addictive and that cigarette smoking caused lung cancer. The litigation dragged on for seven years. In 2006 Judge Gladys Kessler (1938–) of the U.S. District Court for the District of Columbia ruled that the cigarette companies had committed civil violations of the Racketeer Influenced and Corrupt Organizations Act. However, rulings by other courts in 2005 meant that the government could not receive billions of dollars in penalty fines that it had sought from the tobacco companies.

Kessler did issue an injunction ordering the companies to remove terms such as *light* and *ultra light* from cigarette packaging. Both sides filed appeals in the case that proved to be unsuccessful.

These lawsuits represent an unusual occurrence in U.S. history because the state and federal governments brought financial pressure on an entire industry. In 2009 Congress passed the Family Smoking Prevention and Tobacco Control Act, which gave the FDA regulatory control over cigarettes and other forms of tobacco. According to Duff Wilson, in "Senate Approves Tight Regulation over Cigarettes" (*New York Times*, June 11, 2009), the act does not allow the FDA to ban smoking or nicotine, but only to "set standards that could reduce nicotine content and regulate chemicals in cigarette smoke." However, Wilson notes that industry analysts believe the tobacco companies will continue to prosper because "as long as they have a market of addicted customers, even if that clientele is dwindling, they can raise prices to remain profitable."

Corporate Scandals in the 21st Century

During the first decade of the 21st century some of the largest corporations in the United States suffered scandals that seriously eroded public confidence in big business. Most of the misdeeds involved deceptive accounting practices that enriched a handful of top executives, but hurt thousands of employees and investors. The four most notorious cases were:

- Enron—the corporation was an international broker of commodities such as natural gas, water, coal, and steel. During the early years of the 21st century top executives collaborated with Arthur Andersen, the company's accounting firm, to hide debts to make Enron seem more profitable than it actually was. As the deception unraveled, Enron filed for bankruptcy. Thousands of people lost their jobs, along with their health care, retirement funds, and, in many cases, life savings. Even though investors both inside and outside the company lost tens of billions of dollars, Enron wrote $55 million in bonus checks for company executives the day before it declared bankruptcy. Arthur Andersen was found guilty of obstruction of justice. The former Enron executives Jeffrey Skilling (1953–) and Kenneth Lay (1942–2006) and dozens of other people were convicted in the scandal. Lay died of a heart attack before his sentencing hearing. Skilling was sentenced to 24 years in prison and lost subsequent appeals of his conviction.

- WorldCom—in 2002 the federal government uncovered an $11 billion accounting scandal at the telecommunications company. Its resulting bankruptcy left its stock worthless and put thousands of employees out of work. They also lost their pensions and benefits. Several company executives were indicted on fraud charges. The former chief executive officer (CEO) Bernard J. Ebbers (1941–) received a sentence of 25 years in prison.

- Tyco International—in 2002 the company became embroiled in scandals involving its CEO, L. Dennis Kozlowski (1946–), and its chief financial officer, Mark H. Swartz (1960–). Both men resigned and were sued by Tyco in connection with $600 million in loans, salary, and fringe benefits they allegedly took from the company without board approval. The men were indicted for grand larceny and securities fraud. In April 2004 the case was declared a mistrial after a juror who was suspected of communicating with defense attorneys was named in the media and subsequently received threatening letters and phone calls. In 2005 the men were retried, found guilty, and sentenced to up to 25 years in prison.

- Qwest Communications—the government found that executives overstated the company's earnings by more than $2 billion. By the time the scandal became public in 2002 top Qwest executives had sold millions of dollars in company stock, even though they knew the company was in serious financial trouble. Joseph Nacchio (1949–), the former CEO, was sentenced to six years in federal prison, fined $19 million, and ordered to forfeit $52 million he made from illegal stock sales.

Bailout Bonuses

As noted earlier, beginning in 2008 the government decided to bail out several financial and insurance corporations that were in danger of failing. This decision was widely unpopular with the American public because it believed the Great Recession had been caused, in large part, by these corporations. Public dissatisfaction continued to grow when many of the rescued corporations decided to pay large bonuses to their executives.

The furor began in late 2008, when the media reported that the insurance giant AIG still planned to pay out more than $150 million in bonuses after receiving a multibillion-dollar bailout package from the government. The decision was widely criticized as rewarding the risky behavior that drove the company to the brink of financial ruin. However, AIG argued that the bonuses had been promised before the financial meltdown began and still had to be paid. In addition, the company feared that its best-performing employees would quit and go to competing firms if AIG ceased its bonus program.

Throughout 2009 several major corporations in the financial industry were bailed out. They also aroused public outrage by continuing to pay large bonuses. President Obama and many politicians angrily criticized this practice. In December 2009 Obama gave an interview with the CBS show *60 Minutes* (http://www.cbsnews.com/video/watch/?id=5975130n&tag=contentMain;contentBody), in which

TABLE 6.8

Public confidence in societal institutions, June 2012

NOW I AM GOING TO READ YOU A LIST OF INSTITUTIONS IN AMERICAN SOCIETY. PLEASE TELL ME HOW MUCH CONFIDENCE YOU, YOURSELF, HAVE IN EACH ONE—A GREAT DEAL, QUITE A LOT, SOME, OR VERY LITTLE? FIRST, ... NEXT, [RANDOM ORDER]

[In percent]

2012 Jun 7–10 (sorted by "a great deal/quite a lot")	Great deal	Quite a lot	Some	Very little	None (vol.)	No opinion	Great deal/ quite a lot
The military	43	32	18	5	1	1	75
Small business	30	33	29	6	*	1	63
The police	26	30	28	15	1	*	56
The church or organized religion	25	19	29	22	4	1	44
The medical system	20	21	34	23	3	*	41
The presidency	17	20	27	32	4	1	37
The U.S. Supreme Court	15	22	38	20	2	3	37
The public schools	11	18	40	28	2	1	29
The criminal justice system	11	18	41	26	3	1	29
Newspapers	10	15	41	29	3	2	25
Television news	11	10	39	34	4	1	21
Organized labor	11	10	37	34	4	4	21
Banks	9	12	42	33	2	1	21
Big business	9	12	40	34	4	2	21
Health Maintenance Organizations, HMOs	8	11	44	29	3	6	19
Congress	6	7	34	47	5	1	13

*Less than 0.5%

SOURCE: Lydia Saad, "Now I am going to read you a list of institutions in American society. Please tell me how much confidence you, yourself, have in each one—a great deal, quite a lot, some, or very little? First, ... Next, [RANDOM ORDER]," in *Gallup News Service: June Wave 1—Final Topline*, The Gallup Organization, June 7–10, 2012, http://www.gallup.com/file/poll/155261/Confidence_Institutions_Overview_120620.pdf (accessed September 17, 2012). Copyright © 2012 by Gallup, Inc. All rights reserved. The content is used with permission; however, Gallup retains all rights of republication.

he denounced the bonuses and famously proclaimed: "I did not run for office to be helping out a bunch of fat cat bankers on Wall Street."

Jonathan Macey of Yale Law School examines the bailout bonus controversy in "Obama and the 'Fat Cat Bankers'" (*Wall Street Journal*, January 12, 2010). He admits that "many of the banks that got the most bailout money are paying the biggest bonuses." He notes that as of January 2010 Bank of America, Citigroup, Goldman Sachs, JPMorgan Chase, and Morgan Stanley had "allocated about $90 billion for overall compensation, with bonuses comprising more than half." Macey argues that bankers make "relatively modest base salaries," so bonuses for good performance are part of the "basic pay structure" at all major banks, including the bailed-out banks. He believes that bank owners and shareholders (which include the federal government and consequently U.S. taxpayers for many of the bailed-out institutions) actually benefit from the bonuses because they are based on performance. In other words, the bonuses reward the employees who make the largest profits for the companies.

The controversy continued into 2011, when GM announced its plans to pay out bonuses to many of its employees. As noted earlier, GM and its financial subsidiaries received billions of dollars in bailout funds from taxpayers under TARP. Aaron Smith reports in "GM Bonuses to Exceed 50% of Some Salaries" (CNNMoney .com, February 11, 2011) that the company defended the bonuses, explaining that the compensation of its salaried

employees "is based in part on the performance of the company and on their individual performance." In "GM Cuts Benefits for Salaried Staff" (*Wall Street Journal*, February 16, 2012), Sharon Terlep notes that GM also planned to pay out bonuses in 2012 after the company recorded a profit of approximately $8 billion in 2011. However, cost-cutting measures, including reduced benefits, were scheduled to go into effect in 2012 because the company did not meet all of its performance goals in 2011.

Public Perception of Big Business

The Gallup Organization regularly conducts polls that ask respondents about their opinions of various institutions in American society. The results from a June 2012 poll are shown in Table 6.8. Only 21% of those asked expressed a "great deal" (9%) or "quite a lot" (12%) of confidence in big business. In fact, big business rated 14th out of 16 societal institutions that were listed by Gallup for the public's level of confidence. The only two societal institutions that were deemed less trustworthy than big business were health maintenance organizations and Congress. The military garnered the highest rating, with 75% of those asked expressing a "great deal" (43%) or "quite a lot" (32%) of confidence. Small business was the second highest, with 63% of respondents providing a favorable opinion (30% had a "great deal" and 33% had "quite a lot" of confidence). Banks (presumably both large and small) received a much lower rating. Only 21% of respondents had a "great deal" (9%) or "quite a lot" (12%) of confidence in banks.

CHAPTER 7
SAVING AND INVESTING

If you would be wealthy, think of saving as well as getting.

—Benjamin Franklin, *The Way to Wealth* (1758)

Saving and investing are two sides of the same coin. The purpose of saving is to put aside money for use in the future. Saved money can actually make money if it is put into a bank account that earns interest. This is basically a low-risk investment with a low rate of return, but it does preserve the money for the future. Investing is another matter. It means exchanging money for assets that may or may not go up in value over time. Investments that go up in value reap profits for the investor, and those profits can be modest or extravagant. Investments that go down in value are another story. Some or even all the original money invested is lost. Thus, investing entails risk, particularly in a market-driven economy where fluctuations in supply and demand determine the profitability of investments. At a macroeconomic level, the U.S. economy thrives on investing—it provides money for business growth and government expenses. From a microeconomic standpoint, Americans are urged to save and/or gainfully invest some of their earnings to ensure that they have a safety net in the event of a personal financial crisis and to sustain them after they retire.

PERSONAL SAVING RATE

The personal saving rate is a government-measured rate that tracks how much money Americans have available for saving and investing. It is calculated by the U.S. Department of Commerce's Bureau of Economic Analysis (BEA) using data from many sources on income, taxes, government revenues and expenses, and personal expenses. The rate is actually a ratio of two BEA measures: disposable personal income (DPI) and personal saving. The DPI is defined as personal income (e.g., wages and salaries) minus tax and nontax payments made to the government. Personal saving is determined by subtracting personal outlays from the DPI. Thus, personal saving is the money left over. This value is divided by the DPI to show what percentage of the DPI is available for saving and investing.

Because the personal saving rate is based on so many other calculated variables, any small errors in the dependent variables will be exaggerated in the rate itself. In addition, the BEA excludes from its definition of income certain wealth components such as capital gains (which is an increase in the value of an asset). As a result, the BEA admits that the personal saving rate gives an incomplete picture of household savings behavior. However, it is useful for tracking changes over time.

Disposal Personal Income

Table 7.1 shows the amounts and derivations of personal income for 2010 and 2011 and for the first two quarters of 2012 as calculated by the BEA using the National Income and Product Accounts (NIPAs). Note that the quarterly amounts are seasonally adjusted at annual rates. As described in Chapter 1, the NIPAs are estimates of national income. The BEA explains how it compiles the NIPAs in *Concepts and Methods of the U.S. National Income and Product Accounts* (November 2011, http://www.bea.gov/national/pdf/NIPAchapters1-9.pdf). It should be noted that the BEA defines "persons" as "households, NPISHs [nonprofit institutions serving households], private noninsured welfare funds, and private trust funds."

As shown in Table 7.1, personal income consists of the following components:

- Compensation of employees—wages, salaries, and supplements

- Proprietors' income—income earned by the proprietors (owners) of unincorporated businesses, such as sole proprietorships, partnerships, and tax-exempt cooperatives

TABLE 7.1

Derivation of personal saving rate, 2010–11, and first and second quarters 2012

[Billions of dollars]

	2010	2011	Seasonally adjusted at annual rates 2012 I[a]	Seasonally adjusted at annual rates 2012 II[a]
Personal income	12,321.9	12,947.3	13,227.1	13,362.4
Compensation of employees, received	7,970.0	8,295.2	8,495.7	8,562.9
Wage and salary disbursements	6,404.6	6,661.3	6,825.9	6,882.0
Private industries	5,213.3	5,466.0	5,626.8	5,682.0
Goods-producing industries	1,057.5	1,108.6	1,144.0	1,147.3
Manufacturing	674.1	706.6	723.1	726.2
Services-producing industries	4,155.8	4,357.4	4,482.7	4,534.7
Trade, transportation, and utilities	1,005.5	1,050.1	1,083.3	1,096.0
Other services-producing industries	3,150.3	3,307.3	3,399.4	3,438.7
Government	1,191.3	1,195.3	1,199.1	1,200.0
Supplements to wages and salaries	1,565.4	1,633.9	1,669.8	1,680.9
Employer contributions for employee pension and insurance funds	1,097.3	1,139.0	1,159.6	1,167.7
Employer contributions for government social insurance	468.1	494.9	510.2	513.2
Proprietors' income with inventory valuation and capital consumption adjustments	1,103.4	1,157.3	1,184.3	1,197.2
Farm	44.3	54.6	52.3	55.2
Nonfarm	1,059.1	1,102.8	1,132.1	1,142.0
Rental income of persons with capital consumption adjustment	349.2	409.7	445.3	453.4
Personal income receipts on assets	1,598.3	1,685.1	1,696.4	1,735.4
Personal interest income	1,016.6	1,008.8	991.8	1,010.4
Personal dividend income	581.7	676.3	704.6	725.0
Personal current transfer receipts	2,284.3	2,319.2	2,348.0	2,362.0
Government social benefits to persons	2,236.9	2,274.3	2,302.7	2,316.2
Social security[b]	690.2	713.3	753.2	759.4
Medicare[c]	515.3	545.1	555.9	556.9
Medicaid	396.6	403.9	397.6	410.7
Unemployment insurance	138.9	108.0	94.2	83.8
Veterans' benefits	57.9	63.3	68.8	71.5
Other	438.1	440.8	433.0	433.8
Other current transfer receipts, from business (net)	47.4	44.9	45.3	45.8
Less: Contributions for government social insurance, domestic	983.3	919.3	942.6	948.4
Less: Personal current taxes	1,194.8	1,398.0	1,450.8	1,474.7
Equals: Disposable personal income	11,127.1	11,549.3	11,776.4	11,887.7
Less: Personal outlays	10,560.4	11,059.9	11,348.7	11,414.9
Personal consumption expenditures	10,215.7	10,729.0	11,007.2	11,073.7
Goods	3,364.9	3,624.8	3,755.9	3,741.9
Durable goods	1,079.4	1,146.4	1,204.6	1,201.0
Nondurable goods	2,285.5	2,478.4	2,551.3	2,540.9
Services	6,850.9	7,104.2	7,251.3	7,331.8
Personal interest payments[d]	183.8	168.0	175.4	173.0
Personal current transfer payments	160.9	162.8	166.1	168.2
To government	87.4	88.9	90.5	91.3
To the rest of the world (net)	73.5	73.9	75.5	76.8
Equals: Personal saving	566.7	489.4	427.7	472.9
Personal saving as a percentage of disposable personal income	5.1	4.2	3.6	4.0
Addenda:				
Personal income excluding current transfer receipts, billions of chained (2005) dollars[e]	9,035.8	9,340.0	9,435.7	9,523.4
Disposable personal income:				
Total, billions of chained (2005) dollars[e]	10,016.5	10,149.7	10,213.9	10,291.6
Per capita:				
Current dollars	35,920.0	37,012.0	37,571.0	37,862.0
Chained (2005) dollars	32,335.0	32,527.0	32,586.0	32,778.0
Population (midperiod, thousands)[f]	309,774.0	312,040.0	313,443.0	313,976.0

[a]Revised. Revisions include changes to series affected by the incorporation of revised wage and salary estimates for the first quarter of 2012.
[b]Social security benefits include old-age, survivors, and disability insurance benefits that are distributed from the federal old-age and survivors insurance trust fund and the disability insurance trust fund.
[c]Medicare benefits include hospital and supplementary medical insurance benefits that are distributed from the federal hospital insurance trust fund and the supplementary medical insurance trust fund.
[d]Consists of nonmortgage interest paid by households.
[e]The current-dollar measure is deflated by the implicit price deflator for personal consumption expenditures.
[f]Population is the total population of the United States, including the armed forces overseas and the institutionalized population. The monthly estimate is the average of estimates for the first of the month and the first of the following month; the annual and quarterly estimates are averages of the monthly estimates.

SOURCE: Adapted from "Table 2. Personal Income and Its Disposition (Years and Quarters)," in *Personal Income and Outlays: July 2012*, U.S. Department of Commerce, Bureau of Economic Analysis, August 30, 2012, http://www.bea.gov/newsreleases/national/pi/2012/pdf/pi0712.pdf (accessed September 16, 2012)

- Rental income—income from rental properties and royalties received by persons from patents, copyrights, and the rights to natural resources

- Receipts on assets—income from interest and dividends; these are payments that persons earn from their assets and investments and will be explained in detail later in this chapter

- Transfer receipts—payments from businesses and the government; for example, government transfers include unemployment benefits and Social Security payments made to persons

- Personal taxes—taxes that persons pay on their income or personal property, for example, cars

The DPI is the sum of the first five components minus personal taxes. Thus, the DPI is the amount of money that persons have available to spend or save. In 2010 and 2011 the DPI totaled $11.1 trillion and $11.5 trillion, respectively. (See Table 7.1.) In the second quarter of 2012 the DPI totaled nearly $11.9 trillion when seasonally adjusted at annual rates. According to the BEA (2012, http://www.bea.gov/), the DPI grew annually between 1990 and 2008, when it stood at $11 trillion. It declined to $10.7 trillion in 2009 due to the effects of the Great Recession (which lasted from December 2007 to June 2009). The DPI then rebounded to $11.5 trillion as the economy began to strengthen.

Personal Saving

The BEA calculates personal saving by subtracting personal outlays from the DPI. In other words, personal saving is the amount of money that persons have left over for saving. As shown in Table 7.1, personal outlays consist of three components:

- Personal consumption expenditures (PCE)—PCE is the money spent on certain goods and services; a detailed breakdown for the 2011 PCE total of $10.7 trillion is provided in Table 3.1 in Chapter 3

- Personal interest payments—nonmortgage interest paid by households

- Personal transfer payments—payments from persons to the government (e.g., fees and fines) and payments from persons to "the rest of the world"

Table 7.1 shows that personal saving totaled $566.7 billion and $489.4 billion in 2010 and 2011, respectively. In the second quarter of 2012 personal saving was $472.9 billion when seasonally adjusted at annual rates. According to the BEA (2012, http://www.bea.gov/), personal saving fluctuated up and down between 1990 and 2007, but typically stayed in the range of $200 billion to $300 billion annually. In 2007 personal saving was $248.7 billion. It soared to $592.3 billion in 2008 as the economic downturn spurred Americans to spend less and

save more. Personal saving declined somewhat to $508.2 billion in 2009. From 2008 through the second quarter of 2012 personal saving on an annual basis hovered between $470 billion and $500 billion, roughly twice what it was from 1999 through 2007.

Personal Saving Rate Trends

The BEA calculates the personal saving rate by dividing the DPI by personal saving. Thus, the personal saving rate shows the percentage of the DPI that persons saved rather than spent. As shown in Table 7.1, in 2010 and 2011 the personal saving rate was 5.1% and 4.2%, respectively. In the second quarter of 2012 the personal saving rate was 4% when seasonally adjusted at annual rates.

Figure 7.1 shows the personal saving rate on a quarterly basis from the first quarter of 2004 to the second quarter of 2012. The rates were regularly less than 3% per quarter from the first quarter of 2005 to the third quarter of 2007. In late 2007 the rate began a steep upward climb. Throughout 2008 and early 2009 it was typically greater than 5%. Analysts believe this rise was driven by fear. The housing market bust in the latter half of the first decade of the 21st century and the Great Recession gutted home values and greatly reduced the value of other investments into which Americans had put their money (and faith). As the economy improved throughout 2010 and 2011, the personal saving rate generally decreased. In early 2012 it took an upward jog. However, as of November 2012 it remained to be seen whether this increase reflected a lingering upward trend or a short-term fluctuation.

INVESTING BASICS

As noted earlier, personal saving is the amount of money that people have left over for saving. Most people wish not simply to preserve the value of the money, but to use the money to make more money. This is the incentive for investing.

Three of the most important considerations to investors are liquidity, risk, and reward. Liquidity is the ease with which an investment can be transferred into cash. Some people keep cash under their mattresses or in other household hiding places. These savers greatly value liquidity—their cash is quickly and easily accessible whenever they need it. However, the cash is at risk of being stolen or destroyed (e.g., by fire) and it earns no interest. Even worse, the cash actually loses its spending power over time because of inflation.

One of the fundamentals of investing is that reward is usually related to risk; that is, low-risk investments reap relatively low rewards, whereas high-risk investments (if successful) reap higher rewards. Banks, credit unions, and other financial institutions offer accounts in which

FIGURE 7.1

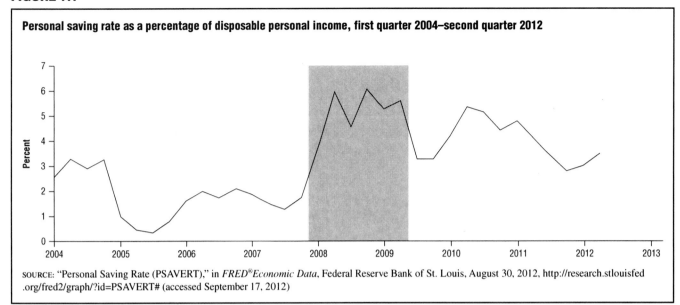

Personal saving rate as a percentage of disposable personal income, first quarter 2004–second quarter 2012

SOURCE: "Personal Saving Rate (PSAVERT)," in *FRED®Economic Data*, Federal Reserve Bank of St. Louis, August 30, 2012, http://research.stlouisfed
.org/fred2/graph/?id=PSAVERT# (accessed September 17, 2012)

cash can be held for safekeeping and perhaps earn interest. The level of liquidity depends on the type of account that is chosen. This is generally a very low-risk investment option. Government entities offer investment options, such as bonds, that are considered to be low risk, because the investments are backed by government money.

The riskiest types of investments, and those with the highest returns, are typically offered by companies. Securities markets (stocks, bonds, and mutual funds) and commodities markets (raw materials and foreign currencies and securities) in the United States are used by corporations to raise money for their business operations and by banks and individuals to build wealth and, in some cases, to pay for retirement. These markets have fueled periods of astounding economic growth (called bull markets), but they have also been at the center of downturns (called bear markets) and disastrous economic crashes, creating the need for an extensive regulatory system. Despite regulations, however, the markets occasionally see high-profile scandals involving major figures in the business world.

Securities are financial assets that give holders ownership or creditor rights in a particular organization. The word usually refers to stocks (which are sometimes called equities). Historically, stocks have appreciated faster than inflation has increased, allowing people to build greater wealth than if they attempted to save money in traditional accounts. Investments can also serve as collateral for certain loans. Besides stocks, there are other types of securities that can be bought and sold on the open market, including bonds and mutual funds. Commodities are typically tangible products (usually raw materials) that are bought and sold in bulk. Financial instruments such as foreign currencies and securities of

the U.S. and foreign governments are also called commodities. Commodities can refer either to the material itself or to a contract to buy the item in the future.

In the broadest sense, any money expenditure that returns a profit is considered to be an investment. Thus, the cost of a college education can be considered to be an investment because it will likely increase earnings potential in the future. However, in this chapter, investments are limited to things that have easily measured financial worth.

FINANCIAL ASSETS

The government does not track the amount of money that people invest, but it does track the value of assets in which households have invested. The Federal Reserve System, the national bank of the United States, in cooperation with the Internal Revenue Service, collects detailed financial information on American families every three years through the Survey of Consumer Finances (SCF). The primary focus of the SCF is to determine Americans' net worth, which will be discussed in detail in Chapter 8. As part of its SCF calculations, the Federal Reserve gathers information about household assets, which it divides into two categories: financial assets and nonfinancial assets. Financial assets include bank accounts, stocks, bonds, investment funds, and other similar assets. Nonfinancial assets include real estate, vehicles, business equity, and other similar assets. This chapter will focus on financial assets, while Chapter 8 will focus on nonfinancial assets.

As of November 2012, the most recent SCF results available were from the 2010 survey. According to Jesse Bricker et al. of the Federal Reserve, in *Changes in U.S. Family Finances from 2007 to 2010: Evidence from the*

Survey of Consumer Finances (June 2012, http://www
.federalreserve.gov/pubs/bulletin/2012/pdf/scf12.pdf), nearly
6,500 interviews were conducted as part of the 2010 survey.
The resulting data are believed to be representative of more
than 117 million U.S. families.

As shown in Table 7.2, 94% of all surveyed families
in 2010 owned some kind of financial asset. The table
provides a listing of the percentage of families holding
different types of financial assets. Demographic and economic information is shown for the families and the
heads of households. The table also shows the median
value (half of the values were less than the median value
and half of the values were greater than the median
value) of the holdings for families holding the assets.

Transaction Accounts and Certificates of Deposit

Bricker et al. note that transaction accounts include
checking, savings, and money market deposit accounts;
money market mutual funds; and call or cash accounts at
brokerages.

Checking, saving, and money market deposit
accounts are accounts held at financial institutions, such
as banks or credit unions, in which customers can deposit
money. In most cases, deposits up to $250,000 are
insured by funds backed by the federal government. This
ensures depositors that their money will be repaid in case
the financial institution goes out of business. The Federal
Deposit Insurance Corporation, an independent government agency, insures funds at banks; the National Credit
Union Administration administers a fund for federally
insured credit unions.

According to the U.S. Securities and Exchange Commission, in "Money Market Funds" (September 23,
2009, http://www.sec.gov/answers/mfmmkt.htm), money
market mutual funds are mutual funds that are "required
by law to invest in low-risk securities." As a result, they
have relatively low risks compared with other mutual
funds. However, unlike deposit accounts at banks and
credit unions, money market mutual funds are not
federally insured. Neither are call or cash accounts at
brokerages, which are accounts in which depositors keep
cash to buy securities.

Compared with other types of investments,
transaction accounts offer high liquidity and very low
risk. The trade-off is that transaction accounts typically
offer lower rates of return, such as interest rates, than
other investments.

Certificates of deposit (CDs) are savings accounts in
which money is placed for a predetermined amount of
time, commonly one to five years, in exchange for payment of a set interest rate throughout that time period.
There are penalties for early withdrawal of the money.
CDs are a low-risk investment; however, because they

offer limited liquidity, their rates of return are generally
better than those for transaction accounts.

As shown in Table 7.2, 92.5% of U.S. families had
transaction accounts in 2010. According to Bricker et al.,
the ownership percentages for these types of accounts in
2010 were:

- Checking account—90.4%

- Savings account—50.5%

- Money market account—17.2%

- Call account—2%

In addition, 12.2% of families held one or more CDs
in 2010. (See Table 7.2.) The median value of the transaction accounts was $3,500. The median value of the
CDs was $20,000.

Savings Bonds and Other Bonds

A bond is basically an IOU (which is short for "I
Owe yoU") from the issuing entity that promises to pay
back the borrowed amount plus interest at a specified
future date (the maturity date). Bonds are sold to investors by government entities, companies, and nonprofit
organizations.

The government issues a variety of securities,
including bonds, with the purpose of earning revenue.
Government entities sell bonds to raise funds for public
projects, such as road improvement or school
construction. The federal government also sells savings
bonds through the U.S. Department of the Treasury.
Savings bonds are not marketable securities. They can
only be sold or redeemed by the Treasury Department. As
shown in Table 7.2, 12% of U.S. families owned savings
bonds in 2010. The median value was $1,000.

Bricker et al. indicate that bonds other than savings
bonds include corporate and mortgage-backed bonds;
federal, state, and local government bonds; and foreign
bonds. Only 1.6% of families surveyed in the 2010 SCF
owned other kinds of bonds in 2010. (See Table 7.2.)
Bond ownership was concentrated in households that
were at the higher income levels. The median value of
family holdings of bonds other than savings bonds was
$137,000. Bricker et al. note that the ownership
breakdown by type of "other bonds" was tax-exempt
bonds (1.2%), corporate or foreign bonds (0.5%),
government bonds (0.3%), and mortgage-backed bonds
(0.2%). Note that tax-exempt bonds are sold by
government entities and nonprofit organizations.

Treasury bills (T-bills) are short-term government
securities sold by the Treasury Department that mature
within a few days or up to 26 weeks. The customer
purchases a T-bill for less than its face value and then
receives face value at maturity. For example, a customer
might pay $90 upfront for a $100 T-bill. When the T-bill

TABLE 7.2

Family holdings of financial assets, 2010

[By selected characteristics of families and type of asset, 2007 and 2010 surveys]

Family characteristic	Transaction accounts	Certificates of deposit	Savings bonds	Bonds	Stocks	Pooled investment funds	Retirement accounts	Cash value life insurance	Other managed assets	Other	Any financial asset
Percentage of families holding asset											
All families	92.5	12.2	12.0	1.6	15.1	8.7	50.4	19.7	5.7	8.0	94.0
Percentile of income											
Less than 20	76.2	5.7	3.6	0.1	3.8	2.1	11.2	10.7	1.7	7.0	79.2
20–39.9	91.1	11.1	6.0	*	6.0	3.5	30.5	17.2	4.2	6.7	93.6
40–59.9	96.4	11.7	10.8	*	11.7	5.8	52.8	19.5	5.5	9.6	97.8
60–79.9	98.9	15.8	16.0	1.3	17.3	8.8	69.7	22.8	6.9	7.3	99.6
80–89.9	99.8	12.1	23.0	2.0	25.7	14.6	85.7	25.8	7.8	8.5	100.0
90–100	99.9	21.5	24.4	8.3	47.8	32.1	90.1	30.9	12.3	10.3	100.0
Age of head (years)											
Less than 35	89.0	5.7	10.0	*	10.1	3.6	41.1	9.6	0.9	9.0	91.3
35–44	90.6	5.7	11.6	0.4	12.1	7.7	52.2	12.3	2.0	8.4	92.7
45–54	92.5	10.0	15.0	1.4	16.0	9.6	60.0	19.8	4.5	7.7	94.2
55–64	94.2	14.6	14.3	2.4	19.5	11.3	59.8	25.7	7.7	8.9	95.8
65–74	95.8	20.6	9.1	3.4	16.1	11.1	49.0	28.4	11.4	7.5	96.2
75 or more	96.4	27.2	10.1	3.6	20.1	11.9	32.8	32.4	14.1	5.0	96.4
Family structure											
Single with child(ren)	84.9	6.7	6.3	*	6.9	3.0	34.0	11.1	3.3	8.3	88.9
Single, no child, age less than 55	88.3	6.0	6.3	*	10.7	5.0	40.2	9.8	1.5	11.3	90.6
Single, no child, age 55 or more	92.8	20.1	7.0	2.5	11.9	9.5	33.7	23.5	9.9	7.7	93.5
Couple with child(ren)	94.3	10.4	18.9	1.2	17.0	9.1	60.1	18.9	3.9	7.6	95.7
Couple, no child	95.9	15.8	12.4	2.9	20.9	12.4	61.6	27.9	8.8	6.7	96.6
Education of head											
No high school diploma	77.4	6.0	2.7	*	2.2	*	17.1	11.9	3.1	5.3	80.8
High school diploma	90.0	10.8	9.1	0.2	8.1	3.2	40.6	19.8	4.2	7.2	92.7
Some college	94.6	11.8	11.7	1.0	11.3	5.4	48.6	17.3	5.5	7.6	95.0
College degree	98.4	15.6	17.7	3.6	27.2	17.6	70.5	23.3	7.9	9.8	98.9
Race or ethnicity of respondent											
White non-Hispanic	96.5	15.0	14.8	2.3	18.6	11.6	58.1	22.6	7.3	8.2	97.3
Nonwhite or Hispanic	84.3	6.5	6.3	0.2	7.9	2.6	34.4	13.7	2.3	7.6	87.2
Current work status of head											
Working for someone else	93.6	9.0	13.7	1.0	13.8	8.1	59.6	17.1	3.6	7.7	95.2
Self-employed	94.8	15.7	12.9	3.5	24.5	14.9	54.7	25.9	8.3	11.1	96.4
Retired	91.7	20.1	9.6	2.6	15.4	8.9	34.4	25.5	10.4	7.3	92.9
Other not working	82.7	3.9	5.8	*	9.5	2.8	24.6	10.2	*	8.3	85.0
Current occupation of head											
Managerial or professional	98.2	14.1	17.3	2.6	24.3	16.0	73.5	21.6	6.8	10.2	99.2
Technical, sales, or services	91.7	7.4	11.0	0.8	10.8	5.8	47.7	17.3	2.8	7.5	93.8
Other occupation	89.6	7.5	11.0	*	8.3	3.1	50.0	15.6	2.4	6.2	91.6
Retired or other not working	89.7	16.6	8.8	2.1	14.1	7.6	32.3	22.2	8.5	7.5	91.2
Region											
Northeast	91.2	12.4	16.9	2.0	16.5	11.7	54.4	20.6	6.1	7.1	93.0
Midwest	94.2	13.5	13.5	0.8	13.8	7.2	54.6	23.3	6.1	7.3	95.5
South	91.1	11.4	9.8	1.5	13.1	7.2	45.9	19.3	5.1	7.2	92.9
West	94.2	12.0	10.1	2.3	18.7	10.4	50.5	16.1	6.0	10.8	95.4

TABLE 7.2

Family holdings of financial assets, 2010 [CONTINUED]

[By selected characteristics of families and type of asset, 2007 and 2010 surveys]

Family characteristic	Transaction accounts	Certificates of deposit	Savings bonds	Bonds	Stocks	Pooled investment funds	Retirement accounts	Cash value life insurance	Other managed assets	Other	Any financial asset
Urbanicity											
Metropolitan statistical area (MSA)	92.8	12.1	12.7	1.8	16.6	9.6	52.2	19.3	6.0	8.1	94.2
Non-MSA	91.2	12.6	8.8	0.8	7.9	4.5	41.9	21.9	3.9	7.5	93.1
Housing status											
Owner	97.4	15.6	15.0	2.3	19.6	11.4	61.7	24.0	7.6	7.6	98.0
Renter or other	82.4	5.2	5.8	0.3	6.0	3.1	27.1	10.9	1.8	8.7	85.8
Percentile of net worth											
Less than 25	78.5	1.4	4.8	*	2.9	*	19.8	7.3	*	5.9	81.7
25–49.9	94.2	5.3	7.0	*	5.6	2.1	42.7	14.2	1.9	8.5	96.1
50–74.9	98.0	14.8	14.2	*	14.0	6.1	58.6	24.1	4.6	7.2	98.7
75–89.9	99.0	27.0	21.6	2.0	26.8	15.5	75.8	30.8	13.1	8.0	99.4
90–100	99.9	27.7	22.8	12.0	54.9	41.8	87.8	36.8	19.3	13.7	100.0
Median value of holdings for families holding asset (thousands of 2010 dollars)											
All families	3.5	20.0	1.0	137.0	20.0	80.0	44.0	7.3	70.0	5.0	21.5
Percentile of income											
Less than 20	0.7	15.0	0.5	20.0	20.0	38.0	8.0	3.1	38.0	2.3	1.1
20–39.9	1.5	15.0	0.5	*	8.0	38.1	11.0	4.2	45.0	2.7	5.2
40–59.9	2.8	18.0	1.0	*	5.6	50.0	22.8	5.0	60.0	5.0	17.1
60–79.9	5.3	16.0	0.7	30.0	13.0	50.0	37.0	7.5	33.0	7.0	39.5
80–89.9	11.1	29.0	0.8	141.0	14.0	65.5	88.0	10.0	82.0	10.0	120.2
90–100	35.0	34.0	2.0	297.2	60.0	200.0	277.0	30.0	150.0	28.0	550.8
Age of head (years)											
Less than 35	2.1	5.2	0.5	*	5.4	8.5	10.5	2.1	9.0	2.0	5.5
35–44	2.5	7.0	0.9	10.0	10.0	41.0	31.2	5.0	10.0	2.7	14.5
45–54	3.5	16.0	0.8	150.0	30.0	110.0	60.0	10.0	50.0	7.0	33.7
55–64	5.0	20.0	1.2	250.0	35.0	110.0	100.0	9.3	65.0	11.0	55.8
65–74	5.7	25.0	4.0	100.0	48.0	115.0	100.0	10.0	95.0	15.0	45.2
75 or more	7.2	32.2	1.0	141.0	45.0	120.0	54.0	7.0	82.0	16.0	43.8
Family structure											
Single with child(ren)	1.0	6.0	1.3	*	15.0	28.0	17.8	2.0	30.0	8.0	4.8
Single, no child, age less than 55	2.0	6.7	0.5	*	7.9	21.0	20.5	5.0	15.0	2.0	7.9
Single, no child, age 55 or more	3.9	20.0	1.7	120.0	37.5	120.0	46.0	4.0	70.0	10.0	22.1
Couple with child(ren)	3.8	14.0	0.8	129.0	15.0	75.0	44.1	8.0	50.0	5.0	25.1
Couple, no child	7.1	30.0	1.2	175.0	33.0	90.0	77.4	11.6	90.0	9.0	57.2
Education of head											
No high school diploma	0.8	40.0	0.5	*	2.7	*	16.3	4.5	50.0	1.3	1.6
High school diploma	2.0	20.0	0.6	49.8	9.5	62.0	25.0	5.2	35.0	3.6	10.3
Some college	2.5	12.0	0.8	40.0	9.9	35.0	27.0	6.0	60.0	5.0	14.1
College degree	9.3	20.0	1.0	150.0	32.0	101.0	76.3	12.0	95.0	10.0	75.7

TABLE 7.2

Family holdings of financial assets, 2010 [CONTINUED]

[By selected characteristics of families and type of asset, 2007 and 2010 surveys]

Family characteristic	Transaction accounts	Certificates of deposit	Savings bonds	Bonds	Stocks	Pooled investment funds	Retirement accounts	Cash value life insurance	Other managed assets	Other	Any financial asset
Race or ethnicity of respondent											
White non-Hispanic	5.0	20.0	1.0	142.0	25.0	91.0	54.0	8.0	73.0	7.5	37.1
Nonwhite or Hispanic	1.6	13.0	1.0	5.0	10.0	50.0	25.0	5.0	25.0	3.0	6.0
Current work status of head											
Working for someone else	3.3	10.0	0.6	100.0	12.5	50.0	35.6	6.0	31.7	3.0	20.0
Self-employed	7.5	30.0	1.3	257.4	50.0	103.6	85.0	19.0	89.0	10.0	50.5
Retired	4.5	30.0	2.0	140.0	35.0	120.0	66.7	7.3	75.0	10.0	29.1
Other not working	1.0	10.0	1.0	*	11.0	120.0	19.3	5.0	*	3.5	2.8
Current occupation of head											
Managerial or professional	8.5	15.0	1.0	170.0	30.0	100.0	73.1	10.0	84.0	9.0	64.5
Technical, sales, or services	2.1	12.0	1.0	36.4	10.0	54.9	25.0	5.0	25.0	2.5	10.6
Other occupation	2.2	10.0	0.5	*	5.6	9.0	25.3	6.0	17.8	2.8	11.7
Retired or other not working	3.0	29.0	1.5	141.0	30.0	120.0	56.5	7.0	73.0	7.0	15.9
Region											
Northeast	4.5	15.0	1.0	104.0	25.0	110.0	60.0	10.0	38.0	6.5	33.4
Midwest	3.4	17.0	0.5	300.0	11.0	52.0	40.0	5.6	80.0	3.0	23.5
South	3.0	20.0	1.0	200.0	20.0	87.5	37.2	7.0	85.0	5.0	16.6
West	4.0	20.0	1.0	100.0	30.0	75.0	45.0	9.0	40.0	8.0	20.3
Urbanicity											
Metropolitan statistical area (MSA)	3.9	19.0	1.0	142.6	23.4	91.0	49.6	8.0	70.0	5.0	23.9
Non-MSA	2.5	20.0	0.5	53.1	10.0	40.0	28.8	5.0	70.0	4.0	13.3
Housing status											
Owner	5.8	20.0	1.0	129.0	26.5	100.0	59.3	8.5	75.0	8.0	45.8
Renter or other	1.0	10.0	0.6	164.0	5.6	20.0	10.0	4.0	16.0	3.0	3.0
Percentile of net worth											
Less than 25	0.6	1.5	0.2	*	1.0	*	5.0	1.5	*	1.0	1.1
25–49.9	1.7	5.5	0.5	*	2.5	5.0	12.0	3.1	10.0	3.0	7.8
50–74.9	5.2	15.0	0.6	*	7.0	20.5	42.0	5.8	30.0	5.0	45.2
75–89.9	14.5	25.0	1.4	50.0	25.0	60.0	133.0	13.7	70.0	10.0	201.0
90–100	60.8	65.0	3.0	220.0	110.0	245.0	413.0	30.0	150.0	70.0	888.0
Memo											
Mean value of holdings for families holding asset	32.4	72.6	6.1	615.0	209.7	388.6	171.2	28.4	247.9	63.9	240.6

*Ten or fewer observations.

Note: For questions on income, respondents were asked to base their answers on the calendar year preceding the interview. For questions on saving, respondents were asked to base their answers on the 12 months preceding the interview. Percentage distributions may not sum to 100 because of rounding. Dollars have been converted to 2010 values with the current-methods consumer price index for all urban consumers.

SOURCE: Jesse Bricker et al., "Table 6. Family Holdings of Financial Assets, by Selected Characteristics of Families and Type of Asset, 2007 and 2010 Surveys—B. 2010 Survey of Consumer Finances," in "Changes in U.S. Family Finances from 2007 to 2010: Evidence from the Survey of Consumer Finances," *Federal Reserve Bulletin*, vol. 98, no. 2, June 2012, http://www.federalreserve.gov/pubs/bulletin/2012/pdf/scf12.pdf (accessed September 14, 2012)

matures, the customer will receive the $100. T-bills can be bought and sold in other markets. Treasury notes (T-notes) have maturity periods lasting two, three, five, and 10 years. They earn a fixed rate of interest every six months. T-notes can be sold by the customer before the maturity date.

Figure 7.2 shows the annual percent yield from 1995 to August 2012 on a 10-year T-note. In general, the interest paid on the 10-year T-note has shown a downward trend since 1995.

Stocks

To raise money to operate and expand a company, its owners will often sell part of the company. A company that wants to raise money this way must first organize itself as a legal corporation. At that time, it creates shares of stock, which are small units of ownership in the company. These shares of stock can then be sold to raise funds for the company. Those who own them are called shareholders in the company. They have the right to attend shareholder meetings, inspect corporate documents, and vote on certain matters that affect the company. Shareholders may also have preemptive rights, which means they are able to buy new shares before they are offered to the public so that existing shareholders can maintain their percentage of ownership in a company.

Not all corporations offer their shares for sale to the public. When a company chooses to do so, its first sale of shares is called an initial public offering (IPO). IPO stock is purchased by investors at a price set by the company.

The money paid for each share of stock is then available to the company for its business operations. In return, shareholders can receive benefits in two forms: dividends and appreciation. Dividends are a portion of the company's profits that are distributed to shareholders. Not all companies that issue stock pay dividends. Those that do usually pay them every quarter (a quarter is three consecutive months of the year; there are four quarters in a fiscal year), and, even though each share of stock might earn only a few pennies in dividends, the total amounts to individual or institutional investors who hold large amounts of shares can be enormous. Appreciation is a gradual increase in the value of a share over time. If a corporation prospers, a shareholder can sell his or her share to someone else for a higher price than he or she originally paid for it. There is no guarantee that a stock will appreciate; however, it is quite possible that it will depreciate over time.

PRICING SHARES. When a corporation creates shares, it determines the price per share for the IPO. From then on the price of each share depends on the public's perception of how well the corporation is doing. If a corporation reports higher profits, then the price per share will likely increase. The challenge for investors is that they cannot predict the future, and stock prices tend to fluctuate up and down over time. A variety of events can influence a stock's price, from the release of a popular new product to news that a company's chief executive officer is being investigated for fraud.

The market for stocks sold by shareholders to other shareholders is called the secondary stock market. It

FIGURE 7.2

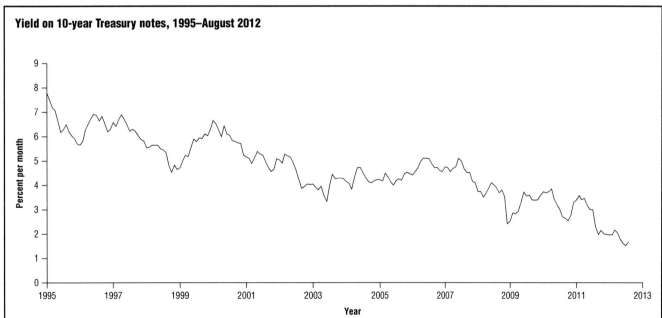

Yield on 10-year Treasury notes, 1995–August 2012

SOURCE: Adapted from "Market Yield on U.S. Treasury Securities at 10-Year Constant Maturity, Quoted on Investment Basis," in *Federal Reserve Statistical Release: H.15. Selected Interest Rates—Treasury Constant Maturities*, U.S. Federal Reserve, September 2012, http://www.federalreserve.gov/datadownload/Output.aspx?rel=H15&series=0809abf197c17f1ff0b2180fe7015cc3&lastObs=&from=&to=&filetype=csv&label=include&layout=seriescolumn (accessed September 17, 2012)

would be almost impossible for all shareholders to find buyers for their shares on their own when they choose to sell. To make it easier for shareholders to buy and sell shares, companies affiliate with a particular stock exchange that handles share transactions. The two most prominent exchanges in the United States are the New York Stock Exchange (NYSE) and the National Association of Securities Dealers Automated Quotations (NASDAQ). The NYSE and NASDAQ are themselves publicly traded companies. The United States also hosts the American Stock Exchange in New York City, the Boston Stock Exchange, the Philadelphia Stock Exchange, the Chicago Stock Exchange, and the Pacific Exchange in San Francisco, California. Additionally, there are stock exchanges in most countries throughout the world.

As shown in Table 7.2, 15.1% of the surveyed families owned publicly traded stocks in 2010. The median value was $20,000.

Corporate Bonds

Another way for a company to raise money is to borrow it. Companies can borrow from banks, just like individuals, but they can also borrow by issuing bonds, which are written promises to pay the bondholder back with interest. Bonds have a face value, called par, and that amount defines the amount of the debt.

A bond offers returns to holders in two ways. The issuing organization will either make regular interest payments on the bond or initially sell the bond at a much lower price than the face value. After a certain amount of time (often many years), the holder can redeem the bond for face value.

Bonds differ from shares of stock in several important respects. First, any organization can issue bonds, whereas only corporations can issue stock. For that reason, unincorporated businesses and federal, state, and local governments use bonds to raise money. Second, bonds provide no ownership interest in the company. The organization's only obligation to the bondholder is to pay the debt and interest. Third, bonds are usually less risky for the purchaser than stocks because the organization is legally obligated to pay the debt, whereas if a corporation has financial difficulties, it is not permitted to pay anything to shareholders until it has paid off its creditors. However, the rate of return on investment for stocks is generally higher than on bonds to compensate for the higher risk factor. Like stocks, though, bonds are traded by investors for prices that may be different from the par value. Investors who buy bonds are buying the right to receive the interest payments and to redeem the bond.

The price of a bond depends on a number of factors, including the organization's creditworthiness and the interest rate. Generally, the better the organization's credit rating, the higher the price of the bond. If the organization begins to have financial problems that will affect its ability to repay the bonds, the price of those bonds will go down. One of the best-known rating companies for bonds is Standard & Poor's, which rates issuing organizations on a scale ranging from AAA to D. Bonds may be short term or long term. Long-term bonds are riskier than short-term bonds and therefore tend to pay higher interest rates.

As noted earlier, in 2010 only 1.6% of U.S. families owned bonds other than savings bonds. (See Table 7.2.) The median value of the bonds was $137,000. Bricker et al. indicate that the ownership breakdown by type of nongovernment "other bonds" was tax-exempt bonds (1.2%; these are sold by government entities and non-profit organizations), corporate or foreign bonds (0.5%), and mortgage-backed bonds (0.2%).

Pooled Investment Funds

Pooled investment funds are funds that combine ownership of various kinds of stocks and bonds. Bricker et al. note that the funds include mutual funds, real estate investment trusts, and hedge funds. Mutual funds are the most common type.

In a mutual fund, the money of multiple investors is pooled and then invested in stocks, bonds, or both. The managers of the mutual fund then buy and sell the stocks and bonds on behalf of the investors. Most investors try to diversify investments; that is, they put money into a number of different types of investments, rather than just one or two (a person's total investments are called his or her portfolio). That way, if one investment loses money, another investment may make enough profit to compensate for the loss.

However, for small investors it can be difficult to diversify. It takes time to evaluate different investments, and small investors may only be able to afford to buy one or two shares of each stock. Most brokers have a minimum purchase requirement that is higher than what the average investor can afford. Mutual funds were developed to solve such problems; by combining their money, small investors are able to diversify.

Unlike the prices of stocks and bonds, the price of a mutual fund is determined by the fund manager, rather than by the open market. This price, called the net asset value, is based on the fund manager's estimation of the fund's value at a particular time. Mutual funds may be purchased either directly from the fund manager or through a broker or other intermediary. The latter is more expensive because the investor will be required to pay fees. Mutual funds provide income to investors in two ways. First, if the mutual fund sells stocks or bonds at a profit or receives dividends or interest payments on bonds, these gains can be paid to investors as distributions. Second, the price of the mutual fund itself may go up, in which case investors can sell their mutual funds for more than they paid.

As shown in Table 7.2, 8.7% of surveyed families owned pooled investment funds in 2010. The median value of the funds was $80,000. According to Bricker et al., the pooled investment funds reflected in the 2010 SCF were largely stock based; that is, 7.7% of surveyed families owned pooled investment funds that were stock based.

Retirement Accounts

Retirement accounts are specially designed to save and invest money deposited by investors while they are young to provide a source of funds when they retire. Retirement fund managers invest the money in various ways, including stocks, bonds, mutual funds, and real estate. Given that Social Security retirement benefits are relatively low compared with a person's career income and that the long-term solvency (the state of having enough money to pay all debts) of Social Security continues to be in question, retirement funds are essential to the baby boom and later generations as they approach retirement age. (Baby boomers are people who were born between 1946 and 1964.)

Retirement accounts were the most commonly held type of financial asset in the 2010 SCF. Just over half (50.4%) of all families surveyed in 2010 had a retirement account. (See Table 7.2.) The median value was $44,000.

According to Bricker et al., the retirement accounts covered in Table 7.2 include both individually purchased and employer-sponsored accounts. The latter are particularly appealing to employees, because some employers contribute money or company stock to their employees' retirement accounts. Some retirement accounts feature appealing tax advantages. For example, 401(k) plans are funds that workers can contribute to on a before-tax basis and that grow tax-free until the money is withdrawn. This is beneficial, because retirees (by virtue of their lower incomes) are typically in lower income tax brackets than they were during their working years.

According to the Investment Company Institute, in *2012 Investment Company Fact Book* (2012, http://icifactbook.org/2012_factbook.pdf), U.S. retirement assets totaled nearly $13 trillion in 2011, up from $7.2 trillion in 2000. In 2011 most of the money ($11.6 trillion, or 90% of the total) was invested in mutual funds.

Cash Value Life Insurance

Cash value life insurance combines the chief benefit of a life insurance policy (i.e., a payout upon the policyholder's death) with an investment vehicle. The policyholder's premiums are invested, for example, in stocks, bonds, or mutual funds, by the fund administrator.

As shown in Table 7.2, 19.7% of surveyed families in 2010 owned cash value life insurance. The median value was $7,300. Bricker et al. note that the SCF accounts for the current cash value of the life insurance policies, not the death penalty that will be paid out at some point in the future.

Other Financial Assets

The 2010 SCF revealed that 5.7% of the surveyed families had a managed asset in 2010 other than the ones described so far. (See Table 7.2.) According to Bricker et al., other managed assets include personal annuities and trusts with an equity interest and managed investment accounts. The median value of these assets in 2010 was $70,000.

As shown in Table 7.2, 8% of the surveyed families owned some other type of financial asset in 2010 with a median value of $5,000. Bricker et al. note that these assets include oil and gas leases, futures contracts, royalties, proceeds from lawsuits or estates in settlement, and loans made by households to other people. Futures contracts typically involve commodities.

COMMODITIES. The term *commodity*, in the narrow sense used in this chapter, means a contract to buy or sell something that will be available in the future. (In a broader sense, anything that can be bought or sold is a commodity.) These sorts of agreements are traded in commodities exchanges. Two important exchanges in the United States are the Chicago Board of Trade and the Kansas City Board of Trade.

There are two basic types of commodities. Futures are standardized contracts in which the seller promises to deliver a particular good to the buyer at a specified time in the future, at which point the buyer will pay the seller the price called for in the contract. Options on futures (which are usually simply called options) are more complicated. Depending on their exact terms, they establish the right of the buyer of the option to either buy or sell a futures contract for a specified price. Options that establish the right to buy a futures contract are call options. Those that establish the right to sell a futures contract are put options. In either case, the buyer of the option only has a limited time in which he or she can exercise his or her right, but the buyer is also free not to exercise the right at all.

The meaning of a commodities contract has changed over the years. Raw materials and agricultural commodities have been traded through commodities exchanges since the mid-19th century. More recently, commodities markets have expanded to include trading in foreign currencies, U.S. and foreign government securities, and U.S. and foreign stock indexes.

Because contracts are made before the goods are actually available, commodities are by their very nature speculative. Buyers purchase commodities because they think their value may increase over time, whereas the sellers think their value may decrease. For example, the seller of a grain futures contract may believe there will be a surplus of grain that will drive down prices, whereas the buyer thinks a shortage of grain will drive up prices. It is the speculative nature of commodities that makes them interesting to investors. Even if they have no need for the goods that the commodities contracts represent, speculative investors can make a profit by buying the commodities contracts at low prices and then selling them to others when prices rise. Commodities respond differently than stocks and bonds to market forces such as inflation; therefore, they can be a valuable part of a diversified portfolio. However, they are riskier and more difficult to understand.

HOMEOWNERSHIP AS AN INVESTMENT

One of the largest investments made by most Americans is the purchase of a home. Because real estate tends to appreciate (increase in value), buying a home is considered to be a relatively low-risk investment. However, this conventional wisdom proved faulty when the housing market bust in the latter half of the first decade of the 21st century enveloped the country. As noted in Chapter 4, home prices actually depreciated (decreased in value) beginning in 2008. Likewise, historical high foreclosure rates meant that many Americans lost both their home and a substantial investment in their future. As shown in Figure 4.4 in Chapter 4, the nation's homeownership rate peaked at 69.4% in 2004 and then declined to 65.6% by the second quarter of 2012.

Home Mortgages

The Federal Reserve compiles home mortgage data on a quarterly and annual basis. These values are published in tabular form in "L.218 Home Mortgages"

as part of the *Federal Reserve Statistical Release Z.1: Flow of Funds Accounts of the United States* (September 20, 2012, http://www.federalreserve.gov/releases/z1/Current/z1.pdf). The Federal Reserve only includes mortgages that are secured by one-to-four family properties, including owner-occupied condominium units. Mortgage types include first and second mortgages, home equity lines of credit, mortgages held by households under seller-financing arrangements, and construction and land development loans that are associated with one-to-four family residences.

Table 7.3 lists outstanding mortgage amounts reported by the Federal Reserve as annual amounts from 2006 to 2010 and from the first quarter of 2011 to the second quarter of 2012. In the second quarter of 2012 outstanding mortgages totaled over $10 trillion. The vast majority of this amount—nearly $9.6 trillion, or 96% of the total—was devoted to the household sector. Another $429 billion in mortgages was attributed to nonfinancial, noncorporate businesses and $9.9 billion was devoted to nonfinancial corporate businesses. After rising from 2006 to 2007, the total amount of home mortgages was relatively flat from 2007 to 2008 and then declined through the second quarter of 2012.

GOVERNMENT REGULATION OF THE MARKET SYSTEM

The prices of stocks, bonds, and commodities fluctuate naturally, which generally is not cause for concern. However, when fluctuations are created as a result of greed or corruption, or by the creation of artificial and unsustainable conditions, the results can be disastrous. Such was the case in 1929, when the stock market crashed and ushered in the period known as the Great Depression (1929–1939). The exact causes of the 1929 crash and the ensuing depression are complex and reach far beyond U.S. borders. However, certain conditions related to the U.S. stock market were significant contributors to the economic disaster. The federal government under President Franklin D. Roosevelt (1882–1945), who served from 1933 to 1945, passed a number of laws that

TABLE 7.3

Home mortgages on 1–4 family properties, including farm houses, 2006–second quarter 2012

[Billions of dollars. Amounts outstanding end of period, not seasonally adjusted.]

						2011				2012	
	2006	2007	2008	2009	2010	Q1	Q2	Q3	Q4	Q1	Q2
Total liabilities	**10,469.8**	**11,194.2**	**11,088.3**	**10,888.9**	**10,422.2**	**10,347.7**	**10,282.0**	**10,223.8**	**10,167.1**	**10,081.0**	**10,028.0**
Household sector	9,879.2	10,566.9	10,514.7	10,369.2	9,950.9	9,884.7	9,826.5	9,773.7	9,721.6	9,640.0	9,589.1
Nonfinancial corporate business	39.4	42.2	32.7	20.3	13.6	12.4	11.4	10.7	10.2	9.9	9.9
Nonfinancial noncorporate business	551.2	585.1	540.9	499.4	457.8	450.7	444.1	439.4	435.3	431.1	429.0

SOURCE: Adapted from "L.218. Home Mortgages," in *Flow of Funds Accounts of the United States; Flows and Outstandings Second Quarter 2012*, Board of Governors of the Federal Reserve System, September 20, 2012, http://www.federalreserve.gov/Releases/Z1/Current/z1.pdf (accessed September 20, 2012)

were designed to prevent the sort of abuses of the market that led to the Great Depression, laws that form the basis for the modern market regulatory system.

An Unregulated System

At the time of the 1929 crash, the stock market was largely unregulated. In the months before the crash, there were signs that the system was beginning to collapse under its own weight, but the industrialists who owned most of the real wealth fed millions of dollars into the market to stabilize it. They were successful for a time, but the artificial conditions created through margin buying (the buying of many market shares at a deflated value) and wild speculation eventually brought the whole system down. Most people lost all, or nearly all, of the money they had invested in the stock market.

Regulation of Securities

Beginning in 1933 Congress enacted a series of laws that were designed to regulate the securities markets. The Securities Act of 1933 (sometimes referred to as the Truth in Securities law) was a reaction against the events that led up to the stock market crash of 1929. Its purpose was relatively simple: to protect investors by ensuring that they receive full information on the securities offered for sale to the public and to prohibit fraud in such sales. The Securities Act set up a system whereby most corporations that wanted to offer shares for sale to the public had to register their securities; the registration information was then made available to the public for review. The required registration forms (which are still being used in the 21st century) contained information on the company's management and business structure, its financial statements, and the securities it was offering for sale. This system was intended to protect investors by making available any information they needed to make informed decisions about their investments, although the truth or accuracy of the information was not guaranteed.

With the passage of the Securities Exchange Act of 1934, Congress established the U.S. Securities and Exchange Commission (SEC), which regulates the entire U.S. securities industry. The SEC expanded the Securities Act of 1933 to require more stringent reporting of publicly traded companies and all other entities involved in securities transactions, including stockbrokers, dealers, transfer agents, and exchanges. Additionally, large companies with more than $10 million in assets and 500 shareholders are required to file regular reports with the SEC detailing their finances and business dealings. The Securities Exchange Act of 1934 also explicitly outlawed illegal insider trading.

Since the 1930s, additional legislation has been passed to increase oversight of the securities and commodities futures trading industries, to prevent fraud, and to reassure investors.

WEAKNESSES IN THE MARKET SYSTEM

Even with careful oversight, fraudulent activities can occur in the securities industry. Securities fraud and the ensuing scandals are devastating to investors and to the markets as a whole. There were many high-profile instances of accounting scandals and securities fraud during the first decade of the 21st century.

Illegal Insider Trading

Insider trading is the buying or selling of stock by someone who has information about the company that other stockholders do not have. Most often, it refers to directors, officers, or employees buying or selling their own company's stock. Insider trading alone is not illegal, but insiders must report their stock transactions to the SEC. Insider trading becomes illegal when it is not reported to the SEC and breaches a fiduciary duty to the corporation; that is, when it violates a duty to act in the corporation's best interests. Most often, this happens when someone within the company has confidential information and uses it as the basis for a stock transaction. For example, if a company officer knows that the company is going to file for bankruptcy the next day and sells his or her shares of the company's stock because the stock price will likely plummet, the trading is illegal. The same goes for someone who gives the information to an outside stockholder so he or she can act on it.

The best-known case of illegal insider trading during the first decade of the 21st century involved the company ImClone Systems, the media mogul Martha Stewart (1941–), and the stockbroker Peter Bacanovic (1962–). The SEC alleged that Bacanovic passed confidential information to Stewart and that she sold her stock in ImClone because of that information. The SEC also accused Stewart and Bacanovic of trying to cover up the matter afterward by lying to federal investigators. The insider trading charge against Stewart was dropped, but she was convicted of lying to investigators and obstruction of justice. Bacanovic was convicted of most of the charges against him. Stewart and Bacanovic were both sentenced to five months in prison.

Overvaluing and Accounting Scandals

Overvaluing is the overstatement of income by companies with the assistance of their accountants to create an inflated impression of financial success among investors, thereby increasing the value of stock. During the first decade of the 21st century Wall Street experienced many scandals concerning such accounting practices at major corporations. The most egregious and notorious breaches of regulations occurred at three companies: Enron, WorldCom, and Tyco International (see Chapter 6). All three became targets of SEC investigations, with company executives brought up on criminal fraud charges and investors losing billions of dollars.

Ponzi Schemes

A Ponzi scheme is a fraudulent investment deal in which the person perpetrating the scheme convinces potential investors that he or she has special investment know-how and can gain them large returns on their investment. The fraudster collects money from an initial group of investors. He or she then convinces additional people to invest and uses part of their money to pay the dividends that the first group is expecting. The initial investors are so pleased that they invest even more money, and so the scheme continues. The fraudster must continually recruit new investors and/or collect more money from existing investors to keep the scam going.

In "The Real Ponzi" (January 2009, http://www.social security.gov/history/ponzi.htm), the Social Security Administration (SSA) notes that the scheme is named after Charles Ponzi (1883–1949), an investment broker who conducted such a scam in 1920 in Boston, Massachusetts. Ponzi sold bonds to his investors and promised them a 50% to 100% return on their investments. He managed to maintain his scheme for seven months before being found out by the authorities. During that time he pulled in an estimated $10 million from around 10,000 investors. Ponzi became a near-instant millionaire and bought a large and expensive house for himself. The SSA reports that after seven years of litigation Ponzi's investors each received, on average, 37 cents for each dollar they had invested.

There are many variations of the classic Ponzi scheme. In 2008 the investment broker Bernard Madoff (1938–) confessed to his sons that he had been running a Ponzi-type investment scam for over a decade. Madoff eventually pleaded guilty and in June 2009 was sentenced to 150 years in prison. In "The Madoff Scam: Meet the Liquidator" (June 20, 2010, http://www.cbsnews.com/stories/2009/09/24/60minutes/main5339719.shtml?tag=currentVideoInfo; segmentUtilities), the CBS program *60 Minutes* reports that Madoff had collected nearly $36 billion from thousands of investors. Approximately half of that money went missing (i.e., could not be found in Madoff's company accounts) before the scam collapsed. As of November 2012, Madoff remained in federal prison. His scam is considered to be the largest Ponzi scheme in U.S. history.

CHAPTER 8
WEALTH IN THE UNITED STATES

All communities divide themselves into the few and the many. The first are the rich and the well-born, the other the mass of the people.

—Alexander Hamilton, 1787

Wealth is collected assets: cash, commodities, stocks, bonds, businesses, and properties. In the United States a small percentage of people have enormous wealth and the rest of the population has far less wealth. Is this a natural and acceptable result of capitalism or an economic injustice that must be righted for the good of society? This is a debate that has raged since the nation was founded. Some people believe the accumulation of great wealth is possible for anyone in the United States as the reward for hard work, ingenuity, and wise decision making. However, other people believe American political, business, and social systems are unfairly structured so as to limit wealth building by certain segments of the population.

WEALTH AND NET WORTH

The components of wealth can be divided into two broad categories: nonfinancial assets and financial assets. Nonfinancial assets are tangible things that have value in and of themselves. Examples include gold, land, houses, cars, boats, artwork, jewelry, and all other durable consumer goods with recognizable value in the marketplace. Financial assets are financial devices that have worth because they have perceived value. The most obvious examples are stocks and bonds. Other devices often counted as financial assets include pensions (which are promises of future income), life insurance policies with cash value, and insurance policies on tangible assets because they protect valuable resources.

The federal government does not measure the overall wealth of individual Americans or the population as a whole. However, it does compile data on related economic indicators that include wealth assets. One of these measures is called net worth.

Net Worth

Net worth is the sum of all assets minus the sum of all liabilities (such as debts). The Federal Reserve System, the national bank of the United States, computes the aggregate net worth of households and nonprofit organizations (NPOs) on a quarterly and annual basis. These values are published in tabular form in "B.100 Balance Sheet of Households and Nonprofit Organizations" as part of the *Federal Reserve Statistical Release Z.1: Flow of Funds Accounts of the United States* (September 20, 2012, http://www.federalreserve.gov/releases/z1/Current/z1.pdf). Table 8.1 shows the net worth data for the second quarter of 2012.

ASSETS. Overall, U.S. households and NPOs had assets of $76.1 trillion at the end of the second quarter of 2012; of this, $24.2 trillion was in nonfinancial assets and $51.9 trillion was in financial assets. (See Table 8.1.) The Federal Reserve includes only four components in nonfinancial assets: real estate held by households ($16.9 trillion), real estate held by NPOs ($2.2 trillion), NPO equipment and software ($325.7 billion), and consumer durable goods ($4.8 trillion). Figure 8.1 shows the breakdown of these assets at the end of the second quarter of 2012. Real estate held by households accounted for the vast majority (70%) of nonfinancial assets, followed by consumer durable goods (20%), real estate held by NPOs (9%), and NPO-owned equipment and software (1%).

Financial assets were much more diverse in type. The largest components of the $51.9 trillion held in financial assets at the end of the second quarter of 2012 were pension fund reserves ($13.7 trillion, or 26% of the total), corporate equities ($9.2 trillion, or 18% of the total), and deposits and currency ($8.7 trillion, or 17% of the total). (See Table 8.1 and Figure 8.2.) Deposits include monies in checking and savings accounts and in money market funds.

Figure 8.3 shows the breakdown of financial and nonfinancial assets for households and NPOs from 2006 to the second quarter of 2012. The total value of assets peaked at

TABLE 8.1

Balance sheet of households and nonprofit organizations, second quarter 2012

[Billions of dollars. Amounts outstanding end of period, not seasonally adjusted.]

	2012
	Q2
Assets	**76,126.9**
Nonfinancial assets	24,201.2
Real estate	19,056.5
Households[a, b]	16,864.4
Nonprofit organizations	2,192.0
Equipment and software owned by nonprofit organizations[c]	325.7
Consumer durable goods[c]	4,819.0
Financial assets	51,925.6
Deposits	8,658.6
Foreign deposits	47.7
Checkable deposits and currency	625.6
Time and savings deposits	6,935.1
Money market fund shares	1,050.2
Credit market instruments	4,788.4
Open market paper	47.1
Treasury securities	878.2
Savings bonds	184.3
Other Treasury	693.9
Agency- and GSE-backed securities	6.5
Municipal securities	1,810.0
Corporate and foreign bonds	1,948.9
Other loans and advances[d]	26.1
Mortgages	71.5
Corporate equities[a]	9,216.3
Mutual fund shares[e]	5,065.7
Security credit	777.7
Life insurance reserves	1,201.1
Pension fund reserves	13,656.2
Equity in noncorporate business[f]	7,691.9
Miscellaneous assets	869.8
Liabilities	**13,458.5**
Credit market instruments	12,895.5
Home mortgages[g]	9,589.1
Consumer credit	2,661.1
Municipal securities[h]	247.6
Depository institution loans n.e.c.	88.5
Other loans and advances	137.6
Commercial mortgages[h]	171.6
Security credit	244.5
Trade payables[h]	290.5
Deferred and unpaid life insurance premiums	28.0
Net worth	**62,668.4**
Memo:	
Replacement-cost value of structures:	
Residential	14,368.3
Households	14,159.4
Nonprofit organizations	208.9
Nonresidential (nonprofits)	1,512.6
Disposable personal income (SAAR)	11,887.7
Household net worth as percentage of disposable personal income (SAAR)	527.2
Owners' equity in household real estate[i]	7,275.3
Owners' equity as percentage of household real estate[j]	43.1

year-end 2007 at $80.3 trillion and then plummeted to $67.6 trillion by year-end 2008. Assets grew slightly in value during 2009 and 2010 and then remained relatively flat through 2011. At the end of the first quarter of 2012 assets were valued at $76.4 trillion. Their value fell slightly to $76.1 trillion at the end of the second quarter of 2012.

LIABILITIES. Assets alone do not provide an indication of the nation's wealth status. Debts and other obligations, known as liabilities, must be subtracted. These liabilities

TABLE 8.1

Balance sheet of households and nonprofit organizations, second quarter 2012 [CONTINUED]

[Billions of dollars. Amounts outstanding end of period, not seasonally adjusted.]

Note: Sector includes domestic hedge funds, private equity funds, and personal trusts.
[a]At market value.
[b]All types of owner-occupied housing including farm houses and mobile homes, as well as second homes that are not rented, vacant homes for sale, and vacant land.
[c]At replacement (current) cost.
[d]Syndicated loans to nonfinancial corporate business by nonprofits and domestic hedge funds.
[e]Value based on the market values of equities held and the book value of other assets held by mutual funds.
[f]Net worth of nonfinancial noncorporate business and owners' equity in unincorporated security brokers and dealers.
[g]Includes loans made under home equity lines of credit and home equity loans secured by Junior liens.
[h]Liabilities of nonprofit organizations.
[i]Households less home mortgages.
[j]Owners' equity in household real estate divided by households.

SOURCE: Adapted from "B.100. Balance Sheet of Households and Nonprofit Organizations," in *Flow of Funds Accounts of the United States; Flows and Outstandings Second Quarter 2012*, Board of Governors of the Federal Reserve System, September 20, 2012, http://www.federalreserve.gov/Releases/Z1/Current/z1.pdf (accessed September 20, 2012)

FIGURE 8.1

Nonfinancial assets of households and nonprofit organizations (NPOs) at end of second quarter 2012

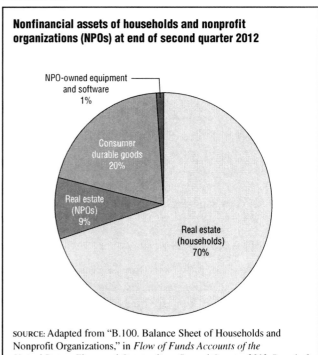

SOURCE: Adapted from "B.100. Balance Sheet of Households and Nonprofit Organizations," in *Flow of Funds Accounts of the United States; Flows and Outstandings Second Quarter 2012*, Board of Governors of the Federal Reserve System, September 20, 2012, http://www.federalreserve.gov/Releases/Z1/Current/z1.pdf (accessed September 20, 2012)

totaled almost $13.5 trillion at the end of the second quarter of 2012. (See Table 8.1.) Credit market instruments accounted for the vast majority of this total, at $12.9 trillion. Home mortgages ($9.6 trillion) were the single largest credit market instrument, followed by consumer credit ($2.7 trillion). Both of these liabilities were described in detail in Chapter 7.

FIGURE 8.2

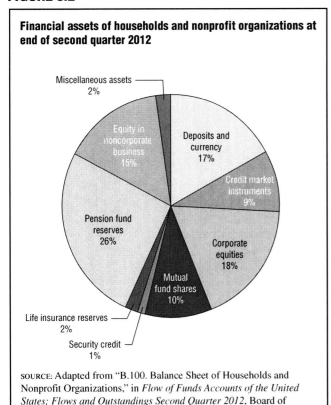

Financial assets of households and nonprofit organizations at end of second quarter 2012

Miscellaneous assets
2%

Equity in noncorporate business
15%

Deposits and currency
17%

Credit market instruments
9%

Pension fund reserves
26%

Corporate equities
18%

Mutual fund shares
10%

Life insurance reserves
2%

Security credit
1%

SOURCE: Adapted from "B.100. Balance Sheet of Households and Nonprofit Organizations," in *Flow of Funds Accounts of the United States; Flows and Outstandings Second Quarter 2012*, Board of Governors of the Federal Reserve System, September 20, 2012, http://www.federalreserve.gov/Releases/Z1/Current/z1.pdf (accessed September 20, 2012)

TRENDS IN NET WORTH. The net worth of U.S. households and NPOs totaled $62.7 trillion at the end of the second quarter of 2012. (See Table 8.1.) Figure 8.4 compares this value to net worth values calculated by the Federal Reserve dating back to 2006. Net worth was approximately $66 trillion in 2006 and 2007 and then plummeted to $53.5 trillion in 2008. Net worth grew slowly, reaching $61.1 trillion at the end of the second quarter of 2011. After falling at the end of the third and fourth quarters of 2011, it bounced back to $62.7 trillion at the end of the second quarter of 2012.

Personal Income and Income Inequality

The U.S. Department of Commerce's Bureau of Economic Analysis (BEA) collects data on the personal income of Americans. As shown in Table 7.1 in Chapter 7, personal income consists of employee compensation (wages, salaries, and supplements), proprietors' income (income earned by the owners of unincorporated businesses), rental income, income from interest and dividends, and transfer receipts (e.g., unemployment benefits or Social Security benefits). Historically, employee compensation makes up the largest component of personal income. In 2011 employee compensation accounted for $8.3 trillion, or 64% of the $12.9 trillion in personal income. Thus, employment factors are extremely important to a discussion of wealth and its distribution.

FIGURE 8.3

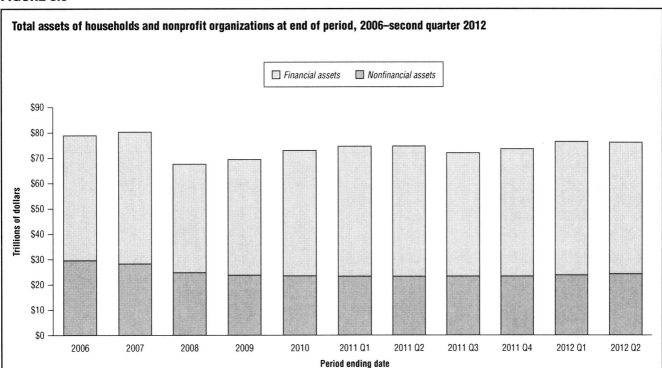

Total assets of households and nonprofit organizations at end of period, 2006–second quarter 2012

☐ *Financial assets*   ☐ *Nonfinancial assets*

Period ending date

SOURCE: Adapted from "B.100.e Balance Sheet of Households and Nonprofit Organizations with Equity Detail," in *Flow of Funds Accounts of the United States; Flows and Outstandings Second Quarter 2012*, Board of Governors of the Federal Reserve System, September 20, 2012, http://www.federalreserve.gov/Releases/Z1/Current/z1.pdf (accessed September 20, 2012)

FIGURE 8.4

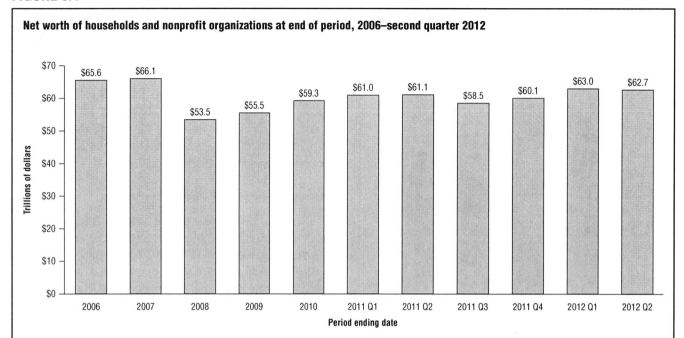

Net worth of households and nonprofit organizations at end of period, 2006–second quarter 2012

SOURCE: Adapted from "B.100. Balance Sheet of Households and Nonprofit Organizations," in *Flow of Funds Accounts of the United States; Flows and Outstandings Second Quarter 2012*, Board of Governors of the Federal Reserve System, September 20, 2012, http://www.federalreserve.gov/Releases/Z1/ Current/z1.pdf (accessed September 20, 2012)

DEMOGRAPHICS OF UNEMPLOYMENT. Table 8.2 shows unemployment data and rates by sex, marital status, race, and ethnicity in 2011. Unemployment rates differed substantially by demographic categories. The rates were higher for men than for women, higher for African-Americans than for other races, and higher for younger people aged 16 to 24 years than for older populations.

The overall unemployment rate among men aged 16 years and older was 9.4%; for men aged 25 years and older the rate was 7.9%. (See Table 8.2.) The highest unemployment rates for men in 2011 were for never-married African-American men aged 16 years and older (24.8%) and aged 25 years and older (20.9%). In general, unemployment rates across all races and ethnicities were highest for never-married men and lowest for men who were married and had a spouse present in the household. The lowest unemployment rate reported for men in 2011 was 5.1% for married Asian-American men aged 25 years and older with a spouse present in the household.

As shown in Table 8.2, the overall unemployment rate among women aged 16 years and older was 8.5% and among women aged 25 years and older was 7.3%. Again, the rates were much higher for never-married women than for married women with a spouse present in the household. The highest unemployment rates for women in 2011 were for never-married African-American women aged 16 years and older (19.3%) and aged 25 years and older (15.9%). The lowest unemployment rate reported for women in 2011 was 5.1% for married white women aged 25 years and older with a spouse present in the household.

As shown in Figure 5.3 in Chapter 5, in August 2012 the overall unemployment rate for people aged 16 years and older was 8.1%. The rate was 24.6% for teenagers aged 16 to 19 years, 14.1% for African-Americans, 10.2% for Hispanics, 7.2% for whites, and 5.9% for Asian-Americans.

Income Inequality

The U.S. Census Bureau collects income data as part of the Current Population Survey Annual Social and Economic Supplement (CPS ASEC), a sample survey of approximately 100,000 U.S. households. Data from 2011 are presented and analyzed by Carmen DeNavas-Walt, Bernadette D. Proctor, and Jessica C. Smith of the Census Bureau in *Income, Poverty, and Health Insurance Coverage in the United States: 2011* (September 2012, http://www.census.gov/prod/2012pubs/p60-243.pdf).

DeNavas-Walt, Proctor, and Smith report that the Census Bureau uses six mathematical and statistical methods to measure income inequality. Three of these methods—mean logarithmic deviation of income, the Theil index, and the Atkinson measure—are complex and not widely used. The remaining three methods and their results are explained in the following sections.

QUINTILE SHARES. The quintile shares method ranks all the households from the lowest to the highest income. The households are divided into five groups of equal population size (i.e., quintiles). The income of each group is then divided by the total income for all groups. If income equality exists, each group will account for 20% of the total income.

TABLE 8.2

Unemployed persons by demographic group, 2011

[Numbers in thousands]

Marital status, race, Hispanic or Latino ethnicity, and age	Men		Women	
	Unemployed 2011	Unemployment rates 2011	Unemployed 2011	Unemployment rates 2011
Total, 16 years and over	**7,684**	**9.4**	**6,063**	**8.5**
Married, spouse present	2,671	5.8	2,031	5.6
Widowed, divorced, or separated	1,186	11.1	1,420	9.7
Never married	3,827	15.1	2,612	12.5
White, 16 years and over	**5,631**	**8.3**	**4,257**	**7.5**
Married, spouse present	2,081	5.3	1,630	5.3
Widowed, divorced, or separated	903	10.3	1,060	9.2
Never married	2,648	13.4	1,567	10.5
Black or African American, 16 years and over	**1,502**	**17.8**	**1,329**	**14.1**
Married, spouse present	385	11.1	218	7.8
Widowed, divorced, or separated	217	16.0	265	11.8
Never married	899	24.8	846	19.3
Asian, 16 years and over	**269**	**6.8**	**250**	**7.3**
Married, spouse present	135	5.2	130	6.2
Widowed, divorced, or separated	20	6.4	42	9.0
Never married	113	10.9	78	9.2
Hispanic or Latino ethnicity, 16 years and over	**1,527**	**11.2**	**1,102**	**11.8**
Married, spouse present	606	8.6	421	10.0
Widowed, divorced, or separated	175	10.5	217	10.7
Never married	745	15.3	464	15.1
Total, 25 years and over	**5,623**	**7.9**	**4,490**	**7.3**
Married, spouse present	2,590	5.7	1,910	5.4
Widowed, divorced, or separated	1,141	10.9	1,353	9.5
Never married	1,892	12.3	1,227	10.0
White, 25 years and over	**4,137**	**7.1**	**3,181**	**6.5**
Married, spouse present	2,013	5.3	1,528	5.1
Widowed, divorced, or separated	871	10.2	1,009	9.0
Never married	1,253	10.6	645	7.8
Black or African American, 25 years and over	**1,082**	**15.2**	**951**	**11.9**
Married, spouse present	378	11.1	207	7.6
Widowed, divorced, or separated	208	15.7	254	11.5
Never married	496	20.9	490	15.9
Asian, 25 years and over	**217**	**6.0**	**209**	**6.8**
Married, spouse present	132	5.1	127	6.1
Widowed, divorced, or separated	19	6.2	41	9.0
Never married	65	9.0	41	7.3
Hispanic or Latino ethnicity, 25 years and over	**1,068**	**9.5**	**788**	**10.2**
Married, spouse present	582	8.6	386	9.6
Widowed, divorced, or separated	163	10.2	203	10.5
Never married	324	11.4	200	11.4

Notes: Estimates for the above race groups (white, black or African American, and Asian) do not sum to totals because data are not presented for all races. Persons whose ethnicity is identified as Hispanic or Latino may be of any race. Updated population controls are introduced annually with the release of January data.

SOURCE: Adapted from "Table 24. Unemployed Persons by Marital Status, Race, Hispanic or Latino Ethnicity, Age, and Sex," in *Labor Force Statistics from the Current Population Survey: CPS Tables*, U.S. Department of Labor, Bureau of Labor Statistics, July 6, 2012, http://www.bls.gov/cps/cpsa2011.pdf (accessed September 18, 2012)

Table 8.3 shows quintile shares of income based on CPS ASEC data from 1971, 1981, 1991, 2001, and 2011. In 2011 the lowest quintile of U.S. households accounted for 3.2% of total income, whereas the highest quintile accounted for 51.1% of total income. The lowest quintile lost income share over time, from 4.1% in 1971 to 3.2% in 2011. The second, third, and fourth quintiles also lost income share over the decades. The second quintile fell from 10.6% income share in 1971 to 8.4% income share in 2011. The third quintile decreased from 17.3% income

share in 1971 to 14.3% income share in 2011. The fourth quintile fell from 24.5% in 1971 to 23% in 2011. The highest quintile gained income share over the decades, from 43.5% in 1971 to 51.1% in 2011. As noted in Table 8.3, the mean (average) household income of the highest quintile in 2011 was $178,020. The mean household income of the lowest quintile in 2011 was $11,239.

GINI INDEX. The Gini index (or Gini coefficient) is a mathematically derived value that is used to describe the inequality in a data distribution. It was developed during the

TABLE 8.3

Selected measures of household income dispersion, selected years 1971–2011

Measures of income dispersion	2011	2001	1991	1981	1971*
Measure					
Household income at selected percentiles					
10th percentile limit	12,000	13,575	11,953	11,532	10,637
20th percentile limit	20,262	22,829	20,277	19,040	18,818
50th (median)	50,054	53,646	48,516	45,260	44,707
80th percentile limit	101,582	106,077	91,407	81,389	75,271
90th percentile limit	143,611	144,351	122,205	106,315	96,564
95th percentile limit	186,000	191,192	155,246	130,981	119,532
Household income ratios of selected percentiles					
90th/10th	11.97	10.63	10.22	9.22	9.08
95th/20th	9.18	8.38	7.66	6.88	6.35
95th/50th	3.72	3.56	3.20	2.89	2.67
80th/50th	2.03	1.98	1.88	1.80	1.68
80th/20th	5.01	4.65	4.51	4.28	4.00
20th/50th	0.40	0.43	0.42	0.42	0.42
Mean household income of quintiles					
Lowest quintile	11,239	12,876	11,638	10,920	10,360
Second quintile	29,204	32,354	29,230	27,202	27,381
Third quintile	49,842	54,155	48,551	45,063	44,392
Fourth quintile	80,080	84,911	74,011	67,172	63,113
Highest quintile	178,020	185,439	141,923	119,990	111,830
Shares of household income of quintiles					
Lowest quintile	3.2	3.5	3.8	4.1	4.1
Second quintile	8.4	8.7	9.6	10.1	10.6
Third quintile	14.3	14.6	15.9	16.7	17.3
Fourth quintile	23.0	23.0	24.2	24.8	24.5
Highest quintile	51.1	50.1	46.5	44.3	43.5
Summary measures					
Gini index of income inequality	0.477	0.466	0.428	0.406	0.396
Mean logarithmic deviation of income	0.585	0.515	0.411	0.387	0.370
Theil	0.422	0.413	0.313	0.277	0.273
Atkinson:					
e=0.25	0.101	0.098	0.078	0.070	0.068
e=0.50	0.198	0.189	0.156	0.141	0.138
e=0.75	0.300	0.282	0.237	0.220	0.214
Household income ratios of selected percentiles					
90th/10th	0.082	0.083	0.082	0.114	0.107
95th/20th	0.094	0.063	0.061	0.059	0.060
95th/50th	0.030	0.023	0.021	0.020	0.016
80th/50th	0.012	0.010	0.011	0.009	0.011
80th/20th	0.042	0.029	0.032	0.030	0.040
20th/50th	0.003	0.003	0.003	0.003	0.004
Mean household income of quintiles					
Lowest quintile	116	46	42	45	49
Second quintile	181	41	41	38	46
Third quintile	256	52	47	47	45
Fourth quintile	387	80	70	62	60
Highest quintile	1,324	1,095	495	370	491
Shares of household income of quintiles					
Lowest quintile	0.03	0.03	0.03	0.03	0.04
Second quintile	0.04	0.06	0.07	0.08	0.10
Third quintile	0.06	0.10	0.12	0.13	0.16
Fourth quintile	0.08	0.16	0.18	0.20	0.22
Highest quintile	0.17	0.35	0.34	0.35	0.39
Summary measures					
Gini index of income inequality	0.0018	0.0030	0.0038	0.0038	0.0063
Mean logarithmic deviation of income	0.0067	0.0051	0.0056	0.0056	0.0061
Theil	0.0050	0.0002	0.0001	0.0001	0.0001
Atkinson:					0.0007
e=0.25	0.0010	0.0014	0.0007	0.0006	
e=0.50	0.0016	0.0022	0.0012	0.0011	0.0013
e=0.75	0.0021	0.0027	0.0018	0.0017	0.0019

*Introduction of 1970 census sample design and population controls.

SOURCE: Adapted from Carmen DeNavas-Walt, Bernadette D. Proctor, and Jessica C. Smith, "Table A-2. Selected Measures of Household Income Dispersion: 1967 to 2011," in *Income, Poverty, and Health Insurance Coverage in the United States: 2011*, U.S. Department of Commerce, U.S. Census Bureau, September 2012, http://www.census.gov/prod/2012pubs/p60-243.pdf (accessed September 16, 2012)

early 1900s by the Italian statistician Corrado Gini (1884–1965). When used to compute income inequality, a value of zero indicates perfect equality, whereas a value of one indicates that all income is made by only one family.

As shown in Table 8.3, in 2011 the Gini index was 0.477. In 1971 it was 0.396. Thus, the Gini index indicates that income inequality increased over these four decades.

RATIO OF INCOME PERCENTILES. The top rows in Table 8.3 list household incomes at selected percentiles. Below the rows are listed household income ratios. Each household income ratio is a percentile income limit divided by another percentile income limit; for example, the 95th/50th ratio in 2011 was $186,000 divided by $50,054, which equals 3.72. In other words, the income of households in the 95th percentile was 3.72 times the income of households in the 50th percentile. These ratios are useful for seeing how income inequality changes over time. In 1971 the 95th/50th ratio was 2.67. Thus, the income gap between high-income households and medium-income households widened between 1971 and 2011. The 95th/50th ratio is commonly called the "top half" inequality measure.

QUINTILE MOVEMENT. It is important to remember that the income inequality measures used by the Census Bureau only provide a snapshot of income distribution at a particular point in time. In reality, many people do not remain in the same quintile continuously, but move up or down depending on their economic circumstances. Quintile movements are tracked by the Census Bureau through the Survey of Income and Program Participation (SIPP). SIPP surveys are conducted monthly and follow the same participants for a multiyear period, called a panel. Each panel typically lasts two to four years. The Census Bureau reports in "SIPP Sample Design and Interview Procedures" (March 15, 2010, http://www.census.gov/sipp/usrguide/ch2_nov20.pdf) that the 2004 SIPP panel lasted from February 2004 through January 2008. The 2008 panel began in September 2008 and was scheduled to end in December 2012; the next panel was scheduled to begin sometime in 2013.

As of November 2012, comprehensive SIPP data were available only for the 2004 panel. According to the Census Bureau, in "Overview of the Survey of Income and Program Participation (SIPP)" (May 9, 2006, http://www.census.gov/sipp/overview.html), the panel included 46,500 households.

DeNavas-Walt, Proctor, and Smith note that 30.9% of households in the bottom income quintile in 2004 had moved up to a higher quintile by 2007. Likewise, 32.2% of households in the top income quintile in 2004 had dropped to a lower quintile by 2007. Quintile movement was tied strongly to the educational levels of the survey participants. Households containing participants with lower educational levels were more likely to drop into lower quintiles over time than were households containing participants with higher educational levels.

WEALTH DISTRIBUTION

In *Changes in U.S. Family Finances from 2007 to 2010: Evidence from the Survey of Consumer Finances* (June 2012, http://www.federalreserve.gov/pubs/bulletin/2012/pdf/scf12.pdf), Jesse Bricker et al. of the Federal Reserve rely on data that were collected for the 2007 and 2010 Survey of Consumer Finances (SCF). The SCF is a survey that is conducted every three years by the Federal Reserve in cooperation with the Internal Revenue Service (IRS) to collect detailed financial information on American families. As explained in Chapter 7, nearly 6,500 interviews were conducted as part of the 2010 survey. The resulting data are believed to be representative of more than 117 million U.S. families.

Bricker et al. rank the families by income percentiles. In 2010 the mean income for each percentile was:

- Less than 20 percentile of income—$12,900 income
- 20 to 39.9 percentile of income—$27,900 income
- 40 to 59.9 percentile of income—$46,300 income
- 60 to 79.9 percentile of income—$73,600 income
- 80 to 89.9 percentile of income—$114,600 income
- 90 to 100 percentile of income—$349,000 income

The families were also assessed for net worth (assets minus liabilities). In 2010 the mean net worth for each income percentile was:

- Less than 20 percentile of income—$116,800 net worth
- 20 to 39.9 percentile of income—$127,900 net worth
- 40 to 59.9 percentile of income—$199,000 net worth
- 60 to 79.9 percentile of income—$293,900 net worth
- 80 to 89.9 percentile of income—$567,200 net worth
- 90 to 100 percentile of income—$2,944,100 net worth

Table 8.4 shows the breakdown by income sources for various net worth percentiles in 2007 and 2010. The data indicate that people at the bottom of the net worth profile (those in the less than 25th percentile) obtained the vast majority (79.9% in 2007 and 75.9% in 2010) of their income from wages. By contrast, people at the upper end of the spectrum (those in the 90th to 100th percentile) obtained only about half of their income from wages. A business, farm, or self-employment provided around a quarter of the income for families in the uppermost percentile.

Nonfinancial Assets

Table 8.5 provides a detailed breakdown of the types of nonfinancial assets that were held by families in 2010. Nearly all (97.4%) the families had at least one nonfinancial asset. The most widely held nonfinancial assets were vehicles (86.7%) and primary residences (67.3%). Bricker et al. note that housing wealth has historically been a large

TABLE 8.4

Before-tax family income distributed by income sources and by percentile of net worth, 2007 and 2010

Income source	Percentile of net worth					All families
	Less than 25	25–49.9	50–74.9	75–89.9	90–100	
2007 Survey of Consumer Finances						
Wages	79.9	80.0	77.7	72.3	46.2	64.5
Interest or dividends	0.1	0.3	0.7	1.9	7.8	3.7
Business, farm, self-employment	1.8	5.3	6.9	7.9	24.7	13.6
Capital gains	0.1	0.4	1.3	2.9	14.4	6.7
Social Security or retirement	9.5	10.9	11.8	14.2	6.2	9.6
Transfers or other	8.6	3.2	1.6	0.8	0.7	1.9
Total	**100**	**100**	**100**	**100**	**100**	**100**
2010 Survey of Consumer Finances						
Wages	75.9	80.7	76.3	69.7	55.8	68.1
Interest or dividends	0.1	0.1	0.4	1.6	8.7	3.6
Business, farm, self-employment	3.5	4.6	4.8	7.2	23.9	12.2
Capital gains	0.1	0.2	0.1	−0.2	2.3	0.9
Social Security or retirement	9.4	9.6	15.9	20.1	7.8	12.0
Transfers or other	11.1	4.7	2.5	1.7	1.5	3.2
Total	**100**	**100**	**100**	**100**	**100**	**100**

SOURCE: Jesse Bricker et al., "Table 2. Amount of Before-Tax Family Income, Distributed by Income Sources, by Percentile of Net Worth, 2007 and 2010 Surveys," in "Changes in U.S. Family Finances from 2007 to 2010: Evidence from the Survey of Consumer Finances," *Federal Reserve Bulletin*, vol. 98, no 2, June 2012, http://www.federalreserve.gov/pubs/bulletin/2012/pdf/scf12.pdf (accessed September 14, 2012)

component of total family wealth. In 2010 primary residences accounted for 29.5% of total family assets.

As shown in Table 8.5, there were substantial differences between net worth percentiles in homeownership and the median values (half of all households were worth more and half were worth less) of their primary residences. Only 21.8% of people in the less than 25th percentile of net worth owned a primary residence in 2010. The median value of their primary residence was $117,000. In contrast, 97.1% of people in the 90th to 100th percentile of net worth owned a primary residence, and the median value was $531,500. Homeownership rates varied based on demographic qualities, including the age and educational attainment of the head of the household, the family structure, and the race and ethnicity of the respondents. For example, just over three-quarters (75.3%) of non-Hispanic white respondents reported owning a primary residence in 2010, compared with 50.6% of nonwhites or Hispanics.

More recent homeownership data by racial makeup are shown in Table 8.6. The data were compiled by the Census Bureau. In the second quarter of 2012 the overall homeownership rate in the United States was 65.5%. The rate was highest (73.5%) for non-Hispanic white respondents. African-American respondents had a 43.8% homeownership rate, and Hispanic respondents had a 46.5% rate. People who described themselves as being of a mixed race or of other races had a homeownership rate of 55%.

Financial Assets

Financial assets include cash, stocks, bonds, and other investments with financial value, such as retirement accounts. Table 7.2 in Chapter 7 includes detailed SCF data on financial assets. In the 2010 survey 94% of all families had at least one financial asset in 2010. The most widely held financial assets were transaction accounts (92.5%). These include checking accounts, savings accounts, money market deposit accounts, money market mutual funds, and call accounts at brokerages.

Just over half (50.4%) of families had retirement accounts. (See Table 7.2 in Chapter 7; it should be noted that this category does not include Social Security benefits and certain employer-sponsored defined benefit plans.) Nearly a fifth (19.7%) of families had cash value life insurance policies. Smaller percentages of families held stocks (15.1%), certificates of deposit (12.2%), savings bonds (12%), pooled investment funds (8.7%), other managed assets (5.7%), and bonds (1.6%). Approximately 8% of families held financial assets of other types.

Overall, Table 7.2 in Chapter 7 shows that families that were the most likely to hold financial assets were those in the highest income brackets, those with a head of household aged 45 years and older, those with a self-employed head of household, and homeowners. Demographic data reveal that 97.3% of non-Hispanic white families held financial assets in 2010, compared with 87.2% of nonwhite or Hispanic families. The largest difference was in retirement accounts. Nearly six out of 10 (58.1%) non-Hispanic white families had retirement accounts, compared with less than four out of 10 (34.4%) nonwhite or Hispanic families.

POVERTY IN THE UNITED STATES

In the United States poverty is officially defined and measured in different ways by different government entities. At the federal level it is measured using two methods:

TABLE 8.5

Family holdings of nonfinancial assets, 2010

Family characteristic	Vehicles	Primary residence	Other residential property	Equity in nonresidential property	Business equity	Other	Any nonfinancial asset	Any asset
Percentage of families holding asset								
All families	86.7	67.3	14.4	7.7	13.3	7.0	91.3	97.4
Percentile of income								
Less than 20	64.9	37.2	4.4	3.9	5.1	2.7	72.0	89.9
20–39.9	85.4	55.9	7.4	5.2	6.6	4.4	90.7	98.0
40–59.9	91.8	71.1	11.6	6.3	10.6	7.3	96.0	99.5
60–79.9	95.4	80.7	16.0	7.9	15.5	9.3	98.6	99.9
80–89.9	96.4	90.6	22.8	11.4	19.3	10.8	99.4	100.0
90–100	95.7	92.4	42.1	18.8	37.6	12.3	99.4	100.0
Age of head (years)								
Less than 35	79.4	37.5	4.5	2.3	8.4	6.1	82.8	95.5
35–44	88.9	63.8	9.7	3.9	11.2	4.2	92.7	97.4
45–54	91.0	75.2	17.0	7.5	16.8	6.7	94.7	98.3
55–64	90.3	78.1	22.1	12.6	19.6	9.6	94.4	98.3
65–74	86.5	82.6	22.8	11.0	15.8	11.0	92.6	97.1
75 or more	83.4	81.9	14.6	13.4	6.0	6.0	93.0	98.7
Family structure								
Single with child(ren)	79.1	52.0	6.2	4.0	5.2	3.9	84.5	94.6
Single, no child, age less than 55	74.6	40.2	6.3	2.4	7.4	5.7	80.7	95.3
Single, no child, age 55 or more	76.3	66.7	11.8	8.2	6.6	8.0	86.8	96.6
Couple with child(ren)	94.8	75.6	15.5	7.1	17.0	5.9	97.0	99.0
Couple, no child	93.2	79.7	22.6	12.8	19.5	10.0	96.3	98.5
Education of head								
No high school diploma	76.2	54.3	5.0	3.3	5.2	1.3	82.2	92.5
High school diploma	85.8	64.7	10.0	6.9	10.9	5.5	90.5	96.5
Some college	85.4	61.5	11.7	6.4	11.2	7.6	89.6	98.2
College degree	91.5	76.6	22.4	10.4	18.9	9.9	95.9	99.5
Race or ethnicity of respondent								
White non-Hispanic	90.9	75.3	16.5	9.4	15.6	8.8	94.9	99.1
Nonwhite or Hispanic	78.1	50.6	9.9	4.2	8.3	3.3	84.0	94.1
Current work status of head								
Working for someone else	89.9	64.8	11.9	5.5	6.6	6.4	92.8	98.3
Self-employed	88.5	78.4	28.3	17.5	71.1	12.0	96.4	98.8
Retired	82.4	74.6	15.0	9.6	4.5	6.8	89.2	96.3
Other not working	72.8	42.9	8.7	2.8	4.1	4.8	78.6	92.5
Current occupation of head								
Managerial or professional	91.0	76.1	22.9	10.7	25.9	9.6	95.7	99.7
Technical, sales, or services	86.7	56.0	9.7	5.1	9.6	5.1	90.1	97.7
Other occupation	91.1	66.6	8.4	5.6	13.8	6.6	93.8	97.1
Retired or other not working	80.3	67.8	13.7	8.1	4.4	6.3	86.9	95.5
Region								
Northeast	78.5	65.0	15.3	5.9	11.1	5.5	85.6	95.1
Midwest	90.1	73.3	11.0	7.6	13.0	5.8	93.8	98.0
South	87.5	67.6	14.1	9.4	12.5	6.6	92.1	97.5
West	88.8	62.5	17.4	6.4	16.6	10.2	92.4	98.7
Urbanicity								
Metropolitan statistical area (MSA)	86.0	65.9	14.9	7.2	13.4	6.9	90.6	97.4
Non-MSA	90.2	73.9	11.9	10.1	12.3	7.8	95.0	97.8
Housing status								
Owner	93.9	100.0	19.1	10.5	17.0	8.4	100.0	100.0
Renter or other	71.9	*	4.6	1.9	5.5	4.2	73.6	92.2
Percentile of net worth								
Less than 25	67.4	21.8	2.8	0.8	2.9	2.5	69.7	89.8
25–49.9	91.6	61.3	4.6	2.1	6.1	4.9	96.8	100.0
50–74.9	93.2	90.1	13.1	7.8	12.9	7.3	99.2	100.0
75–89.9	94.3	95.3	27.1	14.9	20.8	9.2	99.6	100.0
90–100	95.2	97.1	51.7	27.9	46.6	19.7	99.9	100.0

TABLE 8.5

Family characteristic	Vehicles	Primary residence	Other residential property	Equity in nonresidential property	Business equity	Other	Any nonfinancial asset	Any asset
Median value of holdings for families holding asset (thousands of 2010 dollars)								
All families	15.3	170.0	120.0	65.0	78.7	15.0	154.6	187.2
Percentile of income								
Less than 20	5.8	89.0	82.0	36.0	25.0	5.3	23.6	15.2
20–39.9	9.3	110.0	70.0	60.0	25.3	5.0	73.5	75.4
40–59.9	13.8	135.0	82.0	60.0	44.7	10.0	131.2	159.8
60–79.9	20.1	175.0	71.0	50.0	50.0	13.0	198.3	267.0
80–89.9	27.9	250.0	120.0	58.0	82.4	22.0	311.1	448.4
90–100	35.8	475.0	320.0	200.0	455.0	35.0	756.4	1,486.7
Age of head (years)								
Less than 35	12.4	140.0	72.0	24.0	30.0	5.0	34.2	35.7
35–44	16.5	170.0	75.0	50.0	50.0	10.0	142.8	156.3
45–54	18.4	200.0	103.5	50.0	80.0	15.0	191.4	248.4
55–64	17.8	185.0	165.0	102.0	100.0	20.0	206.6	286.6
65–74	16.0	165.0	125.0	60.0	100.0	28.1	199.8	281.7
75 or more	10.6	150.0	125.0	65.0	220.9	26.0	168.2	237.7
Family structure								
Single with child(ren)	9.7	134.0	100.0	50.0	20.0	15.0	79.0	70.0
Single, no child, age less than 55	9.6	135.2	70.0	75.0	43.0	7.0	56.9	50.1
Single, no child, age 55 or more	7.5	130.0	151.0	50.0	80.3	15.0	115.5	143.9
Couple with child(ren)	21.3	190.0	120.0	60.0	75.0	12.0	193.4	233.9
Couple, no child	20.3	180.0	120.0	75.0	109.0	20.0	209.0	306.7
Education of head								
No high school diploma	9.7	95.0	75.0	30.0	27.8	5.0	59.0	47.8
High school diploma	13.3	130.0	62.5	58.0	64.1	8.0	122.2	138.4
Some college	14.5	150.0	65.0	35.0	110.0	14.4	136.2	150.1
College degree	19.5	250.0	190.0	100.0	88.0	20.0	251.5	352.6
Race or ethnicity of respondent								
White non-Hispanic	16.7	175.0	140.0	75.0	97.2	15.0	183.6	238.9
Nonwhite or Hispanic	12.3	139.0	70.0	50.0	43.0	10.0	86.0	76.8
Current work status of head								
Working for someone else	16.3	170.0	96.0	50.0	25.0	10.0	142.7	165.7
Self-employed	21.7	270.0	250.0	132.0	100.0	30.0	370.0	440.2
Retired	11.7	150.0	100.0	62.5	125.5	25.0	155.9	198.0
Other not working	10.7	135.0	60.0	46.6	37.6	10.0	56.7	41.0
Current occupation of head								
Managerial or professional	20.8	250.0	200.0	100.0	102.0	23.0	260.0	347.5
Technical, sales, or services	12.7	153.0	70.0	50.0	27.0	8.0	107.6	115.5
Other occupation	17.2	130.0	57.0	50.0	51.5	8.0	125.0	147.2
Retired or other not working	11.5	150.0	98.0	62.0	81.6	22.0	139.9	163.3
Region								
Northeast	16.2	260.0	154.0	65.0	70.0	30.0	220.4	260.0
Midwest	13.6	135.0	86.5	70.0	100.0	10.0	142.1	174.9
South	15.4	141.7	100.0	50.0	80.3	15.0	134.3	153.1
West	16.3	230.0	170.0	159.4	52.8	15.0	189.1	216.8
Urbanicity								
Metropolitan statistical area (MSA)	15.5	181.0	135.0	70.0	73.6	15.0	168.0	200.0
Non-MSA	14.4	100.0	75.0	60.0	104.5	12.5	111.6	140.1
Housing status								
Owner	18.8	170.0	120.0	70.0	95.0	20.0	217.0	296.2
Renter or other	8.5	*	120.0	22.5	25.0	5.3	9.7	12.6
Percentile of net worth								
Less than 25	6.9	117.0	60.0	3.0	1.2	5.0	9.4	7.4
25–49.9	11.7	95.5	25.0	10.0	11.6	5.0	60.0	69.1
50–74.9	17.7	150.0	48.0	30.0	40.0	13.0	181.6	240.3
75–89.9	22.7	250.0	120.0	65.0	125.0	20.6	360.7	583.8
90–100	32.7	531.5	350.0	250.0	600.0	50.0	1,114.3	2,082.8
Memo								
Mean value of holdings for families holding asset	22.1	261.2	288.9	321.6	788.3	66.5	405.5	612.3

TABLE 8.5

Family holdings of nonfinancial assets, 2010 [CONTINUED]

*Ten or fewer observations.
Note: For questions on income, respondents were asked to base their answers on the calendar year preceding the interview. For questions on saving, respondents were asked to base their answers on the 12 months preceding the interview. Percentage distributions may not sum to 100 because of rounding. Dollars have been converted to 2010 values with the current-methods consumer price index for all urban consumers.

SOURCE: Jesse Bricker et al., "Table 9. Family Holdings of Nonfinancial Assets and of Any Asset, by Selected Characteristics of Families and Type of Asset, 2007 and 2010 Surveys—B. 2010 Survey of Consumer Finances," in "Changes in U.S. Family Finances from 2007 to 2010: Evidence from the Survey of Consumer Finances," *Federal Reserve Bulletin*, vol. 98, no 2, June 2012, http://www.federalreserve.gov/pubs/bulletin/2012/pdf/scf12.pdf (accessed September 14, 2012

TABLE 8.6

Homeownership rates by race and ethnicity of householder, 2008–second quarter 2012

[In percent]

	Homeownership rates				
Year/quarter	United States	Non-Hispanic white alone	Black alone[a]	All other races[b]	Hispanic (of any race)
2012					
Second quarter	65.5	73.5	43.8	55.0	46.5
First quarter	65.4	73.5	43.1	55.1	46.3
2011					
Fourth quarter	66.0	73.7	45.1	56.5	46.6
Third quarter	66.3	73.8	45.6	56.4	47.6
Second quarter	65.9	73.7	44.2	56.0	46.6
First quarter	66.4	74.1	44.8	56.7	46.8
2010					
Fourth quarter	66.5	74.2	44.8	57.7	46.8
Third quarter	66.9	74.7	45.0	57.3	47.0
Second quarter	66.9	74.4	46.2	55.7	47.8
First quarter	67.1	74.5	45.6	57.2	48.5
2009					
Fourth quarter	67.2	74.5	46.0	58.4	48.4
Third quarter	67.6	75.0	46.4	57.8	48.7
Second quarter	67.4	74.9	46.5	57.6	48.1
First quarter	67.3	74.7	46.1	57.4	48.6
2008					
Fourth quarter	67.5	74.8	46.8	58.3	48.6
Third quarter	67.9	75.1	47.8	59.0	49.5
Second quarter	68.1	75.2	47.8	58.4	49.6
First quarter	67.8	75.0	47.1	58.1	48.9

[a]The homeownership rate for second quarter 2012 for householders who reported black whether or not they reported any other race was 43.8 percent.
[b]Includes people who reported Asian, Native Hawaiian or other Pacific Islander, or American Indian or Alaska Native regardless of whether they reported any other race, as well as all other combinations of two or more races.
Note: Beginning in 2003, the question on race on the Current Population Survey (CPS) was modified to comply with the revised standards for federal statistical agencies. Respondents may now report more than one race, but small sample sizes preclude showing all race categories. The question on Hispanic origin is asked separately, and is asked before the question on race.

SOURCE: Robert R. Callis and Melissa Kresin, "Table 7. Homeownership Rates by Race and Ethnicity of Householder: 2008 to 2012 (in Percent)," in *Residential Vacancies and Homeownership in the Second Quarter 2012*, U.S. Department of Commerce, U.S. Census Bureau, July 27, 2012, http://www.census.gov/hhes/www/housing/hvs/qtr212/files/q212press.pdf (accessed September 14, 2012)

poverty thresholds and poverty guidelines. Poverty thresholds are set by the Census Bureau, which also tracks poverty populations in the United States. The thresholds specify minimum income levels for different sizes and categories of families. For example, the Census Bureau (2012, http://www.census.gov/hhes/www/poverty/data/tlsb?>threshld/thresh11.xls) notes that in 2011 the poverty threshold for a family of four including two related children under the age

of 18 years in the household was $22,811 per year. Thus, a family matching this description and making less than $22,811 per year in 2011 was considered by the U.S. government to be in poverty.

Poverty guidelines are published by the U.S. Department of Health and Human Services (HHS) for the 50 states and the District of Columbia. According to the HHS, the poverty guidelines are a simplification of the poverty thresholds and are used for administrative purposes, such as determining eligibility for specific federal programs. The most recent guidelines were published in "Annual Update of the HHS Poverty Guidelines" (*Federal Register*, vol. 77, no. 17, January 26, 2012).

The Poverty Rate

The Census Bureau calculates the number of people in poverty and the poverty rate using the poverty thresholds. The most recent data were collected in 2011 as part of the CPS ASEC and are analyzed by DeNavas-Walt, Proctor, and Smith. As noted earlier, the CPS ASEC surveys around 100,000 U.S. households per year. The data are used to estimate annual poverty levels for the nation as a whole.

According to DeNavas-Walt, Proctor, and Smith, 46.2 million people in the United States lived at or below the federal poverty level in 2011. This represented 15% of the total U.S. population and was up from around 12% in 2000. The number of people in poverty has varied widely over the past few decades. In 1960 approximately 40 million people in the United States lived in poverty. This value dropped to fewer than 25 million people during the 1970s and then began increasing, reaching around 39 million during the early 1990s. The number declined to around 31 million in 2000 and then increased over the ensuing 11 years.

The poverty rate was around 22% during the early 1960s, and then it dropped to around 11% during the early 1970s. It topped 15% during the early 1990s and then decreased to around 12% in 2000, before it began to rise again. The 2011 poverty rate was the highest since 1993.

There were dramatic demographic differences in the U.S. poverty rate in 2011. The differences by race and ethnicity were:

- African-Americans—27.6%
- Hispanics—25.3%
- Asian-Americans—12.5%
- Non-Hispanic whites—9.8%

DeNavas-Walt, Proctor, and Smith note that the 2011 CPS ASEC included native-born Americans, foreign-born naturalized U.S. citizens, and noncitizens. Poverty rate estimates for these groups on a national level were:

- Native-born Americans—14.4%
- Foreign-born naturalized U.S. citizens—12.5%
- Noncitizens—24.3%

Other demographic differences were also significant. The poverty rate in 2011 for those under the age of 18 years was 21.9%, compared with 13.7% for people aged 18 to 64 years and 8.7% for people aged 65 years and older. Among family types, the highest poverty rate was experienced by families headed by unmarried females, at 31.2%. By contrast, the poverty rate for families headed by unmarried males was 16.1% and for those headed by married couples it was only 6.2%.

Poverty rates also differed by work experience. The rate for people who did not work at least one week in 2011 was 32.9%, compared with 16.3% for people who worked part time or part of the year. The rate was 2.8% for those who worked full time year-round. DeNavas-Walt, Proctor, and Smith report that 2.7 million people fell into this category.

Temporary and Chronic Poverty

As noted earlier, there is significant movement between income quintiles over time. Likewise, people can slip in and out of poverty over time. DeNavas-Walt, Proctor, and Smith used data from the SIPP 2004 panel (February 2004 to January 2008) and 2008 panel (began in May 2008 and was ongoing as of November 2012) to gauge these movements on a month-to-month basis. The results indicate that approximately 28% of the U.S. population experienced at least one spell of poverty lasting a minimum of two months during the two-year period of 2009–10. Only 4.8% of the U.S. population is estimated to have lived in poverty continuously throughout this entire period.

Poverty and Economic Well-Being

The poverty rates calculated by the Census Bureau are based on cash income only. There is widespread agreement that these rates do not adequately characterize the standard of living of the nation's poorest people. DeNavas-Walt, Proctor, and Smith acknowledge that the poverty estimates do not consider the value of noncash benefits. These include government assistance programs, such as Medicare (a federal health insurance program for people aged 65 years and older and people with disabilities) and Medicaid (a state and federal health insurance program for low-income people), government subsidies for food and housing, and employer-provided fringe benefits.

The federal government uses other methods to measure what it calls the "economic well-being" of the nation's households. The SIPP surveys described earlier are one of these methods. In "Well Being Main" (2012, http://www.census.gov/hhes/well-being/index.html), the Census Bureau notes that "extended measures of well-being gauge how people are faring at the household level using such factors as possession of consumer durables, housing and neighborhood conditions, and the meeting of basic needs." The SIPP program surveys people about their consumer possessions and seeks to determine if their basic needs are being met for housing and food. As of November 2012, the most recent published SIPP data relevant to "economic well-being" were from 2005. In "Extended Measures of Well-Being: Living Conditions in the United States, 2005" (November 2009, http://www.census.gov/popula tion/www/socdemo/extended-05.html), the Census Bureau includes data tables reflecting SIPP survey results on various topics. For example, in "Table 1. Percent of Households Reporting Consumer Durables, for Householders 15 Years and Older, by Selected Characteristics: 2005," the Census Bureau lists the percentages of households classified as being "in poverty" in 2005 that owned the following consumer goods:

- Refrigerator—98.5%

- Television—97.4%

- Stove—97%

- Microwave—91.2%

- Video-cassette recorder—83.6%

- Telephone—79.8%

- Air conditioner—78.8%

- Clothes washer—68.7%

- Clothes dryer—61.2%

- Cellular phone—48.3%

- Computer—42.4%

- Dishwasher—36.7%

- Food freezer—25.1%

In "Table 2. Percent of Households Reporting Favorable Housing Conditions by Selected Characteristics, for Householders 15 Years and Older: 2005," the Census Bureau indicates that 91.1% of "in poverty" households in 2005 expressed "overall satisfaction" with their housing conditions.

WEALTH INEQUALITY: CAUSES AND CONSEQUENCES

The data are clear that wealth inequality exists and that the gap between rich and poor has widened in recent decades. However, there are varying opinions on the causes for this phenomena and whether it is a wrong that should be righted or an inevitable result of a growing economy.

In *Changes in the Distribution of Income among Tax Filers between 1996 and 2006: The Role of Labor Income, Capital Income, and Tax Policy* (December 29, 2011, http://www.fas.org/sgp/crs/misc/R42131.pdf), Thomas L. Hungerford of the Congressional Research Service lists causes that are commonly cited by analysts:

- High-paying union jobs have declined in availability

- The minimum wage has not risen fast enough to keep up with inflation

- The U.S. business sector increasingly favors highly educated workers and those skilled in particular fields, particularly technological fields, over lower educated workers and workers lacking technological skills

- "Winner-take-all" markets have grown more common in which many people compete, but only a small few reap extremely large rewards

- Politicians have instituted changes, such as tax policies, that have primarily benefited wealthier Americans

Analysts disagree on what exactly has caused wealth inequality, and they also disagree over whether or not it is a problem that should be fixed or is simply a natural consequence of the growth that has occurred in the U.S. economy over time. The debate over wealth inequality has always been a politically partisan issue, with those on the left maintaining that widespread financial inequality causes many social and economic problems and those on the right arguing that the market should be allowed to adjust itself with regard to wages and income.

Wealth Inequality Seen as a Problem to Be Fixed

The Institute for Policy Studies (IPS) is a nonprofit organization that champions progressive social causes. Progressivism as a political movement dates back to the late 1800s in the United States and generally promotes social and economic reforms that reduce all forms of inequality, such as racial segregation and wealth inequality. The IPS alleges in "Inequality and the Common Good" (2012, http://www.ips-dc.org/inequality) that growing income inequality in the United States threatens "U.S. democracy, economic health and civic life." The institute highlights studies that show that growing wealth inequality (or the concentration of wealth among only a few Americans) causes hundreds of specific problems in American society. Examples include worse customer service, less job security, higher credit card interest rates, more overpriced housing, and shorter life expectancies.

Paul Krugman of Princeton University is an outspoken critic of wealth inequality in the United States. In "For Richer" (*New York Times*, October 20, 2002), he asserts that "as the gap between the rich and the rest of the population grows, economic policy increasingly caters to the interests of the elite, while public services for the population at large—above all, public education—are starved of resources. As policy increasingly favors the interests of the rich and neglects the interests of the general population, income disparities grow even wider."

THE OCCUPY MOVEMENT. Income and net worth reports that are compiled by the Federal Reserve and the Census Bureau divide households into fairly broad percentile groups, such as 10th percentile and 20th percentile. In contrast, private researchers use government data to calculate the income and net worth at the 99th percentile limit, that is, for the "richest" 1% of Americans. For example, G. William Domhoff of the University of California, Santa Cruz, indicates in "Wealth, Income, and Power" (October 2012, http://www2.ucsc.edu/whorulesamerica/power/wealth.html) that the top 1% owned more than one-third of the nation's total wealth in 2010. Domhoff cites dozens of studies dating back to the 1990s to support this claim. In addition, a 2011 report from the Congressional Budget Office (CBO) also singles out the top 1% in terms of economic performance. In *Trends in the Distribution of Household Income between 1979 and 2007* (October 2011, http://cbo.gov/sites/default/files/cbo files/attachments/10-25-HouseholdIncome.pdf), the CBO reports the growth from 1979 to 2007 in real (inflation-adjusted) average household income, after government transfers and federal taxes, for the following income groups:

- Top 1%—275% growth in income

- 81st through 99th percentile—65% growth in income

- 21st through 80th percentile—almost 40% growth in income

- Lowest 20%—18% growth in income

Income and wealth inequality sparked public protests during 2011 that were dubbed the Occupy Wall Street Movement or, more broadly, the Occupy Movement. The protests were also driven by the idea that greed and reckless behavior by Wall Street's large financial corporations caused the housing bust and subsequent Great Recession (which lasted from December 2007 to June 2009) that brought economic hardship to so many Americans. As noted in Chapter 7, dozens of struggling companies in the financial industry received government bailouts during the economic downturn. However, even as the companies were accepting the bailouts, many continued to pay out millions of dollars in bonuses to their employees. The net result was a groundswell of popular resentment against "big business." The so-called "1%" were basically guilty by association. Occupy Movement activists adopted the slogan "We are the 99%" and, as of November 2012, continued to hold or inspire protests in which people denounced income and wealth inequality and related social and political concerns.

FIXING WEALTH INEQUALITY. In general, people who consider wealth inequality to be a social and economic wrong believe the government should right the wrong. Progressives support government actions that alleviate wealth inequality, just as the government outlawed racial segregation in schools during the 1950s as a step toward eliminating racial inequality in society at large. Progressives typically advocate "bottom-up" measures, such as raising the minimum wage or improving public education, to "raise the floor" for Americans in the lower- and middle-income classes. Progressives also champion "top-down" measures that shrink the wealth of the higher-income classes to pay for

the bottom-up measures. This concept is known as the redistribution of wealth.

Taxation is the primary tool by which the government can and does "redistribute" wealth among Americans. As will be explained in Chapter 9, the U.S. income tax system is called progressive because it taxes individuals with higher incomes at higher rates than individuals with lower incomes. The tax rates only apply to what the IRS defines as "taxable income." The U.S. tax code allows hundreds of deductions and credits that lessen taxable income amounts. The most well-known example is the deduction for mortgage interest. However, critics complain that wealthy individuals and businesses benefit the most from tax deductions and credits that have been built into the tax code over the years.

Many progressives support raising the tax rates and reducing the tax deductions and credits for people in the higher tax brackets. In addition, they advocate eliminating tax deductions, tax credits, and subsidies (government-provided funds) for wealthy private corporations, particularly those in the oil and gas industry. They also want an increase in the capital gains tax (a tax on the profit that is made when selling capital assets, such as real estate, stocks, and bonds). As shown in Table 7.2 in Chapter 7 and Table 8.5, ownership of such assets is concentrated among higher-income households. Krugman notes in "Taxes at the Top" (*New York Times*, January 19, 2012) that the top capital gains tax rate declined from 29% during the early 1990s to 15% in 2003, a level that was still in place as of November 2012. He complains that "such low taxes on the very rich are indefensible."

President Barack Obama (1961–) supports many progressive causes. For example, the White House states in "Taxes" (2012, http://www.whitehouse.gov/issues/taxes) that the president proposes tax code changes such as "cutting tax preferences for high-income households; eliminating special tax breaks for oil and gas companies; closing loopholes for investment fund managers; and eliminating benefits for corporate jet owners." Obama's tax policy will be discussed at length in Chapter 9.

Wealth Inequality Seen as an Inevitable Result of Economic Growth

On the other side of this issue are those who believe that wealth inequality is an inevitable result of economic growth and does not pose a problem to the U.S. economy and society. This viewpoint is generally associated with conservative political thinking, which holds that market forces must be allowed to adjust themselves without government interference. One idea that is regularly expressed by politicians in this camp is that "what's good for the rich is good for the rest of us." This philosophy was espoused by President Ronald Reagan (1911–2004), who championed a trickle-down economic policy—economic actions (such as tax cuts beneficial to the wealthy) that encourage greater investment in business growth and thereby increase employment, wages, and other benefits for those in the middle and lower classes. Thus, conservatives argue that high-income and high-wealth individuals are job creators who provide opportunities and spur economic growth.

In "Rich Man, Poor Man: How to Think about Income Inequality" (*National Review*, June 16, 2003), Kevin A. Hassett states his belief that the unease over wealth inequality is driven by social views on the "basic justice" of society. However, he argues that there are similarly compelling arguments against taking from the rich to benefit the poor. Hassett notes that taking resources from the rich limits their ability and incentive to start and grow businesses, which will ultimately hurt American workers even more.

This argument is commonly cited by people who oppose wealth redistribution. They also point out that wealth redistribution is an improper term because wealth was not originally "distributed" to its owners, but earned by them.

Michael Tanner argues in "The Income-Inequality Myth" (NationalReview.com, January 10, 2012) that income inequality in the United States is not as large as data suggest. He notes that most studies, including the previously mentioned 2011 CBO study, use taxable income data obtained from the IRS. However, he cites research showing that "changes in the tax code ... have resulted in more wealth being reported as taxable income." In addition, Tanner points out that workers in the low- to middle-income brackets receive valuable noncash benefits, such as employer-sponsored health insurance and retirement funds, that are not counted as taxable income. Likewise, the value of social welfare benefits, such as food stamps and housing subsidies, to Americans in the lowest income brackets are not counted as income. Tanner believes that including non-cash benefits in income comparisons would greatly shrink the perceived inequality gap.

Tanner also argues that any income inequality that does exist has been exacerbated not by tax cuts or other preferential treatment for the rich, but by the large shift in American industry over the past half century from manufacturing to information and technology. This shift has benefitted the more educated over the less educated. Lastly, Tanner disputes the idea that income inequality is necessarily a bad thing. He states:

In what way does someone else's success harm me? Such a viewpoint stems from the misguided notion that the economy is a pie of fixed size. If one person gets a bigger portion of the pie, others of necessity get smaller pieces, and the role of government is to divide up the slices of that pie. In reality, though, the size of the pie is infinite.

Tanner believes that risk takers and innovators who expand the economic pie deserve the rewards that come to them for doing so, and notes that "such rewards inevitably lead to greater inequality."

Public Opinion on Wealth Distribution

In April 2012 the Gallup Organization asked Americans whether certain segments of society "are paying their fair share in federal taxes." In *Taxes* (2012, http://www.gallup.com/poll/1714/Taxes.aspx), Gallup reports that 33% of respondents said "lower-income" people are paying a "fair share." Forty percent believed this segment pays "too much" in taxes, and 24% believed lower-income people pay "too little" in taxes. Just over half (56%) of those asked said "middle-income" people pay their "fair share" in taxes. More than a third (36%) said the segment pays "too much," and 6% thought middle-income people pay "too little" in taxes. Only 25% of respondents said "upper-income" people pay their "fair share" of taxes. Ten percent thought this segment pays "too much," and 62% said upper-income people pay "too little" in taxes.

Less than a quarter (21%) of poll participants said corporations pay a "fair share" in taxes. Eleven percent thought corporations pay "too much," and 64% said corporations pay "too little" in taxes.

Between November and December 2011 Gallup pollsters asked Americans the following question about wealth distribution in the United States: "Do you feel that the distribution of money and wealth in this country today is fair, or do you feel that the money and wealth in this country should be more evenly distributed among a larger percentage of the people?" Nearly two-thirds (61%) of respondents said the nation's money and wealth should be more evenly distributed. Only 35% felt the current distribution "is fair."

In April 2011 Gallup pollsters asked: "Do you think our government should or should not redistribute wealth by heavy taxes on the rich?" Forty-seven percent agreed that the government should redistribute wealth via heavy taxes on the rich. Forty-nine percent disagreed with this approach.

CHAPTER 9
THE ROLE OF THE GOVERNMENT

In general, the art of government consists in taking as much money as possible from one party of the citizens to give to the other.

—Voltaire, *Dictionnaire Philosophique* (1764)

The government has many roles in the U.S. economy. Like other businesses, the government spends and makes money, consumes goods and services, and employs people. Federal, state, and local governments raise funds directly through taxes and fees. They often borrow money from the public by selling securities, such as bonds. A bond is an investment in which people lend money to the government for a specified time and interest rate. Governments also disburse money via contracts with businesses or through social programs that benefit the public.

Finally, the federal government is a manipulator of the U.S. economy. It influences macroeconomic factors, such as inflation and unemployment, through fiscal and monetary policies. Fiscal policy revolves around spending and taxation. Monetary policy is concerned with the amount of money in circulation and the operation of the nation's central banking system.

FUNDING GOVERNMENT SERVICES

Governments are responsible for providing services that individuals cannot effectively provide for themselves, such as military defense, roads, education, social services, and environmental protection. Some government entities also provide public utilities, such as water, sewage treatment, or electricity. To generate the revenue that is necessary to provide services, governments collect taxes and fees and charge for many services they provide to the public. If these revenues are not sufficient to fund desired programs, governments borrow money.

Taxation

The most common taxes levied by federal, state, and local governments are:

• Income taxes—charged on wages, salaries, and tips

• Payroll taxes—Social Security insurance and unemployment compensation, both of which are withdrawn from payroll checks and paid by employers

• Property taxes—levied on the value of property owned, usually real estate

• Capital gains taxes—charged on the profit from the sale of an asset such as stock or real estate

• Corporate taxes—levied on the profits of a corporation

• Estate taxes—charged against the assets of a deceased person

• Excise taxes—collected at the time something is sold or when a good is imported

• Wealth taxes—levied on the value of assets rather than on the income they produce

Taxes are broadly defined as being either direct or indirect. Direct taxes (such as income taxes) are paid by the entity on whom the tax is being levied. Indirect taxes are passed on from the responsible party to someone else. Examples of indirect taxes include business property taxes, gasoline taxes, and sales taxes, which are levied on businesses but passed on to consumers via increased prices.

When individuals with higher incomes pay a higher percentage of a tax, it is called a progressive tax; when those with lower incomes pay a larger percentage of their income, a tax is considered regressive. The federal income tax is an example of a progressive tax because individuals with higher incomes are subject to higher tax rates. Sales and excise taxes are regressive because the same tax applies to all consumers regardless of income, so less prosperous individuals pay a higher percentage of their income.

Borrowing against the Future

Government entities sometimes spend more than they make. When cash revenues from taxes, fees, and other sources are not sufficient to cover spending, money must be borrowed. One method used by government to borrow money is the selling of securities, such as bonds, to the public. A bond is basically an IOU (an abbreviation for "I Owe yoU") that a government body writes to a buyer. The buyer pays money up front in exchange for the IOU, which is redeemable at some point in the future (the maturity date) for the amount of the original loan plus interest. In addition, the federal government has the ability to write itself IOUs—to spend money in the present that it expects to make in the future.

U.S. government bodies borrow money because they are optimistic that future revenues will cover the IOUs they have written. This optimism is based in part on the power that governments have to tax their citizens and to control the cost of provided government services. Even though tax increases and cuts in services can be enacted to raise money, these actions have political and economic repercussions. Politicians who wish to remain in office are reluctant to displease their constituents. Furthermore, the more citizens pay in taxes, the less money they will have to spend in the marketplace or invest in private business, thereby hurting the overall economy. As a result, governments must weigh their need to borrow against the future likely consequences of paying back the loan.

LOCAL GOVERNMENTS

The U.S. Census Bureau performs a comprehensive Census of Government every five years. As of November 2012, the most recent data were from the 2007 census (http://www.census.gov/govs/cog/). In between the censuses, annual surveys are conducted to collect certain data on government finances and employment.

As shown in Table 9.1, 89,004 local government units were in operation in 2012. These units consisted of counties, municipalities, townships, school districts, and special districts. Special district governments usually perform a single function, such as flood control or water supply. For example, Florida is divided into five water management districts, each of which is responsible for managing and protecting water resources and balancing the water needs of other government units within its jurisdiction.

Local Revenues

As of November 2012, the most recent comprehensive data for local government revenues were from 2010. Local governments took in more than $1.6 trillion that year. (See Table 9.2.) Most of the money came from three sources: intergovernmental revenue ($544.2 billion), property taxes ($427.1 billion), and current charges for services ($239.8 billion). Intergovernmental revenue consists of funds that are transferred to the local government from the federal and state governments. State funds accounted for the vast majority of intergovernmental transfers in 2010.

Taxes, particularly property taxes, are an important source of revenue for many local governments. Consumption taxes are also collected on sales and gross receipts. This includes selective taxes that are levied against particular goods, such as motor fuels, alcoholic beverages, and tobacco products. Miscellaneous taxes include individual and corporate income taxes, motor vehicle license taxes, and a wide variety of other taxes.

The revenue included in current charges for services comes from many local sources, including hospitals, sewage treatment facilities, solid waste management, parks and recreation areas, airports, and educational facilities.

Other revenue sources for local governments are miscellaneous general revenue, public utilities, and insurance trusts. Miscellaneous general revenue comes from a variety of sources, including interest payments and the sale of public property. Public utilities primarily supply water, electricity, natural gas, and public transportation (such as buses and trains). Insurance trusts are monies collected from the paychecks of local government employees to pay for worker programs, such as retirement benefits.

RECENT LOCAL TAX DATA. Every quarter the Census Bureau compiles detailed data on local tax collection. Figure 9.1 provides a breakdown of the tax monies that were collected for the four quarters ending with the first quarter of 2012. Property taxes accounted for the vast majority (80%) of the taxes that were collected during that one-year period.

Local Expenditures

Local governments spent nearly $1.7 trillion on annual expenses in 2010. (See Table 9.2.) Education was the largest single component, accounting for $605.9 billion in spending. Lesser amounts were spent on public health, welfare, and hospitals; utilities; environmental and housing concerns; and public safety (e.g., police and fire).

The Census Bureau (2012, http://www2.census.gov/govs/apes/11locus.txt) estimates that in 2011 local governments employed nearly 10.8 million full-time employees and 3.3 million part-time employees.

STATE GOVERNMENTS
State Revenues

According to the Census Bureau, state governments had revenues just over $2 trillion in 2010. (See Table 9.3.) Intergovernmental revenue from the federal government accounted for $555.3 billion of the total. Self-generated state revenue totaled $986.7 billion and consisted largely of collected taxes ($701 billion).

STATE TAXES. The Federation of Tax Administrators (FTA) is a nonprofit organization that provides research services for the tax administrators of all 50 states and the District of Columbia. According to the FTA, in "State Sales

TABLE 9.1

Local government entities, by state, 2012

Geographic area	Total	General purpose						Special purpose		
		Total	County[a]	Subcounty				Total	Special districts	Independent school districts[b]
				Total	Municipal	Town or township				
United States	89,004	38,917	3,031	35,886	19,522	16,364		50,087	37,203	12,884
Alabama	1,208	528	67	461	461	—		680	548	132
Alaska	177	162	14	148	148	—		15	15	—
Arizona	659	106	15	91	91	—		553	309	244
Arkansas	1,543	577	75	502	502	—		966	727	239
California	4,350	539	57	482	482	—		3,811	2,786	1,025
Colorado	2,818	333	62	271	271	—		2,485	2,305	180
Connecticut	644	179	—	179	30	149		465	448	17
Delaware	338	60	3	57	57	—		278	259	19
District of Columbia	2	1	—	1	1	—		1	1	—
Florida	1,554	476	66	410	410	—		1,078	983	95
Georgia	1,365	688	153	535	535	—		677	497	180
Hawaii	21	4	3	1	1	—		17	17	—
Idaho	1,161	244	44	200	200	—		917	799	118
Illinois	6,968	2,831	102	2,729	1,298	1,431		4,137	3,232	905
Indiana	2,694	1,666	91	1,575	569	1,006		1,028	737	291
Iowa	1,939	1,046	99	947	947	—		893	527	366
Kansas	3,806	1,997	103	1,894	626	1,268		1,809	1,503	306
Kentucky	1,314	536	118	418	418	—		778	604	174
Louisiana	530	364	60	304	304	—		166	97	69
Maine	841	504	16	488	22	466		337	238	99
Maryland	347	180	23	157	157	—		167	167	—
Massachusetts	852	356	5	351	53	298		496	412	84
Michigan	2,877	1,856	83	1,773	533	1,240		1,021	445	576
Minnesota	3,633	2,726	87	2,639	854	1,785		907	569	338
Mississippi	991	379	82	297	297	—		612	448	164
Missouri	3,752	1,381	114	1,267	955	312		2,371	1,837	534
Montana	1,240	183	54	129	129	—		1,057	736	321
Nebraska	2,581	1,042	93	949	530	419		1,539	1,267	272
Nevada	190	35	16	19	19	—		155	138	17
New Hampshire	542	244	10	234	13	221		298	132	166
New Jersey	1,344	587	21	566	324	242		757	234	523
New Mexico	854	136	33	103	103	—		718	622	96
New York	3,454	1,603	57	1,546	617	929		1,851	1,172	679
North Carolina	964	653	100	553	553	—		311	311	—
North Dakota	2,666	1,724	53	1,671	357	1,314		942	759	183
Ohio	3,702	2,334	88	2,246	938	1,308		1,368	700	668
Oklahoma	1,854	667	77	590	590	—		1,187	637	550
Oregon	1,509	277	36	241	241	—		1,232	1,002	230
Pennsylvania	4,905	2,627	66	2,561	1,015	1,546		2,278	1,764	514
Rhode Island	134	39		39	8	31		95	91	4
South Carolina	681	315	46	269	269	—		366	283	83
South Dakota	1,979	1,284	66	1,218	311	907		695	543	152
Tennessee	920	437	92	345	345	—		483	469	14
Texas	4,856	1,468	254	1,214	1,214	—		3,388	2,309	1,079
Utah	613	274	29	245	245	—		339	298	41
Vermont	728	294	14	280	43	237		434	143	291
Virginia	497	324	95	229	229	—		173	172	1
Washington	1,831	320	39	281	281	—		1,511	1,216	295
West Virginia	658	287	55	232	232	—		371	316	55
Wisconsin	3,123	1,922	72	1,850	595	1,255		1,201	761	440
Wyoming	795	122	23	99	99	—		673	618	55

—Represents zero.
[a]Excludes areas corresponding to counties but having no organized county governments.
[b]Excludes school districts operated by a state, county, municipal, or township government.
Note: 2012 Counts are preliminary, and subject to change upon final release. Final data are scheduled to be released by September 2013.

SOURCE: "Table 2. Local Governments by Type and State: 2012," in *2012 Census of Governments: Lists and Structure of Government*, U.S. Department of Commerce, U.S. Census Bureau, July 23, 2012, http://www2.census.gov/govs/cog/2012/formatted_prelim_counts_23jul2012_2.pdf (accessed September 18, 2012)

Tax Rates and Food and Drug Exemptions" (January 1, 2012, http://www.taxadmin.org/fta/rate/sales.pdf), 45 states and the District of Columbia assessed sales taxes. As of January 2012, the five states without a sales tax were Alaska, Delaware, Montana, New Hampshire, and Oregon.

In "State Individual Income Taxes" (January 1, 2012, http://www.taxadmin.org/fta/rate/ind_inc.pdf), the FTA provides information on state income tax rates. As of January 2012, 43 states and the District of Columbia imposed income taxes. The states that did not tax income

TABLE 9.2

Local government finances, 2010

[Dollars in thousands. Coefficients of variation in percentages.]

Description	Local government amount[a]
Revenue[a]	**1,631,203,571**
General revenue[a]	1,435,878,592
Intergovernmental revenue[a]	544,231,765
From federal government	68,435,323
From state government[a]	475,796,443
From local government[a]	(X)
General revenue from own sources	891,646,827
Taxes	568,644,464
Property	427,115,829
Sales and gross receipts	89,062,884
General sales	62,356,404
Selective sales	26,706,480
Motor fuel sales	1,292,097
Alcoholic beverage sales	523,429
Tobacco product sales	435,955
Public utilities	13,755,816
Other selective sales	10,699,183
Individual income tax	24,343,849
Corporate income tax	6,120,533
Motor vehicle license	1,628,103
Other taxes	20,373,266
Charges and miscellaneous general revenue	323,002,363
Current charges	239,784,345
Education	27,321,918
Institutions of higher education	12,984,294
School lunch sales (gross)	6,574,468
Hospitals	67,659,617
Highways	5,186,055
Air transportation (airports)	16,659,528
Parking facilities	3,223,576
Sea and inland port facilities	2,837,914
Natural resources	1,853,378
Parks and recreation	7,868,063
Housing and community development	5,333,904
Sewerage	42,889,836
Solid waste management	15,296,261
Other charges	43,654,295
Miscellaneous general revenue	83,218,018
Interest earnings	26,152,777
Special assessments	7,143,416
Sale of property	2,256,148
Other general revenue	47,665,677
Utility revenue	130,585,246
Water supply	48,627,642
Electric power	62,891,734
Gas supply	8,647,407
Transit	10,418,464
Liquor store revenue	1,294,024
Insurance trust revenue[b]	63,445,708
Unemployment compensation	153,875
Employee retirement	63,291,833
Workers' compensation	(X)
Other insurance trust revenue	(X)
Expenditure	**1,666,568,007**
Intergovernmental expenditure	13,998,317
Direct expenditure	1,652,569,691
Current operation	1,296,839,532
Capital outlay	234,780,797
Construction	180,045,100
Other capital outlay	54,735,697
Assistance and subsidies	10,124,431
Interest on debt	72,234,856
Insurance benefits and repayments	38,590,074
Exhibit: salaries and wages	598,764,105

TABLE 9.2

Local government finances, 2010 [CONTINUED]

[Dollars in thousands. Coefficients of variation in percentages.]

Description	Local government amount[a]
Direct expenditure by function	1,652,569,691
Direct general expenditure	1,430,130,796
Capital outlay	190,657,512
Other direct general expenditure	1,239,473,284
Education	605,902,286
Capital outlay	63,991,743
Higher education	39,765,216
Capital outlay	4,920,387
Elementary and secondary education	566,137,070
Capital outlay	59,071,356
Other education	(X)
Libraries	11,574,960
Public welfare	52,377,274
Cash assistance payments	10,124,431
Vendor payments	6,335,657
Other public welfare	35,917,185
Hospitals	84,146,664
Capital outlay	5,898,943
Health	41,432,654
Social insurance administration	48,105
Veterans' services	(X)
Highways	62,773,217
Capital outlay	25,355,486
Air transportation (airports)	21,404,339
Parking facilities	1,672,397
Sea and inland port facilities	4,084,301
Police protection	83,112,238
Fire protection	42,634,639
Correction	26,843,689
Capital outlay	1,761,265
Protective inspection and regulation	5,264,022
Natural resources	9,770,282
Capital outlay	2,764,838
Parks and recreation	35,345,331
Capital outlay	9,701,337
Housing and community development	42,776,968
Sewerage	50,778,201
Capital outlay	20,593,613
Solid waste management	21,485,079
Capital outlay	1,933,463
Financial administration	18,146,604
Judicial and legal	22,033,582
General public buildings	10,783,062
Other governmental administration	24,252,235
Interest on general debt	60,424,091
Miscellaneous commercial activities	5,243,685
Other and unallocable	85,820,889
Utility expenditure	182,677,591
Capital outlay	44,118,375
Water supply	60,620,732
Electric power	64,690,749
Gas supply	8,326,935
Transit	49,039,174
Liquor store expenditure	1,171,230
Insurance trust expenditure	38,590,074
Unemployment compensation	458,452
Employee retirement	38,131,622
Workers' compensation	(X)
Other insurance trust	(X)
Debt outstanding	**1,715,866,346**
Short-term debt outstanding	30,082,191
Long-term debt outstanding	1,685,784,155
Public debt for private purposes	224,371,736
Long-term debt issued	211,544,268
Long-term debt retired	150,696,476

TABLE 9.2

Local government finances, 2010 [CONTINUED]

[Dollars in thousands. Coefficients of variation in percentages.]

Description	Local government amount[a]
Cash and security holdings	**1,489,028,887**
Insurance trust funds	443,357,271
Unemployment compensation	331,190
Employee retirement	443,026,081
Workers' compensation	(X)
Miscellaneous	(X)
Other than insurance trust funds	1,045,671,616
Offsets to debt	302,241,980
Bond funds	153,667,620
Other	589,762,016

(X) Not applicable.
[a]Duplicative intergovernmental transactions are excluded.
[b]Within insurance trust revenue, net earnings of state retirements systems is a calculated statistic, and thus can be positive or negative. Net earnings is the sum of earnings on investments plus gains on investments minus losses on investments. The change made in 2002 for asset valuation from book to market value in accordance with Statement 34 of the Governmental Accounting Standards Board is reflected in the calculated statistics. Note: These data may not be comparable with statistics previously released under the State Government Finance Summary Report due to differences in the data collection and revision cycle.

SOURCE: Adapted from Jeffrey L. Barnett and Phillip M. Vidal, "Appendix Table A–1. State and Local Government Finances by Level of Government: 2010," in *State and Local Government Finances Summary: 2010*, U.S. Department of Commerce, U.S. Census Bureau, September 2012, http://www2.census.gov/govs/estimate/summary_report.pdf (accessed October 9, 2012)

FIGURE 9.1

Breakdown of local tax revenue, four quarters ending first quarter 2012

Individual income tax 4%
Corporation net income tax 1%
General sales and gross receipts tax 9%
All other taxes 6%
Property tax 80%

SOURCE: Adapted from "Table 1. National Totals of State and Local Tax Revenue, by Type of Tax," in *Quarterly Summary of State & Local Tax Revenue*, U.S. Department of Commerce, U.S. Census Bureau, June 26, 2012, http://www2.census.gov/govs/qtax/2012/q1t1.xls (accessed September 18, 2012)

FIGURE 9.2

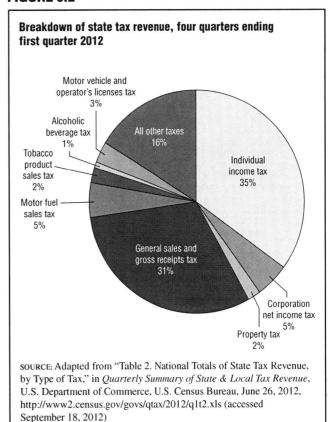

Breakdown of state tax revenue, four quarters ending first quarter 2012

Motor vehicle and operator's licenses tax 3%
Alcoholic beverage tax 1%
Tobacco product sales tax 2%
Motor fuel sales tax 5%
All other taxes 16%
Individual income tax 35%
General sales and gross receipts tax 31%
Corporation net income tax 5%
Property tax 2%

SOURCE: Adapted from "Table 2. National Totals of State Tax Revenue, by Type of Tax," in *Quarterly Summary of State & Local Tax Revenue*, U.S. Department of Commerce, U.S. Census Bureau, June 26, 2012, http://www2.census.gov/govs/qtax/2012/q1t2.xls (accessed September 18, 2012)

were Alaska, Florida, Nevada, South Dakota, Texas, Washington, and Wyoming. Two additional states, New Hampshire and Tennessee, taxed only personal income derived from dividends and interest.

Figure 9.2 indicates the breakdown by type of state taxes that were collected over four quarters ending with the first quarter of 2012. Individual income taxes (35%) and general sales and gross receipts taxes (31%) were the two largest components of the total collected.

State Expenditures

The Census Bureau reports that state governments had expenditures of more than $1.9 trillion in 2010. (See Table 9.3.) Approximately $486 billion of this total was in the form of transfers to other governments, such as local governments within the state. The remainder was devoted to spending priorities at the state level. Public welfare composed the single largest expense ($404.3 billion), followed by education ($254.1 billion). State spending on education is primarily for higher education, such as colleges and universities.

The Census Bureau (2012, http://ftp2.census.gov/govs/apes/11stus.txt) estimates that state governments employed 3.8 million full-time employees and 1.5 million part-time employees in 2011.

TABLE 9.3

Breakdown of state government finances, 2010

[Dollars in thousands. Coefficients of variation in percentages.]

Description	State government amount
Revenue[a]	**2,036,240,449**
General revenue[a]	1,562,240,321
Intergovernmental revenue[a]	575,564,000
From federal government	555,296,681
From state government[a]	(X)
From local government[a]	20,267,319
General revenue from own sources	986,676,321
Taxes	701,005,079
Property	14,544,986
Sales and gross receipts	342,113,482
General sales	222,553,989
Selective sales	119,559,493
Motor fuel sales	36,587,658
Alcoholic beverage sales	5,504,690
Tobacco product sales	16,831,613
Public utilities	14,534,925
Other selective sales	46,100,607
Individual income tax	235,994,401
Corporate income tax	36,739,534
Motor vehicle license	20,870,278
Other taxes	50,742,398
Charges and miscellaneous general revenue	285,671,242
Current charges	169,795,726
Education	94,530,218
Institutions of higher education	93,080,853
School lunch sales (gross)	33,802
Hospitals	42,938,361
Highways	6,928,916
Air transportation (airports)	1,327,248
Parking facilities	12,292
Sea and inland port facilities	1,037,513
Natural resources	2,659,421
Parks and recreation	1,535,723
Housing and community development	696,349
Sewerage	540,200
Solid waste management	420,054
Other charges	17,169,431
Miscellaneous general revenue	115,875,516
Interest earnings	34,581,272
Special assessments	170,739
Sale of property	691,949
Other general revenue	80,431,556
Utility revenue	15,121,578
Water supply	253,843
Electric power	12,267,847
Gas supply	12,505
Transit	2,587,383
Liquor store revenue	6,494,993
Insurance trust revenue[b]	452,383,557
Unemployment compensation	75,037,579
Employee retirement	353,373,854
Workers' compensation	16,591,538
Other insurance trust revenue	7,380,586
Expenditure	**1,943,963,166**
Intergovernmental expenditure	486,025,452
Direct expenditure	1,457,937,714
Current operation	934,147,341
Capital outlay	117,538,296
Construction	100,797,587
Other capital outlay	16,740,709
Assistance and subsidies	37,660,372
Interest on debt	47,387,833
Insurance benefits and repayments	321,203,872
Exhibit: salaries and wages	243,709,711

TABLE 9.3

Breakdown of state government finances, 2010 [CONTINUED]

[Dollars in thousands. Coefficients of variation in percentages.]

Description	State government amount
Direct expenditure by function	1,457,937,714
Direct general expenditure	1,107,983,278
Capital outlay	112,672,836
Other direct general expenditure	995,310,442
Education	254,063,159
Capital outlay	28,641,426
Higher education	202,964,338
Capital outlay	25,899,030
Elementary and secondary education	7,892,395
Capital outlay	1,066,317
Other education	43,206,426
Libraries	448,604
Public welfare	404,330,628
Cash assistance payments	12,569,841
Vendor payments	344,970,051
Other public welfare	46,790,736
Hospitals	58,707,975
Capital outlay	2,653,730
Health	40,064,903
Social insurance administration	5,108,615
Veterans' services	793,609
Highways	93,096,844
Capital outlay	64,754,500
Air transportation (airports)	1,724,180
Parking facilities	7,436
Sea and inland port facilities	1,244,604
Police protection	12,376,317
Fire protection	(X)
Correction	46,095,189
Capital outlay	1,368,218
Protective inspection and regulation	9,018,333
Natural resources	19,335,871
Capital outlay	2,336,778
Parks and recreation	4,939,025
Capital outlay	909,074
Housing and community development	10,715,455
Sewerage	1,117,693
Capital outlay	488,456
Solid waste management	2,281,216
Capital outlay	170,748
Financial administration	21,831,165
Judicial and legal	20,993,935
General public buildings	4,218,724
Other governmental administration	4,587,805
Interest on general debt	45,296,517
Miscellaneous commercial activities	1,699,950
Other and unallocable	43,885,526
Utility expenditure	23,506,881
Capital outlay	4,847,992
Water supply	378,133
Electric power	12,067,802
Gas supply	11,032
Transit	11,049,914
Liquor store expenditure	5,243,683
Insurance trust expenditure	321,203,872
Unemployment compensation	134,908,383
Employee retirement	166,956,051
Workers' compensation	12,508,195
Other insurance trust	6,831,243
Debt outstanding	**1,113,207,691**
Short-term debt outstanding	14,708,791
Long-term debt outstanding	1,098,498,900
Public debt for private purposes	395,097,945
Long-term debt issued	183,132,563
Long-term debt retired	127,648,397

TABLE 9.3

Breakdown of state government finances, 2010 [CONTINUED]

[Dollars in thousands. Coefficients of variation in percentages.]

Description	State government amount
Cash and security holdings	**3,320,750,750**
Insurance trust funds	2,214,658,647
Unemployment compensation	−17,632,312
Employee retirement	2,134,633,277
Workers' compensation	91,242,984
Miscellaneous	6,414,698
Other than insurance trust funds	1,106,092,103
Offsets to debt	498,590,648
Bond funds	52,814,520
Other	554,686,935

(X) Not applicable.
aDuplicative intergovernmental transactions are excluded.
bWithin insurance trust revenue, net earnings of state retirements systems is a calculated statistic, and thus can be positive or negative. Net earnings is the sum of earnings on investments plus gains on investments minus losses on investments. The change made in 2002 for asset valuation from book to market value in accordance with Statement 34 of the Governmental Accounting Standards Board is reflected in the calculated statistics. Note: These data may not be comparable with statistics previously released under the State Government Finance Summary Report due to differences in the data collection and revision cycle.

SOURCE: Adapted from Jeffrey L. Barnett and Phillip M. Vidal "Appendix Table A-1. State and Local Government Finances by Level of Government: 2010," in *State and Local Government Finances Summary: 2010*, U.S. Department of Commerce, U.S. Census Bureau, September 2012, http://www2.census.gov/govs/estimate/summary_report.pdf (accessed October 9, 2012)

FEDERAL GOVERNMENT

For accounting purposes, the federal government operates on a fiscal year (FY) that begins in October and runs through the end of September. Thus, FY 2013 covers the period of October 1, 2012, to September 30, 2013. Each year by the first Monday in February the U.S. president must present a proposed budget to the U.S. House of Representatives. This is the amount of money that the president estimates will be required to operate the federal government during the next fiscal year.

It can take several months for the House to debate, negotiate, and approve a final budget. The budget must also be approved by the U.S. Senate. This entire process can take many months, and sometimes longer than a year. This means that the federal government can be well into, or beyond, a fiscal year before knowing the exact amount of its budget for that year. If a new fiscal year begins and the formal budget for that year has still not passed, then Congress passes temporary spending bills called continuing resolutions that fund federal government operations for a short time, typically a few weeks or a month or two, while negotiations continue on the formal budget.

Budget enactment delays are much more likely when Congress is divided by political partisanship (lack of cooperation between parties). The FY 2011 budget was proposed in February 2010, but not enacted until April 2011 due to fierce disagreements about government spending. Likewise, the FY 2012 budget was proposed in February 2011 and enacted in December 2011. These delays necessitated the passage of several continuing resolutions to keep the federal government operating. Continuing resolutions have expiration dates, which if reached cause the federal government to cease all nonessential operations. Such a government "shutdown" last occurred in 1995 and 1996 and lasted for several months.

The budget negotiations that began in 2010 featured bitter battles between Republican and Democratic lawmakers. This was a result, in part, of the midterm elections of November 2010 that gave Republicans control of the House and Democrats control of the Senate. Many of the newly elected Republican congressional members had been supported by the tea party, a political movement that strongly favors less taxation and smaller government. Consequently, Republican lawmakers as a whole took hardline positions against economic policies that were favored by President Barack Obama (1961–), a Democrat. As will be explained later in this chapter, the bipartisan environment resulted in massive fights over long-term plans for tackling the economic challenges that face the country, including the enormous national debt.

Detailed data on the finances of the federal government are maintained by the Office of Management and Budget (OMB), an executive office of the U.S. president. The OMB assists the president in preparing the federal budget and supervises budget administration. Budget information is available at http://www.whitehouse.gov/omb/budget/Overview. Budget documents include historical tables that provide annual data on federal government receipts, outlays, debt, and employment dating back to 1940 or earlier. The FY 2013 budget includes final values for years to 2011 and estimates from 2012 to 2017.

Federal Revenues

According to the OMB, in *Historical Tables: Budget of the U.S. Government, Fiscal Year 2013* (February 2012, http://www.gpo.gov/fdsys/pkg/BUDGET-2013-TAB/pdf/BUDGET-2013-TAB.pdf), the federal government had revenues (receipts) of $2.3 trillion in FY 2011. The two largest sources of revenue for the federal government in FY 2011 were individual income taxes (47%) and social insurance and retirement receipts (36%). (See Figure 9.3.)

TAXES ON INCOME. In the United States tax rates are approved by Congress and signed into law by the president; the Internal Revenue Service, a bureau of the U.S. Department of the Treasury, enforces the tax codes and collects tax payments, which are due each year on Tax Day, which is typically April 15.

The percentage of an individual's income that he or she pays in federal tax is based on his or her income

FIGURE 9.3

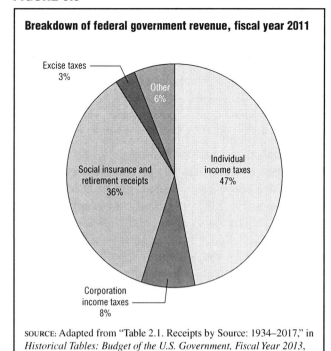

Breakdown of federal government revenue, fiscal year 2011

Excise taxes
3%

Other
6%

Individual
income taxes
47%

Social insurance and
retirement receipts
36%

Corporation
income taxes
8%

SOURCE: Adapted from "Table 2.1. Receipts by Source: 1934–2017," in *Historical Tables: Budget of the U.S. Government, Fiscal Year 2013*, Office of Management and Budget, February 2012, http://www.gpo .gov/fdsys/pkg/BUDGET-2013-TAB/pdf/BUDGET-2013-TAB.pdf (accessed September 10, 2012)

level, which determines the individual's tax bracket. Tax brackets change as Congress modifies the tax codes, but individuals with higher incomes are always taxed at a higher rate than individuals with lower incomes. Through a variety of tax credits and deductions, individuals can lower the amount of income on which taxes are calculated, thereby lowering the amount of tax they pay.

The federal tax on corporate income has been in effect since 1909. Because corporations are owned, and individuals derive income from them, the potential exists for "double taxation," that is, the same income is taxed twice, once as corporate income and, when the profits have been distributed to shareholders, again as individual income. To reduce the effects of double taxation, various credits and deductions have been enacted over the decades to allow income to pass through a corporation without being taxed until it reaches the individual. Credits and depreciation schedules reduce the amount of revenue that is subject to tax.

SOCIAL INSURANCE AND RETIREMENT RECEIPTS. Social insurance and retirement receipts are collected to fund specific programs for people who are retired, disabled, unemployed, or poor. The primary programs are Social Security and Medicare. Social Security provides funds to most workers who retire or become disabled. It also pays money to the survivors of workers who die. Medicare is a federal health insurance program for people aged 65 years and older and people with disabilities.

In "Update 2012" (February 2012, http://www.ssa .gov/pubs/10003.html#a0=0), the Social Security Administration explains that as of 2012 the federal government collected money to pay for these two programs as follows:

• Social Security—a tax of 10.4% on earned annual income up to $110,100. In other words, people who earn more than the annual limit pay the tax on $110,100, regardless of how much they earn.

• Medicare—a tax of 2.9% on all earned annual income.

These taxes are known as payroll taxes because they are assessed based on the amounts that businesses pay their workers. For 2012 part of the tax (6.2% for Social Security plus 1.45% for Medicare) was paid by employers. The remainder (4.2% for Social Security plus 1.45% for Medicare) was paid by wage earners via deductions from their paychecks. Self-employed people had to pay the entire tax bill but could deduct half of it as a business expense when they filed their income tax return for 2012.

As explained in Chapter 5, unemployment insurance is a joint federal-state program that is funded almost entirely by employers. Employers that meet certain criteria (regarding number of employees and amount of payroll) pay both state and federal unemployment taxes.

SALES AND EXCISE TAXES AND OTHER RECEIPTS. Sales and excise taxes are considered to be taxes on consumption. Even though there is no federal sales tax, the federal government does levy excise taxes on items such as airplane tickets, gasoline, alcoholic beverages, firearms, and tobacco products. Excise taxes on certain commodities are often hypothecated, meaning they are used to pay for a related government service. For example, fuel taxes are typically used to pay for road and bridge construction or public transportation, or cigarette excise taxes may be used to cover government-supported health care programs. Excise taxes can be intended to generate revenue or to discourage use of the taxed product (as in high cigarette taxes that raise the per-pack cost in an attempt to discourage smoking).

The "other" category in Figure 9.3 includes estate and gift taxes and customs duties. Estate and gift taxes are taxes on wealth. Estate taxes are levied against a person's estate after that person dies, whereas gift taxes are levied against the giver while the giver is alive. Estate and gift taxes only apply to amounts over specified limits. Customs duties are taxes charged on goods that are imported into the United States. The taxes vary by product and by exporting nation.

Federal Spending

According to the OMB, the federal government spent just over $3.6 trillion in FY 2011. (See Table 9.4.) The OMB breaks down expenditures into broad categories

TABLE 9.4

Breakdown of federal government spending, fiscal year 2011

Superfunction and function	2011 In millions of dollars
National defense	705,625
Human resources	2,414,738
Education, training, employment, and social services	101,233
Health	372,500
Medicare	485,653
Income security	597,352
Social security	730,811
Veterans benefits and services	127,189
Physical resources	161,850
Energy	12,174
Natural resources and environment	45,470
Commerce and housing credit	−12,575
Transportation	92,965
Community and regional development	23,816
Net interest	229,968
Other functions.	177,374
International affairs	45,685
General science, space, and technology	29,466
Agriculture	20,661
Administration of justice	56,055
General government	25,507
Allowances	
Undistributed offsetting receipts	−86,494
Total, federal outlays	**3,603,061**

SOURCE: Adapted from "Table 3.1. Outlays by Superfunction and Function: 1940–2017," in *Historical Tables: Budget of the U.S. Government, Fiscal Year 2013*, Office of Management and Budget, February 2012, http://www .gpo.gov/fdsys/pkg/BUDGET-2013-TAB/pdf/BUDGET-2013-TAB.pdf (accessed September 10, 2012)

called superfunctions and narrower categories called functions. Overall, human resources were the largest expenditure for the federal government, accounting for $2.4 trillion in FY 2011. The largest single component of federal spending was for the Social Security program, which accounted for $730.8 billion of expenditures.

As of November 2012, federal government employment data for 2011 were not available from the Census Bureau. However, the agency (March 2010, http:// www2.census.gov/govs/apes/10fedfun.pdf) indicates that as of March 2010, the federal government employed more than 3 million civilian (nonmilitary) employees.

Federal Surpluses and Deficits

If the government spends less money than it takes in during a fiscal year, the difference is known as a budget surplus. Likewise, if spending is higher than revenues, the difference is called a budget deficit. A balanced budget occurs when spending and revenue are the same.

Figure 9.4 shows the annual budget surplus or deficit from 1901 to 2017 as reported in the OMB's FY 2013 budget (note that 2012 to 2017 are estimated). In general, the federal government had a balanced budget for more than half of the 20th century, excluding slight deficits that occurred during World War I (1914–1918) and World War II (1939–1945). Beginning in 1970 the United States had an annual budget deficit for nearly three decades. The years 1998 to 2001 had budget surpluses. In 2000 the surplus

FIGURE 9.4

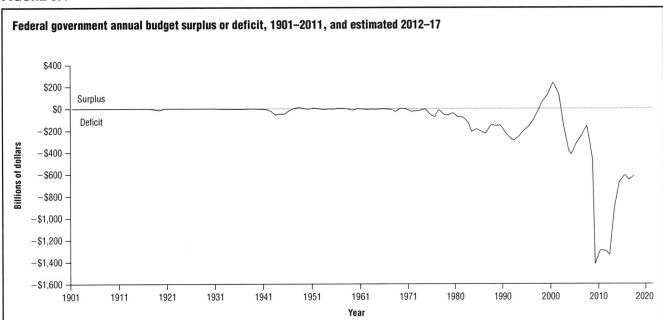

Federal government annual budget surplus or deficit, 1901–2011, and estimated 2012–17

SOURCE: Adapted from "Table 1.1. Summary of Receipts, Outlays, and Surpluses or Deficits (−): 1789–2017," in *Historical Tables: Budget of the U.S. Government, Fiscal Year 2013*, Office of Management and Budget, February 2012, http://www.gpo.gov/fdsys/pkg/BUDGET-2013-TAB/pdf/BUDGET-2013-TAB.pdf (accessed September 10, 2012)

reached a record $236.2 billion. Budget deficits returned in 2002 and reached record lows over the following years. The budget deficit for 2009 was $1.4 trillion, which was a new record low. The OMB predicts that the 2012 deficit will exceed $1.3 trillion. Shrinking budget deficits are expected through 2017.

National Debt

Whenever the federal government has a budget deficit, the Treasury Department must borrow money to cover the difference. The total amount of money that the Treasury Department has borrowed over the years is known as the federal debt, or more commonly the national debt. Budget surpluses cause the debt to go down, whereas deficits increase the debt.

The national debt was low until the early 1940s, when it jogged upward in response to government spending during World War II. (See Figure 9.5.) Over the next three decades the debt increased at a slow pace. During the late 1970s the national debt began a steep climb that continued into the second decade of the 21st century. The budget surpluses from 1998 to 2001 had a slight dampening effect on the growth of the debt but did not actually decrease the amount of debt. The budget deficits of the years that followed sent the debt into another rapid incline. By the end of FY 2011 the national debt stood at $14.8 trillion.

BORROWED MONEY AND IOUS. The national debt has two components: money that the federal government has borrowed from the public and money that the federal government has lent itself. The public lends money to the

federal government by buying federal bonds and other securities. The government borrows the money with a promise to pay it back with interest after a set term. Some of the most common federal securities sold to the public are Treasury bills, Treasury notes, Treasury bonds, and savings bonds. These vary in value, interest paid, and set terms. Public investors include individuals and businesses (both domestic and foreign) and state and local governments.

The federal government also borrows from itself. This is debt owed by one Treasury account to another. Most of the so-called internal debt involves federal trust funds. For example, if a trust fund takes in more revenue in a year than is paid out, it lends the extra money to another federal account. In exchange, the lending trust fund receives an interest-bearing security (basically an IOU) that is redeemable in the future from the Treasury Department. In "Federal Debt and the Commitments of Federal Trust Funds" (May 6, 2003, http://www.cbo.gov/sites/default/files/cbofiles/ftpdocs/39xx/doc3948/10-25-longrangebrief4.pdf), the Congressional Budget Office (CBO) states that "what is in the trust funds is simply the government's promise to pay itself back at some time in the future."

As of November 7, 2012, the Treasury Department (http://www.treasurydirect.gov/NP/BPDLogin?application=np) reported that the national debt was $16.2 trillion, broken down as follows:

• Owed to the public—$11.4 trillion (70% of the total)

• Intragovernmental—$4.8 trillion (30% of the total)

FIGURE 9.5

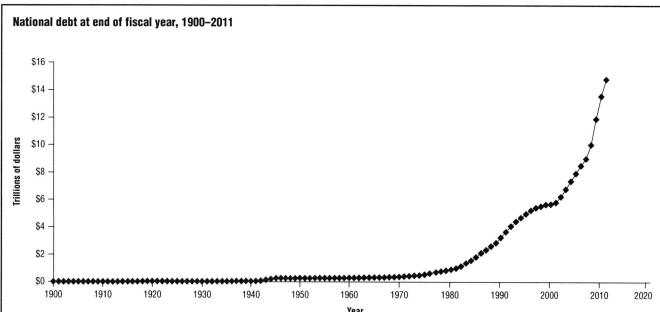

National debt at end of fiscal year, 1900–2011

SOURCE: Adapted from "Historical Debt Outstanding—Annual: 1900–1949," "Historical Debt Outstanding—Annual: 1950–1999," and "Historical Debt Outstanding—Annual: 2000–2010," in *Public Debt Reports*, U.S. Department of the Treasury, Bureau of the Public Debt, October 1, 2010, http://www.treasurydirect.gov/govt/reports/pd/histdebt/histdebt.htm (accessed September 18, 2012); and "Table I. Summary of Treasury Securities Outstanding, September 30, 2011," in *Monthly Statement of the Public Debt of the United States, September 30, 2011*, U.S. Treasury Department, September 30, 2011, http://www.treasurydirect.gov/govt/reports/pd/mspd/2011/opds092011.pdf (accessed September 18, 2012)

FIGURE 9.6

Federal debt held by the public as a percentage of GDP (gross domestic product), 1940–2012 and projected to 2022

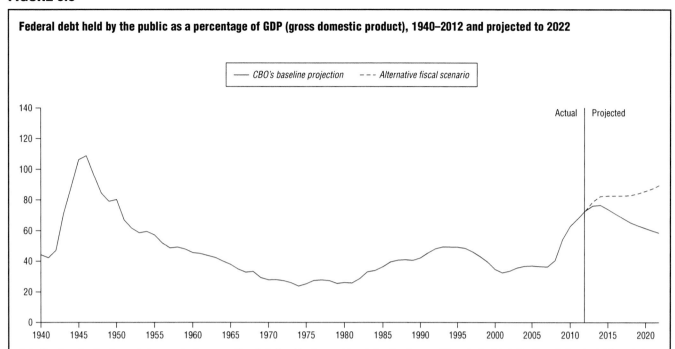

Note: The alternative fiscal scenario incorporates the assumptions that all expiring tax provisions (other than the payroll tax reduction), including those that expired at the end of December 2011, are instead extended; that the alternative minimum tax is indexed for inflation after 2011 (starting at the 2011 exemption amount); that Medicare's payment rates for physicians' services are held constant at their current level; and that the automatic enforcement procedures specified by the Budget Control Act of 2011 do not take effect. The budgetary effects under the alternative fiscal scenario also include the incremental interest costs associated with projected additional borrowing. CBO = Congressional Budget Office.

SOURCE: "Summary Figure 1. Federal Debt Held by the Public, Historically and As Projected in CBO's Baseline and Under an Alternative Fiscal Scenario," in *An Update to the Budget and Economic Outlook: Fiscal Years 2012 to 2022*, Congressional Budget Office, August 22, 2012, http://www.cbo.gov/sites/default/files/cbofiles/attachments/08-22-2012-Update_to_Outlook.pdf (accessed September 18, 2012)

AS A PERCENTAGE OF THE GROSS DOMESTIC PRODUCT. Economists often discuss the national debt in terms of its percentage of the gross domestic product (GDP; the total market value of final goods and services that are produced within an economy in a given year) because a debt amount alone does not provide a complete picture of the effect of that debt on the one who owes it. According to the Central Intelligence Agency (CIA), in *World Factbook: United States* (October 4, 2012, https://www.cia.gov/library/publications/the-world-factbook/geos/us.html), the U.S. national debt owed to the public made up an estimated 67.7% of the nation's GDP in 2011.

Figure 9.6 is a graph prepared by the CBO showing the national debt held by the public as a percentage of the GDP between 1940 and 2012 and projected to 2022. As explained in Chapter 2, the CBO publishes annual budget outlooks that are based on various assumptions about the nation's future economy. For example, Figure 9.6 reflects two far different trajectories for the debt-to-GDP ratio from 2013 onward, depending on congressional actions (or lack thereof) regarding laws related to taxes, spending, and debt reduction.

INTERNATIONAL COMPARISON. In *World Factbook* (2012, https://www.cia.gov/library/publications/the-world-factbook/), the CIA ranks nations of the world in descending

order of national debt owed to the public as a percentage of their GDP in 2011. The United States ranked 35th on this list. The industrialized nation with the largest percentage was Japan (211.7%).

THE BURDEN ON THE ECONOMY. The national debt represents a twofold burden on the U.S. economy. The debt owed to the public imposes a current burden. The federal government pays out interest to investors, and these interest payments are funded by current taxpayers. The debt that the federal government owes to itself is a future burden. At some point in the future the securities that were issued for intragovernmental debt must be redeemed for cash. The government will have to raise these funds by raising taxes, reducing spending, and/or borrowing more money from the public.

THE DEBT CEILING. The debt ceiling is a limit imposed by Congress on the amount of the national debt. The U.S. Government Accountability Office (GAO) explains in *Debt Limit: Delays Create Debt Management Challenges and Increase Uncertainty in the Treasury Market* (February 2011, http://www.gao.gov/new.items/d11203.pdf) that a debt ceiling was first enacted by Congress during World War I. It has been raised numerous times since then. The GAO notes that "the debt limit does not control or limit the ability of the federal government to run deficits or incur obligations. Rather, it is a limit on the ability to pay obligations already incurred." In other words, the debt limit forbids the Treasury Department from borrowing funds to pay for already implemented government programs and activities. This includes paying interest due on bonds that have been sold.

In 2011 the process of raising the debt ceiling turned into a political tussle. Republican lawmakers demanded deficit reduction measures, including deep spending cuts from the Obama administration, as a condition for raising the debt ceiling. The battle raged for months and was "settled" in August 2011, just hours before the United States was going to hit the debt ceiling. The Budget Control Act of 2011 allows the debt ceiling to be raised, but calls for trillions of dollars in spending cuts over coming years.

In "How the Across-the-Board Cuts in the Budget Control Act Will Work" (April 27, 2012, http://www.cbpp.org/cms/?fa=view&id=3635), Richard Kogan of the Center on Budget and Policy Priorities notes that the law reduces funding by more than $1 trillion through 2021 for some government programs. It also calls for the establishment of a special committee to propose legislation to reduce deficits by another $1.2 trillion over the same time period. The law includes a backup plan, called sequestration, that will implement automatic cuts across almost all government programs beginning in January 2013 if the deficit reduction committee cannot reach an agreement. In November 2011 the so-called supercommittee announced that it had failed to reach an agreement. Thus, as of November 2012 the sequestration spending cuts were scheduled to go into effect in January 2013.

PUBLIC INVESTMENT AND TAXES

To fund itself, the federal government uses the money of its constituents. The buying of federal securities, such as bonds, represents a voluntary investment in the government by the public. Federal securities are considered to be a safe low-risk investment because they are backed by an entity that has been in existence for more than 200 years and has a proven track record of fiscal soundness. However, money invested in government securities is not available for private investment. In general, private investments are seen as more stimulating for the economy because they provide direct funds for growth, such as the building of new factories and the hiring of new workers. Public (government) investment may or may not have a stimulating effect on the economy, depending on how the funds are spent.

Taxes represent an involuntary investment by the public in government. The effect of taxes on the economy is a source of never-ending debate in U.S. politics. Taxing personal income decreases the spending power of the public because people have less money to invest in private enterprise or to use to consume goods and services.

Limited taxation is favored by those who believe that workers and companies with more available money to spend will participate to a greater extent in the economy. This, they say, will lead to economic growth. Others observe that cutting taxes without severely reducing government spending leads to large budget deficits and undermines the government programs that provide a social safety net to the disadvantaged.

Tax Breaks

Historically, the federal government has allowed tax breaks (such as deductions) on income or expenses that are related to specific activities. The prime example is mortgage interest. Most taxpayers can deduct the interest they pay each year on their mortgages. The government uses tax breaks to encourage activities it considers good for society in general, such as being a homeowner or donating to charities. However, tax breaks represent substantial amounts of lost revenue to the federal government, perhaps as much as $1 trillion per year. In fact, many individuals and businesses—nearly half by one estimate—end up paying no federal income tax each year. Some analysts call for eliminating or reducing tax breaks so the federal government can collect more revenue to fund programs or reduce the federal deficit. Nevertheless, tax deductions are extremely popular with taxpayers, especially those who are able or potentially able to take advantage of them. Thus, eliminating or curtailing tax breaks would be politically unpopular.

Tax Cuts

In general, the Republican Party advocates smaller government and lower taxes. Even though its preference for lower taxes includes Americans at all income levels, the party is especially concerned about Americans at the highest income levels. The argument is that high-income earners create jobs and invest money, actions that help all Americans and improve the overall economy. By contrast, the Democratic Party typically favors higher taxes on high-income earners.

The Economic Growth and Tax Relief Reconciliation Act of 2001 and the Jobs and Growth Tax Relief Reconciliation Act of 2003 were initiated by the first administration of President George W. Bush (1946–), a Republican, and are collectively referred to as the "Bush tax cuts." The laws instituted a series of tax rate reductions and incentive measures that were phased in over several years. The laws were designed to expire on January 1, 2011, at which time the higher tax rates in effect before the laws were implemented would return.

When President Obama took office in January 2009, the economy was in the midst of the Great Recession (which lasted from December 2007 to June 2009). Republican lawmakers strongly favored extending the

Bush tax cuts, arguing that government should not increase taxes during the economic slowdown. Obama and many fellow Democratic lawmakers favored extending the tax cuts, but only for wage earners with an annual income of less than $200,000 for individuals or $250,000 for married couples. This idea received stiff resistance from Republicans. In a compromise, the Obama administration supported temporary extensions of the tax cuts through the Tax Relief, Unemployment Insurance Reauthorization, and Job Creation Act of 2010. It extended the Bush tax cuts through year-end 2012. As of November 2012, the Obama administration (http://www.whitehouse.gov/issues/taxes/tax-cuts) continued to push for a law that would extend only the income-capped tax cuts, arguing that they would benefit 98% of Americans and 97% of small businesses. This plan, however, was strongly opposed by Republican lawmakers.

THE FUTURE OF SOCIAL SECURITY AND MEDICARE

Social Security and Medicare are two of the most expensive programs that are operated by the federal government. (See Table 9.4.) Together, they accounted for more than $1.2 trillion of spending in FY 2011, or 34% of total expenditures.

As of 2012, people born in 1929 or later qualify for retirement benefits once they have worked for 10 years. Benefit amounts are based on wage history; thus, higher-paid workers will have higher retirement benefits than lower-paid workers. The Social Security Administration indicates in "Retirement Planner: Benefits by Year of Birth" (October 17, 2012, http://www.socialsecurity.gov/retire2/agereduction.htm) the age at which full benefits can be paid:

- People born in or before 1937—aged 65

- People born between 1938 and 1959—sliding age scale ranging from 65 years and 2 months to 66 years and 10 months

- People born in 1960 or after—aged 67

People who have worked for at least 10 years are eligible for permanently reduced retirement benefits starting at age 62. Benefits for widows, widowers, and family members have varying age requirements and other conditions that must be met. Medicare coverage begins at age 65 for everyone except for certain disabled people who can qualify earlier.

Since their inception, the Social Security and Medicare programs have been a source of partisan contention and debate. Much of the debate has centered on how the programs should be funded and the role of government in social welfare. During the 1990s concerns began to arise about how the nation can afford these programs in the future as the population ages and as the number of earners contributing to the plans decreases.

Fewer Contributors, More Beneficiaries

Figure 9.7 shows the percentage of the U.S. population aged 65 years and older from 2000 to 2011 and projections for 2012 to 2037. A huge increase in the aged population is expected to take place after 2015 because of the baby boom that followed World War II. However, as these workers retire, there will be fewer workers contributing to Social Security because succeeding generations have been smaller due to declining birth rates. At the same time, life expectancies have been increasing, meaning that elderly people are living longer past retirement age and collecting benefits for more years.

Funding Social Security

In *A Summary of the 2012 Annual Social Security and Medicare Trust Fund Reports* (April 2012, http://www.ssa.gov/oact/TRSUM/tr12summary.pdf), an annual report on the status of the Social Security trust funds—Old-Age and Survivors Insurance (OASI), Disability Insurance (DI), and Health Insurance (HI)—the Social Security Board of Trustees shows historical trust fund ratios and estimates future ratios. (See Figure 9.8.) The trustees note that assets as a percentage of annual expenditures peaked for the DI and HI trust funds between 2003 and 2007. The OASI trust fund peaked above 400% in 2011. Table 9.5 shows the first years in which the outgoing amounts from the trust funds will exceed the income (including interest) into the trust funds. It also shows the years in which the trust funds will be exhausted. All the trust funds face exhaustion between 2016 and 2035.

FIXING THE PROBLEM. The issue of preparing for future shortfalls in Social Security has become a fierce

FIGURE 9.7

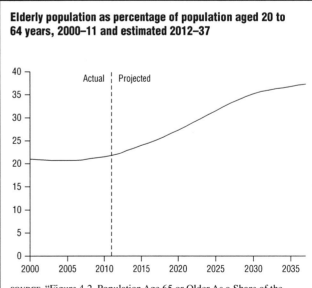

Elderly population as percentage of population aged 20 to 64 years, 2000–11 and estimated 2012–37

SOURCE: "Figure 4-2. Population Age 65 or Older As a Share of the Population Ages 20 to 64," in *The 2012 Long-Term Budget Outlook*, Congressional Budget Office, June 2012, http://cbo.gov/sites/default/files/cbofiles/attachments/06-05-Long-Term_Budget_Outlook_2.pdf (accessed September 19, 2012)

FIGURE 9.8

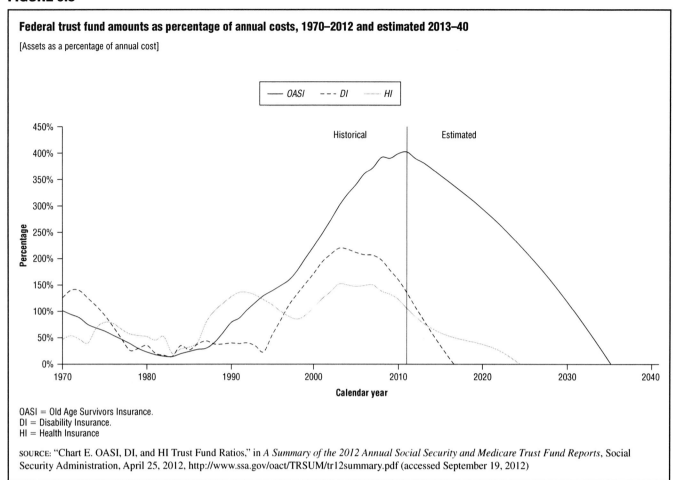

Federal trust fund amounts as percentage of annual costs, 1970–2012 and estimated 2013–40

[Assets as a percentage of annual cost]

OASI = Old Age Survivors Insurance.
DI = Disability Insurance.
HI = Health Insurance

SOURCE: "Chart E. OASI, DI, and HI Trust Fund Ratios," in *A Summary of the 2012 Annual Social Security and Medicare Trust Fund Reports*, Social Security Administration, April 25, 2012, http://www.ssa.gov/oact/TRSUM/tr12summary.pdf (accessed September 19, 2012)

TABLE 9.5

Key dates for the Social Security and Medicare trust funds as of April 2012

	OASI	DI	OASDI	HI
Year of peak trust fund ratio[a]	2011	2003	2008	2003
First year outgo exceeds income excluding interest[b]	2010	2005	2010	2008
First year outgo exceeds income including interest[b]	2023	2009	2021	2008
Year trust fund assets are exhausted	2035	2016	2033	2024

[a]Dates pertain to the post-2000 period.
[b]Dates indicate the first year that a condition is projected to occur and to persist annually thereafter through 2086.
OASI = Old Age Survivors Insurance.
DI = Disability Insurance.
OASDI = Old Age Survivors Insurance and Disability Insurance.
HI = Health Insurance.

SOURCE: "Key Dates for the Trust Funds," in *A Summary of the 2012 Annual Social Security and Medicare Trust Fund Reports*, Social Security Administration, April 25, 2012, http://www.ssa.gov/oact/TRSUM/tr12summary.pdf (accessed September 19, 2012)

debate. Republicans generally favor allowing some privatization of the Social Security system, meaning that workers would be able to partially opt out of the Social Security plan and establish their own retirement savings accounts. However, President Obama is against privatization because he believes that such a plan would tie benefits to the stability of the stock market, which has a history of experiencing major fluctuations. Other possible options include increasing the retirement age and/or decreasing benefits, particularly for wealthier retirees. However, neither of these options would be politically popular with the American public.

FEDERAL GOVERNMENT MANIPULATION OF MACROECONOMICS

The federal government plays a role in the national economy as a tax collector, spender, and employer. Federal policy makers also engage in purposeful manipulation of the U.S. economy at the macroeconomic level—for example, by influencing supply and demand factors. This was not always the case. Before the 1930s the government mostly maintained a hands-off approach to macroeconomic affairs—a tradition that dated back to the founding of the nation. However, the ravages of the Great Depression (1929–1939) brought a level of desperation that encouraged leaders to attempt to influence macroeconomic factors. Even though these efforts were largely futile at soothing deep economic depression, they accustomed Americans to the idea of government interference in economic affairs.

When massive federal spending during World War II helped end the Great Depression, policy makers believed they had discovered a new solution, a government solution, for economic downturns. Government efforts to manage macroeconomic factors became a routine matter over the following decades. These manipulations are commonly divided into two categories: fiscal policy and monetary policy.

Fiscal Policy

The word *fiscal* is derived from the Latin term *fiscalis*, meaning "treasury." It is believed that a fiscalis was originally a woven basket in which money was kept. In modern English, the word *fiscal* has become synonymous with the word *financial*. The federal government's fiscal policy is concerned with the collection and spending of public money so as to influence macroeconomic affairs. Examples of fiscal policy include:

- Increasing government spending to spur businesses to produce more and hire more; this can lower the unemployment rate

- Increasing taxes to pull money out of the hands of consumers; this can lower excessive demand that is driving high inflation rates

- Decreasing taxes to put more money in the hands of consumers; this can increase demand and consequently increase supply (production)

These examples illustrate optimistic outcomes. In reality, the actions of fiscal policy can have complicated and unforeseen effects on the U.S. economy. The situation described in the first example can backfire if production does not grow fast enough to satisfy consumer demand. The result will be rising prices and high inflation rates. Likewise, tax increases and decreases can have unexpected and undesirable consequences. The relationships between the major macroeconomic factors—unemployment, inflation, and supply and demand—are complex and difficult to keep in balance.

Fiscal policy is strongly associated with the economist John Maynard Keynes (1883–1946) and is a cornerstone of Keynesian economics.

Monetary Policy

Monetary policy is concerned with influencing the supply of money and credit and the demand for them to achieve specific economic goals. The actions of monetary policy are not as direct and obvious as the tax and spend activities that are associated with fiscal policy. Monetary changes are achieved indirectly through the nation's banking system. The following are some of the results of monetary policy changes:

- Increasing the amount of money that banks lend to the public—this leads to greater borrowing, which puts more money into the hands of consumers, increasing the demand for goods and services

- Decreasing the amount of money that banks lend to the public—this leads to less borrowing, which slows the growth of the money supply and dampens demand, which can reduce high inflation rates

- Lowering interest rates on loans—this encourages borrowing, which increases the money supply and consumer demand

- Having higher interest rates on loans—this discourages people from borrowing more money, which slows the growth of the money supply and can reduce high inflation rates

Just as in fiscal policy, it is difficult to achieve the desired results. An oversupply of money and credit will aggravate price inflation if production cannot meet increased consumer demand. Likewise, an undersupply can lower consumer demand too much and stifle economic growth. The challenge for the federal government is deciding when, and by how much, money supply and credit availability should be changed to maintain a healthy economy. These decisions and manipulations are made by the Federal Reserve System, the nation's central bank.

THE FEDERAL RESERVE SYSTEM. In 1913 Congress passed the Federal Reserve Act to form the nation's central bank. The Federal Reserve System was granted power to manipulate the money supply—the total amount of coins and paper currency in circulation, along with all holdings at banks, credit unions, and other financial institutions.

The Federal Reserve includes a seven-member board of governors headquartered in Washington, D.C., and 12 Reserve Banks located in major cities around the country:

- Boston, Massachusetts
- New York City, New York
- Philadelphia, Pennsylvania
- Cleveland, Ohio
- Richmond, Virginia
- Atlanta, Georgia
- Chicago, Illinois
- St. Louis, Missouri
- Minneapolis, Minnesota
- Kansas City, Missouri
- Dallas, Texas
- San Francisco, California

In *The Federal Reserve System: Purposes and Functions* (June 2005, http://www.federalreserve.gov/pf/pdf/pf_complete.pdf), the Federal Reserve explains that it uses three techniques to indirectly achieve "maximum employment, stable prices, and moderate long-term interest rates":

- Open market operations—the Federal Reserve buys and sells government securities on the financial markets. The resulting money transfers ultimately lower or raise the amount of money that banks have available to lend to the public and the associated interest rates.

- Discount rate adjustments—the Federal Reserve raises or lowers the discount rate. This is the rate that it charges banks for short-term loans. In response, the banks adjust the federal funds rate, the rate they charge each other for loans. Then the banks adjust the prime rate, the interest rate they charge their best customers (typically large corporations). In the end, these adjustments affect the interest rates that are paid by the general public on mortgages, car loans, credit cards, and so on.

- Reserve requirement adjustments—the Federal Reserve raises or lowers the reserve requirement, the amount of readily available money that banks must have to operate. Each bank's reserve requirement is based on a percentage of the total amount of money that customers have deposited at that bank. Money above the reserve requirement can be lent by the banks. Changes in the reserve requirement influence bank decisions about loans to the public.

CHAPTER 10
INTERNATIONAL TRADE AND THE UNITED STATES' PLACE IN THE GLOBAL ECONOMY

Those who have money go abroad in the world.

—Chinese proverb

Technology has made it easier to go abroad in the world. U.S. companies can sell their goods and services on a global market. Likewise, U.S. consumers can purchase merchandise made around the world—and they do so in large numbers. Global trade is driven by the same forces that control the U.S. market: supply and demand. However, there is the added complication of many very different national governments trying to exert influence over trade and market factors in their favor. The U.S. economy is preeminent in the global economy when it comes to national production. Yet, the United States buys far more from foreign lands than it sells to them. Economists disagree about whether this trade imbalance is good or bad for the U.S. economy.

THE UNITED STATES' PLACE IN THE GLOBAL ECONOMY

The United States' place in the global economy can generally be assessed using three measures: the relative size of the U.S. economy compared with other economies, the role of the U.S. dollar in international trade and capital flows, and the status of the U.S. business sector in terms of financial performance and business environment.

Economy Size Comparisons

The Central Intelligence Agency (CIA) ranks in *The World Factbook* (2012, https://www.cia.gov/library/publications/the-world-factbook/rankorder/2001rank.html?countryName=United States&countryCode=us&regionCode=noa&rank=2#us) the world's economies in terms of gross domestic product (GDP), which is the total market value of final goods and services that are produced within an economy in a given year. According to the CIA, in 2011 the United States ($15.3 trillion) had

the largest GDP of any single nation, followed by China ($11.4 trillion), Japan ($4.5 trillion), and Germany ($3.1 trillion). (See Table 10.1.) The combined nations of the European Union (EU) had a GDP of $15.7 trillion, putting the EU in a position above the United States in terms of economic strength. The GDP values in Table 10.1 were calculated based on purchasing power parity. This is an accounting method that is useful for comparing different economies. The CIA explains that each non-U.S. GDP listed in Table 10.1 was calculated by valuing that economy's goods and services at the prices prevailing in the United States.

The Role of the U.S. Dollar

Another measure of the United States' place in the global economy is the status of the U.S. dollar in international trade and capital flow. Linda S. Goldberg of the Federal Reserve Bank of New York examines in "Is the International Role of the Dollar Changing?" (*Current Issues in Economics and Finance*, vol. 16, no. 1, January 2010) the U.S. dollar's high-level status compared with other currencies. One piece of evidence is that foreign nations hold large amounts of U.S. banknotes. Goldberg cites "the stability of the U.S. dollar" as a key factor in this state of affairs.

In addition, the U.S. dollar is a "central currency" in the exchange rate arrangements that are used by many countries. An exchange rate is to the amount of one currency that can be exchanged for a like value in another currency. According to Goldberg, many countries fix their exchanges rates in relation to the U.S. dollar; likewise, many foreign governments hold U.S. dollars in their exchange reserve accounts.

The U.S. dollar is also important in the invoicing of international trade. Even when foreign countries trade among themselves, they often sell and buy using U.S. dollars. The major exception is within the EU, which uses

TABLE 10.1

Gross domestic product (purchasing power parity) for the world's 30 largest economies, 2011

Rank	Economy	GDP (Purchasing power parity)
1	European Union	$15,650,000,000,000
2	United States	$15,290,000,000,000
3	China	$11,440,000,000,000
4	India	$4,515,000,000,000
5	Japan	$4,497,000,000,000
6	Germany	$3,139,000,000,000
7	Russia	$2,414,000,000,000
8	Brazil	$2,324,000,000,000
9	United Kingdom	$2,290,000,000,000
10	France	$2,246,000,000,000
11	Italy	$1,871,000,000,000
12	Mexico	$1,683,000,000,000
13	Korea, South	$1,574,000,000,000
14	Spain	$1,432,000,000,000
15	Canada	$1,414,000,000,000
16	Indonesia	$1,139,000,000,000
17	Turkey	$1,087,000,000,000
18	Iran	$1,003,000,000,000
19	Australia	$926,200,000,000
20	Taiwan	$887,300,000,000
21	Poland	$781,500,000,000
22	Argentina	$725,600,000,000
23	Netherlands	$713,100,000,000
24	Saudi Arabia	$691,500,000,000
25	Thailand	$609,800,000,000
26	South Africa	$562,200,000,000
27	Egypt	$525,600,000,000
28	Pakistan	$494,800,000,000
29	Colombia	$478,000,000,000
30	Malaysia	$453,000,000,000

SOURCE: Adapted from "Country Comparison: GDP (Purchasing Power Parity)," in *The World Factbook*, Central Intelligence Agency, September 2012, https://www.cia.gov/library/publications/the-world-factbook/rankorder/2001rank.html?countryName=United States&countryCode=us&regionCode=noa&rank=2#us (accessed September 19, 2012)

the euro to conduct cross-border trade. In fact, in the decade following the euro's introduction in 1999, many observers thought the euro would replace the U.S. dollar as the preferred currency for international trade. This was especially true at the height of the Great Recession (which lasted from December 2007 to June 2009), the severe economic downturn that struck the United States. However, many European countries subsequently suffered their own financial crises, weakening the EU's economic growth and the euro's reputation. Also, Goldberg notes that the U.S. dollar has consistently maintained its role as the currency of choice for trade in oil and other high-demand goods. As a result, Goldberg concludes that "while changes in the global status of the dollar are possible, factors such as inertia in currency use, the large size and relative stability of the U.S. economy, and the dollar pricing of oil and other commodities will help perpetuate the dollar's role as the dominant medium for international transactions."

The Status of the U.S. Business Sector

The United States' place in the global economy is also evidenced by the status of the U.S. business sector in terms of economic performance and ease of doing business. As noted in Chapter 6, the business magazine *Forbes* publishes the Global 2000, an annual list of the world's 2,000 largest publicly traded companies. In "The World's Biggest Public Companies" (April 18, 2012, http://www.forbes.com/global2000/), *Forbes* ranks five U.S.-based companies— Exxon Mobil, JPMorgan Chase, General Electric, Berkshire Hathaway, and Wells Fargo—among the top-10 global companies based on sales, assets, profits, and market value. In "A Regional Look at the Forbes Global 2000" (*Forbes*, April 18, 2012), Scott DeCarlo indicates that more than a quarter (524 companies) of the Global 2000 in 2012 were U.S.-based companies—the most for any one country.

In addition, in city-to-city comparisons of economic competitiveness, several U.S. cities receive top rankings. Richard Florida examines in "What Is the World's Most Economically Powerful City?" (*Atlantic*, May 8, 2012) the results of five studies that "gauge the relative economic strengths of global cities and metro areas." He indicates that New York City and Chicago are in all five top-10 lists, with New York City taking the top spot in three of the studies. Other U.S. cities making the top 10 in some of the studies are Boston, Washington, D.C., and Los Angeles.

The United States is also ranked highly by some analysts in terms of its environment for doing business. The World Bank Group is a collection of five international organizations that specialize in aiding developing economies. Through its Doing Business Project (http://www.doingbusiness.org), the World Bank Group annually ranks most of the world's nations in terms of their business environment. The World Bank Group indicates in "Ease of Doing Business in United States" (2012, http://www.doingbusiness.org/data/exploreeconomies/united-states/) that it ranked the United States fourth out of 185 economies in its 2013 rankings based on criteria including the ease of starting a business, dealing with construction permits, getting electricity and credit, paying taxes, and conducting cross-border trade. The three countries that outranked the United States were Singapore, Hong Kong, and New Zealand, in that order.

GLOBAL AND U.S. TRADE

In *International Trade Statistics 2011* (October 2011, http://www.wto.org/english/res_e/statis_e/its2011_e/its2011_e.pdf), the World Trade Organization (WTO) indicates that world trade totaled nearly $22 trillion in 2010. The value of merchandise trade was $17.8 trillion and trade in commercial services was nearly $4.2 trillion.

According to the WTO, the United States was the world's leading trader in 2010 with nearly $3.3 trillion in merchandise trade, or 15% of the total. China and Germany ranked second and third, respectively, in merchandise trade. The United States was also the top trader in commercial services with a total of $976 billion

TABLE 10.2

U.S. international trade in goods and services, 2010, 2011, and January–July 2012

[In millions of dollars]

Period	Balance			Exports			Imports		
	Total	Goods*	Services	Total	Goods*	Services	Total	Goods*	Services
2010 Jan.–Dec.	−494,737	−645,124	150,387	1,842,485	1,288,882	553,603	2,337,222	1,934,006	403,216
2011 Jan.–Dec.	−559,880	−738,413	178,533	2,103,367	1,497,406	605,961	2,663,247	2,235,819	427,428
2012 Jan.–July	−329,687	−437,346	107,660	1,278,350	913,445	364,906	1,608,037	1,350,791	257,246

Notes: Details may not equal totals due to seasonal adjustment and rounding.
*Data are presented on a balance of payments (BOP) basis.

SOURCE: Adapted from "Exhibit 1. U.S. International Trade in Goods and Services," in *U.S. International Trade in Goods and Services, July 2012*, U.S. Department of Commerce, Bureau of Economic Analysis, September 11, 2012, http://www.bea.gov/newsreleases/international/trade/2012/pdf/ trad0712.pdf (accessed September 19, 2012)

in 2010, or 23% of the total. Germany and the United Kingdom followed the United States in this ranking.

U.S. Trade in Goods and Services

Table 10.2 lists the values of U.S. trade in goods and services as measured by the U.S. Department of Commerce's Bureau of Economic Analysis (BEA) for 2010, 2011, and January to July 2012. In 2011 the United States imported nearly $2.7 trillion in goods and services. The vast majority ($2.2 trillion, or 84%) of the total was in goods. The remaining $427.4 billion (16% of the total) was in services. Overall, U.S. imports were up in 2011 compared with 2010, when they totaled $2.3 trillion. U.S. exports totaled $2.1 trillion in 2011. Again, the largest component ($1.5 trillion, or 71%) of the total was in goods. The United States exported nearly $606 billion (29% of the total) in services. Overall, U.S. exports were up from 2010, when they totaled $1.8 trillion.

U.S. Trading Partners

In "Top Trading Partners—Total Trade, Exports, Imports: Year-to-Date December 2011" (February 10, 2012,http://www.census.gov/foreign-trade/statistics/highligh ts/top/top1112yr.html), the U.S. Census Bureau reports that the United States' top-10 goods trading partners in 2011 were:

- Canada—$597.4 billion
- China—$503.2 billion
- Mexico—$460.6 billion
- Japan—$195 billion
- Germany—$147.5 billion
- United Kingdom—$107.1 billion
- South Korea—$100.1 billion
- Brazil—$74.3 billion
- France—$67.8 billion
- Taiwan—$67.2 billion

In 2011 Canada was the leading export market for U.S. goods ($280.9 billion), followed by Mexico ($197.5 billion) and China ($103.9 billion). The United States imported the highest value of goods from China ($399.3 billion), Canada ($316.5 billion), and Mexico ($263.1 billion).

U.S. TRADE BALANCE

The difference between exports and imports over a specific time period is known as the balance of trade (exports − imports = balance of trade). For example, Figure 10.1 shows the U.S. balance of trade in goods and services from July 2010 to July 2012. A positive balance of trade is called a surplus. This is a situation in which the value of exports is greater than the value of imports. A negative balance of trade is called a deficit. This occurs when the value of imports exceeds the value of exports. In July 2012 the United States had a trade deficit of $42 billion.

The United States has had a trade deficit for goods every year since 1976, with record levels reached during the first decade of the 21st century. (See Figure 10.2.) In 2011 there was a trade surplus of nearly $179 billion for services. In other words, the value of exported services exceeded the value of imported services by $179 billion. This surplus was more than offset by an enormous trade deficit of $738 billion for goods. In other words, the value of imported goods was $738 billion greater than the value of exported goods.

The historical trade balance in services has been quite different. It has grown from mildly negative numbers during the 1960s to more than $100 billion in the latter half of the first decade of the 21st century. (See Figure 10.2.)

The Trade Deficit and the U.S. Dollar

The trade deficit is directly linked to the value of the U.S. dollar on foreign exchange markets. As noted earlier, a dollar can be exchanged for equivalent amounts

FIGURE 10.1

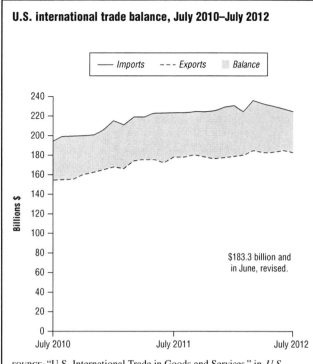

U.S. international trade balance, July 2010–July 2012

— Imports   - - - Exports   Balance

$183.3 billion and
in June, revised.

SOURCE: "U.S. International Trade in Goods and Services," in *U.S. International Trade in Goods and Services, July 2012*, U.S. Department of Commerce, Bureau of Economic Analysis, September 11, 2012, http://www.bea.gov/newsreleases/international/trade/2012/pdf/trad0712.pdf (accessed September 19, 2012)

of any other foreign currency. The exchange rate for any given foreign currency at any given time depends on many complex economic factors, and exchange rates can vary widely over time.

When the U.S. dollar weakens compared with a foreign currency, it means that each dollar buys less of the foreign currency than it did before. Consequently, each dollar buys fewer goods from that nation. By contrast, each unit of the foreign currency is now worth more in U.S. dollars and has more purchasing power of U.S. goods. For example, when the U.S. dollar weakens compared with the Japanese yen, Japanese goods cost more for Americans, but U.S. goods become cheaper for Japanese consumers. As a result, imports from Japan to the United States are likely to decrease, whereas exports from the United States to Japan are likely to increase.

Likewise, when the U.S. dollar strengthens, it buys more foreign currency and more foreign goods than it did before. Thus, a stronger dollar is associated with higher imports into the United States and fewer exports to foreign lands.

Many economists believe the reduced U.S. trade deficit in goods during the late 1980s and early 1990s was associated with a rapid weakening of the U.S. dollar that occurred at the same time. The trade deficit reduction

FIGURE 10.2

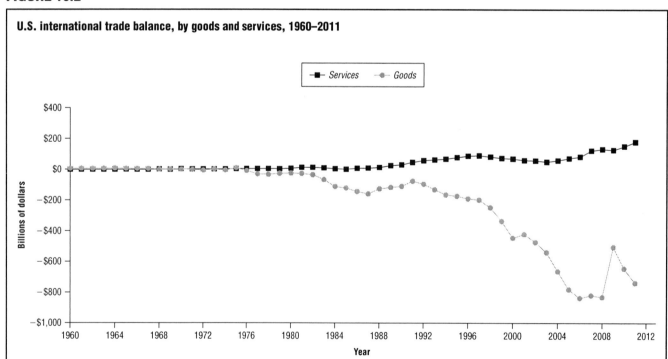

U.S. international trade balance, by goods and services, 1960–2011

■ Services   ● Goods

SOURCE: Adapted from "Table 1. U.S. International Transactions," in *U.S. International Transactions Accounts Data*, U.S. Department of Commerce, Bureau of Economic Analysis, September 18, 2012, http://www.bea.gov/iTable/iTableHtml.cfm?reqid=6&step=3&isuri=1&600=1&601=1960,1961,1962, 1963,1964,1965,1966,1967,1968,1969,1970,1971,1972,1973,1974,1975,1976,1977,1978,1979,1980,1981,1982,1983,1984,1985,1986,1987,1988,1989, 1990,1991,1992,1993,1994,1995,1996,1997,1998,1999,2000,2001,2002,2003,2004,2005,2006,2007,2008,2009,2010,2011,2012&602=0&603=0&604= 0&605=1 (accessed September 19, 2012)

is evidenced as an upward spike in the bottom line in Figure 10.2 during this period. The trade deficit grew increasingly larger each year between 1980 and 1987 and then suddenly reversed its path for several years. During this time Americans were importing fewer foreign goods than before because foreign goods suddenly cost more.

Cédric Tille, Nicolas Stoffels, and Olga Gorbachev indicate in "To What Extent Does Productivity Drive the Dollar?" (*Current Issues in Economics and Finance*, vol. 7, no. 8, August 2001) that the U.S. dollar appreciated by 5.8% against the euro and by 4.8% against the yen on an average annual basis during the 1990s. The relatively strong dollar made foreign goods cheaper for Americans and U.S. goods more expensive for other countries, and unsurprisingly this period coincided with ballooning growth in the U.S. trade deficit. (See Figure 10.2.)

During the first half of the first decade of the 21st century the value of the U.S. dollar began to drop compared with foreign currencies. In contrast to conventional economic wisdom, the U.S. trade deficit continued to grow even as the dollar weakened. This contradiction is examined by Peter S. Goodman and Nell Henderson in "Dollar at 20-Month Low vs. the Euro" (*Washington Post*, November 29, 2006). Goodman and Henderson note that other factors allowed the U.S. trade deficit to grow as the dollar was shrinking—primarily huge buys of U.S. government securities by the governments of China and Japan. However, dollar value changes can take many months to several years to be reflected in the U.S. trade balance. Goodman and Henderson's observation proved to be prophetic as the growth in the U.S. trade deficit was less dramatic between 2005 and 2006 and remained virtually unchanged between 2006 and 2008. (See Figure 10.2.)

The dramatic reduction in the goods trade balance between 2008 and 2009 is attributed to the poor state of the U.S. economy. (See Figure 10.2.) The Great Recession severely dampened imports as U.S. companies and families spent less money on goods. However, as the U.S. economy rebounded in 2010 and 2011, so did the trade deficit.

Is the Trade Deficit Good or Bad?

The United States' enormous trade deficit is a subject of great debate among economists and politicians. Some believe the deficit is bad for the U.S. economy, particularly the country's manufacturing sector, and that steps should be taken by the government to correct the imbalance. Others contend the deficit is a natural consequence of a strong U.S. economy and should not be an issue of concern.

In *The U.S. Trade Deficit: Causes, Consequences, and Cures* (October 11, 2007, http://www.au.af.mil/au/awc/awcgate/crs/rl31032.pdf), Craig K. Elwell of the Congressional Research Service (CRS) outlines the per-

ceived good and bad effects of a large trade deficit. As noted earlier, there is a direct link between the trade deficit and the flow of capital. As Americans buy more foreign goods, foreigners have more money to invest in U.S. financial instruments (e.g., stocks, bonds, and Treasury notes). On the plus side, these investments indicate strong foreign confidence in the security and future growth of the U.S. economy. Also, much of the money flowing into the country is invested in productive capital—that is, invested in growing U.S. industry. However, in many cases these purchases represent debt obligations that the United States will have to pay in the future. In essence, the United States is becoming indebted to foreign nations. Elwell states that "borrowing from abroad allows the United States to live better today, but the payback must mean some decrement to the rate of advance of U.S. living standards in the future."

In a broader sense, large capital inflows demonstrate that Americans prefer spending their money on foreign imports rather than investing it in domestic financial instruments. Put simply, Americans prefer spending to saving. Elwell explains that "so long as domestic saving in the United States falls short of domestic investment and an inflow of foreign saving is available to fill all or part of the gap, the United States will run a trade deficit."

Many critics of the trade deficit claim it hurts the U.S. economy overall, particularly by raising unemployment. Elwell disputes this claim, explaining that the dramatic growth of the trade deficit during the 1990s and the first decade of the 21st century coincided with a generally healthy U.S. economy and relatively low unemployment rates. However, Elwell acknowledges that extensive foreign imports have hurt some U.S. manufacturing industries, particularly textiles, apparel, and steel.

FREE TRADE AGREEMENTS

The U.S. government has long been part of free trade agreements with other individual countries (known as bilateral agreements) and with groups of countries (known as trading blocs). As of October 2012, the United States had free trade agreements in force with 20 countries. (See Table 10.3.)

In this context, free trade means the ability to buy and sell goods across international borders with a minimum of tariffs or other interferences. Tariffs (import taxes) are fees charged by a country to import goods into that country.

Priorities regarding trade policy have shifted over the years according to the state of the economy. During the recession of the late 1970s, U.S. producers called for the government to institute measures—such as high tariffs—to protect them from international competition. During the growth period of the 1980s, however, the focus of

TABLE 10.3

Countries with which the United States has free trade agreements as of October 2012

Australia
Bahrain
Canada
Chile
Colombia
Costa Rica
Dominican Republic
El Salvador
Guatemala
Honduras
Israel
Jordan
Mexico
Morocco
Nicaragua
Oman
Panama
Peru
Singapore
South Korea

SOURCE: Adapted from "Free Trade Agreements," in *Trade Agreements*, U.S. Treasury Department, October 2012, http://www.ustr.gov/trade-agreements/free-trade-agreements (accessed November 30, 2012)

companies turned to their own international expansion, and by the 1990s a push for free trade had gained increased momentum.

According to Bruce Arnold of the Congressional Budget Office, in *The Pros and Cons of Pursuing Free-Trade Agreements* (July 31, 2003, http://www.cbo.gov/sites/default/files/cbofiles/ftpdocs/44xx/doc4458/07-31tradebrief.pdf), opponents to trading blocs argue that when countries with strong economies—such as the United States, Japan, and the countries of the EU—negotiate agreements, smaller nations with developing economies are left at an unfair disadvantage because they are excluded from the favorable terms of the agreements.

North American Free Trade Agreement

The United States, Canada, and Mexico implemented the North American Free Trade Agreement (NAFTA) in January 1994. A primary objective of NAFTA has been the complete elimination of barriers to trade among the three signing countries. Many tariffs were dropped immediately, and others were scheduled to be phased out over time. Agricultural products were an integral part of NAFTA and had some of the longest phaseout schedules. All agricultural provisions of NAFTA were implemented by January 2008.

NAFTA was very controversial in the United States when it was first implemented. Critics claimed that the agreement would encourage U.S. companies to move their manufacturing facilities to Mexico to take advantage of lower labor costs and less government regulation. Robert E. Scott of the Economic Policy Institute estimates in

"The High Price of 'Free' Trade" (November 17, 2003, http://www.epinet.org/content.cfm/briefingpapers_bp147) that between 1994 and 2002, 879,280 U.S. jobs (mostly high-paying manufacturing industry positions) had been displaced as a result of NAFTA's removal of trade barriers. However, the Office of the United States Trade Representative (USTR) disputes the idea that NAFTA has caused a loss of U.S. jobs. In "NAFTA—Myth vs. Facts" (March 2008, http://www.ustr.gov/sites/default/files/NAFTA-Myth-versus-Fact.pdf), the USTR notes that employment in the United States increased by 24% between 1993 and 2007. In addition, the U.S. unemployment rate averaged 7.1% annually from 1980 to 1993 (before NAFTA) and averaged 5.1% annually from 1994 to 2007.

General Agreement on Tariffs and Trade and the WTO

One of the most historically notable trade agreements is the General Agreement on Tariffs and Trade (GATT), which was first signed by the United States and 22 other countries in 1947. This agreement dealt primarily with industrial products and marked a trend toward the increasing globalization of the world economy. The agreement reduced tariffs, removed other obstacles to international trade, and clarified rules surrounding barriers to free trade. For the most part, agriculture was kept out of the initial negotiations. By the end of the 1980s, over 100 countries had ratified GATT.

A series of GATT negotiations that concluded in 1994 created the WTO, which replaced GATT. The WTO now functions as the principal international body that is charged with administering rules for trade among member countries. The new agreements that have been established by the WTO cover a range of topics, including agriculture, food safety, animal and plant health regulations, technical standards (testing and certification), import licensing procedures, trade in services, intellectual property rights (including trade in counterfeit goods), as well as rules and procedures for settling disputes. As of August 2012, the WTO (http://www.wto.org/english/theWTO_e/whatis_e/tif_e/org6_e.htm) consisted of 157 member countries, including the United States.

EUROPEAN UNION

In 1957 six European countries signed the Treaty of Rome, which established the European Economic Community. In 1992 the Maastricht Treaty was signed, which officially established the EU. The leaders of European countries hoped that by engaging in commerce they could create long-term stability and enforce the rule of law in cooperative democratic societies. The EU, which is one of the most important trading partners of the United States, expanded in 2004 from 15 nations to 25, creating the largest trading bloc in history.

According to the EU, in "The Member Countries of the European Union" (http://europa.eu/about-eu/27-member-countries/index_en.htm), in 2012 the EU consisted of 27 member countries: Austria, Belgium, Bulgaria, Cyprus, the Czech Republic, Denmark, Estonia, Finland, France, Germany, Greece, Hungary, Ireland, Italy, Latvia, Lithuania, Luxembourg, Malta, the Netherlands, Poland, Portugal, Romania, Slovakia, Slovenia, Spain, Sweden, and the United Kingdom. The EU (October 10, 2012, http://ec.europa.eu/enlargement/countries/detailed-country-information/croatia/index_en.htm) notes that it signed an agreement with Croatia in December 2011 that will allow that nation to join the EU in July 2013, assuming that all EU members ratify the agreement. As of November 2012, candidate countries for admission to the EU in the future included Iceland, Montenegro, Serbia, Turkey, and the former Yugoslav Republic of Macedonia.

INTERNATIONAL MONETARY FUND

The International Monetary Fund (IMF), a global financial system, was established in July 1944, during the United Nations (UN) Monetary and Financial Conference (more commonly known as the Bretton Woods conference because it took place in Bretton Woods, New Hampshire). The IMF extends short-term loans to members experiencing economic instability. As a condition of receiving its credit assistance, the IMF requires the debtor country to enact significant reform of its economic structure, and often of its political structure as well. The conditions for being granted a loan can include drastic cuts in government spending; privatizing government-owned enterprises, such as railroads and utilities; establishing higher interest rates; increasing taxes; and eliminating subsidies on necessities such as food and fuel.

Supporters of the IMF indicate that these reforms oftentimes eliminate corruption and help establish effective institutions such as courts. In contrast, critics argue that for some countries, these reforms can have devastating social consequences, including severe unemployment, crippling price increases in the cost of basic goods, and political instability resulting from widespread dissatisfaction. Despite this criticism, the IMF membership has grown considerably since its founding. In 1944 it had 45 members. By 2012 the IMF (http://www.imf.org/external/about.htm) consisted of 188 member countries, including the United States.

WORLD BANK

At the same conference that created the IMF in July 1944, the International Bank for Reconstruction and Development (IBRD) was established. In 1960 the International Development Association (IDA) was created. The IBRD and the IDA are commonly known as the World Bank. The World Bank is not a bank in the traditional sense of the word but an agency of the UN. The World Bank works to combat world poverty by providing low-interest loans, interest-free credit, and grants to developing countries. According to the World Bank (http://go.worldbank.org/Y33OQYNE90), in 2012 the IBRD and the IDA consisted of 188 and 172 member countries, respectively.

In its early days, the World Bank often participated in large projects such as dam building. During the first decade of the 21st century it supported the efforts of governments in developing countries to build schools and health centers, provide water and electricity, fight disease, and protect the environment. It is one of the world's largest sources of development assistance.

GLOBALIZATION AND THE ANTIGLOBALIZATION MOVEMENT

The move toward global free trade, or globalization, has generated intense controversy. Proponents maintain that globalization can improve living standards throughout the world. Their arguments include the following:

- Countries and regions will become more productive by concentrating on industries in which they have a natural advantage and trading with other nations for goods in which they do not have an advantage.

- Multinational corporations will be able to realize economies of scale—that is, operate more economically because they are buying in bulk, selling to a much larger market, and utilizing a much larger labor pool. This will increase productivity and lead to greater prosperity.

- Free trade will lead to faster growth in developing countries.

- Increased incomes and the development of job-related skills among the citizens of poorer nations will foster the spread of information, education, and, ultimately, democracy.

Critics of globalization point out the negative effects that multinational corporations have on people in the developing world. They argue that:

- Most of the profits from free trade flow to the United States and to other industrialized countries.

- Local industries can be destroyed by competition from wealthier nations, causing widespread unemployment and social disruption.

- Centuries of cultural tradition can be quickly obliterated by the influence of international companies.

- Multinational corporations often impinge on national sovereignty to protect their profits.

Critics also note that the free trade policies are often applied unfairly, as the United States insists that other countries open their markets to U.S. goods while it protects its own producers from competition. For example, the U.S. government has established many tariffs and regulations that raise the prices of imported food products, denying poor farmers in the developing world access to the lucrative U.S. market. In addition, opponents of globalization point out that the spread of multinational corporations can be detrimental to workers in industrialized nations by exporting high-paying jobs to countries with lower labor costs, and that international competition in the labor market could actually lead to lower living standards in the industrialized world.

The antiglobalization movement is not an organized group but an umbrella term for many independent organizations that oppose the pursuit of corporate profits at the expense of social justice in the developing world. These groups often protest the actions of organizations such as the WTO, the IMF, and the World Bank for their perceived bias toward corporations and wealthy nations. For example, in 1999 a WTO conference in Seattle, Washington, drew more than 40,000 protestors in a massive demonstration that generated intense media attention and completely overshadowed the meeting itself.

ECONOMIC AND TRADE SANCTIONS

The United States uses economic and trade sanctions (stopping some or all forms of financial transactions and trade with a country) as a political tool against countries that are thought to violate human rights, tolerate drug trafficking, support terrorism, and produce or store weapons of mass destruction. Sanctions are enforced by the Treasury Department's Office of Foreign Assets Control (OFAC). As of November 2012, the OFAC (http://www.ustreas.gov/offices/enforcement/ofac/programs/index.shtml) listed economic and/or trade sanctions against dozens of countries, including Cuba, Iran, and North Korea.

The Trade Act of 1974 allowed the United States to impose sanctions on countries with unfair trade policies. The Jackson-Vanik amendment to this legislation required annual certification for communist countries, including China, and barred the president from granting favorable trade status to countries that limited emigration. This amendment was repealed in 2000, marking a major step in the restoration of relations between China and the United States. In December 2001 China was admitted as a member of the WTO. The Chinese market presents an enormous opportunity for U.S. exports.

THE CHANGING FACE OF FREE TRADE
Parity in Labor Standards and Environmental Laws

Discrepancies in labor and environmental regulations among trading nations have formed another barrier to free trade. The administration of President Bill Clinton (1946–) pushed to impose the same labor and environmental standards on trading nations that the United States imposes on itself. The move was designed to discourage trading

partners from exploiting workers and abusing the environment to keep capital costs lower and prices down, thus making their goods and services more competitive than U.S. goods in the global market. Before NAFTA was signed, the United States insisted on assurances from Canada and Mexico that they would enforce labor and environmental laws before ratifying the agreement.

Intellectual Property

Technological advancements have posed new challenges to world trade. As private-sector investment in information technology continues, world economies are becoming even more interconnected. Proponents of free trade, including the United States, have pushed for more protection of intellectual property rights, abuse of which poses a major barrier to world trade. As defined by the UN in the Convention Establishing the World Intellectual Property Organization (2012, http://www.wipo.int/treaties/en/convention/trtdocs_wo029.html), which was signed on July 14, 1967, and amended on September 28, 1979, intellectual property includes:

- Literary, artistic, and scientific works

- Performances of performing artists, phonograms, and broadcasts

- Inventions in all fields of human endeavor

- Scientific discoveries

- Industrial designs

- Trademarks, service marks, and commercial names and designations

- Protection against unfair competition and all other rights resulting from intellectual activity in the industrial, scientific, literary, or artistic fields

WORLD INTELLECTUAL PROPERTY ORGANIZATION. Challenges for the international community include establishing minimum standards for protecting intellectual property rights and procedures for enforcement and dispute resolution. These challenges are not new. The World Intellectual Property Organization (WIPO) explains in "Major Events 1883 to 2002" (2012, http://www.wipo.int/treaties/en/general/) that as early as 1883, with the founding of the 14-member Paris Convention for the Protection of Industrial Property, countries recognized the special nature of creative works, including inventions, trademarks, and industrial designs. In 1886 the Berne Convention for the Protection of Literary and Artistic Works extended the model of international protection to copyrighted works such as novels, poems, plays, songs, operas, musicals, drawings, paintings, sculptures, and architectural works.

In 1893 the Paris Convention and the Berne Convention combined to form the United International Bureaus for the Protection of Intellectual Property, which maintained its headquarters in Berne, Switzerland. This organization eventually evolved into the WIPO, located in Geneva, Switzerland, which carries out a program that is designed to:

- Harmonize national intellectual property legislation and procedures

- Provide services for international applications for industrial property rights

- Exchange intellectual property information

- Provide legal and technical assistance to developing and other countries

- Facilitate the resolution of private intellectual property disputes

- Marshal information technology as a tool for storing, accessing, and using valuable intellectual property information

As of November 2012, the WIPO (http://www.wipo.int/members/en/) consisted of 185 member nations, including the United States.

INTERNATIONAL INVESTMENT

International investment involves the buying and selling of foreign investments (such as stocks, bonds, and other financial instruments) and the investment of cash directly in foreign companies. Also included are investment assets such as foreign-owned gold and foreign currencies.

International investment data are collected by the BEA, the Treasury Department, and the Federal Reserve System (the nation's central bank). The two primary types of international investments that they track are financial investments and direct investments. In *Direct Investment Positions for 2011* (July 2012, http://www.bea.gov/scb/pdf/2012/07%20July/0712_dip.pdf), Kevin B. Barefoot and Marilyn Ibarra-Caton of the BEA explain that a direct investment is an investment in which a resident of one country "obtains a lasting interest in, and a degree of influence over the management of a business enterprise in another country." Legally, a resident can be a person or other entity, such as a corporation or government body. The U.S. government defines a direct investment as ownership or control of at least 10% of a foreign business enterprise.

U.S. Investment in Foreign Assets

The BEA reports in the press release "U.S. Net International Investment Position at Yearend 2011" (June 26, 2012, http://www.bea.gov/newsreleases/international/intinv/2012/pdf/intinv11.pdf) that U.S.-owned assets abroad totaled $21.1 trillion at year-end 2011. This value was up from $20.3 trillion at year-end 2010.

Foreign Investment in U.S. Assets

The United States has historically allowed and often encouraged foreign investment in U.S. assets. The U.S.

Government Accountability Office (GAO) states in *Sovereign Wealth Funds: Laws Limiting Foreign Investment Affect Certain U.S. Assets and Agencies Have Various Enforcement Processes* (May 2009, http://www.gao.gov/new.items/d09608.pdf) that "the United States has an overall policy of openness to foreign investment through policy statements and treaties and international agreements addressing investment." The GAO explains, however, that there are federal laws that limit or otherwise restrict the amount of foreign ownership or control in certain industries—specifically the transportation, energy, natural resources, banking, agriculture, and national defense industries.

Foreign-Owned Assets in the United States

In "U.S. Net International Investment Position at Yearend 2011," the BEA notes that foreign-owned assets in the United States totaled $25.2 trillion at year-end 2011. This value was up from $22.8 trillion at year-end 2010.

It should be noted that the purchase of U.S. assets by foreign entities is funded in large part by U.S. imports. When Americans buy more foreign goods and services, more U.S. dollars flow into foreign countries. This provides greater opportunities for foreigners to invest in U.S. assets.

FOREIGN HOLDINGS OF U.S. FINANCIAL ASSETS. Every five years the U.S. government conducts a comprehensive survey called a full benchmark survey to measure foreign holdings of U.S. securities. As of November 2012, the most recent data available were published in *Report on Foreign Portfolio Holdings of U.S. Securities as of June 30, 2011* (April 2012, http://www.treasury.gov/resource-center/data-chart-center/tic/Documents/shla2011r.pdf) by the Treasury Department. It should be noted that securities include stocks (also known as equities), bonds, and other financial instruments (such as U.S. Treasury bills and notes) and securities sold by U.S. agencies (such as the Federal National Mortgage Association and the Federal Home Loan Mortgage Corporation).

As of June 2011, foreign holdings of U.S. securities totaled $12.4 trillion. (See Table 10.4.) The vast majority of the holdings ($11.6 trillion) consisted of long-term securities (securities with maturity time more than one year). A much smaller value ($878 billion) of short-term debt was in foreign hands.

As shown in Table 10.4, foreign holdings of U.S. securities have more than doubled since 2004, when they totaled $6 trillion. This trend is of major concern to some analysts and politicians, who fear that the United States has become too dependent on foreign money. The danger to the U.S. economy as a whole lies in the possibility that foreigners might suddenly decide to pull out of U.S. financial assets. This could destabilize the financial market and harm U.S. economic growth.

The Treasury Department estimates ownership by country of foreign-owned U.S. securities. However, it

TABLE 10.4

Foreign holdings of U.S. securities, by type of security, as of June 2004–June 2011

[Billions of dollars]

Type of security	June 2004	June 2005	June 2006	June 2007	June 2008	June 2009	June 2010	June 2011
Long-term securities	5,431	6,262	7,162	9,136	9,463	8,492	9,736	11,561
Equities*	1,930	2,144	2,430	3,130	2,969	2,252	2,814	3,830
Debt	3,501	4,118	4,733	6,007	6,494	6,240	6,921	7,731
U.S. Treasury	1,426	1,599	1,727	1,965	2,211	2,604	3,343	4,049
U.S. agency	619	791	984	1,304	1,464	1,196	1,086	1,031
Corporate	1,455	1,729	2,021	2,738	2,820	2,440	2,493	2,651
Short-term debt	588	602	615	635	858	1,149	956	878
U.S. Treasury	317	284	253	229	379	862	743	658
U.S. agency	124	150	147	109	174	90	61	43
Corporate	147	168	215	297	306	197	152	177
Total long-term and short-term	6,019	6,864	7,778	9,772	10,322	9,641	10,691	12,440

*"Equities" include common and preferred stock, all types of investment company shares, such as open-end funds, closed-end funds, money market mutual funds, and hedge funds, as well as interests in limited partnerships and other equity interests that may not involve stocks/shares.
Note: On this, components may not sum to totals because of rounding.

source: "Table 1. Foreign Holdings of U.S. Securities, by Type of Security, as of Selected Survey Dates," in *Report on Foreign Portfolio Holdings of U.S. Securities as of June 30, 2011*, U.S. Department of the Treasury, Federal Reserve Bank of New York, and Board of Governors of the Federal Reserve System, April 2012, http://www.treasury.gov/resource-center/data-chart-center/tic/Documents/shla2011r.pdf (accessed September 19, 2012)

TABLE 10.5

Foreign holdings of U.S. securities, by country, as of June 2011

[Billions of dollars]

Country	Total	Equity	Treas. LT debt	Agency LT debt		Corp. LT debt		ST debt
				ABS[a]	Other	ABS[a]	Other	
China[b]	1,727	159	1,302	218	27	2	14	5
Japan	1,585	302	818	152	106	13	127	67
United Kingdom	982	441	118	6	6	47	347	16
Cayman Islands	889	393	47	29	8	102	229	80
Luxembourg	817	291	88	11	8	40	311	69
Canada	559	415	36	1	4	9	82	13
Switzerland	488	226	106	6	8	18	108	16
Belgium	443	25	85	*	6	35	285	6
Middle East oil-exporters[c]	419	188	117	8	4	5	16	81
Ireland	405	105	31	15	11	33	96	114
Hong Kong	292	43	53	99	17	2	12	66
Country Unknown	138	2	*	*	*	*	136	1
Rest of world	3,696	1240	1,248	169	112	120	462	344
Total	12,440	3,830	4,049	714	317	426	2,225	878
Of which: Holdings of foreign official institutions	4,847	567	3,103	405	230	16	88	438

*Greater than zero but less than $500 million.
[a]Asset-backed securities. Agency ABS are backed primarily by home mortgages; corporate ABS are backed by a wide variety of assets, such as car loans, credit card receivables, home and commercial mortgages, and student loans.
[b]Excludes Hong Kong and Macau, which are reported separately.
[c]Bahrain, Iran, Iraq, Kuwait, Oman, Qatar, Saudi Arabia, and the United Arab Emirates.
LT = Long-term. ST = short-term.

source: "Table 5. Value of Foreign Holdings of U.S. Securities, by Major Investing Country and Type of Security, as of June 30, 2011," in *Report on Foreign Portfolio Holdings of U.S. Securities as of June 30, 2011*, U.S. Department of the Treasury, Federal Reserve Bank of New York, and Board of Governors of the Federal Reserve System, April 2012, http://www.treasury.gov/resource-center/data-chart-center/tic/Documents/shla2011r.pdf (accessed September 19, 2012)

warns that these estimates should be viewed as "rough indicators" because the underlying data are imperfect and are muddied by the complexities of the modern financial system. Certain countries, such as Luxembourg and Switzerland, contain major financial industries that manage or hold securities for residents of other countries. These securities are reported to the U.S. government as owned by Luxembourg and Switzerland, when in fact they are owned by other foreigners. In addition, certain types of securities are allowed to be unregistered as to country of ownership. With these caveats, the Treasury Department provides estimates of foreign holdings of U.S. securities by country in Table 10.5. China had the largest amount ($1.7 trillion), followed by Japan ($1.6 trillion) and the United Kingdom ($982 billion).

China's large holdings of U.S. securities are of particular concern to some analysts. As noted earlier, a country or countries holding large amounts of U.S. securities could, in theory, severely disrupt the U.S. economy by suddenly selling those securities. The probability and consequences of this possible event are examined regularly by the CRS. James K. Jackson of the CRS explains in *Foreign Ownership of U.S. Financial Assets: Implications of a Withdrawal* (March 9, 2010, http://assets.opencrs.com/rpts/RL34319_20100309 .pdf) that a sudden sell-off of foreign-owned U.S. securities could, in theory, cause a dramatic spike in interest rates in the United States. However, Jackson explains that this scenario is highly unlikely because the financial industry responds quickly to market fluctuations. As such, any attempted sell-off would lead to a sudden increase in supply, which would drive down the price of the securities and cause the seller or sellers to lose huge amounts of money. In addition, Jackson notes that the Federal Reserve would not "stand idly by" in such a circumstance, but would act quickly in cooperation with other national banks to stabilize credit markets.

In *China's Holdings of U.S. Securities: Implications for the U.S. Economy* (September 26, 2011, http://www.fas.org/ sgp/crs/row/RL34314.pdf), Wayne M. Morrison and Marc Labonte of the CRS echo these assurances and note that the severe problems experienced by the U.S. financial markets during the Great Recession did not scare off foreign investors. They state, "If these events failed to cause a sudden flight from U.S. assets ... by China or other countries, it is hard to imagine what would." However, Morrison and Labonte acknowledge that the broader problem for the U.S. economy is the nation's lack of saving. They note that "the United States must boost its level of savings in the long run in order to reduce its vulnerability to a potential shift away from U.S. assets by foreign investors."

FOREIGN DIRECT INVESTMENT IN THE UNITED STATES. As noted earlier, foreign direct investment entails foreign ownership or control of at least 10% of a U.S. business enterprise. Barefoot and Ibarra-Caton report that foreign direct investment totaled $2.5 trillion at year-end 2011. This value was up from nearly $2.3 trillion at year-end 2010. The largest holders of foreign direct investments in the United States at year-end 2011 were the United Kingdom ($442.2 billion), Japan ($289.5 billion), and the Netherlands ($240.3 billion). For comparison, China had only $3.8 billion in direct investment in the United States at year-end 2011.

IMPORTANT NAMES
AND ADDRESSES

Agency for Healthcare Research and Quality
540 Gaither Rd.
Rockville, MD 20850
(301) 427-1364
URL: http://www.ahrq.gov/

American Bankruptcy Institute
44 Canal Center Plaza, Ste. 400
Alexandria, VA 22314
(703) 739-0800
FAX: (703) 739-1060
E-mail: Support@abiworld.org
URL: http://www.abiworld.org/

Bureau of Economic Analysis
1441 L St. NW
Washington, DC 20230
(202) 606-9900
E-mail: CustomerService@bea.gov
URL: http://www.bea.gov/

Congressional Budget Office
Ford House Office Bldg., Fourth Floor
Washington, DC 20515-6925
(202) 226-2602
E-mail: communications@cbo.gov
URL: http://www.cbo.gov/

Consumer Federation of America
1620 I St. NW, Ste. 200
Washington, DC 20006
(202) 387-6121
E-mail: cfa@consumerfed.org
URL: http://www.consumerfed.org/

Economic Policy Institute
1333 H St. NW, Ste. 300, East Tower
Washington, DC 20005-4707
(202) 775-8810
FAX: (202) 775-0819
E-mail: researchdept@epi.org
URL: http://www.epi.org/

Federal Communications Commission
445 12th St. SW
Washington, DC 20554

1-888-225-5322
FAX: 1-866-418-0232
E-mail: fccinfo@fcc.gov
URL: http://www.fcc.gov/

Federal Home Loan Mortgage Corporation
8200 Jones Branch Dr.
McLean, VA 22102-3110
(703) 903-2000
URL: http://www.freddiemac.com/

Federal Housing Finance Agency
400 Seventh St. SW
Washington, DC 20024
(202) 649-3800
FAX: (202) 649-1071
E-mail: FHFAinfo@FHFA.gov
URL: http://www.fhfa.gov/

Federal National Mortgage Association
3900 Wisconsin Ave. NW
Washington, DC 20016-2892
(202) 752-7000
1-800-732-6643
URL: http://www.fanniemae.com/

Federal Reserve System, Board of Governors
20th St. and Constitution Ave. NW
Washington, DC 20551
(202) 974-7008
URL: http://www.federalreserve.gov/

Federal Trade Commission
600 Pennsylvania Ave. NW
Washington, DC 20580
(202) 326-2222
URL: http://www.ftc.gov/

Federation of Tax Administrators
444 N. Capitol St. NW, Ste. 348
Washington, DC 20001
(202) 624-5890
URL: http://www.taxadmin.org/

Internal Revenue Service
1111 Constitution Ave. NW
Washington, DC 20224
1-800-829-1040
URL: http://www.irs.gov/

International Monetary Fund
700 19th St. NW
Washington, DC 20431
(202) 623-7000
FAX: (202) 623-4661
URL: http://www.imf.org/

Investment Company Institute
1401 H St. NW, Ste. 1200
Washington, DC 20005
(202) 326-5800
URL: http://www.ici.org/

Office of Management and Budget
725 17th St. NW
Washington, DC 20503
(202) 395-3080
FAX: (202) 395-3888
URL: http://www.whitehouse.gov/omb/

Organisation for Economic Co-operation and Development
2 rue André Pascal, 75775
Paris, Cedex 16 France
(011-33) 1-45-24-82-00
FAX: (011-33) 1-45-24-85-00
URL: http://www.oecd.org/

Social Security Administration
Windsor Park Bldg.
6401 Security Blvd.
Baltimore, MD 21235
1-800-772-1213
URL: http://www.ssa.gov/

U.S. Bureau of Labor Statistics
Postal Square Bldg.
2 Massachusetts Ave. NE
Washington, DC 20212-0001

(202) 691-5200
URL: http://www.bls.gov/

U.S. Census Bureau
4600 Silver Hill Rd.
Washington, DC 20233
(301) 763-4636
1-800-923-8282
URL: http://www.census.gov/

U.S. Commodities Futures Trading Commission
Three Lafayette Centre
1155 21st St. NW
Washington, DC 20581
(202) 418-5000
FAX: (202) 418-5521
E-mail: Questions@cftc.gov
URL: http://www.cftc.gov/

U.S. Consumer Product Safety Commission
4330 East-West Hwy.
Bethesda, MD 20814
(301) 504-7923
FAX: (301) 504-0124
URL: http://www.cpsc.gov/

U.S. Department of Commerce
1401 Constitution Ave. NW
Washington, DC 20230
(202) 482-2000
E-mail: TheSec@doc.gov
URL: http://www.commerce.gov/

U.S. Department of Health and Human Services
200 Independence Ave. SW
Washington, DC 20201
1-877-696-6775
URL: http://www.hhs.gov/

U.S. Department of Housing and Urban Development
451 Seventh St. SW
Washington, DC 20410
(202) 708-1112
URL: http://www.hud.gov/

U.S. Department of Labor
Frances Perkins Bldg.
200 Constitution Ave. NW
Washington, DC 20210
1-866-487-2365
URL: http://www.dol.gov/

U.S. Department of the Treasury
1500 Pennsylvania Ave. NW
Washington, DC 20220
(202) 622-2000
FAX: (202) 622-6415
URL: http://www.treasury.gov/

U.S. Equal Opportunity Employment Commission
131 M St. NE
Washington, DC 20507
(202) 663-4900
1-800-669-4000
E-mail: info@eeoc.gov
URL: http://www.eeoc.gov/

U.S. Government Accountability Office
441 G St. NW
Washington, DC 20548
(202) 512-3000
E-mail: contact@gao.gov
URL: http://www.gao.gov/

U.S. International Trade Commission
500 E St. SW
Washington, DC 20436

(202) 205-2000
URL: http://www.usitc.gov/

U.S. Securities and Exchange Commission
100 F St. NE
Washington, DC 20549
(202) 942-8088
E-mail: https://tts.sec.gov/oiea/
QuestionsAndComments.html
URL: http://www.sec.gov/

U.S. Small Business Administration
409 Third St. SW
Washington, DC 20416
1-800-827-5722
E-mail: answerdesk@sba.gov
URL: http://www.sba.gov/

World Bank
1818 H St. NW
Washington, DC 20433
(202) 473-1000
FAX: (202) 477-6391
URL: http://www.worldbank.org/

World Intellectual Property Organization
34, chemin des Colombettes,
CH-1211
Geneva 20 Switzerland
(011-41-22) 338-9111
FAX: (011-41-22) 733-5428
URL: http://www.wipo.int/

World Trade Organization
Centre William Rappard
Rue de Lausanne 154, CH-1211
Geneva 21, Switzerland
(011-41-22) 739-5111
FAX: (011-41-22) 731-4206
E-mail: enquiries@wto.org
URL: http://www.wto.org/

RESOURCES

Several government agencies provided invaluable economic data and information for this book: the U.S. Department of Commerce's Bureau of Economic Analysis (BEA), the U.S. Census Bureau, the U.S. Department of Labor's Bureau of Labor Statistics (BLS), and the Federal Reserve System.

The BEA compiles the *National Income and Product Accounts*, which include detailed financial information on gross domestic product, personal income and outlays, saving, corporate profits, and international trade and balance of payments.

The BLS publishes statistical data on wages, benefits, and income; inflation and economic indexes; employment and unemployment; industries and occupations; employment demographics; and worker health and safety standards. In addition, the BLS posts many of its publications online, including *Employment Situation, Occupational Outlook Handbook, Monthly Labor Review*, and *Occupational Outlook Quarterly*.

The Census Bureau provides comprehensive economic and demographic data. Particularly useful for the study of the U.S. economy are the census publications *Historical Statistics of the United States, Colonial Times to 1970, Bicentennial Edition, Part 1* (September 1975), *Income, Poverty, and Health Insurance Coverage in the United States: 2011* (Carmen DeNavas-Walt, Bernadette D. Proctor, and Jessica C. Smith, September 2012), the *American Fact Finder: 2007 Economic Census* (July 2010), and *Statistical Abstract of the United States: 2012* (2012).

The Federal Reserve System publishes economic data and papers on a variety of economic subjects, including housing, consumer spending, interest rates, consumer credit, net worth, wealth distribution, and debt. Especially useful is the series *Federal Reserve Statistical Release*.

Other government agencies and offices consulted during the compilation of this book include the U.S. Government Accountability Office, the Congressional Research Service, the Social Security Administration, and the White House. The latter provided budgetary information and the annual *Economic Report of the President*.

Important information was also obtained from the Federal Trade Commission; the U.S. Commodities Futures Trading Commission; the U.S. Departments of Agriculture, Education, Energy, Health and Human Services, Housing and Urban Development, and the Treasury; the U.S. International Trade Commission; the U.S. Department of Homeland Security's Office of Immigration Statistics; the Internal Revenue Service; the Congressional Budget Office; the Office of Management and Budget; the Federal Housing Finance Agency; the Central Intelligence Agency; and the U.S. Small Business Administration.

International organizations that provided input include the Organisation for Economic Co-operation and Development, the World Trade Organization, the International Monetary Fund, the World Bank, and the World Intellectual Property Organization.

A number of independent, nonpartisan think tanks and private organizations were consulted to obtain various points of view on socioeconomic issues. These organizations include the American Bankruptcy Institute, the Center for Corporate Policy, the Center for a New American Dream, the Center for Responsive Politics, the Consumer Federation of America, the Dollars & Sense Collective, the Economic Policy Institute, the Levy Economics Institute of Bard College, the Tax Foundation, and United for a Fair Economy.

Finally, the Gallup Organization was the source for numerous public opinion polls that were conducted to gauge American attitudes on economic topics.

INDEX

CPSIA information can be obtained
at www.ICGtesting.com
Printed in the USA
FFOW01n0119060415
12420FF

9 781414 481319